Haiti, History, and the Gods

Haiti, History,
and the Gods

Joan Dayan

UNIVERSITY OF CALIFORNIA PRESS

Berkeley / Los Angeles / London

University of California Press
Berkeley and Los Angeles, California

University of California Press
London, England

Copyright © 1995 by Joan Dayan

Library of Congress Cataloging-in-Publication Data
Dayan, Joan.
    Haiti, history, and the gods / Joan Dayan.
        p.   cm.
    "A centennial book."
    Includes bibliographical references and index.
    ISBN 0-520-08900-6 (alk. paper)
    1. Haiti—Civilization—Philosophy.   2. Haiti—Religion.
3. Nationalism—Haiti—Religious aspects.   4. Social psychology
and literature—Haiti—History.   I. Title.
    F1916.D39   1995
    972.94—dc20   94-46352
                                                                              CIP

Printed in the United States of America

1 2 3 4 5 6 7 8 9

The paper used in this publication meets the minimum requirements
of American National Standard for Information Sciences—Perma-
nence of Paper for Printed Library Materials, ANSI Z39.48–1984 ⊚

For Edmond Dayan (1907–1992)

Baton ki bat chen nwa se li ki bat chen blan
(The stick that beats the black dog also beats the white dog)

—Haitian proverb

Contents

Prologue

Haiti tempts impassioned representation, as well as proprietary impulses. Writers, grappling with their own identity, from Jules Michelet to William Seabrook, turned to Haiti as a land of conversion, where Africa could become France or a white man could become black. My mother, trying to tell me about her childhood in Port-au-Prince, never sure if she was French, Syrian, or Haitian, and light enough not to think of herself as black, always returned to the nuns at Sacré-Coeur. Her stories also focused on transformation and miraculous identity shifts:

They never told us about the slave trade. I did not know about that. In the beginning, they said, there were some little light pygmies that were here. And they grew bigger and darker. I always wondered how they got so black and so big so fast.

They told Jews in the class: all you have to do is swallow a wafer and you'll be Catholic.

I begin with these conversion narratives, these broken recollections, because I am interested in how stories get told, what gets remembered, and which details matter. This book does not aim at conclusiveness. Since I am committed to allowing conflict and collision among texts that differ in origin, purpose, and effect, these voices from the past are not encased in a chronological grid or clarifying summary argument. Rather, I try to dramatize a complex and perplexing social history too often lost in exposition. The violence, mimicry, and belief I lay bare in these pages preserve an ambivalent, provisional, and convertible locale that would be masked by privileged beginnings or propositions.

Let me admit at the outset that I am obsessed by Haiti, for reasons that have much to do with my own vexed and haunted childhood, the uncertainty of my family origins, and my confrontation with an always blocked, silenced, or unspeakable history. Since I disdain what is now called "identity politics" or "personal criticism," that savvy recentering of the self one claims to be decentering, I will take my reader on no backward-turning journey into childhood terror, fragments of denial, and lies that kept me forever outside, always on the margins of any place or self that could be called my own. Instead, let me begin by trying to recover a few memories of Haiti.

In 1970 I held a ball and chain in my hands. I asked the oungan (priest) if these were used in service. He did not answer me. I wondered if his father and grandfather had kept these instruments of slavery. Now they were part of the sacred objects on the altar, laid out with bottles of rum, plates of food, chromolithographs of the saints, candles, sacred stones, rattles, beaded flags, and crosses. How did the relic of a horrible past fit in with the offerings to the gods? What did it mean to the people who chanted, prayed, or gathered before it? I do not remember where I saw this thing.

When "Baby Doc" Duvalier had been helped to flee Haiti by the United States, glory days had begun. Jubilation in the streets. T-shirts with the slogan "Haïti libérée." "Uprooting" of tontons macoutes. Looting of centers of vodou, collecting drums, all trappings of devotion, and burning oungan alive. These priests were suspected of working with Duvalier. Many priests were killed. I knew that Catholic priests had also accommodated themselves to the regime. They were spared.

I recalled the ounfò I had visited fifteen years before this fanfare of mutilation and hope. Near Fontamara, not far from Port-au-Prince, this religious compound seemed to me to say something about how "politics," once brought into the sphere of the spiritual, undergoes changes that even a consummate and cunning politician like "Papa Doc" Duvalier could not have dreamed of. I have chosen a photo of the wall paintings of the sanctuary as the cover for this book because it exemplifies a particular way of putting things together: condensing epic stories into visual claims on the imagination. The sanctuary, also referred to as the kaymistè, the house of spirits, had two rooms: on the right, one called "Chambre Petros"; on the left one called "Cham Radas." Two rooms for two nations of gods. The Rada—named for the people taken from Arada, on the coast of Dahomey— the supposedly benign, "sweet" spirits. The Petwo, the violent, hungry, and "stiff" revolutionary gods born during slavery on the soil of Saint-Domingue. A veve, the symbolic design of a lwa, or spirit, was painted on the Petwo door; a faded painting was tacked on to the Rada door. All I could make out was the Haitian flag, vertical bands of black and red. Jean-Jacques Dessalines had torn the white from the French tricolor, leaving blue and red. "Papa Doc" had changed blue to black

Ball and chain in the altar room to the spirit Simbi lakwa (Simbi-the-cross). Haiti, 1970. Photograph by Leon Chalom.

in order to clarify the black gist of the union of "mulatto" and "negro." To the right of the door a cloth image of the flag was tacked on the wall. In the middle of the flag was a picture of Duvalier. Painted on the right-hand corner of the wall, Duvalier appeared again, as if peeping over the pile of wooden folding chairs that leaned against the wall. I recognized him by his glasses. His wife, Simone, wearing one white glove, was shown walking away from him. Did this mean the oungan supported Duvalier? What would such support mean? I thought about the many other symbols, images, and words painted on these walls. I suspected that in this space of absorption, renewal, and adaptation, the image of Duvalier, even the word "Doc," did not carry the weight of a macoute pistol. Rather, I thought about these elements as a visual encrustation, where things thought disparate or incongruous appeared simultaneously, and on an equal footing. These accretions

Wall painting on the kay-mistè (sanctuary of the spirits) in the temple of Vincent Dauphin, oungan. Fontamara, Haiti, 1970. Photograph by Leon Chalom.

had more to do with a philosophy of knowing and belief than with politics. But how can these materials be deciphered in conventional narration? How do we read out this synchronic history? Scales of justice, the male and female serpent gods Danbala and Ayida Wèdo, Azaka with his pipe, his broad straw hat, his blue denim garments, and his bottle of clairin. A sickle of labor, the shaded silhouette of the coconut palm that formed the coat of arms of the Republic of Haiti. And there, above Azaka, god of farming, in between the snakes, the coat of arms with the palm fronds, the six flags of red and black with a splotch of white in the center, either marking the place of absence, where once the white had been, or simulating the photo of Duvalier in the center of the flag on the wall. At the bottom of the seal, the motto: "L'Union Fait La Force," The Union (of blacks and yellows, negroes and mulattoes) Makes Strength. Symbols and mottos from the French revolutionaries formed the emblems of the new Republic; and here, on this wall, "Société L'Afrique Guinin" brushes up beside the advertisement for Radio and TV. On the left "La Sirène," one of the powerful female spirits, blows the lambi or conch shell.

The oungan chanted what a friend of mine called a four-day genealogy of the gods. Once every seven years the teller of histories sat for three or four days, as visitors and participants came and went, talking about the gods. I only heard a couple of hours of the names in what seemed to me then a gradual and easy transition from hero to legend to dead spirit to powerful god. It was my first time in Haiti. Many times since that summer day in 1970, I have wished I had stayed in Bel-Air and listened. I hold on to the fragments now recalled too late. When I was introduced to the oungan, he said "Salam Alechem" (Peace be with you). Wondering why he spoke Arabic to me, I simply asked what language that was. He answered, "ce langaj," which means a secret language with its sources in Guinea, used by initiates. What kind of history in Africa was behind the Arabic greeting that had been transformed into magic, the mystical speech of vodou. Did the songs tell stories of slavery? How much feeling, hope, remembering, and admonition did the oungan preserve in this condensation of history? I did not ask these questions. Instead, I walked away, puzzled by why exploits of Dessalines, a hero of the Haitian Revolution, followed what sounded like novenas to the Virgin Mary.

The three parts of *Haiti, History, and the Gods* should be read as three superimpositions that reinforce one another, while discouraging a unified point of view. I tell the same story again and again in different ways. Readers might well ask: "Why do we have to step in the same waters twice, three times?" I answer that the communion I intend in this narrative is much like ritual. The more a detail, scene, or theme is repeated, the more of its meaning is established. Syncretism, hybridity, and contamination usually apply to places on the "periphery," in this case the colonies, while the metropole is allowed to stand as an icon of purity. I not only think of colonies as safety valves for metropolitan excess, but envision metropolitan societies with their heads in the dirt they thought they had exported to the "tropics." While treating colonial Saint-Domingue as ground or impetus for many of the processes that would shape republican France, I also describe what happened when France came to Saint-Domingue, most notably, when Napoleon Bonaparte, wanting to reinstitute slavery in his possessions, sent his best troops to Saint-Domingue in order to bring down Toussaint Louverture and make sure no epaulette remained on any black shoulder. The final section takes the despotism, sensuality, romance, and bondage so central to these restored narratives and pushes them to their extremes in an Americas that kept Haiti as its silenced but crucial interlocutor, and to a large extent its ancestor spirit.

In charting the cultural imagination of a place, I summon many characters, bodied and disembodied. The idea of bodies, alternately idealized or brutalized, is at the heart of this retrieval. I spend an unusual amount of time on scenes that activate remnants of illicit identities and promiscuities. Slavery variously affects these figures of excess: Donatien Rochambeau's inheritance of Toussaint's "colored" seraglio in Port-au-Prince; the pieces of Dessalines's body reassembled by the unhinged woman Défilée; Pauline Bonaparte Leclerc's representation as a goddess who mimicked mourning as she donned the dress of adoring Creoles; the stereotype of the luxurious *mulâtresse*; and the invocation of Ezili, the spirit of love who denies or prohibits love.

I began writing this book by asking how Haiti functioned as the necessary element in early historical constructions, how its two-sided nature (alternately "Black France" and the "African Antilles") helped to delineate Western constructions of "civilization" and "savagery." The first chapter, "Rituals of History," retains much of this initial inquiry. What happens if we read the history of events in France from the ground of Haiti, where the call for "Liberté, Egalité, Fraternité" crashed hard upon the facts of Property, Labor, and Race? The events and their protagonists—whether Toussaint, Henry Christophe, or Dessalines—have long been fixtures in Haiti's own political or literary storytelling. These stories are often conflicting, depending on who tells the story and for what purpose. I thus turn from Western or "mainstream" historical accounts to those written by Haitians themselves. How did Haiti as an "idol of liberty" influence the way Haitian writers saw themselves?

The ground underlying this project of reconstruction remains *vodou,* even to the point of pressing Catholicism into its service. Recognizing that this term for serving the spirits has become a hollow word, a chunk of life ripped out of context and used for all kinds of popular fictions ("voodoo politics," "voodoo dolls," and "voodoo economics"), I take vodou as impetus for another kind of inquiry. In 1972, as I wrote about the gods in order to explain the poetic masterpiece, René Depestre's *Un Arc-en-ciel pour l'occident chrétien* (A Rainbow for the Christian West), where vodou spirits in the blood of a poet descend one by one into a judge's house in Alabama, I was struck by Sidney Mintz's introduction to Alfred Métraux's classic ethnography, *Voodoo in Haiti*. Here, for the first time, someone clarified what it meant to interact with the spirits, how the rituals that seemed so extraordinary were really quite ordinary, and therein lay their power. The daily, the everyday, the commonplace worked wonders: in his words, "the apparently bizarre becomes ordinary." But what most haunted me was the sense of thought pressing down on the mind and in the spirit: as Mintz put it, "when African slaves from a score of different societies first attempted to implant their symbolic pasts in the hearts and minds of their children." From images of the heart and thoughts of the mind, Mintz, in a phrase enclosed by dashes that I never forgot, supplies what he meant by "a core of belief": "—one might almost say a series of philosophical postulates about reality."

The idea of philosophy, of thought thinking itself through history, compelled me. I began to consider not only the historical functions of vodou—its preservation of pieces of history ignored, denigrated, or exoticized by the standard "drum and trumpet" histories of empire—but the project of thought, the intensity of interpretation and dramatization it allowed. Facing what remains to a large extent an unreconstructible past—the responses of slaves to the terrors of slavery, to colonists, to the New World—I try to imagine what cannot be verified. I do not treat vodou as an experience of transcendence, an escapist move into dream or frenzy. Instead, I emphasize the intensely intellectual puzzlement, the process of thought working itself through terror that accounts for what I have always recognized as the materiality of vodou practice, its concreteness, its obsession with details and fragments, with the very things that might seem to block or hinder belief. This sense of invention goaded by thought leads me to claim that vodou practices must be viewed as ritual reenactments of Haiti's colonial past, even more than as retentions from Africa. The shock of Creole society, I emphasize, resulted in strange bedfellows, spiritual connections that had as much to do with domination as resistance,

with reinterpretations of laws laid down, tortures enacted, and the barbarous customs of a brute white world. The spirits are not, as Melville
Herskovits suggested, simply African imports, retained and reinterpreted in the New World, nor are they pale imitations of pre-Christian
and Christian images, idolatrously copied, without intellectual content.

Kamau Brathwaite in *Creole Society in Jamaica* alluded to a two-
way process of giving and getting, a colonial creolization that allowed
for exchange rather than merely domination or obeisance. Underlying
each part of my book is the encounter with religious practice, a philosophy that seems to deny as much as it gives. Why would such demanding gods, apparently counterposed to the historical realities of
Haitian life, be invented by people in need of supernatural assistance?
This book traces the experience of "possession," "service," and "attachment" through a treatment of spirits as deposits of history, and as
remnants of feelings that cannot be put to rest.

I have been seduced by the extremism of certain situations, moments that seem harrowing reembodiments of an enlightenment ideal.
This seductive space summons a bondage that catches, enthralls, and
stills me. Trying to break out of conventional historical, literary, and
ethnographic analyses, I risk writing the kind of text that I wanted
to combat in writing *Haiti, History, and the Gods.* Yet in highlight-
ing complexities and ambiguities that have been obscured in writings
about Haiti, about France, and even about the United States, I hope
to set the stage for what might be called literary fieldwork. In the second chapter, "Fictions of Haiti," concentrating on the novels of Marie
Chauvet, I experience the difficulties posed by using a literary source
as data that can test, confirm, or enhance facts from other sources.
Chauvet's fictions are compared with other texts, literary and nonlit-
erary. Perhaps the greatest writer of Haitian fiction, Chauvet, exiled
from Haiti in 1968, has been the most suppressed and the most misunderstood. Deliberately occupying her space as light-skinned bourgeoise in Duvalier's *noiriste* Haiti, she wrote in order to refuse clarity,
to attack the assumptions of Haitian nationalism and historical identity, to knock down heroes and to confront the embarrassing claims of
color that plague Haitian society.

Images of women, scenes of affectionate appropriation, and cha-
rades of love permeate this text. Whether called Ezili, Sister Rose,
Défilée, whores or ladies, virgins or vampires, or summoned by Mary
Hassall in her *Secret History; or, The Horrors of St. Domingo* or by Chau-

vet in her fictions, certain symbols of women lurk throughout as keys
to the nature of this quest. In *Marianne au combat: L'Imagerie et la
symbolique républicaines de 1789 à 1880,* Maurice Agulhon wonders:
"Why doesn't Marianne have a twin sister across the Atlantic?" He
mentions that the United States, with its Protestantism, did not allow
for the kind of iconization engendered by the Catholic population of
France. His superb exploration of "Marianolâtry," as a reversal and
deepening of "Mariolâtrie," ignores the Caribbean and Latin America
as other sites for doubling, conflation, and the reinvestment in erotics
that shaped republics. If, as Agulhon laments, "the American Republic, in which the founding principles of 1776 are so close to ours in
'89, did not engender a feminine myth comparable to ours," I would
add that the stories of virgins, saints, and weeping, childless, demonic
beauties were powerfully fleshed out in those places that not only held
onto but dismembered, renewed, and reinvented these vessels of a
dominant culture. Sometimes gruesomely corporealized, these bodies
survived in new worlds that had much to do with the old.

In the most haunting passage that Matthew Gregory ("Monk")
Lewis ever wrote (not in *The Monk* but in his *Journal of a West India
Proprietor,* published posthumously in 1834), he arrives at his lodging
in Savannah la Mar, and sees a "clean-looking negro," who gives him
water and a towel. Thinking that he belongs to the inn, Lewis takes
"no notice of him." After some time, the servant introduces himself:
"Massa not know me; *me your slave!*" The "sound," Lewis admits,
"made me feel a pang at the heart." What does knowledge mean in
the context of a sound like *slave*? Where does the pathos of the heart
figure? I recalled Emerson's "Ich diene. I serve. A royal motto." What
does it mean to say "I serve"? I wondered about names spoken by
masters, words like *love, slave, white, black,* names given and names
taken away, and what these words meant to those thought to have no
history, no thought, no feeling. What did those constructed as "things"
but sometimes desired as "lovers" make of words that, once heard,
could then change in meaning, according to expediency, to circumstances, to whim? As I have said, one of the critical turns in my study—
the query about the subjective reactions of slaves—is perilous. But the
question must be asked. Only then can we begin to probe a "memory" that demolishes such straightjacket pairs as victim and victimizer,
colonized and colonizer, master and slave.

I have always suspected, as did Thomas Carlyle in "The Nigger Question" (bracketing his racist disquisition on pumpkin-eating emancipated

blacks and the "dog kennel" and "jungle" of Haiti), that "SLAVERY, whether established by law, or by law abrogated, exists very extensively in the world . . . and in fact, that you cannot abolish slavery by act of parliament, but can only abolish the *name* of it, which is very little!" Recall Ishmael's "Who ain't a slave? Tell me that." How did terms like *bondage, service,* and *property* get transferred to fictions of appropriation and love? Though I sense the danger in looking at stories and novels as depositories for the experience of slavery (its transmutation into remarkable "histories" for the readers' delectation), I suspect that domination and servitude worked reciprocally for those who lived with the terrors of the "peculiar institution." They, too, transported these terms, the facts of life in servitude, to places free from the control of commerce, production, and commodities. Once inserted into religious practices and expressed in spiritual beliefs, these experiences returned, transfigured as they pulsed through the spirits worshipped in the night.

Terror is the place of greatest love. When I ask, "How are gods made?" I am also asking, "How are histories told?" I want to reveal the blur at the heart of hierarchy. A mutually reinforcing double incarnation, or doubling between violation and sentiment, purity and impurity, is essential to my project. In forcing proximity on categories or claims usually kept separate, I invoke that convention called "gothic." Rude, barbarous, and rank with multiple narrations, my text concedes slippages that make codes of law complicitous with sadistic fantasies, supernatural haunts wedded to natural histories, and national myths synonymous with gothic romance.

"If you want somebody bad enough and can't have them, then you try to become them," a friend told me as we walked to the cemetery in Port-au-Prince, where "Papa Doc" Duvalier's tomb had been smashed, stones scattered. On an inside wall of the tomb, the *mulâtresse* Michèle Bennett (wife of "Baby Doc") had been sketched out in white and red, participating in an orgy, with a fleur-de-lis painted in black on her breasts.

Acknowledgments

I want to begin by thanking the Haitians who have inspired and shared in this work in various ways during the past twenty years: René Depestre, René Bélance, Franck and Paul Laraque, and those who first introduced me to the discipline of vodou and the resilience of Haitian thought and aesthetics: Evelyne, Philippe Bernard, La Merci Benjamin, Vincent Dauphin, the sculptors Georges Liautaud and André Dimanche, and the painters Gérard Valcin and André Pierre. In the course of working on this project, I have owed a great deal to various friends, colleagues, and institutions. I am grateful for fellowships in 1985–1986 from the National Endowment for the Humanities and the Social Science Research Council, and to Yale University for granting me a sabbatical. During my year at the Davis Center for Historical Study at Princeton, I had the opportunity to test my sense of literary history in seminars that raised questions I would otherwise not have known to ask. I thank Natalie Davis, the director of the center, for her continued presence as a model of graceful inquiry, and Richard Rathbone and Gayatri Spivak for their wit and unfailing acuteness.

In writing this book, I spent fruitful hours in the library of the Institut Saint-Louis de Gonzague in Port-au-Prince. There, Frère Ernest not only helped me to locate materials necessary to my study of religiosity in Saint-Domingue but told me stories that led me to know how beliefs, thought superficial, revealed the gist of a sacred history. Drexel Woodson's rigorous questions about texts and social contexts in Haiti taught me a great deal. Kamau Brathwaite has inspired me for many years now. I give thanks for his presence. I owe an ongoing intellectual debt to Sidney Mintz, Vincent Crapanzano, Gananath Obeyesekere, and Erika Bourguigon for their critical readings of the manuscript and their generosity in sharing their work with me. Thomas Cassirer and Rudy Troike have continued to be provocative interlocutors. The support, good humor, and understanding of my editor, Stanley Holwitz, helped shape this book as far back as our first talk in 1990.

I greatly value the support I received from editors who first published sections of the book in their journals. I want to thank Cathy Davidson at *American Literature*, Richard Poirier at the *Raritan Review*, Ralph Cohen at *New Literary History*, and Abiola Irele at *Research in African Literatures* for their permission to reprint. I also thank Gyan Prakash for inviting me to contribute an earlier version of chapter 1 to his collection, *After Colonialism: Imperial Histories and Postcolonial Displacements*, and Maryse Condé and Madeleine Cottenet-Hage for printing another version of chapter 4 in *Penser la créolité*.

Out here in the desert, I completed a book that was a long time in the making. My gratitude to the University of Arizona Special Collections and Interlibrary Loan for their unstinting help in my research, and to Gary Kabakoff for his help in the production of this book. Friends on the East Coast have not only read this manuscript in pieces over the years but continue to ask the necessary questions: Allen Mandelbaum, Ronald Paulson, and Schuldt. Kenneth Gross, Lizabeth Paravisini, and my graduate students in Tucson, especially Jennifer Ellis and Sharon Harrow, have goaded me on to thought. I am most grateful to Wendy Wipprecht, consummate editor and critic, and to Tom Miller, who, more than once, became my best reader.

I recall my mother hanging over the railing of a Hilton somewhere in the Caribbean, when I was very young, trying to pick mangoes. Though separated from Haiti and tempted into forgetting her life there, she shared with me, perhaps unwittingly, her attachment. When I was sixteen, my uncle Leon Chalom showed me a painting by Jean-Enguérrand Gourgue called *Vodou*. He then accompanied me on my first trip to Haiti, and without him I could never have made the contacts so important to my later work. Finally, I dedicate this work to the memory of my father, whose discussions of Spinoza and Maimonides no doubt led me to know the import of trying to articulate the spiritual life.

Note on Orthography

Haitian orthography is varied, and the phonetic variants numerous. The fight over the orthography of Haitian Creole was especially virulent during the 1940s and 1950s: an argument about English or American orthography (associated with Protestantism) as opposed to French (associated with the Catholic Church). Between 1940 and 1945, the Protestant missionary H. Ormonde McConnell developed an orthography for Haitian Creole that was then revised, following the advice of Frank Laubach, and adapted to French. French speakers opposed the McConnell–Laubach orthography as too American, and another adaptation by Charles-Fernand Pressoir, which the Haitian elite favored, became the official orthography recognized by the Haitian government in 1961. I have, in most cases, adopted the most accessible phonemic orthography, which closely approximates that in official use in Haiti since 1979: Albert Valdman et al., *Haitian Creole-English-French Dictionary*, 2 vols. (Bloomington: Creole Institute, University of Indiana, 1981). Because some Haitian novelists and ethnographers continue to use a French transliteration of Creole, I have standardized the Creole spelling in my translations from their works. In the English texts, I have retained the author's choice of spelling, so readers should expect some inconsistency in orthography. Those familiar with my earlier publications will note that, in now using the standard, popular Haitian spelling of Creole, I have abandoned my attempt to preserve the range of gallicized Creole terms used by various writers, depending on author and time period. Therefore, *vodoun, loa, Erzulie, Petro(s)*, for example, now appear as *vodou, lwa, Ezili, Petwo*.

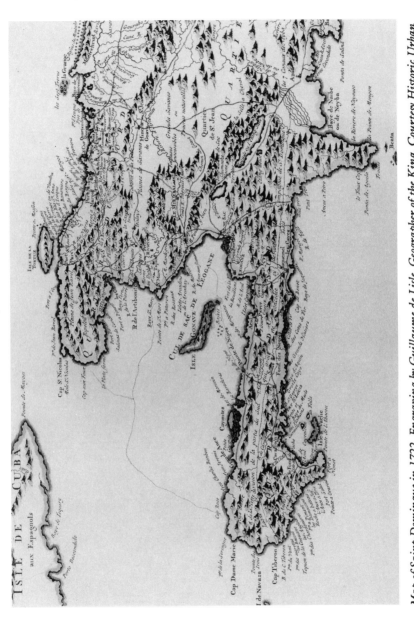

Map of Saint-Domingue in 1722. Engraving by Guillaume de Lisle, Geographer of the King. Courtesy Historic Urban Plans, Ltd., Ithaca, New York.

PART ONE

1

Rituals of History

The child of savage Africa,
Sold to fall under the colonist's whip,
Founded independence on the soil of slavery,
And the Hill, in its voice, echoed the language of Racine
and Fénélon!
—M. Chauvet, *Chant lyrique,* 1825[1]

"Rid us of these gilded Africans, and we shall have nothing more to wish," Napoleon Bonaparte wrote to his brother-in-law General Victor-Emmanuel Leclerc in 1802. Though successful in Guadeloupe and Martinique, Napoleon's soldiers, commanded first by Leclerc and then by Donatien Rochambeau, failed to reestablish slavery in Saint-Domingue. The only locale in history for a successful slave revolution, Saint-Domingue became the first Black Republic in 1804. As the Martiniquan writer and politician Aimé Césaire put it, "The first epic of the New World was written by Haitians, by Toussaint, Christophe, and Dessalines."[2] When Jean-Jacques Dessalines articulated the meaning of "independence" for Haiti, he realized what Césaire called a transformative, "prodigious history" of the Antilles. Dessalines tore the white from the French tricolor—"Mouché, chiré blanc là qui lan drapeau-là" (Tear out the white from the flag, Monsieur)[3]—as he would remove the name Saint-Domingue from the former colony. He called the new nation "Haiti," from the original Amerindian word (*Ayti*) for the island meaning "mountainous lands."

On January 1, 1804, in Gonaïves, Dessalines proclaimed independence. Speaking in Creole, he recalled French atrocities and urged Haitians to fight to the death for their country. Boisrond-Tonnerre, Dessalines's "high-brown" secretary, demanded—in a formal French that recalled Maximilien de Robespierre's speeches in 1792—"a solemn abjuration of the French nation" in the name of Dessalines: "If there remains among you a lukewarm heart, let him retire, and tremble to pronounce the oath that must unite us. Let us swear to the whole world, to posterity, to ourselves, to renounce France forever and to die rather than live under its domination; to fight to the last breath for the independence of our country."[4] In the attempt to drive a wedge between France and Haiti, Dessalines ordered nearly 3,000 French men, women, and children killed with hatchets, sabres, bayonets, and daggers. No gunshot was allowed, no cannon or musketry. Silence and calm were necessary so that from one town to the next no one would be warned of the approaching slaughter.

Yet no declaration of independence, whether spoken in French or Haitian Creole, could sever the bonds between the former colony and its "Mother Country." Speaking of this massacre, which began in February (after the French had been promised protection) and ended on April 22, 1804, Dessalines declared in French: "Haiti has become a red spot on the surface of the globe, which the French will never accost." The violence was consecrated in the language of those who had been annihilated. We should not underrate the horror of this ventriloquy: the implications of a liberation that cannot be glorified except in the language of the former master. Even as Boisrond-Tonnerre warned of the dangers not of the "French armies," but "the canting eloquence of their agents' proclamations," he perpetuated the rhetoric he condemned. Dessalines's proclamation of April 8 (drafted by his mulatto secretary-general, Juste Chanlatte) is also a highly stylized, Jacobin document. By avenging himself on the "true cannibals," the Haitian, no longer vile, earned his right to "regeneration" and understood at last what it meant to breathe "the air of liberty, pure, honorable, and triumphant." Dessalines concluded by making the Haitian Revolution transferable to the Americas: "We have rendered to these true cannibals, war for war, crime for crime, outrage for outrage; yes, I have saved my country; I have avenged America."[5]

For whom does Dessalines speak? The majority of the revolutionaries did not know French (it is claimed that Toussaint Louverture knew how to read and write, but Dessalines, like Henry Christophe, was illiterate and could barely sign his name). Yet historians, both Haitian and foreign, present them, with some exceptions, as able to speak

French. When Boisrond-Tonnerre declared independence in the name of Dessalines on January 1, 1804, he recognized this linguistic colonialism with lyric prescience: "The French name still darkens our plains." Though French shadowed Haiti, with writers articulating the Haitian Revolution retrospectively in French, Creole also shared in the task of coercing difference into governable homogeneity. During the revolution, Creole was imposed as the national language by the Creole (Haitian-born) leaders Toussaint, Dessalines, and Christophe. This emerging language, initially used as a means of communication between slaves and masters, was an amalgam of French vocabulary and syntactic contributions from West Africa, as well as Taino, English, and Spanish. The African-born former slaves, who spoke one of at least two or three African languages, were silenced and subjugated to the Creole linguistic monopoly, a creolization that made for a linguistic accord conducive to political control by Creoles.[6] What strikes a reader of the various French proclamations during and after the revolution is the astonishing homogeneity of what was said, no matter who speaks or for what purpose. Debates in the revolutionary assemblies in Paris, the words of Georges-Jacques Danton and Robespierre especially, once printed in newspapers in Saint-Domingue, were recycled as formulas or favored shibboleths by those who took on the burden of politics and the prerogative of French in the new republic.

Called variously "Black France" by one nineteenth-century observer (Jules Michelet), this "France with frizzy hair" by another (Maxime Raybaud), and merely a "tropical dog-kennel and pestiferous jungle" by Thomas Carlyle, Haiti forced imagination high and low: expression moved uneasily between the extremes of idealization and debasement. In the background of this textualized and cursedly mimetic Haiti, however, remained certain legends, blurred but persistent oral traditions that resisted such coercive dichotomies as genteel and brute, master and slave, precious language and common voice. Though Haiti's "Africanness," like its "Frenchness," would be used by writers for differing purposes, the business of *being Haitian* was more complex—and the slippages and uneasy alliances between contradictions more pronounced—than most writerly representations of Haiti ever allowed.

Romancing the Dark World

A series of articles on Haiti appeared in the *Petite Presse* in Paris from September 8 to December 31, 1881. Written by the black

Martiniquan, Victor Cochinat, the columns reported on everything
from vodou to the military, calling attention to the Haitians' love of
artifice, their propensity to exaggerate and mime, and their apparent
indifference to the continuing and bloody revolutions that followed
independence in 1804. Cochinat also turned to vodou and to tales of
cannibalism and magic in order to prove to his French audience that
Haiti remained unregenerate.[7]

Louis-Joseph Janvier published his alternately strident and elegiac
response to Cochinat in Paris in 1883.[8] Janvier, born in Port-au-
Prince, descended from peasants, was the first in his family to be
educated. In 1877, when he was twenty-two, he received a scholar-
ship from the Haitian government to study in France. There he remained, for twenty-eight years, until 1905. His collection of meditations, called *La République d'Haïti et ses visiteurs*, contained long
passages from the abolitionist Victor Schoelcher, Oliver Wendell
Holmes, and M. Victor Meignan, and a preface packed with quota-
tions from Jules Michelet, René de Chateaubriand, Victor Hugo,
Ernest Renan, Georges-Jacques Danton, Alphonse de Lamartine, and
Henry Christophe. Janvier claimed that Haitians were on the road to
civilization, arguing that the bloodiest political crimes in his country
simply proved that "Haiti always imitates Europe."

Be indulgent, oh sons of western Europe!

Recall—I am citing at random, unconcerned about chronology—recall the
Sicilian Vespers, the *holy* Inquisition . . . the Albegensian massacre, the war of
the Two Roses, the massacre of Strelitz, the sacking of ghettos, the religious
wars in England, which is to say the papists hanged by the anti-papists, and
the anti-papists burned by the papists, Saint-Bartholemew, the days of September 1792, the 10th of August, the red Terror, the 13th Vendemiaire, the
18th Brumaire, the white Terror, the June days of 1848, December 2, 1851;
the month of May 1871. . . . be indulgent.[9]

The historian Michelet was Janvier's idol, "this sublime thinker." When
confronting the succession of coups d'état that imperiled the young
nation, Janvier claimed Haiti to be the incarnation of history in Michelet's sense of resurrection: "The history of Haiti is a series of mar-
velous resurrections."

That Haitian independence had to be sealed in a ritual of blood
and vengeance made even more urgent the need to "rehabilitate the
black race," to prove that in Haiti everything is French. If we recall
Dessalines's proclamation abjuring the French nation after the massacre, which he called his "last act of national authority," we can

appreciate the high costs of such symbolic violence. The imagination of future generations of Haitians would be handicapped by the theatricality of the past.

When Janvier wrote his defense of Haiti, the population was about 90 percent peasants. Romanticized for their pastoral innocence and endurance, those whom foreigners had condemned as remnants of "dark Africa" were transformed by Janvier into French-speaking, God-fearing laborers. The ground upon which he constructed his fable of the Haitian nation—proud, vital, earthy, and black—they served as an appropriate symbol of the new Haiti: a gothic Eden resurrected on the ashes of colonial Saint-Domingue. Whether they inhabited the plains or the *mornes* (hills), the peasants Janvier idealized were fiercely independent, attached to their lands and devoted to their gods. Yet Janvier's sense of "the Haitian" depended on his refutation of vodou, which he denounced as "primitive." He assured his readers that all Haitians were now Catholic or Protestant, that all traces of barbarism had disappeared, and that most Haitians spoke French. After all, Janvier concluded, "French prose, Haitian coffee, and the philosophical doctrines of the French Revolution are the best stimulants of the Haitian brain."[10]

Black Skin, White Heart

The turning of Saint-Domingue into Haiti, colony into republic, demanded a new history that would be written by people who saw themselves as renewing the work of the French who had once abolished slavery and declared slaves not only *men* but *citizens.* Yet the reactionary conceptual flotsam of the Old Regime, and the appropriate tags of "civilization," "order," and "dignity" would clash with a "fanaticism" that had no proper language and no right to history. Could the history of the Haitian Revolution be told in the language of France? As Haitian historians attempted to gain access to "civilization," someone else's language (and at least part of the history that went with it) was necessary to their entitlement.

In his 1774 *The History of Jamaica,* the Jamaican Creole Edward Long turned to an Africa he had never seen, wrote of its unimaginable savagery, compared negroes to orangutans, and did his best to prove "the natural inferiority of Negroes." Yet, there was one chance for the black individual to distinguish himself from his dark surround. Long tells the story of Francis Williams—a native of Jamaica and son of Dorothy and John Williams, free blacks—who, once educated into literature, defined himself "as a *white* man acting under a *black* skin." Williams had been chosen to be

the subject of an experiment, which, it is said, the Duke of Montague was curious to make, in order to discover, whether, by proper cultivation, and a regular course of tuition at school and the university, a Negroe might not be found as capable of literature as a white person.[11]

Williams gets a "new" language. He acquires a convertible history. That he composes his poetry in Latin should alert us to the artifices possible in a New World that could be more ancient than the Old. Writing "An Ode" to Governor George Haldane, he disclaims the color of his skin in order to gain acceptance for his poem. Toward the end of the ode, recognition, or proof of rehabilitation, depends not only on the labor of language but the sudden disavowal of an epidermal trait: "Tho' dark the stream on which the tribute flows, / Not from the *skin,* but from the *heart* it rose."

> "Oh! *Muse,* of blackest tint, why shrinks thy breast,
> Why fears t'approach the *Caesar* of the *West!*
> Dispel thy doubts, with confidence ascend
> The regal dome, and hail him for thy friend:
> Nor blush, altho' in garb funereal drest,
> *Thy body's white, tho' clad in sable vest.*"[12]

If the justification of slavery depended on converting a biological fact into an ontological truth—black = savage, white = civilized—the descendant of slaves must not only pay tribute to those who enslaved but *make himself white, while remaining black.* Further, acquisition of the forever unreal new identity is paid for by negation of the old self.

What is significant about Williams's "An Ode" is that he talks both to his black Muse and his white patron: he keeps her black, "in garb funereal drest," yet he also makes her white, assuring his "muse" and his white readers: "Thy body's *white, tho' clad in sable vest.*" Finally, the poet concludes, "the sooty *African*" will be white in "manners," in the "glow of genius," in "learned speech, with modest accent worn." These adornments constitute the whiteness that transforms the heart and, once this has happened, turns the man inside out.

The complex working out of personal identity through a duplicity or doubling of color proves crucial to the making of a nation, and shapes the way the first two major Haitian historians, Thomas Madiou and Beaubrun Ardouin, introduced themselves. Though a mulatto who lived in Paris for ten years, Ardouin focused on his African ancestry. He announces himself in his introduction as "Descendant of this African race that has been so long persecuted," and at the end of his eleven-volume history (published between 1853 and 1860), he exclaims: "Glory to all these children of Africa. . . . Honor to their memory!"[13] Madiou, also mulatto, lived in France from the age of ten until he was twenty-one. Unlike Ardouin, who defended the *affranchis* (freedmen) and ignored their interest, after the decree of May 15, 1791, in preserving slavery, Madiou refused to account for Haitian history in accord with the "official" mulatto view. He would later be claimed by Haitian ideologues as the *noiriste* historian of Haiti. His fiery assessment of Dessalines as a Haitian Robespierre, "this angel of death," based on interviews in the 1840s with former revolutionaries, departed from the critical disdain of the more moderate and elite *éclairées* (enlightened). If Dessalines was savage, Madiou countered that he remained the "Principle incarnate of Independence; he was barbaric against colonial barbarism."[14]

For both Madiou and Ardouin the labor of writing history demanded that the historian be seen as human while remaining Haitian. They turned to France and the white world, but claimed blackness and repaired the image of Africa, by making Haiti—purified of superstition, sorcerers, and charms—the instrument of reclamation. Throughout Haitian history the recovery or recognition of blackness (*négritude* or *noirisme*) never depended exclusively on color or phenotype.[15] Reading Madiou's and Ardouin's introductions to their histories, it is difficult to specify their color. Sir Spenser St. John—Great Britain's minister resident and consul general in Haiti, intermittently from 1863 to 1884—reminded his readers in *Hayti, or the Black Republic,* in a tautology that makes indefinite the need to define: "Thomas Madiou (clear mulatto) . . ."; "M. Beaubrun Ardouin (fair mulatto) . . ."[16] Their ability to reclaim and represent their "native land" to a foreign audience depended on their variously authentic and partly spurious claims of color but, most important, on the wielding of proper language. Both Madiou and Ardouin concluded their introductions by apologizing not for color but for style. In Ardouin's case, especially, the apology helped him to prove his nationality, affirmed by nothing less than his resolutely faltering or broken French. He articulated, perhaps for the first time, what Edouard Glissant much later would name *antillanité,* and what Césaire, speaking about his choice to write poetry in French and not in Creole, would qualify as French with the *marque nègre.*

If this work finds some readers in Paris, they will see many infelicities of style, still more faults in the rules of grammar: it will offer them no literary merit. But they should not forget that, in general, Haitians stammer the words of the French language, in order to emphasize in some way their origin in the Antilles.[17]

Ardouin had no doubt remembered Madiou's introduction. In *Histoire d'Haïti* Madiou had addressed his readers:

I beseech the reader to show himself indulgent concerning the style of my work; all I did was attempt to be correct, since at 1,800 leagues from the hearth of our language, in a country where nearly the entire population speaks Creole, it is quite impossible that French would not suffer the influence of those idioms I have meanwhile tried to avoid.[18]

Between Civilization and Barbarism

In Port-au-Prince on April 16, 1848, the very black and illiterate President Faustin Soulouque began the massacre of mulattoes he suspected as conspirators. In Paris a "prince-president," Louis Napoleon, who had just emerged from the other side of the barricades and blood of the June 1848 revolution, exclaimed, "Haïti, Haïti, pays de barbares!"

Soulouque, following Dessalines's and Napoleon Bonaparte's imperial example, declared himself Emperor Faustin I on August 25, 1849. Spenser St. John thought this act typical of a racially particular obsession: "All black chiefs have a hankering after the forms as well as the substance of despotic power."[19] Imitating his French model, Soulouque crowned himself, then crowned the empress, and created a nobility of four princes, fifty-nine dukes, two marquises, ninety counts, two hundred barons, and thirty knights. About three years later, in France, Louis Napoleon became emperor and brought the Second Republic to an end. The nephew of Napoleon—Karl Marx's "caricature of the old Napoleon"—did not have it easy. When he declared himself emperor a year after the coup d'état of December 2, 1851, he

SOULOUQUE ET SA COUR

CARICATURES

PAR

CHAM. *(pseud.)*

Noé, Amédée de.

— Attention, grenadiers, du haut de ces cocotiers quarante
singes vous contemplent !

AU BUREAU DU JOURNAL LE CHARIVARI,
16, RUE DU CROISSANT.

—

IMPRIMERIE LANGE LÉVY ET COMP., 16, RUE DU CROISSANT.

Soulouque and His Court, *by Amédée de Noé (pseudonym: Cham). Paris,
1850. Courtesy Schomburg Center for Research in Black Culture, New York
Public Library.*

found himself not only described as Hugo's "Napoléon le petit" but compared to the Haitian Soulouque.

In *The Eighteenth Brumaire of Louis Bonaparte* (1851), Marx compared what he called "the best" of Louis Napoleon's "bunch of blokes" to "a noisy, disreputable, rapacious bohème that crawls into galooned coats with the same grotesque dignity as the high dignitaries of Soulouque."[20] Referring to the counterfeit Bonaparte, Victor Hugo wrote a poem about "A monkey [who] dressed himself in a tiger's skin" ("Fable or History," *Les Châtiments*, 1853). Though most obviously referring to the dubious royalty and bombast of Louis Napoleon, the horrific slaughters of Hugo's poem could not fail to remind readers of Soulouque's outrages. Hugo's parting shot in "Fable or History" could be taken as a product of racialist ideology: "You are only a monkey!"

Gustave d'Alaux (the pen name of Maxime Raybaud, the French consul during part of Soulouque's reign), wrote *L'Empereur Soulouque et son empire*, parts of which appeared as a series of articles in the metropolitan *Revue des Deux-Mondes* (1850–1851) and finally as a book in 1856. He introduced his readers to a place where you could find "civilization and the Congo," and "newspapers and sorcerers."[21] Even the American Wendell Phillips, rendering homage to Toussaint and the Haitian Revolution in 1861, reminded his listeners in Boston and New York how much events in Haiti mattered to the new Napoleon in France: "the present Napoleon . . . when the epigrammatists of Paris christened his wasteful and tasteless expense at Versailles, *Soulouquerie*, from the name of Soulouque, the Black Emperor, he deigned to issue a specific order forbidding the use of the word."[22]

A later Haitian historian, Dantès Bellegarde in *La Nation haïtienne* (1938), lamented that the reputation of Soulouque suffered from the illegitimate actions of Louis Napoleon. Soulouque's character was defamed when the French, seeking a safe way obliquely to attack power, made him the vessel for their disdain of their own emperor. Bellegarde's words are crucial to understanding how different history might be if we jostle our ideas of cause and effect:

The crowning of the emperor, celebrated with unmatched magnificence, resulted in cruel jokes about Soulouque in the liberal French press and thus avenged the coup d'état of December 2, 1851, by Prince-President Louis Napoleon. And when, by the plebiscite of November 20, 1852, he had himself proclaimed emperor, they accused him of having aped [*singé*] Faustin I, and the more one blackened Soulouque, the more odious appeared the imitation of his grotesque act by the old member of the Italian Carbonari. The hatred of Napoleon the Little, as the poet of the *Châtiments* referred to him, contributed much to giving the chief of the Haitian State his unfortunate reputation as a ridiculous and bloodthirsty sovereign.[23]

Rereading events in France through the quizzing glass of Haiti is to clarify the reciprocal dependencies, the uncanny resemblances that no ideology of difference can remove. Who are the *true* cannibals? Who is "aping" whom? Recall Dessalines's words after his massacres of the French: "Yes, we have repaid these true cannibals, war for war, crime for crime, outrage for outrage." The question must have haunted Beaubrun Ardouin when he found himself in Paris, having escaped from the murderous Soulouque, happy to find himself in the "Republic" he praised in a letter to Lamartine, only to see liberty turn again into monarchy: the country he had turned to as example for his "young Haiti" flipping over, again, into empire. Ardouin, more opportunist than Madiou and an accomplished bureaucrat, had few problems with the change, as long as he was in France and not in Haiti. But he still had to justify his country to a people, many of whom were busy condemning Napoleon III, the very emperor he praised, and gladly advancing their attack by compounding black and white, Haiti and France, Soulouque and Louis Napoleon.

To justify revolution when despots were being recycled as simulacra was no easy matter. And to celebrate Haiti when Joseph Arthur de Gobineau had just published *De l'inégalité des races humaines* (1853–1855), a book that uses Haiti to signal the degeneracy of the black race ("depraved, brutal, and savage"), is a task we should not underestimate. The first volume of Ardouin's *Etudes sur l'histoire d'Haïti*, published in 1859, enjoyed such success that a second printing followed within a year.[24]

No Easy Liberty

Ardouin no doubt appreciated the business of politics. Friend and partisan of the tough mulatto, Major General Jean-Pierre Boyer (an *ancien affranchi*), who governed Haiti from 1820 to 1843, Senator Ardouin had negotiated the initial financial settlement with France in 1825: 150 million francs indemnity to be paid in five years to the dispossessed French planters of Saint-Domingue in order to obtain French recognition of the independence of its former colony, which was given in a royal ordinance from King Charles X. This edict, which conditionally recognized the Republic of Haiti as a "Free, independent and sovereign state," was backed up by force, leaving no doubt that the rhetoric of sovereignty would always be subject to severe qualification. France conveyed its recognition to President Boyer by a fleet of fourteen warships bearing 494 guns.[25]

But Madiou, never one to mince words, imagined what the heroes of the revolution would do if they left their tombs only to see the French flag flying in the cities of the new republic, while Haitians curried favor and became indebted to the descendants of colonial torturers. But it was Boyer's *Code Rural* (signed at the National Palace in Port-au-Prince on May 6, 1826) that reduced most Haitians, especially those who did not occupy positions of rank in the military or civil branches of the state, to essentially slave status. A small fraction of Haiti's population could live off the majority, collecting fees—with the help of their lackeys, the rural *chefs de section*—for produce, for the sale, travel, and butchering of animals, and even for the cutting of trees. In *Les Constitutions d'Haïti* (1886), addressed primarily to a Haitian audience, Janvier described Boyer's code as "slavery without the whip." Jonathan Brown, an American physician from New Hampshire who spent a year in Haiti (1833–1834), recalled his impressions of Boyer's regime in *The History and Present Condition of St. Domingo* (1837): "The existing government of Hayti is a sort of republican monarchy sustained by the bayonet."[26]

Boyer did not like "vice" or "laziness" displayed in dancing, festivals, or unsupervised meetings among the population. He demanded order, propriety, and hard work. He would have agreed with Ardouin who later condemned vodou in his *Etudes* as "the barbarism . . . that brutalizes souls." Borrowing from the *Code Henry* (that of Christophe in 1812), Boyer reinstituted strict regulations of punishment, work schedules, and forced labor. The *Code Rural* contained 202 articles, aimed at delimiting and identifying those who are "bound" to the soil. Article 3, for example, prescribes cultivation for those who "cannot justify their means of existence."

It being the duty of every Citizen to aid in sustaining the State, either by his active services, or by his industry, those who are not employed in the civil service, or called upon for the military service; those who do not exercise a licensed profession; those who are not working artisans, or employed as servants; those who are not employed in felling timber for exportation; in fine, those who cannot justify their means of existence, shall cultivate the soil.[27]

In 1843 and 1844 there were two revolutions that Ardouin would later describe as the "tragedy" of his generation: the popular army of Praslin, led by Charles Rivière-Hérard, and, the next year, the Piquet rebellion (named for the *piquiers,* the stakes or spears made by the militant peasant cultivators), led by the black Southerner and police lieutenant Louis-Jean Acaau "to defend the interests of the poor of all classes." The crises of 1843 and 1844 compelled Ardouin to write his history. The "Proclamation de Praslin," though ostensibly speaking for the people, and condemning Boyer's officials (including Ardouin) as traitors, was really a document contrived by Rivière-Hérard and other mulattoes, disgruntled Boyerists who wanted some of the power. The struggle of Acaau's *l'armée souffrante* (the suffering army), along with the resistance of members of the black elite, like Lysius Salomon, resulted in Rivière-Hérard's overthrow. Salomon's petition to the provisional government of Rivière-Hérard (June 22, 1843) is a marvel of recall and revision: "Citizens! Dessalines and Pétion cry out to you from the bottom of their graves. . . . Save Haiti, our communal mother; don't let her perish . . . save her. . . . The abolitionists rejoice and applaud you."[28]

Recognizing that it would be useless to resist these variously contrived liberation movements, Boyer had addressed the Senate for the last time on March 13, 1843, before leaving—like subsequent overthrown Haitian presidents—for Jamaica. Then began five years of instability comprising four short-lived presidencies. The phenomenon of Faustin Soulouque and Haiti's crisis of legitimacy resulted from what could be called a *comedy of color.* The mulatto oligarchs of Haiti reacted to the possibility of yet another revolution by contriving what became known as *la politique de la doublure.* The politics of the understudy allowed the light-skinned elites to remain in power, but under cover of blackness. The *dédoublement* of color, the *splitting in two,* qualifies Francis Williams's ritual of conversion. If the Jamaican black Williams proclaimed his *white heart with a black skin,* in Haiti, mulattoes in the turbulent 1840s were the heart of power, while selecting black skins as masks.

After a trinity of elderly and tractable black illiterates (Philippe Guerrier, 87 years old, directed by Beaubrun and Céligny Ardouin; Jean-Louis Pierrot, 84; and Jean-Baptiste Riché, 70), Soulouque (then 59) was chosen by those whom Spenser St. John called "the enlightened Ministers of the late General Riché." Beaubrun Ardouin, as head of the Senate, proposed the illiterate, black, and apparently malleable

General Soulouque as president of Haiti on March 1, 1847. When, a year later, Soulouque killed Ardouin's brother Céligny—the former minister of Haiti to the French government—Ardouin returned to France where he wrote his *Etudes*. But he never lost, even in exile, the capacity to name heroes or to please his patrons. Whether praising the republic of 1848 or the subsequent empire of Napoleon III, Ardouin held fast to France. But he carefully excluded the slave owners, those who fought for the colonial system, from those he called "the true French."

Who is the true Haitian? Ardouin's answer to the question gives definition the utility of not defining. Though he claimed himself as a "Descendant of Africa" and condemned the injustices of the colonial government against "the men of the black race which is my own," he asserted that the road to being Haitian must progress away from the dark continent toward his present audience, those he appreciated as representing enlightened France. He remained uncomfortable with "oral and popular traditions," and most of all with "superstitious practices derived from Africa." Again and again, he emphasized those things that made Haiti worthy of the France he esteemed (and identified Haitians who thought like him as most qualified to command): same religion, language, ideals, principles, customs, and, he concluded, "a taste preserved for French products." For France, he writes, "has deposited the germ of its advanced civilization." Now, under "the reign of a monarch [Napoleon III] enlightened and just," Haiti can profit from the "lights [*les lumières*] of its former mother country."

"Sucking from the breasts of France," as Ardouin had once put it in a letter to Lamartine (who, as minister for foreign affairs in the provisional government of 1848, would definitively abolish slavery in the French colonies), Haiti would turn, emptied of its gods and its magic, to both "the revolution of 1789 . . . this torch of French Genius" and to the Napoleonic eagle. On January 15, 1859, General Fabre Nicholas Geffrard overthrew Soulouque. Ardouin returned briefly to Haiti and then departed again for Paris as minister plenipotentiary.[29]

Dessalines, Dessalines Demanbre

On October 17, 1806, Jean-Jacques Dessalines, "chef suprême des indigènes," the first president and emperor of Haiti, was murdered in an ambush at Pont-Rouge by soldiers from the South on the road from Marchand (now Dessalines) to Port-au-Prince. The assassination order came from a clique of mulattoes and blacks from the West and South, including his friend General Alexandre Pétion. General Christophe knew of the plan. A young officer shot Dessalines. General Yayou stabbed him three times. Vaval filled him with bullets from two pistols. Then he was stripped naked, his fingers cut off so that the jeweled rings could be removed. Stories vary about the details of the mutilation. Even Ardouin, not given to melodrama, hesitated before recounting what happened to the corpse after Dessalines was assassinated by the men with whom he had fought: "one must pause at this appalling outrage."[30]

By the time the body reached Port-au-Prince, after the two-mile journey, it could not be recognized. The head was shattered, the feet, hands, and ears cut off. In some accounts, Dessalines was stoned and hacked to pieces by the crowd, and his remains—variously described as "scraps," "shapeless remains," "remnants," or "relics"—were thrown to the crowd. According to Madiou, American merchants hustled to buy his fingers with gold. "They attached an importance to the relics of the founder of our Independence that Haitians, transported by such horrible fury, did not then feel."[31] That foreign merchants bargained for Dessalines's fleshly remnants tells us something about the role of Dessalines as martyr of liberty. Yet this is only part of the story, for popular vengeance turned Dessalines into matter for resurrection. Dessalines, the most unregenerate of Haitian leaders, was made into a *lwa* (god, image, or spirit) by the Haitian people. The liberator, with his red silk scarf, was the only "Black Jacobin" to become a god. Neither the radical rationality of Toussaint nor the sovereign pomp of Christophe led to apotheosis. Yet Dessalines, so resistant to enlightened heroics, gradually acquired unequaled power in the Haitian imagination.

Dessalines was born sometime in 1758 on the Cormiers plantation, in a parish now known as the Commune of Grande-Rivière du Nord. Jean Price-Mars, in *Silhouettes nègres* (1938), describes the sordid beginnings of the "redeemer of the Negro race in Haiti" in Vié Cailles (Old Homes). In Price-Mars's logic of conversion, the most degraded slave becomes the most admired hero. Dirt forms the backdrop for projected splendor.

Vié Cailles, ramshackle huts, deformed, made ugly by filth, abodes grimacing with a drove of disgraceful beings, lost in misery, it is among you in the sin of

Jean-Jacques Dessalines. Reproduced from Michele Oriol, Images de la révolution à Saint-Domingue *(Port-au-Prince: Editions Henri Deschamps, 1992).*

promiscuity and in the gestation of the new world that was born, one day, the redeemer of the race, this Duclos who, by the transformative power of destiny, became Jean-Jacques Dessalines.[32]

According to the Haitian historian Horace Pauléus Sannon, Dessalines began fighting on the side of the rebel Georges Biassou's band as early as 1791.[33] Madiou describes the black Creole Biassou as a vodou adept, surrounded with *oungan* (priests) whose advice he sought.[34]

In 1794 Dessalines became Toussaint's guide through Grande-Rivière du Nord. At the time of the revolution, Toussaint was a literate coachman, and later steward of all the livestock on the Bréda plantation. Christophe (born in Grenada) was a waiter, then a manager, and finally an owner of La Couronne, an inn at Cap Français. Dessalines, first owned by a brutal white named Duclos, was then sold to a black master. Whenever Dessalines wanted to justify his hatred of the French, it is said that he liked to display his scar-covered back.[35] We should think for a moment about the figure of the hero who was once a slave, a man who would refer to himself as "Duclos" (his name in servitude), recalling for his listeners, even as emperor, his identity as an item of property. Out of detritus came the redeemer. Then, Dessalines, torn into bits and pieces, would return to the filth, only to rise again as hero, legend, and spirit.

Rejecting things French, unconcerned about social graces, and turning away from the customs, language, and principles Ardouin would see as that part of the Haitian inheritance that made his country worthy of recognition by "civilized" Europe, Dessalines made a vexed entry into history. Perhaps more than either Toussaint (who had the habit of asking the women who visited him, in a tender but nasal twang, "Have you taken communion this morning?") or Christophe, Dessalines recognized the temptations of civilization, which for him meant a new, more subtle servitude. He understood how easily rebels or republicans could themselves become masters. Speaking of the *anciens libres,* those freed *before* Léger-Félicite Sonthonax's General Emancipation decree of August 1793—which abolished slavery in the North of Saint-Domingue—Dessalines warned that the actions of "sons of colonists" could disadvantage those he called "my poor blacks." He exclaimed: "Beware, negroes and mulattoes! We have *all* fought against the whites. The goods that we have won in spilling our blood belong to every one of us. I intend that they be shared fairly."[36] Madiou emphasized Dessalines's preference for steering clear of the established

cities, "so that European corruption could not reach him," choosing
to establish himself at Marchand, situated in the plain of the Artibonite at the foot of the Cahos hills.[37]

Spenser St. John recognized "the only quality" of Dessalines as "a
kind of brute courage . . . he was nothing but an African savage."[38]
Dessalines's adamant refusal to be coaxed into spectacles of civility
meant that he would be a less acceptable subject for mainstream biog-
raphers. Though Toussaint is celebrated in numerous biographies as
"the Black Consul," "this gilded African," or "the Black Napoleon,"
and Christophe is heralded as "Black Majesty" or "King of Haiti," not
one English biography of Dessalines has yet appeared. Further, the two
most important twentieth-century poets of Martinique, Aimé Césaire
and Edouard Glissant, do not write about Dessalines. Glissant wrote
the play *Monsieur Toussaint* (1961). Césaire turned to Toussaint in his
Toussaint Louverture: La Révolution française et le problème colonial
(1981), as well as writing *La Tragédie du Roi Christophe* (1963). Perhaps they had difficulty (in spite of their rhetoric or their desire) ac-
knowledging the chief who called his people to arms with the command, "Koupe tèt, boule kay" (Cut off their heads, burn their houses),
a command recast by Haitians today as "Koupe fanm, boule kay" (Fuck
their women, burn their houses).

In his first published work, *Henri Christophe,* published in Barbados
in 1950, Derek Walcott presented Dessalines as a butcher, obsessed by
rituals of blood. After the massacre of the French, Walcott's "Messenger" recounts:

> Two hours we raged the city, raping, rioting,
> Turning with slaughter the chapels into brothels.
> I skewered a white martyr under an altar,
> We flung one girl in an uncertain arc
> Into the bloody bosom of the pier, and over us
> This king rode, looking as though he chewed his corpses.

Why is it that Haiti and its heroes conjure up legends and romanticized gestures of defiance or fustian power? Here is Walcott again in
his essay, "What the Twilight Says":

They were Jacobean too because they flared from a mind drenched in Eliza-
bethan literature out of the same darkness as Webster's Flamineo, from a flick-
ering world of mutilation and heresy. . . . Dessalines and Christophe, men
who had structured their own despair. Their tragic bulk was massive as a cita-
del at twilight. They were our only noble ruins. . . . Now, one may see such

heroes as squalid fascists who chained their own people, but they had size, mania, the fire of great heretics.[39]

Such spurious but compelling heroics led Walcott to sigh in his long poem, *Another Life* (1973), "for a future without heroes, / to make out of these foresters and fishermen / heraldic men!"

Historians have thus had a difficult time writing about the general whose uncompromising ferocity had become legendary. More embarrassing still were stories of the surfeit and abandon of his reign. Surrounded by cunning ministers, Dessalines recognized too late the need to curb their excesses. Madiou and others recount Dessalines's notorious passion for dancing and women. His favorite mistress was the much-admired dancer Couloute, whom Dessalines met in Jérémie in 1800. The emperor's ardor for her inspired a celebrated and much popularized dance, the *carabinier* (a wilder, more energetic and undulating kind of *meringue*), which was accompanied by the chant: "The Emperor comes to see Couloute dance."[40] At one particularly luxurious ball, when a dancing Dessalines leapt into the air and landed on his knee before Couloute, Christophe is reported to have remarked (loud enough for Dessalines to hear him): "See His Majesty! Aren't you ashamed to have such a *sauteur* [meaning both "jumper" and "temporizer," or "chameleon"] as our leader!"

Hyperbolized by Madiou as a "thunderbolt of arbitrariness," Dessalines fought at different times against the French and the African-born former slaves (*nèg bosal, nèg ginen,* or *nèg kongo,* or in French, *nègres bossales*) who never collaborated with the French. These *maroons,* such as Ti-Noël, Sans Souci, Macaya, Cacapoule—and other unnamed insurgents of the hills who formed armed bands of nearly a thousand men—refused to surrender to Leclerc, as did Christophe and Dessalines after the loss of the battle of Crête-à-Pierrot and the removal of Toussaint in 1802.[41] It is said that when Leclerc—who had earlier praised Dessalines as "butcher of the blacks" in a letter to Napoleon in September 1802—learned of his defection from the French not a month later, he cried out, "How could I have been so deceived by a *barbare*!" Yet, if we trust the account of the French naturalist Michel Etienne Descourtilz, imprisoned in Crête-à-Pierrot during the siege that preceded Dessalines's cooperation with Leclerc, Dessalines left no doubt about his cunning: "Listen well! If Dessalines surrenders to them a hundred times, he will betray them a hundred times."[42] According to the historian Hénock Trouillot, writing about Dessalines in the Haitian newspaper, *Le Nouvelliste*: "His name alone, in spite of the contradictions of his attitude, was a symbol among blacks."[43] In December 1802, his authority was so great that the mulatto general Pétion knew he had no choice but to fight under the black who had, only two years before, under Toussaint's orders, bathed the south of Haiti in the blood of mulattoes.

A number of oral traditions haunt the written remains of Dessalines, general in chief of the Army of Independence. In a story reported by both Trouillot and Mentor Laurent, African bands called *takos,* including a rebel named Jean Zombi and "other types full of fire," surrounded Dessalines in Plaisance, refusing to listen to him, saying "we do not deal with whites." According to Trouillot, Dessalines replied:

Look at my face. Am I white? Don't you recognize the soldier of Crête-à-Pierrot? Was I white at the Petite-Rivière of the Artibonite when the expedition arrived? Ask these hills covered with French bones. They will nominate Dessalines as the hero of these trophies.[44]

Historians disagree about the languages Dessalines could speak. Some say he spoke in "Congo," a general attribution for the specific African "nations" or "tribes" in Saint-Domingue (Arada, Nago, Congo, Fon, Ibo, Bambara) that would also be used to refer to the "secret" or "magic" language of initiates in vodou. In *Les Limites du créole dans notre enseignement,* Trouillot cites words from Antoine Métral's *Histoire de l'expédition française au St. Domingue* which suggest that even though he did not speak their language, Dessalines could gesturally, figurally become African: "His savage eloquence was more in certain expressive signs than in words." Trouillot concluded: "By fantastic gestures Dessalines managed more than once to make himself understood by Africans, so it seemed, when he did not speak the dialect."[45] We are dealing, therefore, with a Creole who could take on the role of an African as easily as he could serve the French when he and Christophe fought with the expeditionary force of Leclerc.

Dessalines controlled his own passage between apparent extremes and thrived on the composite histories of his locale. According to Madiou, Dessalines called the populations subject to his authority "Incas or children of the sun," memorializing the 1780 Inca uprising in Peru. For the Haitian Marxist historian Etienne Charlier, when Dessalines called the new black republic "Haiti," retrieving its original Amerindian name, he "transcends his race and presents himself as the avenger of the Indians."[46] A story I have heard told in Creole by unlettered informants, in Port-au-Prince, after "Papa Doc" Duvalier's death in 1971, is more puzzling. Dessalines would ask an *indigène* (a "native" in Haiti) a question in French, and if the person answered, he would be killed for not being a "true" Haitian (i.e., he had not answered in Creole). That this fiction of historical prohibition has no date is not surprising. As I have argued, stories about Dessalines are construed with different meanings by diverse groups over time. I understood the story reinterpreted here as proof of Dessalines's exigence and uncompromising purity. Not only kill off the French, but anyone who speaks French. Though the origins of this story are unknown, its repetition in the streets of Port-au-Prince, after the passing of another imperious Haitian leader, attests to the drama of mimesis and transformation in Haitian history. Whether or not this story was invented by those who despised Dessalines—the mulatto, literate elites, if not the French themselves—does not matter as much as its survival among the unschooled.

A "folk tale" reported to George Simpson by his collaborator Jean-Baptiste Cinéas, who heard the story from his great-grandmother, tells how Dessalines did "magic" at the Battle of Crête-à-Pierrot.

Before each battle the spirits enabled him to make himself invisible so that he could inspect the enemy's camp. The most striking example of this protection was at Crête-à-Pierrot where eighteen thousand French soldiers surrounded his fort with its fifteen hundred men. The French sent a spy to give Dessalines poison, but he threw up the poison. Each night he left the fort, slipping through the French army without being seen, and conferred with Haitian officers outside the fortress. At Crête-à-Pierrot he solemnly sacrificed a magnificent bull, and his spirits told him he would have the honor of winning independence for his people.[47]

Yet, Dessalines, though believed to have been a vodou adept—and in some stories, sorcerer—was also known to have massacred cult leaders and their devotees. Madiou recounts how Dessalines, as Toussaint's inspector general of cultivation in the West, pursued "the secret societies where they practiced African superstitions." Discovering a meeting of "those sorcerers called Vaudoux," led by "an old black woman" and a number of cultivators who had abandoned their fields in order to participate in these rites, Dessalines and his battalion surrounded the area, seized fifty of the Vaudoux and killed them with bayonets.[48] Gustave d'Alaux in *L'Empereur Soulouque et son empire* explained that while Toussaint and Christophe—obsessed with the trappings of culture—pitilessly suppressed vodou practitioners, "Dessalines, in spite of his either sincere or pretended infatuation with African savagery, was himself mixed up with the papas [conjure-men]." D'Alaux reported that once, before going into battle, Dessalines covered himself with magic talismans in order to become invulnerable. But wounded in the first discharge of fire, Dessalines beat up the "sorcerer" and took back the money he had paid for the consultation.[49] In another version of the story, when the protective charms failed to work their magic, Dessalines, after asking for his money, killed the "charlatan."[50]

Any attempt to reconstruct Dessalines historically involves ambiguities, obscurity, and details that do not cohere. But perhaps that is how gods are born. As Zora Neale Hurston wrote in *Tell My Horse,* her ethnographic account of religious belief and practice in Jamaica and Haiti: "Some unknown natural phenomenon occurs which cannot be explained, and a new local demigod is named."[51] The popular and oral canonization of Dessalines, unlike the public and written, is quite comfortable with a Dessalines apotheosized but not purged of incoherence. Practitioners today remember Dessalines as "Papa," a memorial preserved in a Creole poem by félix morisseau-leroy, which concludes:

Pou tou sa l fè m di: papa Desalin, mèsi
Pou tou sa l pral fè
M di: mèsi, papa Desalin.[52]

(Papa Dessalines, thank you
For everything you did:
For everything you're going to do
I say thank you, Papa Dessalines.)

What then did Dessalines do? Two of the concerns that accounted for the admiration and disdain summoned by his name were race and land. In the Constitution of 1805, he declared that no white, whatever his nation, could set foot on the territory of Haiti as master or owner of property (article 12). Who could be Haitian? For Dessalines, certain whites could be naturalized as Haitians: for example, white women who have conceived or will bear Haitian children, and those Germans and Poles who deserted Leclerc's army during 1802–1803 in order to fight with the indigènes (article 13). Further, Haitians, whatever their color, would be known as *blacks,* referred to "only by the generic word *black*" (article 14).[53] Since the most problematic division in the new Haiti was that between *anciens libres* (the former freedmen, who were mostly *gens de couleur,* mulattoes and their off-spring) and *nouveaux libres* (the newly free, who were mostly black), Dessalines attempted by linguistic means and by law to defuse the color issue.

If Dessalines promised a reconciliation of persons of differing grades of color, it was nevertheless a conversion that depended, at least ver-bally, on the blackening so feared by both colonists and the mulatto elite. In colonial Saint-Domingue the reminder of the stain or corrup-tion of black blood was necessary to the law of difference demanded by racial superiority. "In a word, one could say that a colored popula-tion, left to itself is fatally destined to become black again at the end of a very few generations." In *Saint-Domingue: La Société et la vie créoles sous l'ancien régime,* Pierre de Vassière described this lapse, the mixture that can transform white into mulatto and then mulatto "to the most absolute black," as the colonist's greatest fear: the "law of regression" or "reversion."[54]

Consider what remained of colonial divisions in Saint-Domingue in 1804:

color	"native land"	status
whites	France	free
people of color	Saint-Domingue	freed
blacks	Africa	slaves

Though blacks were also *libres* (free) and not all whites were mas-ters, this tripartite organization of white masters at the top and servile blacks at the bottom, with freed *gens de couleur* (people of color) in be-tween, operated as the crucial ideological structure in Saint-Domingue. How else could servitude be sustained, except through an accentua-tion of the color distinction? Dessalines took the "lowest" rung and made it a synecdoche for the whole.[55]

In his *Description topographique, physique, civile, politique et histor-ique de la partie française de l'Isle Saint-Domingue* (written between 1776–1789, published in 1797), Médéric Moreau de Saint-Méry dis-tinguished 128 parts of "blood" that, variously combined, result in the possible nuances of skin-coloring among *free coloreds.*[56] The combina-torial fiction, surely one of the more remarkable legalistic fantasies of the New World, reminded the mulatto, especially, that no matter how white the skin, the tainted blood haunts the body. Dessalines's answer to the hair-splitting subtleties of Moreau de Saint-Méry was to get rid

of the distinctions, but some would argue that he created an overweening category even more coercive than Moreau de Saint-Méry's
fable of color.

Dessalines tried to accomplish nothing less than an epistemological
conversion: a curse would be removed, and then reproduced as salvation. To be called black on the soil of Haiti would be proof of Haitian
identity. Dessalines knew that the elimination of the stain of color and
the alliance between *noirs* and *jaunes* (blacks and yellows) were necessary to the future of independent Haiti. As Madiou records Dessalines's words: "Maintain your precious concord, this happy harmony
between you; it is the gauge of your good fortune, of your salvation,
of your success: it is the secret of being invincible."[57]

But it was Dessalines's attempt to redefine the ownership of land
that probably cost him his life. In 1804 he had rescinded all transfers
of property made after October 1802, thus removing mulatto claims
to valuable plantations. In 1805 he decided that all land titles would
have to be verified. Tradition has it that Dessalines would check for
the authenticity of land titles by smelling them to discover those faked
by smoking into looking old: "ça pas bon, ça senti fumée" (it's no
good, it smells smoked). According to many, this was a direct attack
on the *anciens affranchis,* those who had taken, or had been given
land formerly owned by their white planter fathers.

In his constitution Dessalines had given equal rights to both legitimate children and those recognized by their fathers but born out
of wedlock, thus accepting the prevalence of *plasaj,* or consensual
union, not wishing to coerce his people, those he called "natives of
Haiti," to follow the marital rituals of the whites. According to Madiou, Dessalines's law of May 28, 1805, decreed that it would be un-
just to establish unequal rights in inheritance among men who had
come out of servitude and degradation, since these "*indigènes* had all
been . . . legitimized by the revolution." However, for Dessalines
there could be no kinship with a white colonist. No mulatto could
claim that he was entitled to his father's land. Ardouin, a descendant
of the disenfranchised *anciens affranchis,* argued that land reform was
"an attack on the sacred right of property." But for Janvier, and other
later Haitian historians, Dessalines "wanted to make the genuine independence of the peasant possible by making him an owner of land."[58]

When we ask what made possible the second coming of Dessalines
as hero and god, we must attend to his vision of the *true* Haitian. He
gave property to those slaves who had, only recently, been consid-

ered property themselves. The division of land, his attempt to destroy "false" property titles, and the violence with which he tried to carry out what has been called "an impossible reform of the mentality of the ruling classes, and perhaps his own mentality,"[59] would make him the favorite of left-leaning, twentieth-century novelists René Depestre and Jacques-Stephen Alexis.[60] As the sociologist and anthropologist Anténor Firmin put it in *De l'égalité des races humaines* (his 1885 response to Gobineau's *De l'inégalité des races humaines*):

> For us, sons of those who suffered the humiliations and martyrdom of slavery, we could see there [in Dessalines's actions] the first manifestation of the sentiment of racial equality, a sentiment which Dessalines still personifies in Haiti.[61]

Between Dessalines's death in 1806 and the speech of Lysius Salomon (the finance minister during *la politique de la doublure*) in memory of the "emperor-martyr" in 1845, the transition from oblivion to glory had taken place. Speaking at the parish church of Cayes on October 17, 1845, Salomon proclaimed: "Avenger of the black race, liberator of Haiti, founder of national independence, Emperor Dessalines! today is your glory, the sun today burns for you as radiantly as it did in 1804." Before Salomon's daring speech, which blamed "the aristocracy of color" for Dessalines's death (and earned Salomon, who was later called "the eater of mulattoes," their lasting fury), previous governments had ignored or condemned "the Liberator."

One exception was the cunning political move by the mulatto Charles Rivière-Hérard in January 1844, during the forty-first anniversary of the founding of the state of Haiti. As Madiou put it: "He made a speech where, for the first time since the death of Dessalines in October 1806, these words came out of the mouth of a President of the Republic: 'It is to the glorious Dessalines, it is to his immortal comrades that the Country owes the new era into which she enters.'" Madiou reminded his readers that Rivière-Hérard was part of the class that despised Dessalines, the large landowners of Cayes, who had most to lose when Dessalines began his call for property reform. He "belonged to a class of citizens who saw in Dessalines nothing but a barbaric despot that they had sacrificed; but since they planned a *coup d'état,* they had to draw on the sympathies of the people by glorifying the founder of independence."[62] Yet, Madiou concluded, the people were not dupes of these "empty words," for they had heard that Dessalines's remains—unworthy of a mausoleum—still lay in a deserted grave, marked only by a brick tomb with the inscription in Creole:

"Ce-git Dessalines, / Mort à 48 ans" (Here lies Dessalines, / Dead at 48 years old).[63]

Some fifty years after Rivière-Hérard claimed the figure of Dessalines for his own political designs, President Florvil Hyppolite built in France a modest monument in memory of Dessalines. Later, for the centenary celebration of the Haitian nation, which actually marked the beginning of the state cult of Dessalines, Justin Lhérison composed the national anthem, the "Dessalinienne." Sung for the first time on January 1, 1904, the song begins:

> For our Ancestors
> Let us march together
> No traitors in our ranks
> Let us be the only masters of the land,
> Let us march together
> For our Country
> For our Ancestors

But the monumentalization that turned October 17 from a day that heralded liberation from a dictator to a day of mourning for his death was devised by literate Haitians in the cities. Repressive governments, such as that of Louis Borno under the U.S. occupation of 1915–1934, found the erection of a mausoleum for the Liberator easier than affording their subjects liberation from internal oppression and foreign control.

Called by the literate elite "the Great One," "the Savior," "the Lover of Justice," and "the Liberator," the Dessalines remembered by vodou initiates is far less comforting or instrumental. They know how unheroic the hero-turned-god could be. The image of Dessalines in the cult of the people remains equivocal and corruptible: a trace of what is absorbed by the mind and animated in the gut. How inevitable are the oscillations from hero to detritus, from power to vulnerability, from awe to ridicule: a convertibility that vodou would keep working, viable, and necessary.

Not simply master or tyrant, but also slave and supplicant, Dessalines and the religious rituals associated with him keep the ambiguities of power intact. "Do you have the heart to march in blood all the way to Cayes?" Dessalines asked the soldiers of his third brigade before his assassination in October 1806. Unlike the spectacles of sanctification endorsed by the urban literati and the politicians, the history reconstructed by the gods and their devotees is not always one of revolt and triumph. Gods held in the mind and embodied in ceremony reenact what historians often forget: the compulsion to serve, the potency and virtue of atrocity. The very suppressions, inarticulateness, and ruptures in ritual might say something about the ambivalences of *the* revolution: it was not so liberating as mythologizers or ideologues make it out to be, and the dispossessed, who continue to suffer and remember, know this.

Dismemberment, Naming, and Divinity

Vodou enters written history as a weird set piece: the ceremony of Bois-Caïman. The story is retold by nearly every historian, especially those outsiders who enjoyed linking the first successful slave revolt to a gothic scene of blood drinking and abandon. David Geggus has written in *Slavery, War, and Revolution: The British Occupation of Saint Domingue* that "the earliest mention of the famous Bois Caïman ceremony seems to be in Dalmas's *Histoire* of 1814." Though the French colonist Antoine Dalmas's lurid account in his *Histoire de la révolution de Saint-Domingue* seems an unlikely source for the spirit of liberation, what matters is how necessary the story remains to Haitians who continue to construct their identity not only by turning to the revolution of 1791 but by seeking its origins in a service quite possibly imagined by those who disdain it.[64]

On the stormy, lightning-filled night of August 14, 1791, in the middle of the Caïman woods, Boukman (a *oungan,* or priest) and a *manbo* (priestess) conducted the ceremony that began the fight for independence. Madiou, though given to much melodramatic detail, did not include the ceremony in his history. But vodou, once displaced, reared its head a few pages following his descriptions of the uprising in the North. Madiou described Biassou, who, with General Jean-François, led the revolt, surrounded by "sorcerers" and "magicians." His tent was filled with multicolored cats, snakes, bones of the dead, and other objects of what Madiou calls "African superstitions."[65] Ardouin described the ceremony of Bois-Caïman, but told his reader that he was "transcribing here an extract from the unedited works of Céligny Ardouin" that included information he received from an old soldier who resided in Saint-Domingue, in service of the King of Spain.[66]

Both Madiou and Ardouin recounted how blacks, *"phantasiés,"* as Madiou put it, by sorcerers, threw themselves at cannons, believing the balls dust. When blown to pieces, they knew they would be reborn in Africa. The naturalist Descourtilz (his life was saved during the retaliatory slaughter of whites by Dessalines's wife, Claire Heureuse, who hid him under her bed) remembered how "the Congo Negroes and other Guineans were so superstitiously affected by the utterances of Dessalines that they even let him persuade them that to die fighting the French was only a blessing since it meant that they were immediately conveyed to Guinea, where, once again, they saw Papa Toussaint who was waiting for them to complete the army with which he proposed to reconquer Saint-Domingue."[67]

The colonized are not necessarily, as Albert Memmi has written, "outside of the game" of history. Gods were born in the memories of those who served and rebelled, and they not only took on the traits or dispositions of their servitors but also those of the former masters, tough revenants housed in the memories of the descendants of slaves. While de-idealizing, by reenacting to the extreme, a conceit of power, the figure of Dessalines became a proof of memory: something gained by those who were thought to have no story worth the telling.

To reconstruct a history of the spirits in Haiti is no easy matter. How does our thought about a glorified, if ambiguous, past become palpable? How do we get from now to then, to a history beyond the reach of written history? Until the American occupation—and one could argue, the publication of Jean Price-Mars's *Ainsi parla l'oncle* (1928)—the Haitian elite looked upon vodou as an embarrassment. Even Duverneau Trouillot—who published his "esquisse ethnographique" (ethnographic sketch), *Le Vaudoun: Aperçu historique et evolutions* in 1885—while listing (for the first time, as far as I know) the individual spirits, felt that vodou in Haiti demonstrated the inevitable degradation of ancestral practices, reduced to "a tissue of rather ridiculous superstitions." Trouillot prophesied that Christian civilization would soon absorb these atavistic "remnants" or "debris."[68]

Born in Haiti, Dessalines is called a *lwa krèyol* (Creole god). As *Ogou Desalin* he walks with the African Ogou, the gods of war and politics that remain in Haiti in their multiple aspects. Duverneau Trouillot warned that after the revolution, African beliefs and rituals would continue to degenerate. But the old traditions and gods remained powerful, embracing new events and leaders like Dessalines.

With independence, the underground opposition to the now defeated white oppressor did not disappear, for the spirits, and the people's need for them, was not contingent on being suppressed. Rather, vodou came, to some extent, out into the open to thrive. But haltingly so, as though the people were keeping some of the old secrets hidden, ready to serve in other repressive situations that did not fail to occur.

In transcribing a popular song addressed to Dessalines, a student of oral history faces nearly insurmountable problems of translation and retrieval. Alfred Métraux in *Voodoo in Haiti* and Odette Mennesson-Rigaud and Lorimer Denis (Duvalier's comrade in folkloric exploration in the 1940s) in "Cérémonie en l'honneur de Marinette" record the following song, which I heard during a four-day genealogy of the gods in Bel-Air, Haiti, in 1970. The singer, who was also a oungan, concentrated on stories of the spirits or *mistè* (mysteries) who inspired the revolutionaries, particularly the spirit of François Makandal, the prerevolutionary maroon leader and prophet, who, the tale goes, warned Dessalines before his death not to go to Pont-Rouge.

> Pito m'mouri passé m'couri (Better to die than to run away)
> Pito m'mouri passé m'couri
> Dessalines, Dessalines démembré
> Vive la liberté.[69]

According to Mennesson-Rigaud, this song was sung by Haitian soldiers during the revolution and is preserved in the militant Petwo ceremonies.[70] Both Métraux and Mennesson-Rigaud translate *démembré/demanbre* as "powerful." Yet in Creole the word means "dismembered," "beaten," or "battered." How did these two ethnographers come up with power from accounts of Dessalines shot, kicked, and dismembered?

If we take both meanings as possible—indeed, as necessary—records of the human capacities for knowledge, courage, and composure, then we have a Dessalines who is battered and powerful, dead and living. Talking with practitioners in Port-au-Prince in 1986, I heard another form of the word, which might be transcribed as *denambre*. Could *denambre* be a form of *dénombrer* or *dénommer* (to count or to name)? Both activities—numbering and naming—carry great power for those who believe in the magic of numbers or the secret of naming; hence the translation "powerful." Further, in Haiti *nam* means

Oungan sings the genealogy of the gods. Bel-Air, Haiti, 1970. Photograph by Leon Chalom.

spirit, soul, gist, or sacred power. So, Dessalines denambre either has his spirit taken away, or, since he was feared to be a sorcerer, he has the power to de-soul, to steal someone's spirit.[71]

The history told by these traditions defies our notions of *identity* and *contradiction*. A person or thing can be two or more things simultaneously. A word can be double, two-sided, and duplicitous. In this broadening and multiplying of a word's meaning, repeated in rituals of devotion and vengeance, we begin to see that what becomes more and more vague also becomes more distinct: it may mean *this*, but *that* too.

In spite of this instability, or what some argue to be the capriciousness of spirits and terminologies, something incontrovertible remains: the heritage of Guinea maintained in Haiti by serving the gods. Those who live are reclaimed by the ancestors who do not die—who return as vengeful revenants if not properly served—and by the gods who cajole, demand, and sometimes oppress the mere mortals, the *chrétiens-vivants* who forget their ancestral origins. The gods are not only in your blood but in the land. In parts of contemporary Haiti the *demanbre*, or sacred plot of land, marks the "spiritual heritage of the group."[72] Defined as "the basic unit of peasant religion," "the common family yard," and "the center of the veneration of the dead," this ancestral land cannot be divided, sold, or given away.[73] Haiti was conceived as earth blooded with the purifying spirit of liberation. Serving Dessalines thus reinspirits what many believe to have been his legacy: the indivisible land of Haiti consecrated by the revolution and projected in his Constitution of 1805 as uncontaminated by foreign proprietors or masters. Dessalines demanbre, the dismembered but potent Dessalines of the song, intimates this promise of indivisibility and proof of devotion. Having lost his personal identity, he becomes the place. The dismembered hero is resurrected as sacred locale.

Service for Dessalines records an often grueling attachment to a recalcitrant land, as well as bearing witness to a cruel and demanding intimacy. The song about Dessalines demanbre joins the hero to a powerful "she-devil" or "sorceress," known as Kita demanbre. When Kita or Dessalines demanbre appears in a ceremony, usually in the violent *sèvis zandò*, they reenact a ferocity that annihilates any socialized, or fixed, opposition between male and female. The feared Marinèt-bwa-chèche (Marinèt-dry-bones, dry-wood, brittle or skinny arms) said to *mange moun* (eat people) is also called Marinèt-limen-difé (light-the-fire). Served with kerosene, pimiento, and fire, she is the lwa who put

Sèvis zandò, at Alvarez's compound. Between Gressier and Léogane, Haiti, 1970. Photograph by Leon Chalom.

Song to "Papa" Dessalines, sèvis zandò. Oungan Alvarez wears the red scarf of Ogou Desalin. Between Gressier and Léogane, Haiti, 1970. Photograph by Leon Chalom.

the fire to the cannons used by Dessalines against the French. Marinèt, with the possible subtext of the French Marianne, as a national image of revolution and republican fervor, also reconstitutes legends of ferocity distinctly associated with black women. In one of many letters to Napoleon, Rochambeau warned from Cap Français: "If France wishes to regain San Domingo she must send hither 25,000 men in a body, declare the negroes slaves, and destroy at least 30,000 negroes and négresses—the latter being more cruel than men."[74] The other Petwo gods that bear the names of revolt, the traces of torture and revenge, like Brisé Pimba, Baron Ravage, Ti-Jean-Dantor, Ezili-je-wouj (Ezili with red eyes), and Jean Zombi, recall the strange promiscuity between masters and slaves; white, black, and mulatto; old world and new. These rituals of memory could be seen as deposits of history. Shreds of bodies come back, remembered in ritual, and seeking vengeance: whether blacks fed to the dogs by Rochambeau or whites massacred by Dessalines.

The lwa most often invoked by today's vodou practitioners do not go back to Africa; rather, they were responses to the institution of slavery, to its peculiar brand of sensuous domination. A historical streak in these spirits, entirely this side of metaphysics, reconstitutes the shadowy and powerful magical gods of Africa as everyday responses to the white master's arbitrary power. Driven underground, they survived and constituted a counterworld to white suppression. It is hardly surprising that when black deeds and national heroic action contested this mastery, something new would be added to the older traditions.

The dispossession accomplished by slavery became the model for possession in vodou: for making a man not into a thing but into a spirit. In 1804, during Dessalines's massacre of the whites, Jean Zombi, a mulatto of Port-au-Prince, earned a reputation for brutality. Known to be one of the fiercest slaughterers, Madiou described his "vile face," "red hair," and "wild eyes." He would leave his house, wild with fury, stop a white, then strip him naked. In Madiou's words, he "led him then to the steps of the government palace and thrust a dagger in his chest. This gesture horrified all the spectators, including Dessalines."[75] Jean Zombi was also mentioned by Hénock Trouillot as one of the takos who had earlier threatened Dessalines in Plaisance. Variously reconstituted and adaptable to varying events, Zombi crystallizes the crossing not only of spirit and man in vodou practices but the intertwining of black and yellow, African and Creole in the struggle for independence.

The ambiguities of traditions redefined by changing hopes, fears, and rememberings are exemplified by the brief mention of Jean Zombi in the 1950s by Milo Rigaud in *La Tradition voudoo et le voudoo haïtien*. "Jean Zombi is one of the most curious prototypes of vodou tradition. He was one of those who, on Dessalines's order, massacred the most whites during the liberation of Haiti from the French yoke. Jean Zombi is actually one of the most influential mysteries of the vodou pantheon: as lwa, he belongs to the Petwo rite."[76] According to the anthropologist Melville Herskovits, in Dahomean legend the zombis were beings without souls, "whose death was not real but resulted from the machinations of sorcerers who made them appear as dead, and then, when buried, removed them from their grave and sold them into servitude in some far-away land."[77] Born out of the experience of slavery, the sea passage from Africa to the New World, and revolution on the soil of Saint-Domingue, the zombi tells the story of colonization.

An especially important definition is that of Moreau de Saint-Méry, who presents for the first time in writing the night world of what he names *revenans* (spirits), *loupgaroux* (vampires), and *zombis,* which he defines as a "Creole word that means spirit, revenant."[78] The name zombi, once attached to the body of Jean, who killed off whites and avenged those formerly enslaved, revealed the effects of the new dispensation. Names, gods, and heroes from an oppressive colonial past remained in order to infuse ordinary citizens and devotees with a stubborn sense of independence and survival. The undead zombi, recalled in the name of Jean Zombi, thus became a terrible composite power: slave turned rebel ancestor turned lwa, an incongruous, demonic spirit recognized through dreams, divination, or possession.

In contemporary Haiti, however, the zombi calls up the most macabre figure in folk belief. No fate is more feared. The zombi, understood either as an evil spirit caught by a sorcerer or the dead-alive zombi in "flesh and bones," haunts Haitians as the most powerful emblem of apathy, anonymity, and loss. Maya Deren locates the terror incited by the zombi not in its malevolent appearance but in the threat of conversion projected by this overwhelming figure of brute matter: "While the Haitian does not welcome any encounter with a zombie, his real dread is that of being made into one himself."[79] This incarnation of negation or vacancy is as much a part of history as the man Jean Zombi. In Guadeloupe and Martinique, zombi simply means evil spirit, but in Haiti the zombi undergoes a double incarnation, meaning both spirit and, more specifically, the animated dead, a body without mind or, as the Jamaican novelist Erna Brodber, in her recent *Myal,* has so aptly put it, "flesh that takes directions from someone."

The phantasm of the zombi—a soulless husk deprived of freedom— is the ultimate sign of loss and dispossession. In Haiti, memories of servitude are transposed into a new idiom that both reproduces and dismantles a twentieth-century history of forced labor and denigration that became particularly acute during the American occupation of Haiti. As Haitians were forced to build roads, and thousands of peasants were brutalized and massacred, tales of zombis proliferated in the United States. The film *White Zombie* (1932) and books like William Seabrook's *The Magic Island* (1929) and John Huston Craige's *Black Bagdad* (1933) helped to justify the "civilizing" presence of the marines in "barbaric" Haiti. This reimagined zombi has now been absorbed into the texture of previous oral traditions, structurally reproducing the idea of slavery in a new context.

As lwa, then, Jean Zombi embodies dead whites and blacks, staging again for those who serve him the sacrificial scene: the ritual of consecration that makes him god. In this marvel of ambivalence, the zombi is also consumed by the dead who continue to undergo zombification. In *Un Arc-en-ciel pour l'occident chrétien* (1967), René Depestre summons "Cap'tain Zombi," who consolidates the pieces of history preserved in the name.

> I am teeming with corpses
> Teeming with death rattles
> I am a tide of wounds
> Of cries of pus of blood clots
> I graze on the pastures
> Of the millions of my dead
> I am shepherd of terror.[80]

Let us return to Dessalines's Constitution of 1805, and to the logic of the remnant turned god. "The law does not permit one dominant religion" (article 50). "The freedom of cults is tolerated" (article 51). Freedom of religion would not again be allowed, in the many constitutions of Haiti, until 1987. Both Toussaint and Christophe had recognized only Catholicism ("La religion Catholique, apostolique et romaine") as the religion of the state. Dessalines remained close to the practices of the Haitian majority. But Dessalines betrayed the gods he served in Arcahaie, in the West of Haiti. According to Milo Rigaud, who does not give sources for his unique details of Dessalines possessed and punished, Dessalines suffered the vengeance of the spirits for ignoring their warnings not to go to Pont-Rouge. Rigaud concludes, "The case of Dessalines recalls an axiom well known by all those who serve the gods in Africa: 'You must never make a god lose face.'"[81] Nor did the gods forget the general's attack on their servitors when he followed Toussaint's orders in 1802. But what Ardouin called the "misfortunes" of popular vengeance on Dessalines could be a record of something less verifiable and more disturbing. The mutilation of Dessalines not only records a collective frenzy visited on the once-powerful body but reinvests the corpse with the possibility of transfiguration. Such a hankering after resurrection, repeated and theatrical, still plagues Haiti, with each new hero, with each new government, with every dispensation.

General Yayou, when he saw the body of Dessalines, proclaimed: "Who would have said that this little wretch, only twenty minutes ago, made all of Haiti tremble!" When an initiate is "possessed" by the "emperor," the audience witnesses a double play of loss and gain. The "horse" (in the idiom of spirit possession, the god "mounts" his horse) remains him- or herself even when ridden, but is stripped bare, as was Dessalines, of habitual characteristics, the lineaments of the everyday. In this transformative articulation, the essential residue, gist, or spirit, the nam remains. What emerges after the first moments of disequilibrium and convulsive movements is the ferocity commonly associated with Dessalines. It is as if the self is not so much annihilated as rendered piecemeal. Out of these remnants comes the image of the god or mystery who overtakes what remains.

In *Divine Horsemen,* Maya Deren writes, "*The self must leave if the loa is to enter,*" alerting us to the risky dependency of the god on the human vessel.[82] Each lwa has a variety of character traits—speech patterns, body movements, food preference, or clothes—but he or she cannot express them except by mounting a horse. Deification is never simply a spiritualization of matter. Spirit and matter, defilement and exaltation do not dwell unperturbed in harmony. The wrinkle or hitch in the business of divinity is what makes vodou resistant to annihilation, whether by the constant persecutions of the Church or, more recently, by "Papa Doc" Duvalier's use of it for political ends.

Défilée

In the last year of the revolution, General-in-Chief Dessalines led an army whose spirit and courage was recorded in numerous accounts by the French military. A song from the days when Dessalines and his columns of men (figures vary from 16,000 men in four columns to 27,000) marched toward victory at Butte de la Charier and Vertières was sung to a generation of students at the Ecole de Médecine in Port-au-Prince by an old man named Brother Hossé or José. Timoléon Brutus, one of the students who heard it around 1901, records it in his homage to Dessalines as the battle song celebrating the march of Dessalines to the North, where he would assault Cap Français and force the surrender of General Donatien Marie Joseph de Vimeur, vicomte de Rochambeau:

Dessalines sorti lan Nord
Vini vouè ça li porté. (bis)
   Ça li porté.
Li porté Ouanga nouveau, (bis)
   Ouanga nouveau (bis)

Dessalines sorti lan Nord
Vini compter ça li porté (bis)
   Ça li porté.
Li porté fusils, li porté boulets, (bis)
   Ouanga nouveau (bis)

Dessalines sorti lan Nord
Vini prend ça li porté. (bis)
   Ça li porté.
Li porté canons pour chasser blancs, (bis)
   Ouanga nouveau (bis)[83]

(Dessalines is coming to the North
Come see what he is bringing
   What he is bringing.
He is bringing new magic,
   New magic

Dessalines is coming to the North
Come notice what he is bringing
   What he is bringing.
He is bringing muskets, he is bringing bullets,
   New magic

Dessalines is coming to the North
Come take what he is bringing
   What he is bringing.
He is bringing cannons to chase away the whites,
   New magic)

A woman marched with Dessalines's troops, peddling provisions to the soldiers. Known as Défilée, she was born to slave parents near Cap Français. When she was about eighteen years old, Défilée was raped by a colonist, her master.[84] During the revolution, she must have escaped, though nothing is known about her until she became sutler to Dessalines's troops. But with Dessalines's death, Défilée became the embodiment of the Haitian nation: crazed and lost, but then redeemed through the body of their savior. A woman's lamentation converts a sudden gruesome act into a long history of penitential devotion. The historian and dramatist Hénock Trouillot, in *Dessalines ou le sang du Pont-Rouge* (1967), gives Défilée the task of condemning her people: "What the French could not accomplish, have they really done it, these monsters? . . . Haiti has dared what Saint-Domingue tried in vain. Dessalines? Dessalines? Him? The titan? The father of our country? What will they say about us, tomorrow? . . . The blood of the black Christ! The blood of the Emperor!"[85]

The fall of Dessalines and the excesses committed on his corpse are overshadowed by this final, bizarre drama that writers as diverse as Madiou and Ardouin record. As the people defiled the remains of their "supreme chief," Défilée entered the scene. She is mad, though neither Madiou or Ardouin tells how or why she became so. Madiou recounted how numerous children, joyously shouting, threw rocks at Dessalines's remains. A wandering Défilée asked these "innocent beings who abandon themselves to good as to evil," who this bundle of something *was*. They answered Dessalines, and her wild eyes became calm: "a glimmer of reason shone on her features." She found a sack, loaded it with his bloody remnants, and carried them to the city cemetery. General Pétion then sent soldiers who, for a modest sum, buried Dessalines.[86]

Ardouin, who would have been ten years old in 1806, claimed to have been an eyewitness to the popular vengeance in Port-au-Prince. Refuting Madiou's version, Ardouin explained that he knew Défilée, and she could not have carried Dessalines. "Perhaps Madiou did not recall that Dessalines was hefty, weighing perhaps 70 to 80 kilos: how could a rather weak Défilée carry such a weight?" According to Ardouin, she followed the officers, and for a long time returned to the site, where she threw flowers over the grave.[87] Though Défilée was helped to carry the sack by a well-known madman named Dauphin, most accounts choose to ignore what is possible in favor of the miraculous: Défilée's lone journey with the hero's remains.

The poet and dramatist Massillon Coicou wrote a drama in two acts, *L'Empereur Dessalines,* performed for the centenary of Dessalines's death in Port-au-Prince on October 7, 1906. In his preface to the published version, Coicou, who was assassinated by President Pierre Nord Alexis in 1908, reminded his readers that "Dessalines, beaten, massacred, abandoned to execration, regained his prestige."[88] In this version, Défilée took Dessalines's members, clotted with mud and blood, scorned by everyone, bathed them in tears, and carried them in the folds of her dress. Coicou asks, "Isn't she the most beautiful incarnation of our national consciousness, this madwoman who moved amidst those who were mad but believed themselves sane?"[89]

"Oh! the murderers!!!
Look! Défilée the madwoman takes you away
The monster. Look at him who sleeps in my dress
I will take care of him, my dear love, for a long time.
I will watch over you, for ten, twenty, thirty, one hundred years."[90]

Hénock Trouillot, in *Dessalines ou le sang du Pont-Rouge*, leaves little
to the imagination when he presents Défilée busily collecting, examining, and naming the emperor's remains, then putting them in her sack:

"That, it is his head . . . The center of the volcano that activated the hero . . .
Here is the trunk . . . he was powerful . . . So many scars! . . . Tokens of his
unparalleled bravery . . . Shreds of battered flesh!"[91]

Other writers, eager to translate social drama into healing miracle,
described the encounter between the emperor-turned-fleshly-remnant
and the madwoman-turned-sane as a ritual of reciprocal salvation.
Windsor Bellegarde asks all Haitians to remember "*Défilée-La-Folle*
[Madwoman] who, on the sad day of October 17, 1806 . . . saw the
Founder of Independence fall under Haitian bullets, and when the
people of Port-au-Prince seemed suddenly to go mad, she gave to everyone an eloquent lesson of reason, wisdom, and patriotic piety."[92]
Others described the encounter as verbal confrontation and exorcism,
patterned loosely after the stunning vigil of Mary Magdalene. Rid of
"seven devils" in Mark and Luke, in the Fourth Gospel she is sole
witness of the risen Christ. She waits by an empty tomb, Jesus calls
her name, and she then recognizes her resurrected "Master." Défilée
names Dessalines (whom she called "this martyr" in the Frenchman
Edgar La Selve's account), and this act momentarily chases the demons
from her mind.[93]

Oral tradition, while remembering Défilée, does not try to ratio-
nalize or sanctify the terrors of vengeance. Unlike the written accounts,
the following song does not depend on schematic reversal: the exchange between sentiment and enlightenment or, more specifically, the
possession of the woman in love by the dismembered hero that makes
him whole and her reasonable in an ecstasy of expiation.

Parole-a té palé déjà
Dessalines gangan
Parole-a té palé déjà
Tous lé jours Macandal apé palé Dessalines
Dessalines vé pas couté . . .
Défilée ouè;

Défilée pé! . . .
Général Dessalines oh! gadez misè moin,
Gadez tracas pays-là
Pays-là chaviré
L'empérè Dessalines oh! . . .
Ou cé vaillant gaçon
Pas quitté pays a tombé . . .
Pas quitté pays a gâté[94]

(The word has already been spoken
Dessalines the priest
The word has already been spoken
Everyday Makandal is going to speak to Dessalines
Dessalines doesn't want to listen . . .
Défilée yes;
Défilée is frightened! . . .
General Dessalines oh! look at my misery,
Look at the troubled country
The capsized country
Emperor Dessalines oh! . . .
You this courageous boy
Don't leave the fallen country . . .
Don't leave the ruined country)

Here, the drama depends on her attachment to the vicissitudes of secular, political life, as well as to the supernatural legend, reported by Rigaud in *La Tradition voudou et le voudou haïtien*, that the spirit of the one-armed maroon hero, Makandal, warned Dessalines not to go to Pont-Rouge.

It is not possible to verify when the Haitian people began to sing this song of worldly regret for the death of their "Papa," their *gangan* or priest. I suspect that sometime before the literate elite decided it would be wise to resurrect Dessalines as hero, those who suffered under the rule of Christophe and Boyer began to recall Dessalines and their own momentary "madness" in rejoicing over his death. At their moment of greatest failure, still crushed by confounding, persistent oppression, the poor deified Dessalines. This imperiled and particularized deification, so unlike the cult of resurrection adopted by the state, does not necessarily promise a new order of things, nor does it offer Haitians a fantasy of conversion. Note that the Haitian historian Jean Fouchard, reconstructing history according to a dominant agenda, records this song as if it were offered up to the dead hero immediately after his assassination as if by a startled, ignorant, and childlike populace: "the dumbfounded people then sang and still sing in their vodou ceremonies the ardent supplication of orphans mingled with the terrible omens they did not know about."[95]

Can a biographical subtext affirm the centrality of the figure of Défilée to both public and popular renditions of revolutionary history? In her "Bibliographie Féminine, Epoque Coloniale et XIX Siècle," Ertha Pascal-Trouillot, one of Haiti's numerous acting presidents since the 1986 departure of "Baby Doc" Duvalier, gives a reality to the legendary Défilée. Her name was Dédée Bazile. She had spent part of her youth in Port-au-Prince at Fort Saint-Clair, where she followed Dessalines as a *vivandière* (sutler) for the indigenous army. According to Pascal-Trouillot, "she had a wild passion for Dessalines that exacerbated the mental troubles caused by the slaughter of her parents by French soldiers." She was not simply a marketwoman or meat vendor, who followed the Haitian Revolutionary Army as it marched (hence her name Défilée, meaning parade or procession), but, unstrung by the loss of her parents and her love for Dessalines, she supplied the soldiers with sex.[96]

Another story was recalled by the hundred-year-old Joseph Jérémie, known as Monsieur Jérémie, identified in one manual of Haitian literature as "talented writer, storyteller" and "dean of Haitian letters," who told the story to Jean Fouchard in the 1950s.[97] According to him, one night Défilée's two sons and three of her brothers, all of whom were enlisted in the army, did not return from a party in the Cahos mountains, where the "slaves" often secretly got together. About six hundred "slaves" were surprised and "pitilessly massacred by the *sbirri* [sergeants or officers] of the bloodthirsty General Donatien Rochambeau." The news unhinged Dédée's mind, but she continued to follow Dessalines's army as a sutler, "with the same spirit, the same faith in final victory." Joseph Jérémie describes how she got the name Défilée. "As soon as the soldiers stopped somewhere to rest, Dédée also stopped. Abruptly, the madwoman raised the long stick [used for a crutch] held in her hand, and bravely cried out: *défilez, défilez* [march, march]. They obeyed her." Whereas Pascal-Trouillot alludes to the effects of unrequited passion—Dédée's infatuation with Dessalines—Jérémie is impressed by her inspiring effect on the soldiers and Dessalines's fatherly love for his devotee.[98]

Défilée, who presided over Dessalines's battles for independence as his sutler and sometime-partner, is the first to stand by him after his dismemberment. Dessalines, turned into pieces of meat, gets reassembled by the woman who used to sell meat to him and his soldiers. She alone touches the befouled remains. Like Mary Magdalene and "the other Mary," and varying unnamed women who appear in the resurrection scenes in the Gospels (later known in medieval tradition as the "two Marys" or the "three Marys"), Défilée mourns and cares for the body of the Liberator.[99] Though Catholic emblems of love, penitence, and devotion pervade the story of Défilée and Dessalines, other elements undergird this national narrative. If Défilée summons the tale of a republic, fallen and then resurrected through transformative love, she also remains an image that goes beyond this blessed conversion. Not only does Dédée Bazile, or Défilée, flesh out the sacred in popular incarnations that intermingle promiscuity and power, sex and sacrament, but her drive to collect Dessalines's body parts has more to do with preventing resurrection than enhancing or witnessing it.[100]

Rather than merely representing patriotic fervor or unmitigated generosity, as the legitimizers of the official cult of Dessalines would have it, Défilée's actions also suggest a preoccupation with proper rituals of burial and fear of the unquiet dead. In describing the West African roots of the ancestor cult in Haiti, Maya Deren notes a concern with the corpse rendered as pieces of magical matter used for harm: "Care is taken . . . that no parts rightfully belonging to the dead matter should remain in circulation in the living world. Such precautions against a false life, which might also be put to magic and malevolent use, are numerous."[101] The figure of Défilée transcends the role of witness and devotee. More like the oungan or manbo who prevents the dead from returning to life to harm the living, Défilée assembles Dessalines's remnants in order to make sure they are suitably buried, thus thwarting their resurrection by a sorcerer. Read in this way, the figure of Défilée transposes apparently contradictory traditions with fluent and convincing ease: the penitent devotee turns into the wise diviner, and the fear of stunted burial is joined to the promise of glorious resurrection.

Lurking in every effusion of ennobling love is the terror of dehumanization. The status of Dessalines as hero and god is restored by the double incarnation of Défilée and Dédée Bazile: a problematic but mutually reinforcing union of regenerate love and strong sexuality, legitimate and forbidden practices. To Dédée Bazile is attributed the only song of farewell to Dessalines, which Joseph Jérémie says she sang while kneeling before Dessalines's unmarked tomb, and after kissing it three times:

Jacquot tol lô cotoc
Tignan
Jacquot, Jacquot, tol lô cotoc
Tignan
Yo touyé Dessalinn
Dessalinn papa moin
Tignan
Moin pap jam'm blié-ou
Tignan[102]

(Jack *tol lô cotoc*
Ti-Jean
Jack, Jack, *tol lô cotoc*
Ti-Jean
You killed Dessalines
Ti-Jean
Dessalines my papa
Ti-Jean
I will never forget you
Ti-Jean)[103]

Fouchard explains that the refrain *tol lô cotoc* was the creolized form of the French *tralala*. One of Haiti's oldest songs, still repeated as the most moving elegy to Dessalines, it was reputedly composed by Défilée to "her Jacquot that she had loved, admired and so faithfully served, braving bullets, in the retinue of the Army."[104]

What does the conjunction of hero and madwoman tell us about Haitian history? The trope of long-suffering or mad *négresse* and powerful *noir* became a routine coupling in contemporary Haitian as well as Caribbean texts. The parallels between literary and historical writing raise questions about the myth of the Haitian nation and the kinds of symbols required to make a "national" literature. Haitian history has been written by men, whether colonizers who distort or negate the past, or the colonized who reclaim what has been lost or denied. What is the name of the manbo who assisted the priest Boukman in the legendary ceremony of Bois-Caïman? According to most stories, the black manbo began the attack. "As history tells it she made the conspirators drink the blood of the animal she had slaughtered, while persuading them that therein lay the proof of their future invincibility in battle."[105] Arlette Gautier has argued in *Les Soeurs de solitude* that, as opposed to the men of the revolution, women left no records. "They have remained nameless except for Sanite Belair, Marie-Jeanne Lamartinière for Saint-Domingue and the mulatta Solitude in Guadeloupe."[106]

Both Madiou and Ardouin mention women during the revolution. Not only the fierce Sanite Belair, who refused to be blindfolded during her execution, and Marie-Jeanne Lamartinière, who led the indigènes in the extraordinary Battle of Crête-à-Pierrot, and Défilée, but also Claire Heureuse (her real name was Marie Claire Félicité Guillaume Bonheur), the wife of Dessalines, who saved many of the French he had ordered massacred.[107] Yet we need to consider how these women are mentioned, how their appearances work within the historical narrative. Their stories are something of an interlude in the business of *making history*. Bracketed off from the descriptions of significant loss or triumph, the *blanches* raped and butchered or the *noires* ardent and fearless became symbols for *la bonté, la férocité,* or *la faiblesse* (goodness, ferocity, or weakness). More significant, at least in most standard histories, especially those written by foreigners, the mulatto women who fought with the black rebels, and even took part in the ceremony of Bois-Caïman, are not mentioned. One of the manbo in the ceremony was named Cécile Fatiman. The description of her in Etienne Charlier's *Aperçu sur la formation historique de la nation haïtienne* is striking in its portrayal of a light-skinned product of colonial mixing:

Cécile Fatiman, wife of Louis Michel [Jean-Louis] PIERROT, who commanded an indigenous battalion at Vertières and later became President of Haiti, participated in the Ceremony of Bois-Caïman: she was a manbo. Daughter of an African Négresse and a Corsican Prince, Cécile FATIMAN was a Mulâtresse with green eyes and long black and silky hair and had been sold with her mother in Saint-Domingue. Her mother also had two sons who disappeared during the trade, without leaving a trace. Cécile FATIMAN lived at Le Cap until the age of 112 years of age, in full possession of her faculties.[108]

Although Oswald Durand's popular poem "Choucoun" (1883) celebrated the figure of the *mulâtresse,* the brown-skinned, silky haired "marabout / with eyes as bright as candles," the official poetic dogma of négritude—boldly politicized in Haiti with Duvalier's cult of *noirisme*—summoned the black woman as muse. The *négresse* Défilée, poor and abandoned, became part of a conceptual framework necessary to twentieth-century Haitian writers as diverse as Carl Brouard, Jacques Roumain, and Jacques-Stephen Alexis. How do we read sexuality when locked into the evocation of *nationalism* or *black soul*? Alexis's militant novel *Compère Général Soleil* (1955) begins with Hilarion, a nearly naked negro in the night, "blue because of his shadow, because of his blackness." He wanders, thinking about misery, which means thinking about a particular image of woman.

Misery is a madwoman, I tell you. The bitch, I know her well. I've seen her in the capitals, the cities, the suburbs. . . . This enraged female is the same everywhere. . . . Angry female, skinny female, mother of pigs, mother of whores, mother of all assassins, sorceress of every defeat, of every misery, ah! she makes me spit![109]

He will later meet Claire Heureuse (his beautiful helpmate named after Dessalines's wife), who promises regeneration from a barbarism represented as female. Hilarion's négritude, as in so many other dramas of men finding themselves, defines itself against the familiar conceit of the double Venus, women cloven in two as beneficent or savage, virginal or polluted.

What happened to actual black women during Haiti's repeated revolutions, as they were mythologized by men, metaphorized out of life into legend? It is unsettling to recognize that the hyperbolization necessary for myths to be mutually reinforcing not only erases these women but forestalls our turning to these *real* lives. But such a turn is not my purpose here. Let me attend then to the nature of the feminine emblems underlying and sustaining the nation. The legend of *Sor Rose* or Sister Rose is a story of origins that depends for its force on rape. In this story, the Haitian nation began in the loins of a black woman. The ancestress must be ravished for the state to be born. Yet, Sister Rose, like Défilée, forms part of a narrative that does not always depend on the facile opposition of virgin and whore. Things are much more complicated. Like the religious calling embedded in her name, the colonial past, once remembered in these reconstructions, is sometimes like a sudden sighting of forced intimacies.

I know of only two written references to this ancestress, both from the 1940s, complementary to the noiriste revolution of 1946: Timoléon Brutus's biography of Dessalines, *L'Homme d'airain* (1946), and Dominique Hippolyte's play about Dessalines and the last years of the revolution (1802–1803), *Le Torrent* (1940). In *La Tradition voudoo* (1953), Milo Rigaud noted that the mulatto André Rigaud, ultimately Toussaint's enemy, issued from the coupling of a Frenchman and "a pure négresse of the Arada or Rada race [in Dahomey], Rose. On his habitation *Laborde*, he 'served' the Rada mysteries [spirits] from whom his mother had recovered the cult."[110]

The legend of Rose, like that of the land of Haiti (and, implicitly, like the tale of Défilée), begins with a woman "brutally fertilized," as Brutus puts it, "by a slave in heat or a drunken White, a criminal escaped from Cayenne [the French colonial prison]; or a degenerate from feudal nobility in quest of riches on the continent." Summoning this myth of violation, Brutus argues that it is senseless to put mulatto over black or vice versa, since "the origin of everyone is common." No superiority can be extricated from the color and class chaos that began Haitian society. Yet, in this locale of blacks, whites, mulattoes, criminals, slaves, and aristocrats, Rose, represented as the generic "black woman," is singular. In an amalgam of neutralized distinctions, she stands out as victim and martyr.

Let us turn briefly to the legend as dramatized in Hippolyte's *Le Torrent,* a play celebrating the "flood" and "tempest" of popular revolution that overwhelmed the colonial masters and Napoleon's soldiers. (This apocalyptic drama was recently replayed: Jean-Bertrand Aristide was the leader of the mass movement called *Operasyon Lavalas,* meaning "flood" or "deluge" in Creole.) *Le Torrent,* written in collaboration with the historian Placide David, won first prize in a competition of dramatic art organized in 1940 by the self-proclaimed dictator and "Second Liberator," the mulatto President Sténio Vincent.[111] In the preface to his *Dessalines ou le sang du Pont-Rouge,* Hénock Trouillot describes *Le Torrent* as the "true beginnings of historical drama in Haiti." Praising the play as a "return to the historical sources of the origins of the Haitian nation," Trouillot locates mythic power in the popular struggle against the elites, who lack "national aspiration."[112] Performed on May 18, 1940, the play was published in 1965, during the regime of "Papa Doc" Duvalier. The play is expertly packaged: its text is preceded by a "communication" from Dumersais Estimé, secretary of state and minister of education under Vincent— and in 1946, elected the first black president of Haiti in thirty years— and by the official report of the jury examining manuscripts, which included Dr. J. C. Dorsainville and Dr. Jean Price-Mars, two leaders of *Les Griots,* writers who sought a return to the African sources of Haitian life, to Creole, to vodou, and to "authentic" identity. As a government-sponsored spectacle, then, *Le Torrent* was resurrected in print as a drama worthy of "exalting Haitian patriotism and enhancing the teachings of our National History."[113]

The folklore manipulated in *Le Torrent* goes deep into the psyche of the black nation, reconstituted after the national affront of the American occupation, which ended six years before this play was produced at the Theater Rex in Port-au-Prince. Sister Rose presides over the play as the coalescence of all those symbols most gripping to the black intelligentsia and, hypothetically at least, to the imagination of the black masses: the African ancestral heritage, vodou, revolutionary struggle, and Haitian Creole. Sister Rose is the only character who consistently speaks Haitian, although in the text of the play it is transliterated as French. Her brother Ti-Noël, taken from Dahomey with Rose and sold to the French planter Robert Delcourt, generally speaks French, even when talking with her. *Le Torrent* takes place in Haut-du-Cap, not far from Cap Français, in Master Delcourt's colonial habitat. This place of wealth and privilege is contaminated not only by the struggle outside but by the question of legitimacy, color, and race in the domestic sphere. The prototypical mythic act is that of white Delcourt sleeping with black Rose, the mistress and housekeeper, who gives birth to the mulatto twins Jean and Pierre. Pierre loves his "dream" of whiteness, Mademoiselle Emilie, the daughter of Captain Jougla, an officer of the Expeditionary Army. The story unfolds as news of General Antoine Richepanse's reinstitution of slavery in Guadeloupe leads to Dessalines's desertion of Leclerc and his temporary alliance with the insurgent black masses led by Ti-Noël, Macaya, and Jean Zèclè.

The gratifying fantasy of the play is the triumph over colonial color prejudice. Even if you are light-skinned and have fine manners, if your mother is black you will never be accepted by the "pure-blooded" French. Yet, Pierre's initial disavowal of his mother, Sister Rose ("as soon as the young white lady arrives, you will disappear"), turns into recognition when he tells the black woman in the shadows to come forward ("Mom, go get dressed. Go put on your beautiful Indian dress. You will wear your Madras handkerchiefs"). What is most striking about the celebratory reversals of the play—Dessalines's defection from the French, the mulatto sons joining with the African-born Ti-Noël, and the recognition of "the African soul" and "the regeneration of the race" by none other than the planter Delcourt, as he praises his "black madonna"—is that Sister Rose remains constant. In her varying guises, she abides all the changes. Whether called "slave," "mother," "wife," or "servant," whether praised as the incarnation of "love" or "kindness," "luck" or "lady of sorrows," she is the passive recipient of history. Rose, icon of Haiti, ends the play in solitary epiphany. As the white father, the mixed-blood sons, and the black rebels leave (Delcourt returns to France, and his sons go off with Dessalines and his rebels to fight Leclerc), Rose stays where she is told, obedient to the wishes of those who make history: "Sister Rose, alone, the image of the future victorious Country, watches them depart."[114]

In the legend of Sister Rose, *to give oneself to a man*, voluntarily or not, is *to give Haiti a history.* But what kind of history? And who gets to claim it? In *La Femme* (1859), Jules Michelet, who had praised Madiou's *Histoire,* greeted Haiti: "Receive my best wishes, young State! And let us protect you, in expiation of the past!" Yet, while extolling the spirit of this "great race, so cruelly slandered," he turns to Haiti's "charming women, so good and so intelligent."[115] A few pages earlier, he had tried to show that those races believed to be inferior simply "need love." Tenderness toward women, as colonial historians had argued in their justifications of slavery, was the attribute of civilized men alone. But Michelet extended the possibility of enlightenment to women in love, specifically to black women who want white men: "The river thirsts for the clouds, the desert thirsts for the river, the black woman for the white man. She is in every way the most amorous and the most generous." Her beneficent desire entitles her, in Michelet's mind, to a particular kind of reverence. Not only is she identified as an icon of loving surrender, but she becomes the land: generalized as an Africa named, tamed, and dedicated to serving Europe. "Africa," Michelet concluded, "is a woman."[116]

Michelet's words recall descriptions of the *femme de couleur* in colonial Saint-Domingue, most pronounced in Moreau de Saint-Méry and Pierre de Vassière, but found in "natural histories" throughout the Caribbean. Not only sensual, but beings who lived for love, they embodied the forced intimacies and luxuriant concubinage of the colonial past. In Haiti, Michelet's Black Venus becomes Sister Rose, beautiful but violated. Yet, it remained for a Haitian, Janvier, in his *La République d'Haïti et ses visiteurs,* to be explicit about a perilous history understood as courtship with one aim: possession.

The history of Haiti is such: difficult, arduous, thorny, but charming, filled with interpenetrating, simultaneous deeds, subtle, delicate, and entangled.

She is a virgin who must be violated, after long courtship; but how exquisite when you possess her! . . . She is astonishing and admirable.[117]

The emblems of heroism or love recuperated in written histories of Haiti often seem to be caricatures or simulations of French "civilization." In this recycling of images, as in the case of Louis Napoleon and Soulouque, we are caught in a mimetic bind. The heterogeneity of vodou syncretism, however, offers an alternative to such blockage. Vodou does not oppose what we might call "Western" or "Christian" but freely associates seemingly irreconcilable elements, taking in materials from the dominant culture even as it resists or coexists with it.

On May 18, 1803, at the Congress of Arcahaie, General-in-Chief

Dessalines ripped the white out of the French tricolor that covered the table. Trampling it under his feet, he commanded that the red and blue—symbolizing the union of mulatto and black—be sewn together as the new flag and that "*Liberté ou la Mort*" (Liberty or Death) replace the old inscription, "*R.F.*" (*République Française*).[118] In "The Legend of the First Flag" (1927), Luc Grimard renders the theatrical heroics of that memorable night in verse. The gesture of tearing "the white" from "the heart of sublime tinsel" announces the birth of a "new people":

> In the nascent Republic, it was for him
> A gage of union, a symbolic flag,
> It was this somber blue, it was this light red
> The mulatto and the black against all the Leclercs![119]

But in the minds of many Haitians, the gods or spirits become part of the narrative. In Léogane in the 1970s I heard people recount that Dessalines cut out the white strip of the French flag while possessed by the warrior spirit Ogou. Brutus in *L'Homme d'airain* (1946) presents an even more compelling version. He tells a story "of undying memory," heard and passed on by Justin Lhérison in his history class at the Lycée Pétion in Port-au-Prince in the 1930s. It was not a spirit of African origins that possessed Dessalines, but "the Holy Virgin, protectress of the Blacks." Then, Dessalines cursed in "Congo *langage*" (the sacred language for direct communication with the spirits) and "then in French against the Whites who dared believe that 'the Independents wanted to remain French.'" Brutus concludes, "He was in a mystic trance, possessed by the spirit when he said: '*Monsieur, tear out the white from that flag.*'"[120]

But who is this spirit? What is the Virgin Mary doing speaking in Congo and in French? Dessalines possessed speaks the language of the spirit who has entered his head and who addresses him as "Monsieur." Ogou, transmogrified as the Virgin Mary, speaks both French and "Congo language" (the generic term for "African languages" and, more specifically, the tongue of vodou initiates). The inherently unreformable quality of this myth goes beyond sanctioned histories and, most important, de-idealizes a "pure" type such as the Virgin. We can begin to understand what happens to the idea of virginity or violation when hooked into the system of local spirituality. If priests violated local women while teaching chastity, if they produced impurity—*the mixed blood*—while calling for purity, how was this violation absorbed into the birth of new gods?

During the chaotic ten-month regime of Jean-Louis Pierrot (April 16, 1845–March 1, 1846), the peasant rebel leader Acaau's black lieutenant and chaplain, Frère Joseph, had great influence in Port-au-Prince. Pierrot, the brother-in-law of Christophe and Acaau's close friend, had, according to Etienne Charlier, married Cécile Fatiman, the mulatto manbo of Bois-Caïman, though her role in the sinister practices that reportedly characterized his time in office is not known. Gustave d'Alaux, in *L'Empereur Soulouque et son empire,* describes how Joseph (whom he called a "bandit") walked, candle in hand, amid Acaau's bands and edified them with his novenas to the Virgin, and mastered them because of his influence with the vodou spirits.[121] D'Alaux makes Joseph's fame coincide with his role as the Virgin's intermediary. One of the most famous political rallying cries from the turbulent years 1843 to 1846 is put in the mouth of the Virgin, who here cooperates with the popular struggle by speaking Creole. Here are Joseph's words, as d'Alaux records them: "Acaau is right, because the Virgin said: *Nègue riche qui connaît li ni écri, cila mulâte; mulâte pauve qui pas connaît li ni écri, cila nègue* [A rich negro who knows how to read and write is a mulatto; a poor mulatto who does not know how to read or write is a negro]."[122] After communicating this Manichean color-and-class conflict as if it were a divine utterance, Joseph began to call himself Frère Joseph, dress completely in white, and perform his devotions and prayers. He also continued to make prophesies.[123]

Madiou, writing about the "tempestuous" struggle in 1845 between the two "superstitious" or "pagan" sects, called *guyons* and *saints,* revealed how confused spirituality in Haiti had become after independence. African and European materials converged: bags with fetishes, human bones, and snakes were employed in Catholic rituals, while vodou practitioners, called "frères," carried out priestly functions and recited Catholic liturgy. The guyons, called "loups-garous" by Madiou, and reputed to be cannibals, were thought to carry human flesh in their *macoutes* (sacks). The saints, equally "fanatical" and "partisans of vodou," considered the guyons "the damned," and "dreaded" and "executed" them. Madiou describes the saints as believing in "the immortality of the soul and in eternal punishments and rewards." They practice vodou, "but under the forms of Roman Catholicism."[124]

Duverneau Trouillot had argued that after independence, vodou ceremonies had become so "Frenchified," so acculturated to French Catholicism, that the old cult would eventually disappear under the weight of Christian civilization. The "advantages of liberty" could not help but contribute to the disintegration of what he perceived as increasingly disordered and uncodified beliefs and gods.[125] But what Trouillot praised as the benefits of liberation were never available to the Haitian majority. For them, the God, saints, and devils of French dogma, never fully accessible, were accommodated by being remade on Haitian soil. Endowed with new qualities, they lost their missionary or conquest functions. Remnants of texts and theologies, reinterpreted by local tradition, articulated a new history. The Virgin who possessed the militant Dessalines or Frère Joseph would also haunt Haitians as the *djablès*: the feared ghostly she-devil condemned to walk the earth for the sin of dying a virgin.

To serve the spirits is to disrupt and complicate the sexual symbolism of church and state. In answer to Janvier's correlation between the virgin, long desired and finally violated, and Haiti's history, intractable but ultimately apprehended, the most feared spirits, like the most beloved Virgin, were formed out of the odd facts that made up the discourse of mastery permeated by the thought of subordination. A vodou history might be composed from materials such as oral accounts of the possession of Dessalines and his emergence as lwa, god, or spirit, and equally ambivalent accounts of figures like Ezili, Jean Zombi, or Défilée. Sinkholes of excess, these crystallizations of unwritten history force us to acknowledge inventions of mind and memory that destroy the illusions of mastery, that circumvent and confound *any* master narrative.

Ezili

The despotism of the senses
constitutes the source of tyranny.
—Emmanuel Levinas, "Freedom and Command"

What is the best kind of submission? You cannot surrender your will, you cannot be possessed unless your body becomes the vessel for the master's desire. The body must be owned, made into property, for possession to take place. In vodou practice, however, such an instrumental seizure does not describe the relationship between a god and mortal. And to talk about possession is somewhat

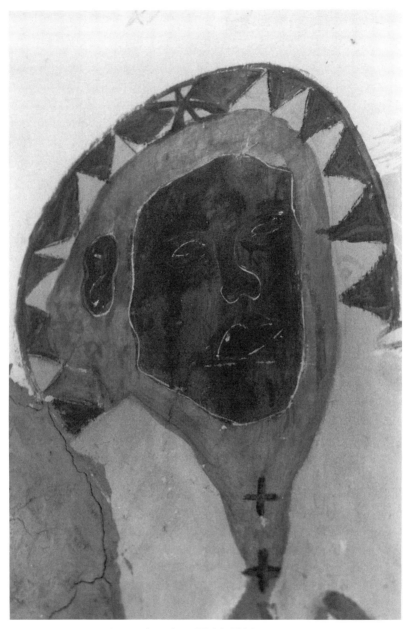

Wall painting of Ezili Dantò. Bainet, Haiti, 1986.

misleading, since those who serve the gods do not use the term. Most often, the experience of being entered, inhabited, and seized by a spirit is described as being mounted (as the horse is by the rider). I want to reflect on a goddess called Ezili in Haiti by thinking about the ways in which a word like *possession,* so powerful in the Western imagination, becomes in the figure of Ezili something like collective physical remembrance. The history of slavery is given substance through time by a spirit that originated in an experience of domination. That domination was most often experienced by women under another name, something called "love."

In that unnatural situation where a human became property, love became coordinate with a task of feeling that depended to a large extent on the experience of servitude. In his *Description . . . de la partie française de l'Isle Saint-Domingue,* Moreau de Saint-Méry got at what most characterized Creole society in the colony by concentrating on a cult of desire: "Love, this need, or rather this tyrant of the sensitive soul, reigns over that of the Creole." Love, promiscuity, pleasure, and abandon are words that recur throughout French accounts of the colony of Saint-Domingue. In plantation society—and the same was true on other Caribbean islands and in the United States—domination encouraged the brutalization of "enlightened man" and enflamed his unbridled appetite for lust and cruelty. Writing his *Notes on the State of Virginia,* Thomas Jefferson warned: "The whole commerce between master and slave is a perpetual exercise of the most boisterous passions, the most unremitting despotism on one part, and degrading submissions on the other."[126]

But no matter how degrading, how despotic the effects of slavery, there remained a place for love, a kind of excrescence from the everyday oppression and torture, an experience that could be named and claimed by the "civilized" agents of an odious system. How easily the sentiments, when attached to women other than white, became emblematic of lust and debauchery. Yet, the mixed-blood or mulatto mistress somehow became the concrete signifier for lust that could be portrayed as "love." Moreau de Saint-Méry envisioned her as "one of those priestesses of Venus" and then explained: "The entire being of a Mulâtresse is given up to pleasure, the fire of this Goddess burns in her heart only to be extinguished with her life. This cult is her law, her every wish, her every happiness. . . . To charm all her senses, to surrender to the most delicious ecstasy, to be surprised by the most seductive ravishing, that is her unique study."[127]

If, in the perverse ethics of the planter, the spiritualized, refined images of white women depended on the violation of black women, the bleached-out sable Venus accommodated both extremes. In the crossing and unsettling of enforced (and contrived) duality, the free woman of color would be served, fed, honored, and adored, and at the same time excluded from marriage, threatened by poverty, and often abandoned. The pervasiveness of this coupling is noted by C. L. R. James in *The Black Jacobins*: "In 1789, of 7,000 mulatto women, 5,000 were either prostitutes or the 'kept mistresses' of white men."[128] But Bryan Edwards reassured his readers in his *History, Civil and Commercial, of the British Colonies in the West Indies* (1793) that the "free women of color universally maintained by white men of all ranks and conditions, are not prostitutes, as flourished in Europe at that time." In the hybrid New World of forced intimacies and artificial hierarchies, terminologies were conveniently redefined and manipulated. Later, reflecting in *Absalom, Absalom!* on this cult of desire in the former French colony of Louisiana, William Faulkner would present the Creole octoroon courtesan as exemplary. Wafting through his pages as some "fatal insatiation," she is so highly prized ("they are more valuable as commodities than white girls") and fulfills so well "a woman's sole end and purpose: to love, to be beautiful, to divert," that she goads the male fantasist on to trials of redefinition: "No: not whores. Not even courtesans. . . . No, not whores. Sometimes I believe that they are the only true chaste women, not to say virgins, in America."

What Pierre de Vassière, writing about Saint-Domingue in the years between 1629 and 1789, called "a very strange familiarity" between those who made themselves masters and those who found themselves slaves, made the old practices of exclusivity unworkable.[129]

These white women live with their domestics under the weight of the most bizarre intimacy. Nearly every young white Creole owns a young mulâtresse or quarteronne, and sometimes even a young négresse, whom they make their *cocotte*. The cocotte is the confidant of all the thoughts of the mistress (and this reliance is sometimes reciprocal), the confidant of her loves.[130]

In plantation isolation, differences were sometimes collapsed in a reciprocity that made those supposedly inferior absolutely necessary to those who imagined themselves superior. Such intimacy in human bondage also has been noted between black slaves and the free mulatto women they served. As Jean Fouchard puts it, "How could the slave avoid being drawn to . . . that intermediary class whose insolent ostentation gave birth to the war of lace and clothing that involved the entire colony in an all-out competition?"[131]

Colonial historians of Saint-Domingue were obsessed by the rites of love and the pleasures of the toilette, ceremonies of propriety and consumption. Ezili, known in written representations as "the Black Venus," "the Tragic Mistress," or "the Goddess of Love," remains a commentary on the harrowing reality of Saint-Domingue. A goddess was born on the soil of Haiti who has no precedent in Yoruba or Dahomey. Far more specific in her attributes than Oya, Yemanja, or Oshun, the Ezili (whether Ezili Dantò, Ezili Freda, Ezili-je-wouj, or Marinèt) recalls the violent yoking of decorum and lust.

Served by her devotees with the accoutrements of libertinage— lace, perfume, jewels, and sweets—this spirit carries the weight of a history that testifies to the union of profligacy and virtue, thus making a mockery of piety. For not only does Ezili, like Défilée, signal the transcending of violation and whoring through infinite love, but she also tells a rather banal and keenly materialist story. Let me emphasize here that the elaborate dress and the details of service articulate a specific experience of Saint-Domingue that goes beyond the scattered scriptural, classical, and West African materials assembled in the manifestations of Ezili.[132] A rage for devotional practices, instead of demanding divestment or abstention, encouraged embellishment and a veneration of luxury. Henry Breen, though writing of Saint-Lucia in the 1840s (which the English and French fought to possess for over a hundred years), explains this rapacious staging of belief, the bond between religious fervor and fashionable ostentation: "In a word, dress and devotion are the order of the day—the all-engrossing topics of female society; and both are so harmoniously blended that the greatest *dévotée* is often the greatest coquette."[133]

In his *Histoire d'Haïti*, Madiou reflected, "If the Spanish and French, in possessing the Queen of the Antilles [Saint-Domingue], left there the bloody traces of their domination, they also left their languages, their mores, their customs, ultimately the germs of this new 'civilization.'" Let us take the spirit surviving today under the name of Ezili as a medium for apprehending the particulars of a society that was not African, not French, and certainly not a civilization as a dominant historiography has taught us to understand it. Transported Africans, uprooted French, and native Creoles found themselves participating together in unprecedented spectacles of civility and barbarism. Imagine a world where grace and "the charm of evenings on the Faubourg St.-Germain" (the Haitian Madiou) coexisted with "a nearly absolute lack of sensibility and even a certain native cruelty resulting from the harsh and brutal way that they [the planters] treated their slaves" (the Frenchman Vassière).

Recognized as the most powerful and arbitrary of gods in vodou, Ezili is also the most contradictory: a spirit of love who forbids love, a woman who is the most beloved yet feels herself the most betrayed. She can be generous and loving, or implacable and cruel. As mystery of love, assistance, and beauty, she appears at night to her devotees in the form of a pale virgin. As spirit of vengeance, she is fiercely jealous and sometimes punishes wayward devotees with death, impotence, or frigidity if they dare drink or have sex on those days devoted to her.

In writing about Ezili, most ethnographers, Haitian and foreign, have had recourse to analogy. She is Venus. She is the Virgin Mary or "the sinner" of the Gospels (whether understood as the unnamed penitent or Mary Magdalene). She is Ishtar or Aphrodite. If we forgo limiting ourselves to these external impositions, we can apprehend how Ezili, and the names and practices associated with her, store and reinterpret the unwieldy images of the past. Let us recall the incongruous origins of the cult of the Virgin, the strength of Mariolatry arising from its syncretism of pre-Christian cults of willful goddesses and harlot saints. In practice, there are slippages and uneasy alliances between gods described as antagonistic: Ezili Freda, the pale, elegant lady of luxury and love, identifed with the Virgin Mary or the Mater Dolorosa, represented in Catholic chromolithographs as a young girl, wearing necklaces of pearls and gold, her heart pierced with a golden sword; Ezili Dantò, the black, passionate woman identified with the Mater Salvatoris, her heart also pierced, with a dagger; and Ezili-je-wouj, Ezili Mapian, and Ezili-nwa-kè (black heart) of the militant Petwo family of gods.

When her roles are described, and thus circumscribed in writing, even by Maya Deren in *Divine Horsemen* and Zora Neale Hurston in *Tell My Horse,* the discourse on Ezili has most often perpetuated masculine fantasies of women. Split between the "good" Ezili Freda and the "evil" Ezili-je-wouj, between the beautiful coquette "Mistress Ezili" and the old, stooped "Gran Ezili" or Ezili-kokobe (the shriveled), she dramatizes the cult of mystification: the splitting of women into objects to be desired or feared.

In ritual performances this dichotomy is both entangled and blurred. Songs tell of an Ezili Freda abandoned and betrayed, both married and prostituted (both institutions equated by their claims alternately to entitle or dispossess): "Ezili marye, li pa genyen chans! / Ezili jennès,

Veve of Ezili Freda. Croix-des-Missions, Haiti, 1980.

li pa genyen chans!" (Ezili is married, she's unlucky! / Ezili is prostituted, she's unlucky!). Depending on locale, on the particular ceremony, or the composition of the *ounfò* (in the West of Haiti, ounfò
refers to either the temple surroundings or the ceremonial altar), Ezili
appears as Ezili-towo (the bull), Ezili-do-ba (low back), Ezili Zandò,
and Ezili-séverine-belle-femme, as well as Ezili Freda, Ezili Dantò, and
Ezili-je-wouj. Nowhere is the demolition of an ideal type so pronounced as in the subversive erotics of Mistress Ezili. The pale "lady,"
alternately sweet and voracious, enters into the head of the black
devotee, and together they re-create and reinterpret a history of mastery and servitude. What some have called the "eternal feminine" or

Veve of Ezili Dantò. Port-au-Prince, Haiti, 1974.

Veve of Ezili Dantò. Bel-Air, Haiti, 1970.

"maternal libido" is reconstituted by varying incarnations that question the very nature of domination.

Though she seems to be the vessel for Western values, bearing the trappings of exquisite formalism and femininity, she subverts the roles she affects. In her many aspects, Ezili reveals a sexual ambiguity and a convertibility of class so pronounced that study of this goddess and her relations with other spirits and mortals—as well as her use in literary representations—would help articulate a phenomenology of eros in Haiti. Her symbol is the heart, or the heart pierced with a dagger, and it appears not only in chromolithographs but in the ritual *veve* traced out in flour made from corn, or even coffee grounds.

Called the lwa of love, Ezili demands that the word be reinvented. In her rites, notions of affection or attachment undergo strange but instructive metamorphoses. She possesses men as well as women: both sexes take on her attributes and accede to her mystique of femininity. Ezili also chooses women as well as men in "mystic marriage." The customary gendered relations between men and women do not matter. She is no fertility goddess, and except for a song about her lost child Ursule (product of her union with Ogou Badagri), who disappeared under the waters of the Caribbean sea, she is not a mother:

Moin pa gangnin chance, mézan-mi ô!
Moin pa gangnin chance!
Moin pa gangnin chance, mézan-mi ô!
Moin pa gangnin chance!

Gnou sèle ti pitite moin gangnin
L'allé, navigué lan la mè.
Can-note chaviré, avè li!
Lan la mè, cannote chaviré![134]

(I'm unlucky, my friends, oh!
I'm unlucky!
I'm unlucky, my friends, oh!
I'm unlucky!

One little child that I had
She went sailing on the sea.
The boat sunk with her!
The boat sunk in the sea!)

Even Gran Ezili, conceived as a stooped matron of prostitutes, is not really maternal. The indeterminacy of this spirit, served by prostitutes, homosexuals, and virgins, is thus oversimplified when portrayed by Maya Deren in *Divine Horsemen* as "Lady of Luxury" or "Goddess of

Love" or by Zora Neale Hurston in *Tell My Horse* as the "ideal of the love bed."

What the *négresse* observed as a slave in the house of the whites could have contributed to producing a spirit both caring and tender, indifferent and savage—she who is not as lavish with her love as some writers would like, but who alternately hinders and promotes consummation. If we consider the recorded intimacy between slave and mistress, it is less surprising that Ezili changes from Deren's "Goddess of Love" who "protests that she is not loved enough" to "that combined rage and despair which is Erzulie-Gé-Rouge."[135]

Writing a journal of his voyage to Saint-Domingue in 1782, Justin Girod de Chantrans was concerned about the attachment of white men to free *négresses* and mulattas, the devotion to pleasure, the money spent on linen, lace, and jewels for the *filles de joie,* and the white women's "cruel tyranny," their "extreme brutality" toward their slaves.[136] If, as I have argued, the lwa were born out of the slave's awareness of the demands and finery of their masters, the appearance of Ezili in ceremony repeats, perpetuates, and subverts the colonial relation. Whether reactivated in her garb of grace as Ezili Freda or in the fury and violence of her other incarnations, she is not so much a "dream of luxury," as Deren wrote, as a mimicry of excess.

Vodou could be said to signal indigence: a recognition of essential poverty, an economic and cultural lack. But Ezili appears to summon plenitude. In the poverty of rural Haiti, the poorest country in the Western hemisphere, what does serving the implacable, demanding, and luxurious Ezili mean? Never metamorphosed out of history or embellished into dream, Ezili's appearance prods memory, not fantasy. We should not therefore romanticize her as serving the desire for unattainable love or longed-for treasures. Though Maya Deren, in her writing about the spirit, claims to have been possessed by Ezili, she is tempted to render homage to a dream of beauty. "Erzulie is the loa of the impossible perfection which must remain unattainable." Or, "Vodoun has given woman, in the figure of Erzulie, exclusive title to that which distinguishes humans from all other forms: their capacity to conceive beyond reality, to desire beyond adequacy. . . . In Erzulie, Vodoun salutes woman as the divinity of the dream, the Goddess of Love, the muse of Beauty."[137] In Deren's portrayal, Ezili yields to a supreme labor, man's right to dream. But she is also served by women, and the bits of lace, the elaborate toilette, the wine and perfumes are part of a social and collective drama that has less to do with a "gorgeous, gracious, and beneficent" woman, who gives herself "in radiant ecstasy" to men (Hurston's description), than with the continued invitation to retain or repel these extravagances. For Haiti's poor, whether in an urban ghetto or the countryside, she compels an exuberance of devotion that plays itself out in a surfeit of matter. Those who do not have are possessed by the spirit of those who did.

Moreau de Saint-Méry was astonished by the opulence and tyranny exhibited by the white Creoles of Saint-Domingue. We get a picture of men losing control in a tumult of passion, of women burning themselves out in quest of love, victims of jealousy and greed. Writing about "the sensitivity" of the New World mistress, he concluded, "their temperament makes them unable to live without love." He described what happened when white Creole women, overstimulated by chocolate, candies, and café au lait, learned of their husbands' betrayals. "Nothing equals the anger of a Creole woman who punished the slave that her husband had perhaps forced to dirty the nuptial bed. In her jealous fury she doesn't know what to invent in order to satisfy her vengeance."[138]

What some ethnographers have described as fantasies of luxury or collective wish fulfillment might more accurately be seen as the blunt recollection of what those who were abused first by the master and then by the mistress had come to know. This time, however, the rigors of knowing demand a reenactment that goes beyond imitation. The place of torture becomes the scene for a charade of love. The knowledge has to do with the costs and the perils of mastery: a grotesque distortion performed in Ezili's moves from deification to defecation, her confounding of angelic and brute. On a sliding hinge of convertibility, white "ladies," mulatto "mistresses," and black "wenches" merge and expose the falsity of these terms. When men made myths to justify the union of reason and animality—a relation absolutely necessary to the perpetuation of slavery—adoration, like abuse, animated and sustained servility, but it was always called by other names.

Service

The lwa don't use bullwhips.
—Manbo La Merci Benjamin, Bel-Air, 1970

The lwa depend on sacrifice, on blood and flesh, for life and vigor. One of the problems in discussing the practice of vodou is that, like the shifting languages of the Haitian Revolution, the

Manbo La Merci Benjamin offering food to Legba. Bel-Air, Haiti, 1970.

terminology used to describe the phenomenon is imbued with a magical or supernatural meaning that originates in European narratives of witches, vampires, and devils. The codes and trappings of Europe contributed to how the spirits of Africa would be received, comprehended, and sustained in the New World. In the appendix to *Life in a Haitian Valley,* Melville Herskovits referred to the accommodation or "adjustment" to disjunction, to the tension between Europe and Africa, "the two ancestral elements" that "have never been completely merged," as *socialized ambivalence.* He used the idea to explain the "vacillation" in individuals' behavior and to account for "the political and economic instability of Haiti."[139] Ritual services in Haiti exemplify the syncretism, the dual processes of association and interpenetration that Herskovits describes as "selection," "working over," "revamping and recombining the elements of the contributing cultures, with the result that the ensuing combinations, though of recognizable derivation, differ from their aboriginal forms."[140]

I refer to Herskovits here because the divergence between a vital African spiritual heritage and European traditions, polarized as either sacred or demonic, makes it difficult to think about what serving the spirits might mean to the devotee for whom the written agenda of priests or ideologues might not matter, or at least not matter as texts do for the literate practitioner.[141] Dehumanization or bondage, so much a part of displays of servitude or possession in Europe, where domestic slavery or the bond of property could become a metaphor for unparalleled intimacy or perfect devotion, worked differently for those who were not inventing the institution of slavery, accumulating property, or trying to justify mastery.

The lwa live in the blood (*nan san ou*). They are not vampires, though their need for blood might suggest this comparison. There are vampires, called *lougawou* in Haiti (not like the figure of the werewolf, though the name is the same), who can change themselves into dogs, trees, or horses, shed skin, suck blood, and terrify those who dare walk abroad in the night. The lougawou resemble the European idea of vampire, but they remain totally separated from the lwa and the ancestors; they lurk in a society of evil, cohabiting with other shape-shifters like *baka, bizango, djab,* or *djablès*. Though the lwa drink the blood of sacrificed animals and inhabit the blood and bodies of their human devotees, they do not take away but rather enhance the life of the mortal vessel.

In Haiti the very notion of what constitutes a person or identity is indelibly tied to the lwa, whose lineaments are in turn dependent on the human. The relation between human and god is reciprocal. It is said that when the people are happy, the lwa are happy and show their pleasure by appearing more often. The *pitit bon anj* or *ti bon anj* (little good angel), the *gwo bon anj* (big good angel), and the *kò kadav* (body cadaver) constitute the three parts of individual identity in Haitian thought. According to "Papa Doc" Duvalier's colleague in ethnographic investigation, Lorimer Denis—in his essay "Le Cimetière" (1956)—the ti bon anj, a "guardian" and the source of consciousness, affect, and dreams, depends on the lwa for protection, for keeping the little good angel steady and bound to the person. The gwo bon anj, also called *lonb-kadav* (shadow-corpse), is the double of the material body—something like the idea of *spiritus*—but is understood as the shadow cast by the body on the mind. The gwo bon anj can easily detach itself from the body. As Denis puts it, "when you dream you're in New York, in Paris, it's the gwo bon anj who visits these places." When Denis's gwo bon anj wanders, it might be seized by a sorcerer, never to return to its fleshly abode.[142]

The three-part structure of Haitian identity is difficult to comprehend, and accounts are often contradictory. What matters here is that the ti bon anj remains inseparable from all that constitutes our personality—or thinking matter—and the lwa, penetrating the ti bon anj during possession, depends on its force for support. Without the lwa, the ti bon anj in turn loses its necessary anchor: the ti bon anj will be free-floating, attaching itself to anything, or in its dislocation may be stolen by a sorcerer and turned into a zombi. Once the lwa is not supported by the ti bon anj, and no longer possesses (or manifests itself to) its chosen identity, the lwa is lost. And dispossessed, it roams the countryside, bereft and rapacious.

The intimate, constant, and sometimes combative relation between god and servant is perhaps difficult to describe because of the use of the word *possession,* and the stunning of self into spirit.[143] Not everyone can be possessed. This temporary experience, also called by French ethnographers the *crise de loa* (crisis of spirit), overshadows the constancy of relation, the gradual discipline of mind necessary for the momentary phenomenon to take place. As I have said, "possession" is not the term used by practitioners. Instead, they describe the experience in active terms and, most important, as an interaction: "the lwa descends"; "the lwa mounts the horse" (*monte chwal*); "the lwa dances in the head." Although it has been said that the self must leave for the lwa to enter, the self is not erased. The experience of alternating attenuation and expansion prods us to envision a configuration of wills, recognizing each other through their relation.

Though the human vessel is filled with spirit to the point of manifesting altered physical movements, changed expressions, and a new identity, the self is also liberated from normal conventions and societal or economic constraints. The god is insatiable, but the unrelenting desire for food, sex, or drink works with and evolves through the human's desire for expression. In this two-way process, postures or masks of servitude act as the medium for renaming and redefinition. Let me begin with Derek Walcott's analysis of conversion and consumption in his essay *The Muse of History*:

What seemed to be surrender was redemption. What seemed the loss of tradition was its renewal. What seemed the death of faith was its rebirth. . . .

Manbo La Merci Benjamin goes into trance, supported by ounsi. Bel-Air, Haiti, 1970.

Good, the missionary and merchant must have thought, once we've got them swinging and clapping, all will be peace, but their own God was being taken away from merchant and missionary by a submerged force that rose at ritual gatherings, where the subconscious rhythm rose and took possession and where in fact the Hebraic-European God was changing color, for the names of the sub-deities did not matter, Saint Ursula or Saint Ursulie; the Catholic pantheon adapted easily to African pantheism. Catholic mystery adapted easily to African magic. Not all accepted the white man's God. As prologue to the HAITIAN REVOLUTION, Boukman was invoking Damballa in the Bois Cayman. Blood sacrifices, warrior initiations, tortures, escapes, revolts, even the despair of slaves who went mad and ate dirt, these are the historical evidence, but what is finally important is that the race or the tribes were converted, they became Christian. But no race is converted against its will. The slave-master now encountered a massive pliability. The slave converted himself, he changed weapons, spiritual weapons, and as he adapted his master's religion, he also adapted his language, and it is here that what we can look at as our poetic tradition begins. Now began the new naming of things.[144]

I have quoted Walcott at length, because his is a provocative if somewhat general interpretation of how a covert history of mastery and appropriation was being created, even as the historians of empire wrote their narratives of conquest. But mastery in this transformative process did not mean the same thing as it did to the Europeans, nor was usurpation effected for the same ends.

"Master of the head" (*mèt tèt*). "I serve the gods" (*M sèvi lwa*). "Ceremony" (*sèvis*). Let us consider how the terminology of vodou repeats or reenacts the experience of slavery but allows the speakers to hold on to a freedom that goes beyond such intentional signification. Here, I am aware that contemporary practice cannot be adduced as proof of what happened in the slave cults of colonial Saint-Domingue. Even the best of colonial reporters did not agree on what vodou was. Furthermore, it is presumptuous to think that one can say precisely what it meant to serve the gods in the eighteenth century. As Gabriel Debien warns in *Les Esclaves aux Antilles françaises,* referring to the written documents: "To describe the lives of slaves after these sources is a paradox. They are never the ones who speak, who bear witness, but the overseers or masters."[145]

I want, however, to argue that most of the written evidence of domination or blind submission (Moreau de Saint-Méry, for example, observing a Rada rite in the late 1770s, described it as "monstrous absurdity") oversimplifies the complex rethinking of a brutal institution. Those who had no recourse to written texts or maxims, who could not respond to the *Code Noir* of Louis XIV (which ordained "the Discipline and Commerce of Negro Slaves in the French Islands of America"), responded with prescripts of their own. Slaves, separated from their kith and kin, enduring the Middle Passage to the New World, were introduced to another kind of daily relationship, a perverted family life on the plantation. Because they were things or "chattel" in the words of the Black Code, they were tyrannized by the master, but, as Orlando Patterson argues in his insightful *Slavery and Social Death,* they never became utterly degraded:

Slavery, for the slave, was truly a "trial by death," as Hegel called it. Out of this trial the slave emerged, if he survived at all, as a person afire with the knowledge of and the need for dignity and honor. We now understand how very superficial are assertions that the slave internalized the degraded conception of him held by the master; or that his person was necessarily degraded by his degraded condition. Quite the opposite was the case, Hegel speculated, and what evidence there is fully supports him.[146]

Repeating the terminology of constraint became a way to provoke an alternative epistemology that was not necessarily conveyed in language.

Herein lies a key to the ambiguous nature of ritual practice. Let me pursue this hypothetical reconstruction. Slaves learned snippets of Catholicism, including the names of saints. Indeed, they were named after saints—as well as after heroes, Greek and Roman gods, places of origin, days of the week, or physical characteristics—once their old names were taken away: Clare, Patrick, Paul, Priam, Hector, Jupiter, Cupid, Mina, Senegal, Long-Arms, High-Buttocks.[147] As they absorbed these new names and new terms, they transferred them to the experience (or heritage) that had never left them, the memories of spirits and ancestors that would now have to fill new vessels (much as the lwa would always choose new and different bodies for their manifestations). If newly baptized slaves could be renamed as saints, why couldn't their African spirits be identified with, or imbue, a saint? The old gods were called by new names. In this disguise, slaves could still serve their gods.

The Jesuits tried hard to convert the slaves. According to most accounts, the Jesuits distinguished themselves among the denominations operating in Saint-Domingue by caring more for the souls of slaves than for material gain. Instead of calling the transplanted Africans "slaves" or "negroes," the Jesuits used the term *serviteurs,* a thoughtfulness that, along with their dedicated teaching, resulted in their expulsion in 1763.[148] Those who serve the lwa today call themselves *sèvitè* (servants). Thus, we find the same words—master, servant, service, and the names of saints—but the meanings are different. Note also a curious detail mentioned by Moreau de Saint-Méry in his discussion of African slaves: "the Africans that one shouts at, calling them *Horses,* are eager to get themselves baptized."[149] Could *chwal* (horse), the word used by practitioners for one who is possessed by the spirits, have originated with the name whites used to identify slaves who wanted to be baptized? The old meanings are questioned, replayed, kicked around, and, finally, dismissed. In place of the "master," you get the new law embodied in the lwa, the master of your head that debunks the other mastery, while substituting its own discipline of thought, its own ritual of knowing. In Creole the term for law is *lwa* or *lalwa*. When pronounced in Creole, lwa sounds like *loi* in French. It would be interesting to know what those possessed by the *loi d'état* (laws of state) thought that slaves were doing when they prayed to and served their lwa.

In Haiti in 1970 Manbo La Merci Benjamin explained how the lwa might seem to oppress their followers but advised me to remember that these spirits did not have bullwhips. She was trying to help me understand that submission to these spirits was *not* another form of slavery. As she put it, "instead of being turned into a thing, you become a god." Whereas the zombi is the husk of the human emptied of substance—nothing more than a thing—the human "possessed" can satisfy needs and impulses, can open up to a plenitude possible only because of the ultimate nonidentity of the spirit and the spirit-possessed.

To conceive the *image* of the god in oneself is to be possessed. It is a deed of the most serious conception. Thought realizes itself in the imaging of the gods. A recurrent formation of consciousness and a conception realized within the limits of religious study, the experience of possession localizes and materializes what, for the uninitiated, might remain abstract or vague. This discipline of mind and task of imagination are too often ignored in Western accounts of vodou.

To be ridden by the mèt tèt, to be seized by the god, is thus to destroy the cunning imperial dichotomy of master and slave, or colonizer and colonized. Submission to the god thrives on the enhancement of ambiguity, which could be described as follows: you let yourself be taken over by something outside of you, a force you want and don't want, control and don't control, and you get a sense of yourself that you did not have before. And spirits unfold their potential in the lineaments of the human, getting what they did not have before, the material envelope through which they experience life on earth. In this

Oungan André Pierre. Croix-des-Missions, Haiti, 1986.

exchange of spirit and matter, sacred and profane, the alleged disjunction is suspended. Finally, the forms of this experience of letting go and opening out do not depend on ownership. The lwa "rides" or "dances" or "descends," but does not coerce his/her partner into "possession."

"I do not mean domination. . . . The spirit is dancing in the head of his horse." So explained André Pierre, the painter and oungan, when I visited him in Croix-des-Missions in 1986. For the "possessed," that dance is not a loss of identity but rather the surest way back to the self, to an identity lost, submerged, and denigrated. In the horrors of the New World, the ability to know the god in oneself meant survival, which is nothing other than the ability to keep *expressing* the self, and acceding, if only temporarily, to a form of power that defies compromise.

PART TWO

2

Fictions of Haiti

*Take the still rude brain of one of our peasants. . . . his mind
contracted and stunted, so to speak, by misery. . . . their
wretchedness seems to them natural like winter or hail.*
 —Hippolyte Adolphe Taine,
 The Ancient Regime, 1875[1]

*If, in her simplicity, she confounded the God of her white father
with that of the vodou cult, she loved the mild mother of the
Crucified as much as she feared Ezili-gé-wouj, female lwa of her
black ancestors.*
 —Adeline Moravia, *Aude et ses fantômes*[2]

"—We are all dying . . .—and she plunges her hand
into the dust." With these words Jacques Roumain began his classic
novel *Gouverneurs de la rosée* (1944).[3] It was in literature that the
Haiti of dust, suffering, and death became the ground for the most
powerful and, to a large extent, most accurate fictions about its peasantry—a group that had been appropriated by polemicists as diverse as
Louis-Joseph Janvier, Hannibal Price, or, later, François "Papa Doc"
Duvalier in his ethnographic and "scientific" writings on the Haitian
nation. "Papa Doc" Duvalier idealized the peasantry as the source of
what remained *uniquely* Haitian, while he followed the governmental
tradition of expropriating peasants' lands, taxing their produce, and ignoring their right to education and health care. Some novelists showed
the abject underside of the more poetic and monumental productions

of Haitian history: starvation, fear of the powers connected to the government in Port-au-Prince, the endless laws, constitutions, and injunctions that the rural masses could not read, and the illnesses that crippled and rotted the flesh.

How chilling, then, to read Janvier's homage in *La République d'Haïti et ses visiteurs* (1883) to the Haitian worker. His pastoral vision turns into a prophesy of what would happen in twentieth-century Haiti:

> Haitian peasant, my brother, you are very happy. Live, love, run, chase, dance, breathe with full lungs in the copses and in the great deaf woods; make children . . . do not give up a parcel of earth to anyone, and wait. The time will come.
>
> Long days will pass before the hour of true misery comes to you; you will be miserable only when the mangoes and guava no longer pave the roads, when the woods will be shut up between walls, when the rivers will be less full of fish, the earth less fertile, and when there will be someone who can devour in a night the artisan's or peasant's work of a hundred days.[4]

Nowhere in his response to the scornful account of Haiti by Victor Cochinat does Janvier allude to the peasants' ignorance or exploitation, nor does he mention those conditions that would lead to his hypothetical landscape: roads no longer surrounded by fruits and earth no longer fertile. Yet his description of the time when some unnamed person or thing will consume in one night the labor of many days was no fantasy but an accurate portrayal of Haitian reality, and he knew it. In his less idealizing analysis of the peasantry, *Les Affaires d'Haïti* (1885), Janvier wrote: "One would have to say that, although they constituted the substratum of the nation, the nation deemed them pariahs."[5]

One hundred years later, Glenn Smucker, an anthropologist studying the coffee-producing area of L'Artichaut, a mountain peasant community in northern Haiti, described the "unequal exchange," the implacable social hierarchy that separates peasants from the "town gentry" or "urban dwellers": "This is a setting where coffee buyers may 'fix' the scales or misread the weight when dealing with *moun sòt*, 'stupid people,' i.e., non-literates. . . . Creole makes a clear distinction between *nan bouk* (in town) and *andeyo* (on the outside, i.e., in the country)."[6] Stigmatized even to the point of having "peasant" stamped on their birth certificates (Orders in Council of January 11 and 18, 1945), they are marginalized, defined as "exiles" or "outlaws."[7]

Certain stereotypical views of the peasantry contributed to a distinctly Haitian literary tradition. We cannot ignore the great divide between the treatment they received at the hands of the elites, who considered them to be subhuman, slaves or savages, and their hyper-idealization by writers who were themselves part of the traditional bourgeoisie. What still needs to be examined is the nature of this purified account—the fictive distillation of a complex and harsh reality. A rather striking, and incongruous, example of the apotheosis of those peoples who cannot write back, let alone read, is the poem by Léon Vieux, "Au Printemps" (1915):

> Slaves resigned to the native soil,
> They have the deep pleasure of happiness.
> . . . .
> These heroes of useful labor, they don't have
> Any vain illusion of useless glory.[8]

What does it mean when an educated, upper-class writer, estranged from vodou through instruction and an acquired *langue de culture,* returns to the cult of the ancestors? What does the ethnographic precision of Haitian novelists say about the constraints of what is generally called "history"? What do we learn about the demands of theodicy when the gods and those who serve them appear in texts that call themselves "fiction"? Though often denounced as "superstition" in the presentable past of historians like Thomas Madiou and Beaubrun Ardouin, vodou is anchored to the intelligible plot of Haitian nationalist thought.

Writing Misery

The novels of Jacques Roumain, Jacques-Stephen Alexis, and Marie Chauvet examine the causes and effects of a misery unalleviated and brutal. These writers historicize the Haitian majority by attending to the one thing that remains in a landscape of loss: the heritage of Guinea preserved in services for the gods. Trees inhabited by or sacred to the spirits can be uprooted by American companies, but the lwa still come into the heads of their people. Whether we turn to the dust of Roumain's *Gouverneurs de la rosée* or the scorched earth of his *La Montagne ensorcelée* (1931), to the enforced deforestation in Alexis's *Les Arbres musiciens* (1957), or to Chauvet's cursed world of beggars, torturers, cripples, and martyrs (1954–1986), the gods remain. In his 1987 dissertation on conjugality and family in Duverger, at the western end of the Fonds-des-Nègres plateau, Ira P. Lowenthal explains that the gods are part of the land but are also experienced as "part and parcel" of the Haitian's "corporate and personal 'substance.'" Most Haitians live "in the palpable presence of their gods," who depend on their human devotees for their embodiment on earth.[9]

Why portray misery? Chauvet wrote *Fonds des Nègres* (1960) during the years Alexis was completing *Les Arbres musiciens* (1957) and *L'Espace d'un cillement* (1959).[10] Yet the questions she asks about death, ethics, love, and mastery turn us more directly to Roumain's village of Fonds-Rouge in *Gouverneurs de la rosée* and to the mysterious deaths and terrible vengeance of *La Montagne ensorcelée*. Chauvet, unlike her two male precursors, has not been popular. She writes as a bourgeoise, locating herself emphatically outside the majority of women in her culture; and unread by those of her own class, she is scorned by those whose more "political" agenda demands that they speak for and with the people.

Going beyond the "peasant novel" or proletarian visions of Roumain or Alexis, Chauvet defies mythologizing or mystification. No passion for change can fool her into assuming she can speak for those whom she cannot know. Therefore, in attempting to contextualize Chauvet's work, we cannot turn to the revolutionary redefinition of identity and culture that is so much a part of the life and work of Roumain and Alexis. Roumain founded the Haitian Communist Party in 1934. After being imprisoned and then exiled for political activities, he returned to Haiti in 1941 and founded the Bureau of Ethnology in order to study the historical factors that conditioned the cultural development of the nation. In 1942, following his defense of the rights of Haitians to practice vodou, he was again exiled. In a kind of honorary banishment, he was named chargé d'affaires in Mexico. He died two years later. Alexis became known for his activities in the Partie Démocratique Populaire de la Jeunesse Haïtienne (in which he was joined by Theodore Baker and René Depestre) that resulted in the overthrow of President Elie Lescot in the so-called bloodless revolution of January 1946. After living in exile in France and traveling to Moscow, Peking, and Cuba as representative of the Parti Entente Populaire, a communist group established in 1958, Alexis returned to Duvalier's Haiti in 1961. With four other Haitians and about twenty thousand dollars cash, he landed at Môle St. Nicholas with the intention of "liberating" Haiti. Arriving in the countryside with that much money aroused suspicions, and peasants turned the revolutionaries over to the army. Alexis was not only imprisoned but tortured and, according to most accounts, stoned to death.

When we turn to Chauvet, whose politics do not correlate with the traditional male roles of martyr, "man of culture," or "black Orpheus," we must rethink our definition of politics. The Haitian elite incarcerated their women within conventions and rules at once idealizing and demeaning. Vessels for luxury, respectability, and beauty, they were forced into lives not of their own making. If male writers felt themselves torn between their "native land" and the metropole—words from France taming their heart from Senegal, to paraphrase the words of the Haitian poet Léon Laleau—women writing not only experienced Gallic conventions (French as a literary language) as a wedge between two worlds but also had to confront their own positioning outside *all* forms of production, whether literary or popular. Taught for the most part by nuns, bourgeois women were raised to be "a kind of superior domestic"; they learned a pious passivity and practiced what Jacques Barros has called a *"dressage intellectuel."*[11]

While following in *Fonds des Nègres* the tradition of the peasant novel, Chauvet forces us to reassess the claims of romance and politics. In her preface, Chauvet explains why a bourgeoise from Port-au-Prince visited the hills of Fonds-des-Nègres in the Département de la Grande Anse in the middle of Haiti's southern peninsula. She also reveals that what might have begun as an homage to Méliance Destina, her children's "faithful servant," becomes a funeral rite that gives the novelist—an outsider to the place and people she writes about—the capacity to remember and to lament.

After she died of cancer, I had her buried on the mountain of Fonds-des-Nègres where the hut of her mother was built and where she was born. Her burial has been recounted in the second chapter of this book. Many of the characters who played a role still live. A brief stay by the bedside of this poor girl allowed me to discover those agricultural problems that explain the terrible misery of the peasants.

She closes with a jeremiad, addressing those of her class who exploit the poor and scorn them for their bare feet, calling them *"nègres-pieds-à-terre," "nègres-va-nu-pieds"*:

There exist in every country in the world certain corners forgotten by God and by man, where ignorance and superstition reign as mistresses.

To the four winds, I hurl my cry of alarm, hoping that my feeble voice will be heard by God and men.

Chauvet does not mention vodou in her preface. She relegates the term to a note at the bottom of the page: "N.B.—The vodou ceremonies have been derived from the study of Dr. Louis Maximilien: *Le Vodou haïtien.*"[12] This derailing of what remains most unique about her project is significant. Chauvet will not claim that she knows or has experienced vodou, but she cannily attributes her expertise to a text. As "tante Rosalie"—the African-born grandmother of Mimola in Antoine Innocent's *Mimola, ou l'histoire d'une cassette* (1906)—used to say to her Haitian daughter: "Min, ca criol pas connin gran passé criol! [There are secrets that the Creole cannot know!]."[13] But Chauvet's project is to let her bourgeois, Haitian-born readers in on a few secrets. No doubt they have read Maximilien's classic 1945 study, which attempted to recuperate vodou for a Christian audience. He drew upon Western religion and pagan practice, quoting from Lucien Lévy-Bruhl, Hippolyte Taine, and Léo Frobenius in order to explicate and defend vodou. Maximilien's treatise, however, does not illuminate the vodou of Chauvet's *Fonds des Nègres*. Whereas Maximilien comfortably expounds on vodou as a system of beliefs and forms of worship, Chauvet details the pressing needs of abject lives. This difficult pragmatism leaves little room for anything so sacrosanct as worship, so abstract as belief. She refuses to idealize what remains for the Haitian poor a costly and constant attention to the spirits. Hers is no mere inventory of ritual, no catalogue of divinities or ceremonial symbols, but an expression of how the gods can be served, how they can be fed, when those who serve them can barely survive. Before they drink, her characters remember to spill a few drops of coffee or rum to the thirsty gods. The action is not remarkable but ordinary, as much a part of their lives as breathing. That Chauvet's work comes out of an experience of mourning, and that she fulfills her duties toward the dead by writing about what does not die, compels the most radical fiction about vodou ever written.

How could Chauvet have known so intensely the drama of the gods and their attachment to their servitors? If elite women in Haiti are separated from the poor and raised to be objects of luxury, then Chauvet's attempt to write a "peasant novel" in the late fifties raises some questions about representation. What happens when a woman writer turns to "the people" who have been heavily metaphorized by the male writers who preceded her? Most revolutionary calls to négritude—whether Duvalier's "totalitarian" appropriation of the vodou-believing peasantry or Frantz Fanon's "The Intellectual before His People," or Depestre's "The Responsibilities of a Man of Culture"—ignored women as agents of reclamation or revolt.

When the Martiniquan Frantz Fanon attacked Mayotte Capécia in *Black Skin, White Masks* (1952), she was, at that time, the only woman from Martinique to have published in Paris. He begins his dismissal by giving women a special role in *his* rhetoric of return. "The person I love will strengthen me in my assumption of my manhood."[14] In Chauvet's *Fille d'Haïti* (1954), the mulatto heroine Lotus carried on the tradition of women standing by their men already established by Roumain and Alexis. But in *Fonds des Nègres* Chauvet's bourgeois Marie-Ange remains recalcitrant, both in her relationships with men and with the lwa. Marie-Ange, having left her home in Port-au-Prince, comes to Morne Brice, in the hills above the town of Fonds-des-Nègres, to visit her grandmother and conjure-woman Sister Ga. Her real quest has less to do with courting the various men in her proximity than with the gods, and with what remains for her their most compelling articulation, the oungan Papa Beauville.

To understand how unique is Chauvet's ambiguous tale, how daring her complication of the roles of gods and humans, how total her reversal of the claims of progress or enlightenment, we should reconsider Roumain's *Gouverneurs de la rosée*. In Roumain's book, hope returns with the return of Manuel—who worked in the fields of Cuba—to his native land, where the peasants are described as "resigned pulp" who have no "sense," but who can be redeemed by the intellectual who knows. Although that possible renewal is fraught with ambiguity—the competing claims of traditional gods and new ideology—Manuel dies a hero. In *Fonds des Nègres,* the promise set forth in the dreams of Papa Beauville is embodied in Marie-Ange, who comes to visit a land in which she has no intention of remaining. The story of why she stays undermines any claim to heroism.

As Manuel momentarily recognizes in *Gouverneurs de la rosée* (much as did Roumain in his complex defense of vodou in *A propos de la*

campagne "anti-superstitieuse" in 1942), the variety of African traditions and subsequent rituals of resistance in Haiti cannot be ignored.
Manuel owes respect not only to his ancestral past but also to the gods
who persecute those who think they can choose to forget. Gripped by
the irresistible remnants of belief, Roumain writes about Manuel's history of revolt, but every call to action is haunted by the deep call of
another past. Words of rebellion struggle against the incantations of
destiny: "Life is a continual return. The dead, it is said, return to
Guinea and even death is only another name for life." Manuel's "pa-
roles conséquentes" cannot inhibit "these *revenants* in broad daylight,
these bloody and obstinate phantoms."

Roumain's story begins and ends with the spirits. As soon as Manuel returns from Cuba, his father scolds him. "You have forgotten our
customs [*l'usage*]," he grumbles. "You do not care about the dead;
they are also thirsty." Manuel smiles at his father's reminder that before he drinks, he should make an offering to the earth which houses
the gods and the dead. Yet he is troubled by the gods. He watches as
Legba enters the peasant Fleurmond, changing him "into his own
venerable image, in keeping with his ageless age. His shoulders bent
and his body panting with fatigue, he leaned on the improvised crutch
of a twisted branch." Unexpectedly moved during this vodou ceremony, he later tells his beloved Annaise: "The other night, at this service for Legba, I danced and I sang to my complete satisfaction: I am
nègre, no?" Manuel does not, however, tell her how Ogou erupted
into the ceremony uninvited, waving his red handkerchief and saber,
singing the song of prophesy that dooms Manuel. Ogou warns Manuel not to dig the canal that will water the parched lands of Fonds-
Rouge ("N'a fouillé canal la, ago . . . / Veine l'ouvri, sang coulé,
ho!"). Manuel digs for water, ignoring the god's command, and he
thus fulfills the omen: he dies, bleeding before his mother Délira's
portrait of Ogou. "The god brandished a saber and his red coat enveloped him in a cloud of blood."[15]

Chauvet's *La Folie* (the climax of her 1968 trilogy, published as
Amour, Colère et Folie), the story of four "mad" poets who have locked
themselves in a stinking room to hide from the *tontons macoutes* (called
"the devils"), focuses on the inexplicable power of the objects of vodou, the heritage packed up in a trunk and left to René by his dark
mother. Chauvet knows that no claims to modernity or civilization
can destroy the call of the past, the pull of blood. In *Fonds des Nègres,*
fear of the gods and of evil-working neighbors stalks the minds of

all the characters, no matter how educated or rich. Chauvet offers no other alternative. The vodou revealed through the experiences of the inhabitants on that desolate hilltop in Fonds-des-Nègres promises no escape from thought or recognition. The narrative, like the social drama of vodou, builds on varying embodiments that deepen fear, urging commitment to what is fragmentary and contingent. In *Le Roman haïtien* (1982), François Hoffmann claims: "The resignation, the passivity, the fatalism of the peasant class in the Haitian novel can only devalorize it in the eyes of the reader. The individuals who make up that class, are they worthy of admiration? I do not think so."[16] Yet, when a writer such as Chauvet turns to a grammar and syntax that resist the written, things are far more equivocal than Hoffmann allows. And something vital is lost in so casual a transferral of deceptively simple words like "resignation," "passivity," or "fatalism" to the social context of vodou practice.

Even Papa Beauville's dreams evolve out of his experiences in the "real" world and become goads to change. Services for the spirits are always inscribed in phenomena: things are variously reconstituted, relationships destroyed or healed. Though stories of *baka*, or evil spirits, of dead children abound in the world of *Fonds des Nègres* (as they inhabit Roumain's Fonds-Rouge and Alexis's Fonds-Parisien), Chauvet wants her readers to ask: What is the logic of vodou? What does serving the gods mean to those who think about them? In a community of unseen powers, pessimism, and death, what remains of value? That none of these questions is easily answered attests to Chauvet's honesty. *Fonds des Nègres* opens up a place of terror and bewilderment, out of which comes something like conversion. In her delineation of incoherence, of characters who are neither free nor happy, Chauvet does violence to any belief that could be imagined as incorruptible or certain. And, in her world, understanding, like belief, is provisional.

A Rhetoric of Lament

The French ethnographer Paul Moral begins his *Le Paysan haïtien: Etude sur la vie rurale en Haïti* (1961) with a recollection and a regret: "In less than ten years, Haiti has changed its face. 1950: *la belle époque.* . . . 1959: the country, still engaged in a crisis of exceptional gravity. . . . natural richness wrecked by anarchic exploitation of the soil and a delinquent governmental inconsistency; the alarming increase in population; general misery and its string of calamities; the precarious situation of an elite culture isolated in the midst of an illiterate majority." In the preface to his work, Moral laments that "the peasant of 1959 is no longer that of 1950." What is the difference? Not poverty, not hard labor, but "despair."[17]

Moral is shocked because the period of the fifties, before Duvalier's election, boasted a kind of euphoria: tourism increased, business flourished, and life in the rural areas encouraged idyllic writings on ancestral customs and collective labor. Yet, like so many other periods in Haitian history, the relative ebullience of the fifties was superficial. For the peasant cultivators (*abitans* in Creole) or the *nègres des mornes* (men of the hills or *nèg mon* in Creole), the crisis has been perpetual. As Michel-Rolph Trouillot argued, "from the early nineteenth century on, export taxes on peasant products including logwood and especially coffee were passed on by the exporters to the producers. . . . It is not too much to suggest that the peasantry, almost alone, was subsidizing the Haitian state."[18] Oppressed by the "rural police" or "chefs de section," the peasantry has always (except perhaps in 1843–1844) remained marginal to Haitian political life. Their struggle to own and maintain a parcel of land—and to conduct the services for the gods and ancestors who inhabit inherited land—has not ceased since independence was declared in 1804.

Chauvet wrote *Fonds des Nègres* at the time Moral was completing his ethnographic work in Haiti. Her novel refers to a history of writing—fictive and ethnographic—about the peasantry. Chauvet interrogates the textualized Haiti of extremes: that apparently cyclical, iterated history of lost glory. Where is the "golden age" of Haitian history? How do we locate a time of promise, a crucible of invention and creativity in the succession of revolutions that always seem to leave the majority of people in the same place? In *Amour* (1968), Chauvet exposes the illusion of change, so much a part of both political strategy and the romanticism of writers like Roumain or Alexis, who believe there was a time when the peasantry, though impoverished, could look back to a time *before*, when things were different. As Bienaimé recalls in Roumain's *Gouverneurs de la rosée*: "In that period, they all lived in good harmony, united like the fingers of the hand, and the *coumbite* [collective agricultural work] joined together the neighborhood for the harvest or for the clearing of land for cultivation."[19] A few years later, even the ethnographer Rémy Bastien in *Le Paysan haïtien et sa famille* was seduced into belief in a paradise lost. Talking to his informants about "family life in the nineteenth century," he reflects, "we found ourselves introduced to another world: we discovered an era of abundance, prosperity, and happiness, revealed by the veneration and respectful memories that they keep for the old heads of the family."[20]

From Jean-Baptiste Cinéas—in *Le Drame de la terre* (1933), *La Vengeance de la terre* (1933), and *L'Héritage sacré* (1945)—to Roumain, Alexis, and Chauvet, certain rituals of nationalism and loss are repeated, almost formulaic in their intensity. The land has been mistreated, the trees have been cut down, the sun blasts the barren earth, while the peasants remain ignorant, oppressed, and miserable. Like Roumain and Alexis, Chauvet writes about the tragedy of deforestation, whether instigated for profit by outside interests in collusion with the Port-au-Prince elite, or carried out by the peasants themselves to build huts or make charcoal. But in *Amour,* Chauvet, even while writing about the erosion and loss of once-fertile lands, reminds her readers of a more general tragedy which flattens out the veneer of extremes, the ups and downs of Haitian history, into a statement about the nature of Haitian independence:

By what miracle has this poor people for such a long time remained good, hospitable, benign and gay in spite of its misery, in spite of injustice and social prejudice, in spite of our multiple civil wars? We have become used to slaughtering each other since Independence. The claws of the people get ready to extend themselves and are sharpened. Hate between us is born and begets torturers. They torture before they slaughter. It is to our colonial heritage that we cling, as we cling to French. We excel in the former and are still mediocre in the latter.[21]

When Roumain and Alexis create characters who reflect on what has been lost, they are writing for the most part out of the negative experiences of the forties, when the United States, with the help of a Vichy-allied government in Port-au-Prince, obtained large amounts of land to start a rubber production program. On August 14, 1941, SHADA (Société Haïtiano-Américaine de Développement Agricole) was formed. SHADA expropriated peasant land, destroyed their houses, devastated their fields, and cut down their trees. Not a single ton of rubber was produced. Since the land and the gods give the majority of Haitians their identity, it is not surprising that the taking of land was accompanied by what became known as the "antisuperstition" campaign, also called *la renonce* (the act of revoking), led by the Catholic Church (also a Vichy collaborator, called by Roumain "cette église pétainiste") and supported by the government.

In *Les Arbres musiciens,* Alexis documents the effects of the terrors of 1941, the double deprivation of property and soul, in the small peasant community of Nan-Rémembrance. He tells the story of "this raving Inquisition," which aimed to "destroy the gods of immemorial Africa," and the simultaneous violations by the bulldozers of SHADA: "Such a cavalry of white men, in khaki, galloped on strange horses of iron, with a mad speed, such a cloud of destructive archangels." The earth, sacred to the peasants—the primary source of livelihood and their ancestral legacy—suffers, mutilated: "The living god which was the soil struggled in agony with wild convulsions, feeling its flesh, its meadows, its fields, its trees, its animals, its stomach of warm humus, all its members torn to pieces."[22]

Since Alexis, more than any other writer in what Hoffmann has called "the generation of 1946," locates the moment of possibility and liberation in revolution, the absolute effects of which were made incontrovertible by Jean-Jacques Dessalines, we should note the panegyric to Dessalines which comes near the conclusion of *Les Arbres musiciens.* Though a Marxist, Alexis takes on the mythologizing of nationalists, including Duvalier, who spoke on the part of their "African brothers" and singled out the *true* Haitian as the black majority: a teeming, oppressed populace became the voice of an authentic and uncompromised Haiti. The world of Nan-Rémembrance destroyed, the sanctuaries leveled, and the inhabitants scattered, the oungan Bois-d'Orme asks the intellectual Carméleau, "Perhaps you can explain to me? Why then did our ancestors fight? Why did Dessalines exist, if the Whites must come to recapture our lands?" Carméleau answers with a litany of lost heroes.

"You have spoken to me about Dessalines. . . . Acaau was also of the people, they assassinated him; Anténor Firmin, the general Jean-Jumeau were also the people, they have assassinated them . . . Charlemagne Péralte was the people, they sold him and crucified him alive, they left him like fodder to the ants and hawks . . . Those who govern us are not the people, papa Bois d'Orme . . . They live on our earth, but they are not joined with her, mingled with her, soldered to her, for better and for worse. . . . And, each day, the true children of Dessalines are slaughtered at some Pont Rouge. . . . Me, I know that one day Dessalines will return to the earth of Haiti, he will return to put an end to groaning, to laments, and to fight at the head of his children."[23]

Throughout her writings, Chauvet exposes how the revolution, proclaimed in the name of the people, did not change the broad outlines of the social system. Mulattoes and blacks merely took over the top ranks of society. As Jean Price-Mars wrote in *Ainsi parla l'oncle* (1928), "The great planters of the past were simply dispossessed by the new political leaders who gave themselves these privileges and prerogatives." The condition of the people, once "reduced to the cultivation of small and isolated farms . . . in a century of liberal and political independence, is that of servitude minus the presence of the Code Noir and the whip of the commander. Yet the moral philosophy remained quite unscathed since the magic formula—liberty, equality, and fraternity—was inscribed on the facade of the reconstructed edifice."[24] Chauvet questions the apparently endless making of heroes in Haitian history: the cult of the founder, the father, and the protector who betrays, or is betrayed. She proves how damaging the cult of the hero is, how the image of a savior plays into the totalitarian designs of the dictator. How different is Alexis's rhetoric of salvation (located in the second coming of a man like Dessalines) from that of Duvalier, who saw himself, much as did Dessalines or Henry Christophe, as the father of the nation, the caretaker of his Haitian children?

For ethnographers as diverse as Rémy Bastien, Alfred Métraux, and Paul Moral, the turn to vodou summons judgment as well as lamentation. Writing about the results of the 1941 "antisuperstition" campaign in the Marbial Valley, Métraux betrays his emotion: "I shall not soon forget the awed and heart-stricken tones of the peasant who, having declared that his family had always revered the lwa of Africa, cried out, 'No, no my lwa are not devils.'"[25] Bastien, in *Le Paysan haïtien et sa famille,* like Moral, emphasizes the decline in ancestral practices that is conjoint with the erosion of the soil and the continued division and diminution of family property. Thinking about Marbial, Bastien declares:

Today, no one dances anymore, the sacred drums have been burned, the children reject paternal authority, the women emancipate themselves. . . . And the old ones, who are passing on, believe that with them, the valley will end up dying.[26]

The most disturbing part of Moral's *Le Paysan haïtien* is his chapter "The Degeneration of Vodou," an examination of the peasants' desperation, most fully illustrated in the decline of the rituals of former times. Moral sees the "progressive weakening of ancestral practices" as "a sort of degradation." The elaborate ceremonies and altars to the gods (noted, for example, in the works of Métraux or Rigaud) are no longer. What remain are services for the dead, the often-elaborate funeral rites, as well as healing practices or magic. Yet, what Moral called degeneration does not accurately portray the way that the gods and those who serve them persist. As inherited land gets sold or stolen, the gods wander, and ancestor spirits, bereft of their sacred places, take vengeance. Nonetheless, the spirits do not disappear.

Chauvet does not deal with vodou as a metaphor for all that remains vital in Haitian culture, nor does she use a ceremony or god as symbol for what is "true" or "empowering." Refusing to take beliefs, services, and devotion out of a context of attitudes, ideas, and feelings that are at best ambiguous, vodou becomes an element in a network of forces, part and parcel of changing economic, social, and emotional needs. Vodou, constantly redefined by the practitioners themselves, is further complicated by the finite and temporal predicaments of those who suffer. Chauvet's *Fonds des Nègres* deals with what remains: the bare bones of rituals, the remnants of an undying attachment to the lwa, a constant dialogue with the dead. How can we describe the experiences of those who serve the gods? Chauvet begins with what, to outsiders and to the privileged, elite intellectuals of Haiti, might well look like nothing. Out of that nothing, she reveals the essence of vodou. But this phrase is too abstract to describe Chauvet's labor: her effort to show how a fear or love of the spirits exacts services that entangle money, sex, and the sacred and compels devotion in what looks to some like the junkyard.

The economics of Haiti provoke the anger of the lwa and the vicissitudes of vodou. In *Fonds des Nègres,* the oungan Beauville warns: "Do you know what the drums are used for now? To make the rich in the city dance. They are taken around the parlors, they are taken down the streets to be sold . . . Ah! misery could make you sell your teeth and your skin . . . But negroes displease the lwa: they are selling their beliefs and even their ceremonies. But not a cent will remain in the hollow of their hands. It is the curse of the lwa."[27] As the family lwa and root lwa (*lwa fanmi* and *lwa rasin*) disappear, the bought lwa (*lwa achte*) increase. Money makes possible unspeakable bargains.

Those who believe in "progress" argue that the "cure" of civilization and development will end the problem of "superstition." And capricious spirits, no longer served, will vanish. No more service, no more gods. Carles Osmin, the roving, despondent intellectual of *Les Arbres musiciens,* tells the oungan Bois-d'Orme:

The Lwa come out of the earth like bananas, manioc or corn . . . The Lwa come out of our earth because our earth is miserable . . . The Lwa will die only on the day that electricity chases away the darkness of the huts, the day when agricultural machines whinny in the fields, the day when the peasants know how to read and write.

And Bois-d'Orme had earlier declared: "The Lwa will live as long as hunger endures, as long as misery endures, as long as illness endures, as long as blood is spilled!"[28]

The argument that the lwa or gods of the land will die only when electricity, light, and literacy come to the countryside had been made by Jacques Roumain in *A propos de la campagne "anti-superstitieuse"* (1942): "If one wants to change the archaic religious mentality of our peasant, it is necessary to educate him." Further, "What we should direct in Haiti, is not an antisuperstition campaign, but an antimisery campaign. With school, hygiene, a more elevated standard of living, the peasant will have access to this culture and the decent life which one cannot refuse him."[29]

Jean-Baptiste Cinéas, in his preface to *L'Héritage sacré* (1945), described the life of the Haitian peasant as "interwoven with all these demonological speculations, all these lapsed gods, stuck to these poor people like a straightjacket. They will disentangle themselves when, in the future, the face of the world appears to them in its scientific truth, rid of all phantasms."[30] Are the lwa dependent for their existence on lack, on an essential indigence? Do they persist on the soil of Haiti because the inhabitants of that land are poor? If the peasants learned to read and write, would they no longer need their spirits, no longer think about their dead? We must wonder, as we read Chauvet's story of Papa Beauville, Sister Ga, Marie-Ange, Madame St. Flè, Docé and his wife, the blind girl Marilia, and other unnamed and starving children, whether the spirits persist *because* of misery.

By choosing to deal in the most detailed way with those who remain *most* miserable, in a life punctuated by the dead and the dying, Chauvet seems to urge this conclusion: more misery equals more fear; less food means more irrationality. Yet Chauvet's *Fonds des Nègres* suggests that there is something about the spirits that lingers, that clings to those who are educated and lead a "decent" life. Sister Ga, a "leaf doctor" (healer or conjure woman), counsels Marie-Ange: "You must learn to live in the hills." Enlightenment consists in serving the lwa and the dead, keeping silent about what you suspect about your neighbors, and fearing evil spirits. Yet for Chauvet's Facius Louissant—the young, militant large landowner (*gwo nèg* in Creole) who was educated in Port-au-Prince by the "Fathers of the Seminary," whose lands are rich with coffee—knowledge and wealth are not incongruous with service and belief. Facius (Ti Fa) serves Azaka, the peasant spirit or lwa of agriculture. Like "Cousin Zaka," who is identified by his blue denim pants, knapsack, and broad-brimmed straw hat, Facius first appears "dressed in blue denim pants and a white cotton shirt, he wore shoes—which distinguished him from other peasants—and sported a straw hat trimmed with a black band." To Marie-Ange's complaint "You lay out the road to progress, but you remain in vodou," Facius responds, "It's a great refuge for the negro." Though Marie-Ange wonders if such belief brings resignation, Facius assures her that his struggle to help the poor people in the countryside to reclaim their land from the thieving urban bourgeois by forming a cooperative is not inconsistent with serving the gods. Far from weakening the will or inhibiting successful rebellion, vodou remains the necessary basis for political action.[31]

Chauvet's oungan, Papa Beauville, welcomes Marie-Ange's attempts to teach reading and writing to the children of Morne Brice. He respects and does not feel threatened by the agronomists from the city, and he appreciates the practical benefits of agricultural technology. He will even turn to Marie-Ange in his quest to understand fully what the dead who throng around his mat every night mean when they say he will save this earth:

It's a big thing, belief, my child. . . . It's a heritage. . . . Listen to this: I've frequented the city, I've seen three generations die and the good Lord has given me eyes to see and I have seen. I've seen how in other places they weed the land, how they plant and how they harvest. And when I saw, I said: here is why we are poor over here; we do not know how to plant, or harvest, or how to defend our rights. I've seen a big machine . . . just like that, go for a drive over the earth and do in an hour what a thousand hands would do in a thousand days. They call them tractors, have *you* ever seen tractors?

In this redemptive vision of progress, ritual *konesans* (knowledge) remains pragmatic, as the spirits themselves convey the need for incorporating new practices into old belief structures. As he confesses to

Marie-Ange, "I don't know how to read or write but I have the science of vodou in my head. The annoying thing is it's not enough."[32]

Holy Earth, We Are among Your Children

E si ou pa gen tè, ou pasé pou zonbi
(*If you don't have land, you pass for a zombi*)[33]

On a patch of land, surrounded by mountains "peeled like mangy dogs and trees with stumped branches," a man, as yet unidentified, walks under a burning sun. He thinks about the earth: "To probe her, no big deal, her bones are as visible as those of a skinny woman, and she is dying like a consumptive in her last moments." Then, aloud, he says: "All misfortune comes from the cut trees, they have cut them down, even the calabash trees, even the trees of Ogou." With his mention of Ogou, old iron god and warrior, a cry of lamentation shatters his reflection. The narrator of *Fonds des Nègres* then describes the man: he is Papa Beauville, a oungan identified with Ogou Feray, who has sold his land except for the ground under his hut. The tree sacred to his spirit, the calabash tree, is the only tree that remains on the yard or compound (*lakou*) of which he is head.[34]

His face black and smooth, ascetic and lean, framed by a thick beard, his sparrow hawk eyes, his long and impeccable height was disconcerting. Young? Old? Poor certainly, his rags attested to that, but rich also since he possessed the treasure most desired by a man of the hills, the "points" of Ogou. Misery does not lead to despair when the all powerful force of a vodou god exalts his servitor. Misery was an old acquaintance; it had corroded him and so relentlessly that he had lost all his teeth: just punishment!

Here, the "points" (magic power, or *pwen* in Creole) of Ogou should be distinguished from the points bought from a sorcerer, which are spirits bound to serve the buyer under certain conditions.[35] Like Alexis's Bois-d'Orme, Beauville has inherited the points from his father. The priestly function, the access to ritual knowledge is ancestral. His father, a "great, venerable priest, master of all the secrets of vodou," served the spirits in a landscape of ripe coffee, with "cows grazing in the distance" and the "hot smell of the earth." But Beauville has committed an error, and he has earned, as he says again and again, "the vengeance of the vodou gods." He has divided his family property into small plots and sold his inheritance "in a moment of madness, for a miserable sum of money which had passed between his fingers like sand."

Chauvet describes Beauville's first interaction with his followers: "Someone touched the calabash tree, my Lord God! . . . Someone touched the calabash tree . . . someone touched the calabash tree. . . . You cut down all the trees, and the earth is no longer protected. Look, she's going away and shows you her teeth in revenge."[36] Not only is the calabash tree, or *reposoi*, the place where the spirits dwell, but its leaves, fruit, and syrup have long been indispensable to the peasantry: used in popular medicine for the treatment of headaches, sunstroke, fever, whooping cough, asthma, and other diseases. In the calabash fruit, the peasant transports and keeps fresh water, syrup from sugar cane, *palma-christi* oil, or milk. Utensils necessary for housekeeping are made from the fruit of the calabash. Finally, the calabash fruit—emptied, dried out, and then covered with a net in which are enmeshed colored beads or snake vertebrae—is used for making the priest's ritual rattle (*ason*) that summons the lwa. The phrase *pran ason* means to become a vodou priest.

Most significant for Chauvet's representation of Beauville is that the calabash tree (identified in the mind of Marie-Ange with Beauville) is taken by some as a sign of legitimate strength and endurance, as opposed to demonic, ill-gotten power. In "The Meaning of Africa in Haitian Vodu," Serge Larose describes at length what the calabash tree means to his informants in Léogane in the 1960s. Larose quotes a peasant who explained his fidelity to Guinea, the vodou of his ancestors: "You see that calabash tree. It protects you; it protects the yard. And it allows one to live. Here are three gourds that you can sell; enough to live. There is no need to go to the crossroads, calling for bulls and other demons. These acts are satanic."[37]

The oungan Bois-d'Orme, in *Les Arbres musiciens,* warns: "This earth has secrets, values, and customs that no one can profane without being severely punished." For Beauville, however, the land he has lost is more than a symbolic vessel for tradition. Beauville has sold his land to those he calls "women without men," Sister Ga, Madame St. Flè, Céphise, and Madame Docé, who allowed Mr. Carena—the "fat bourgeois" and foreigner from the town—to convince them to cut down trees so that he could produce oil for export. As Beauville retells the story, Carena promised: "Deforest, deforest, and you'll make money." Beauville blames the outsider for greed—a rapaciousness he demonstrates throughout *Fonds des Nègres*—but he also condemns the inhabitants who curse the land. Even though they denigrate the land, deeming it not "good enough to give dogs to eat," Beauville, urged on by the spirits of the dead (*lemò*), is passionate about saving the land.

Last night I saw all of my dead: my five brothers, my seven sons, my father, and my grandfather. Bent over me, they said: they must know, the men of the hills, you must speak. You did not speak for yourself and your life is over, but you will speak for the others. My dead have told me again: if the peasants of the hills here are poorer every day, it's because they scorn the earth. They scorn it and abandon it. Then my father, brandishing his shovel, cried: it is the land that will save you.[38]

Unlike some oungan, who take advantage of their spiritual power and seize their followers' land, Beauville recounts his dreams in order to convince those who bought his land to retain it and together resist those whom Sister Ga calls "vultures from the capital."

In Chauvet's *Amour,* though one of the peasants knows that to obey Monsieur Long of Edward H. Long and Company Imports is to be left with nothing ("this money will pass through our fingers, keep our trees intact"), his words cannot stand against Long's band of thugs, who bludgeon the peasants on Long's orders. But in *Fonds des Nègres,* Chauvet sustains the confrontation between those in the hills and the conniving bourgeois from the town of Fonds-des-Nègres as background to Beauville's story, which he has told, he says, "one hundred times." Repeated yet again at the request of the blind Marilia, his tale enacts the original scene of abuse that compels his prophesy of salvation. This oral performance, like his dream narrations, entrances his audience. After selling his land, he goes to the capital Port-au-Prince to establish himself as a vodou priest in a magnificent ounfò, but is scorned because of his peasant garb and the pittance he demands for consultations. He goes on to work as an estate manager, is falsely accused of stealing and then is beaten and imprisoned for six months. Beauville warns: "If you go down to the cities to work for the bourgeois . . . sooner or later, you'll return with your tail between your legs. . . . I worked for those folks there and you know what happened to me."[39]

Chauvet's peasants are not, however, passive victims to the machinations of the authorities, the scorn of the powerful. Instead, Chauvet, who wants her novel to reflect the realities of peasant life, shows how they devise behaviors that go along with the expectations of the city folk (*gwo boujwa*) and that appear deferential to the rural policemen (*chef seksyon*) and their cohorts. They play a role and perform it well. What appears to be resignation is instead their thorough apprehending of how local social and economic life organizes itself. The anthropologist Glenn Smucker records the peasant view of pragmatic decorum in *Peasants and Development Politics*:

> The state is not your friend
> It is not family
> It's not your mother
> It's not your father
> It's neither brother nor sister.
> There is no resistance
> In the face of force.
>
> Hate the dog
>
> But tell him how white his teeth are.
> Never tell a chief
> He's not the boss!
> Roll him around
> Flatter him.
> The authority does what he wishes
> It's already ratified.
> The cockroach is never in the right
> Before the chicken.
> There's only one king—the state.[40]

In *Fonds des Nègres,* compliance with authority is less a sign of servility than a ruse of respect and deference. As Sister Ga counsels Marie-Ange, when she sees the chief of police and the son of the cheating lawyer Lobin pay a visit to Papa Beauville in order to get power and luck (*pwen*): "In the hills, it's good not to see, and most of all, to never understand. . . . You put stupidity on your face and you answer yeeeesa or noooosa, even if you aren't stupid, or although you get annoyed and they hate you. . . . Put wax in your ears, coal in your eyes, and you hear nothing and see nothing." The "notables" from the town not only confiscate the plots in the hills but decide to plant sisal on the savannah of Fonds-des-Nègres and arrive with their order of eviction: "State land, now you must return it to the State, get on, move . . . and they chased them away like chickens."

Chauvet's representation of dispossession and the peasants' self-possessed response to one of the most routine aspects of their lives is so accurate that I cite it in its entirety:

—Where are your papers?
And desperate hands dug through trunks, looking for a yellowed, crumpled paper, embellished with illegible writing.
—What's that?
—Papers.
—If you mock the State, you'll go to prison. We're giving you eight days to get out . . .
—Yeeeesa, master, thank you, yeeeesa, master.

When the authorities, who had previously been "assiduous clients of the oungan," get to Beauville's hut, they act as if they had never seen him; and Beauville, who "could have made them straggle behind his feet like dogs," acts the same way, exemplifying "discretion" before those who call the land "rat caca." With seeming meekness, he says, "You must never obstruct a *nègre*" (here "man," as in the Creole saying, "Haiti, where negro means man").[41] Submission to those seen as thieves and plunderers becomes a strategy for survival; such behavior indicates a way of thinking about mastery that is quite distinct from the assumptions of those who consider themselves masters.

Dying to Serve

The drama of *Fonds des Nègres* takes place in a world where the spirits do not die, even though, as Papa Beauville says, people "are dying like flies in these hills." Marilia likes to talk about how she lost her eyes. Her body swelled up, her skin dried out and fell off in white scraps. Then, the black of her eyes fell out like small balls, and Papa put them into a *govi* (the earthen jar or bottle that belongs to the spirits of the dead). The city-dweller Marie-Ange inhabits a place where women blow their noses on their clothes, spit, and curse; where starving children press around her as she eats ("they crawled fearfully toward the boiling pot"); where howls of ritual mourning punctuate her gradual realization of what it means to serve. Death, decay, and betrayal push her toward an enlightenment articulated through gestures of prostration. She feels as if she has been buried alive in the bottom of a hole; she shivers at the sight of Papa Beauville's face, but remains riveted, just as she can't tear herself away from the calabash tree; and, finally, overwhelmed by a terrible knowledge, she falls down, her eyes closed, "annihilated, her face in the hot and dry earth, her back to the sun."

No matter how we look at it or try to avoid it, the business of possession, initiation, and service is suffused with sex or, more precisely, with the idea of submission. Yet Chauvet urges her readers to think about what it means to submit. Neither Marie-Ange nor Beauville acts in ways that are easily reconciled with assumptions about mastery and servitude. Marie-Ange is no servile *ounsi* (spouse of god), and Beauville is as "taken" by Marie-Ange as she is possessed by him.

When Marie-Ange first visits Beauville in his hut, he is standing before the altar with a print of Sen Jak Majè that is balanced above an earthen pot surrounded by necklaces. As she smells something terrible and indescribable, he proclaims: "Look . . . it's me, Ogou-Feray, the lwa of power, the lwa of courage, the lwa of battle. It's me, Ogou-Feray, man of iron. Do you believe in me?" Marie-Ange tiptoes out of the dark hut, and, thinking he is asleep, she does not see him looking at her, "full of lust." After leaving Beauville, Marie-Ange, not understanding why she feels an "insurmountable malaise" in her heart, looks up at the sky. It is so close that it seems she can touch the stars: "One by one and in her hands they formed an immense shower of sparks." Amidst this glory, she "wondered at her recent emotion before the oungan. In order to put herself to the test she sat down under the calabash tree and smiled at the stars." Chauvet externalizes in the image of the calabash tree what lust in the sacred signifies.

Under the moon, the cut branch opened like an arm and its trunk took on the form of a man's long body. The tree of Ogou! she thought and she shook with a shudder. A terrible irrational fear flooded over her and made her abruptly get up and run to the hut of Sister Ga. She had forgotten until then the presence of the stars.

Resignation to the lwa and to Papa Beauville brings recognition. Things long buried, whether we want to understand them as instincts or desires, are released. Chauvet represents liberation as a discipline of surrender, an experience that makes it difficult to understand the surrender as capitulation. "Her blood boiled as if it carried hidden things, so great was this new need in her for savage communion with everything that surrounded her." Although Sister Ga speaks to Marie-Ange of submission as deference or obedience to Beauville—"Before papa, you will be without will"—every colloquy with Beauville compels Marie-

Mural of Azaka and Ogou Feray (who is identified with Sen Jak Majè or St. James the Elder), with a knight in the background. Port-au-Prince, Haiti, 1974.

Ange to learn not subjugation or deference but instead to thrill to fear and desire without servility. Chauvet suggests an elation that merely physical possession would remove.

Marie-Ange asks Beauville to help her "enter into the religion of the lwa," which she later explains by admitting, "I want to serve Ogou."[42] To recognize Beauville's spiritual power does not mean to submit sexually, and Marie-Ange never grants Beauville the sexual possession he desires. Yet, the passages that describe their encounters evoke an erotic intensity unmatched anywhere in the text. For vodou practice does not deny the flesh but rather confers on sexuality a sense of exaltation that surpasses fleshly desire or sentimental satisfaction. The feeling of sacred enhancement, shared equally by men and women, has little to do with abstract belief or morality. The experience is purely corporeal: a surfeit of matter so extreme it becomes utterly mystical. The European notion that lust is an expression of animality—the low, dark, or bestial side of humanness—Chauvet demonstrates to be quite limited.

To describe this spectacle of servitude as Marie-Ange's transformation into a god-possessed soul would suggest an uplift, moral or psychic, that does not capture her experience. This passionate bourgeoise lusts for the fields of Facius, excites another admirer, Docé ("while smiling she undulated her round buttocks against the trunk of the mango tree"), longs for something indefinable in Papa Beauville (engrossed by the "young look" in the old man's eyes), and, finally, surrenders to the mysteries surrounding her:

This atmosphere of anxiety and fear slowly awakened in her the slightest trace of hereditary shadows repressed by education and instruction. The mysterious power of vodou fascinated her but in thinking about it she could not avoid associating with it the magic practiced by some of its adepts, and this discouraged her. But soon she yielded to its encompassing influence.

In Chauvet's conglomeration of remnants, those things that have most attracted outsiders to "temple vodou" (the drums, dances, altars, cult objects, and ceremonial trappings) are stripped away. Chauvet does not idealize vodou practice, nor does she, like some critics, condemn it as mere lubricity. Even Marie-Ange's surrender to "the holy will of the lwa" is not absolute: she never loses her right to doubt the gods and their influence.

Into Fonds-des-Nègres Marie-Ange brings her communion garb that recalls the precious lace demanded by Ezili. Starving children surround her, thrilled "at the sight of her communion dress, embellished with flounces and lace." When she arrives, like the extravagant Ezili Freda, she demands a fork, desires a bed, a plate, and a glass, and reminds Sister Ga that she has grown up with "propriety" and "instruction." Yet, though identified with Ezili, Marie-Ange is not deified or made more glorious. She teases Docé, "puts her claws" into him, exciting him with a "knowing coquetry"; she turns toward and away from Facius. For it is Beauville who reclaims her, first in the dreams he recounts, and then, finally, in his capacity as Ogou, the spirit who dances in his head. "I have seen you a hundred times in my dreams. Ezili held your hand, and you walked by her side. For me that has great significance." Chauvet's footnote to Ezili reads simply "wife of Ogou."

Even after her initiation ceremony, when she becomes *ounsi bosal* (*ounsi* means "spouse of god" and *bosal*, "untamed" or "wild"), a body that "the lwa can inhabit," Marie-Ange is dispassionate:

Left alone, she was astonished at her lack of fervor. She had no desire to pray or to thank the lwa. Once the emotion of the first moments had passed, there remained only a kind of unsatisfied curiosity that directed her gaze around the room, fixing it especially on the veve, then on the Crucifix.[43]

The vodou servitors, most often women, are called ounsi, or "spirit wives." As Deren notes, "in terms of the family structure of which the religious organization is an extension, the ounsi are, theoretically, as wives to the oungan" or " 'chief of spirits.' " Although some interpret this to mean that the oungan has sexual relations with his initiates, Deren explains: "The original reference, undoubtedly, in a polygamous culture, was to the several wives of the chief who was usually priest and king. Today the relationship between the hounsis . . . and houngan is, at its most intimate, rather that of father and daughters."[44] In Chauvet's representation of crumbling rites, resistant and angry gods, and resigned mortals, the relation between "Papa" Beauville and the acolyte he calls "my child" denies Deren's simplistic rendering of familial attachment.

Those who have been initiated into the mysteries and have passed the *boule zen* (trial by fire) are born anew as *ounsi kanzo* (initiated by fire), as opposed to the ounsi bosal (from the Spanish *bozal*, and originally applied to the slaves newly arrived from Africa, as opposed to the Creole slaves born in the New World). When lwa possess the ounsi bosal, the experience is dangerous and unpredictable, for the lwa can be as undisciplined as their "horses." As Beauville told Marie-Ange in her initiation ceremony:

Here you are ounsi-bosal, my child, he said to her. Now the lwa can inhabit you. Do not be afraid if you fall while you walk, it's always like that the first time, the lwa are not on their feet. But, when papa elevates you to rank of ounsi-kanzo, you will know truly what we call being possessed by a lwa.[45]

In order to become ounsi kanzo, you must master—not abandon—yourself, be prepared to receive the lwa and, most of all, to localize and control what for the uninitiated remains vague or unreal. Instead of representing the formal ceremony of uplift (*haussement* in French, as used by Haitian writers; practitioners do not use the term, which denotes elevation or raising up), Chauvet has the ritual part of an exchange between Marie-Ange and Beauville take place in his room. She demonstrates how sensuous and matter-of-fact real knowledge must be. The intensely embodied presence of Beauville leads Marie-Ange to her initiation as ounsi kanzo.

Let me cite Louis Maximilien in *Le Vodou haïtien* to demonstrate Chauvet's displacement of the sacred by the down-to-earth, and to show how Maximilien's desire for ideals of eternity and purity contrasts with Chauvet's demand for a surplus of thought in the body.

This initiation which makes him break out of everyday servitude and which permits him "to attain the free atmosphere of the beyond"; this initiation which is this instant when he turns away once and for all from what is happening, when he affirms his absolute will to attain the eternal, signals his entering into the road of the test. Speaking theosophically, "he is going to prepare himself gradually to meet his master face-to-face."[46]

Unlike this scene of heavenly enthrallment, that of Marie-Ange engirded by the stars, with her sensation of Beauville in the long shadow of the calabash tree, makes us think about an intensely personal relation no longer in terms of love. Chauvet construes Beauville's power as knowing how not to reduce Marie-Ange to a servile soul. Unabashedly virile, Beauville sustains his power, because its very perpetuation depends upon what might seem to question or undo it. This is an astonishing drama by which the meanest, or most common, desire becomes grand, because of what it evokes in its object. Consider the terms of their exchange:

—Speak, tell me what you have in your heart.
She opened her mouth and he interrupted her.

—Tell me what you want to say or close your mouth, my child.
His tone was cutting. Prudently, Marie-Ange held her tongue. He leaned over her and she saw dancing in his eyes like stars.
—Look at me, Marie-Ange.
It was the first time he pronounced her name and the last syllable, deformed by his lack of teeth, came out of his mouth like breath.
—Give me your hands, Marie-Ange.
He threw his pipe to the ground, seized her by her hands and made her gaze enter into his own. Yet again, the incomprehensible youth of this gaze surprised her. "What a beautiful face he has," she said to herself, "without wrinkles or furrows."
Marie-Ange's hands were set on his as lightly as dragonflies. Yet, she had the impression of weight on them.
—I am soon going to make you a ounsi-kanzo, my child, but before, you will belong to Ogou before belonging to any man on earth.
He continued to fix her with his eyes and she felt her will faltering like that day when the drums hammered at her temples.
—Stretch out, he brusquely ordered her.
—Oh, papa, she sighed, quivering.
—Stretch out.
As soon as she laid down on the mat, a sweet languor overcame her. She felt a hand graze her breasts then go down the length of her stomach.
—Oh, papa, no, no, and she struggled with all her force.
—It's not me, it's Ogou.
—No, no . . .
He caressed her so brutally that she lost her breath. With a thrust, she threw herself to one side and freed herself.
—Good, good, you do not want to, all right. You refuse all to Ogou, he won't give you anything either.
She looked at him without a word, leaned back against the door. The papa again took up his pipe and began smoking, impenetrable.

This unsettling exchange replays upon the body an earlier catechism. Beauville baits her: "What do you know about the men of the hills?" They "waste their money to honor the lwa, and they walk in rags, they serve the lwa and they eat dry spud. That's true, isn't it?" Marie-Ange answers simply, "It's you who told me." Beauville's method, which operates in terms of both the natural and the supernatural, is to challenge Marie-Ange, while never denying his desire for her.

Though Marie-Ange leaves the hut saying "Yes, papa" to his next challenge ("but the moment will come when you will obey me"), both of them know that their words do not match their actions. "'Yes, papa, yes, papa,'" he repeats, "one might believe you to be docile." In an earlier supplication, Marie-Ange, adopting Beauville's intense gaze, "fixes him with her eyes" and urges: "I want to understand what

is happening, that's what I want. I want you to enlighten my spirit."
Beauville laughs, and answers: "You give me orders, heh? And meanwhile you say to me, 'Enlighten my spirit, papa.'"[47] What they are
both after is an intimacy that resists and transcends the structures of
mastery and servitude, a mutual breaking of the rules. As so often in
Haiti, words spoken, a principle invoked, even the representation of a
thing, do not necessarily refer to practice, to the lived reality of stress,
accommodation, and complementarity. Furthermore, if Beauville had
wanted to take Marie-Ange (just as if he had wanted to punish the
greedy officials who are among his clients), Chauvet leaves no doubt
that he could have.

Ezili, Marinèt, Agwe, and Ogou

*They manifest themselves. They become incarnate in the bodies of
their servitors. They eat, drink, talk, dance in the person of their
medium. Some gods make themselves men all day long. . . . And
the person possessed . . . becomes god, he is the god in flesh and
bones.*

—Louis Mars[48]

If these gods are "in the image of men," as Alexis's rev-
erent Bois-d'Orme describes them, Chauvet asks: How does this image constitute itself? What does it mean to embody the spiritual?
Moving beyond folklore and its attractions, Chauvet denies the delights of fantasy, the possibility of veneration. Beauville's rituals cannot
be read in the terms that Alexis uses for Bois-d'Orme: "He maintained pure from all defilement an old tradition." The devotee refers
to his lwa not only as angels (*zanj*), mysteries (*mistè*), saints (*sen*), or
the invisibles (*envizib*), but also as devils (*djab*). As we have seen, the
crossing of languages and terms is very much a part of the transformative and adaptive processes of vodou. The practitioner has internalized
the language of Christian demonization, taught to him by the priest
or pastor in order to wean him from belief, but usually reinforcing the
presence of the gods. According to some accounts, the oungan distinguishes himself from the *boco,* who uses his supernatural powers
for evil, with these words: "He serves with both hands" means he
works for both good and evil. Like most progressive Haitian intellectuals, Alexis separates the Rada nation of lwa, "the pure vodou Arada"

practiced by Bois-d'Orme, from the satanic sorcery of Danger Dossu, "le gangan macoute" (the bogey priest). In practice, however—and in Chauvet's novel—the distinction between religion and sorcery made by aligning gods according to whether they are Rada or Petwo, and by opposing the oungan and the boco, is not always so absolute. In some situations you have to "fight the devil with the devil," as one oungan in Léogane told me. The oungan must be familiar with black magic in order to combat the spells of sorcerers. The Jamaican Erna Brodber, in her novel *Jane and Louisa Will Soon Come Home* (1980), helps us to understand Chauvet's ritual drama: "People had a great deal of strength and power in their hearts; they wanted to use it kindly for you, but like dammed up water, it had no morals: it could as easily be let towards you as against you."[49]

Beatrice St. Jean, a Haitian friend of mine who grew up in Port-au-Prince but now lives in New York, described her experience of the gods. Her terror gives some idea of the overwhelming life of the spirit in Chauvet's *Fonds des Nègres*. Spirits can be lusty, greedy, or tyranni-cal, as well as protective and comforting. And jealous neighbors can brutally use secret power. As Beatrice explained, "Vodou is a thing of evil, of gods asking for what you cannot give, of looking to the right and to the left, fearing that someone somewhere might have put the meat on you. If you have one foot in this world and one foot in the next, then everything is out of control and in control of alternately the right and the wrong people." She thought of the lwa as the Mafia: "They come into your life and they don't leave you alone. Do this. Do that. You can never be happy. You live in fear. And the worst thing is that they speak in a language you can't always understand. I once told them, 'Don't speak to me if you can't speak clearly.'" Though she turned away from her gods, they still visit in her dreams, "tall in her head." When her grandmother in Haiti became a Seventh-Day Adventist, she threw her lwa's wine, food, playing cards, and candles into the toilet, and the lwa went underground. But then they came into her mother's head, and she became ill. "Her mind shook, and she lost it, until she let the family lwa come back."[50]

Sister Ga explains to her granddaughter Marie-Ange why she must serve the lwa if she lives in the hills. "Serve the lwa, join their religion. You live in the hills, my child, where Jesus and his saints are also nec-essary, but they sometimes have a hard time climbing up the paths of these hills, Jesus and his saints."[51] For Chauvet, the gods are products of a purely local imagination, not part of some abstract mythology.

Rather than offering her readers an explanatory theology, the spirits are substantiated by the personalities who serve them, and their powers are accentuated by the vicissitudes of life in Fonds-des-Nègres. Participants in a drama of enlightenment, violation, and revenge, the lwa, though identifiable in terms of their traditional traits, change and adjust to the peculiarities of their devotees.

Chauvet sometimes distinguishes between the traditional and benign Rada spirits—said to come from Dahomey—and the revolutionary Petwo or Zandò spirits. But the actions of Beauville (identified with Ogou Feray) and Sister Ga (identified with Agwe) complicate the dichotomy between tradition and innovation. Chauvet thus questions the hierarchy of pure types that is tainted by a colonial ideology of "civilized" versus "barbaric." The spirits change over time, "walk" in different rites, mix with other "nations" (the African ethnic groups of which Haitians are descendants), and take on traits that refute the idea of innate character.[52]

Let us once again consider Ezili, best known as the elegant lady of love. Not only does she walk as Ezili Freda in the mild Rada rites, but she walks in the Petwo or Zandò rites as well, as Ezili-je-wouj or Ezili Mapian. It is as if the extremes of love and restraint, enacted for the community by the generosity, tears, and surrender of Ezili Freda, lead to a more savage transformation: the flowers, perfume, and basil of Ezili Freda turn into (or merge to form) the blood, flesh, and dirt of Ezili-je-wouj. For some Haitians, the beautiful coquette is linked to the terrifying Marinèt-bwa-chèche, who evolves as another aspect of Ezili. Ezili the gracious mulatto, enraged by too much coercive praise and worn out by too much use, turns into the cunning and cannibal woman of the night, Marinèt, the spirit of the bush.

This mutability is crucial to our understanding of the drama enacted on Morne Brice, where Madame St. Flè, who looks like a *mal fraisé* (screech owl) and gradually takes on the traits that will identify her with Marinèt-bwa-chèche, spits out her disdain for Marie-Ange, the French-speaking mulatto from Port-au-Prince, identified with Ezili. Madame St. Flè reviles her as "the princess" and the "cursed seed vomited by the Capital."[53] As the narrative progresses, the connection—or rather the necessary if somewhat unsettling alliance—between the old hag and the young virgin suggests that the community's perception of deification is related to what might seem to oppose it.

Praise or exaltation summons the curse that undergirds any exalted ideal. Chauvet shows how ritual enactments of love, service, or abandon are themselves coordinate with facts some readers would prefer to ignore. I turn briefly to Alexis's *Compère Général Soleil* as a background to Chauvet's more extreme resistance to figures of romance. In *Compère Général Soleil,* Alexis discloses something unspeakable that lurks in (or too easily possesses) any ideal image. He consecrates the vodou ceremony to Ezili Mapian, "a political lwa," described as the "amorous goddess, pronouncing her words in precious French," and to Marinèt-bwa-chèche (though she remains undescribed). Although the altar of the greedy oungan Frère Général (also identified with Ogou), displays a chromolithograph of "Ezili [Freda], the majestic white woman with her blue veil [who] smiled over the image, her hands crossed, with little angels flying around her," the force underlying the possessions that will ensue is not that of Saint Mary—nor that of the luxuriant Ezili Freda—but are instead the spirits of the frenetic, vengeful Petwo and Zandò nations of spirits.

Alexis interrupts this vodou ceremonial set piece (the catalogue of "saint lwa" named by the possessed Frère Général, "purified of all his moral turpitude . . . becoming again the son of Africa . . . the *papaloi* whose body trembles in trance") with the sudden, chilling appearance of an abandoned, bestial little girl. This "Child-beast of terror and phantasmagoria" with "furtive and animal eyes," who digs in the remains of the ceremonial food with "a furious frenzy," belies the victimization that undermines every previous invocation of "La Belle Vénus" or "La Vièrge."[54] Alexis mires the sacred realities of vodou in the lives of the poor. And, without pushing too far the import of this "apparition" in the muck, I want to argue that Chauvet further emblematizes this complicity.

In *Fonds des Nègres,* Chauvet makes the society itself the impetus for supernatural sanction. Madame St. Flé, the woman most identified with bitterness and rage, suspected of theft and maleficent doings, sets in motion the embodiment necessary for the gods to become manifest. The lwa Marinèt, known to be an evil spirit involved in magic, is said to "eat" children (usually meaning "kill") and to protect thieves. She is depicted with arms extended out back, body stooped forward, and head lowered (known as "beak to earth"). Bent like a bird of prey, her fingers twisted like claws, she mounts her "horse." Here, Chauvet particularizes Marinèt's traits in Madame St. Flè's person: not only is she stooped and brittle with harsh, sharp gestures, but she has a "rusty laugh."

The ceremonial scene is preceded by a series of calamities on Morne

Brice. Someone has stolen Sister Ga's pig, her only means of sustenance; someone has taken Marie-Ange's life savings; and Marilia, the fourth child to die a terrible death, expires while warning of supernatural baka, though Marie-Ange suspects Marilia has been poisoned by someone in their yard. The threat posed by the amorphous and ever-present baka covers a range of representations: zombi spirits stolen by a sorcerer; bought lwa enticed into service by contract with a boco; and evil spirits that wander in the form of cats, dogs, pigs, cows, or other domesticated animals-turned-monsters. The unbridled syncretism in these recycled, proliferating, and chaotic images of evil will eventually coalesce in Madame St. Flè, the one person incriminated by the community.

At the moment of greatest fear, hunger, and suspicion, Sister Ga is possessed by her guardian spirit, Agwe. The possession of her body by Agwe seems to be connected to her increasing anxiety about Marie-Ange's safety. Having confided in Marie-Ange, Sister Ga now sees her granddaughter turn to the gods "in moments of distress or to attract good luck and toughen hope." Marie-Ange now follows Sister Ga in praying, " 'aïe, loas yo, en moué' " (Oh, lwa come into me). When Chauvet describes for her readers Sister Ga's possessing god, she refuses to sensationalize what it means to serve the spirits:

Her own lwa was Agwe, a good Arada lwa just like Ogou Feray. He was the master of the waters and when her husband used to go with other men in the area to fish, she called on the protection of the god for the fishermen. . . . Her prayers had been answered, because her husband had not died from drowning, but from a bad fever that a jealous peasant had thrown upon him.

Sister Ga's portrayal of Agwe's *veve,* or symbolic drawing, usually made from cornmeal, flour, or coffee grounds, is not only accurate but tells a story, rare in the pages of Haitian fiction or ethnography, of how unassuming, contingent, and even unknowable real *konesans* (spiritual knowledge) must be:

"It has the shape of a lovely boat. Once, during a ceremony, Agwe descended into the veve and he entered me: without knowing it, I emptied a dozen calabashes of water. That's what someone told me because when the lwa is in you, you do not know any more what you do, you become strong, powerful, happy in spite of your misery. After my death, you also will serve Agwe, my child: this will be your most beautiful heritage. Because to be in communion with the lwa, to serve them, it's to obey the religion of true negroes."[55]

Chauvet devotes an entire chapter to the grueling confrontation between Sister Ga/Agwe and Madame St. Flè/Marinèt. Chauvet pro-

Veve of Agwe. Port-au-Prince, Haiti, 1974.

vides a context for the spirit's entry, so that readers cannot comfortably dismiss the god as a bit of decor or a backdrop to her story. Chauvet is not interested in titillating her readers with sensationalized re-creations of possession. Instead, she tries to represent, even at the risk of a tedium of detail, the most misunderstood and arduous experience in vodou: the mounting of the horse by the spirit rider.

I want, for a moment, to turn to Maya Deren's description of possession in "The White Darkness" in *Divine Horsemen*. "Never have I seen the face of such anguish, ordeal and blind terror as at the moment when the loa comes." Deren ends the chapter and the book by describing her own possession by Ezili, a dazzling journey under the waters. Hers is a glorious surrender, a loss that she can only remember in images of the rolling sea, fog, light, "a white darkness, its whiteness a glory and its darkness, a terror."[56] In comparing Chauvet's representation with that of Deren's, I am drawn to the way that a certain kind of language, even when used with the greatest respect for the subject described, can wear away at or, more precisely, leave no room for the experience itself.

Deren's idealizing, impressionistic, and gothic passage into the unknown contrasts with Chauvet's attempt to locate precisely Sister Ga's alteration in the particularities of her immediate environment: the priest, participants, and spectators, and, of course, the social or secular problems the god personality addresses. In thinking about how Chauvet's "fiction" about vodou accords with the best kind of ethnography, I am reminded of Sidney Mintz's introduction to the 1971 edition of Alfred Métraux's *Voodoo in Haiti* (first published in English in 1959): "We properly expect an ideological subsystem to be highly responsive to changes in the sociology of local life, to economic pressures of all kinds, and even—at times—to fads, vogues, and new customer demands. . . . Thus one expects to find a delicate interdigitation of belief and belief system, on the one hand, and of the specific character of social life, on the other."[57]

Chauvet's attempt to conceive the gods in the literary text succeeds most when she gives full rein to the confused motives of her characters and the sometimes gratuitous behavior of the spirits. When oral tradition, a series of fragmented versions of ceremony and service, becomes the ground for literary representation, Chauvet scrupulously avoids hyperbole. Neither rhapsody nor gore contributes to this ceremony. Madame St. Flè, wrapped in a tattered black shawl, is the first to greet her companions in the yard. Complaining of cold and fever, she stares fearfully at Papa Beauville. Then, Sister Ga trembles, her eyes riveted on Beauville. Marie-Ange tries to reach her, but she is stopped by Beauville. Chauvet announces Sister Ga's possession: " 'By power of Agwe-Taroyo, negro-tadpole-of-the-pond, negro-of-saltwater, negro-shell-of-the-sea, after God, after God, after God' . . . recited Sister Ga, talking through her nose. She whirled around, her head turned backwards, her lips dry and as if burned by a sudden alteration." Part of Chauvet's recitation follows the familiar invocation to Agwe that Milo Marcelin notes at length in the first volume of his *Mythologie vodou* (1950), which Chauvet would have known:

—By power of Mr. Agwe T Arroyo, Master Agwe Woyo. Negro-shell-of-the-sea, Negro-tadpole-of-the-pond [fish of fresh waters], Negro-zangui [eel], Negro-of-saltwater, Negro-of-strong hands, Negro-under-the-sea. After God, after God, after God.[58]

Once possessed by Agwe, Sister Ga demands, cajoles, and finally startles St. Flè into recognition. How does this relationship of taut communion occur? How does power become intelligible as matter in a ritual that can convert an incorporeal idea into image and gesture?

Painting of Agwe and Lasyrenn by André Pierre. Collection of Leon Chalom.

Sister Ga rows her arms as if they were oars, and states, "'Agoué, ou mouté moin, Agoué ô.'" ("Agwe, you have mounted me, Agwe oh"; translated by Chauvet into French in a footnote.) Transfigured by "an unknown feeling from the depths of her being," Sister Ga becomes a young girl, pitching from front to back, as she tacks toward her interlocutor.

"Someone in this company has blood on their hands, blood," she suddenly cried out with a voice that was not hers. "Blood on their hands, blood . . . What is this person waiting for in order to stop killing? Me, Agwe, I speak, it's me, Agwe."

As if in answer to Agwe's accusation, the symbol of Marinèt is heard: "The hooting of an owl" . . . "the voice of screech owls!" Then St. Flè responds, "laughing derisively," and involuntarily imitates "the cry of the malevolent bird."

When the god's urges are corporealized in Chauvet's characters, the intimacy between spirits and their fleshly counterparts becomes clear. As Sister Ga becomes Agwe, Marinèt reveals herself as St. Flè. The gods' appearance in the visible world has externalized these women's inner needs, impulses, and thoughts. Sister Ga, exhausted, falls into a sitting posture and returns to her usual behavior, exhibiting, to Marie-Ange's surprise, no animosity toward St. Flè. But St. Flè's transformation continues. She submits and becomes the embodiment of the convulsed Marinèt: "She spoke of clouds that were falling over her head. . . . She lifted her hand to her brow and without a cry fell over backwards."[59]

After Sister Ga's possession, Beauville convenes a ceremony for the god Ogou. During the ceremony, Marie-Ange is unaccountably transported: "The drums were calling her. Their rhythm was in her blood, in her flesh. No, it was impossible, conceiving and tasting them with such intensity—that she had never participated in such rites." Beauville returns from the market with "a red hen and cock—victims for sacrifice—a red candle and red scarves." Legba, "master of the barriers," is invoked, Ogou's veve drawn, and his forge lit. Beauville sacrifices the cock and hen, and Chauvet's description is to the point: "He had torn off their necks, kissed their wounds, and dropped their blood into the fire." Suddenly, Ogou mounts Beauville and begins to ride him. "'And it's me Ogou, Daramin Daco, and it's me under the lwa,' intoned the papa, in a metallic voice." As the presiding priest, Beauville seems serenely aware, though transformed. He experiences none of the violence Sister Ga experienced when the spirit entered her.

Vincent Dauphin "mounted" by Ogou Desalin. Fontamara, Haiti, 1970.
Photograph by Leon Chalom.

"Transfigured, all the muscles of his body hardened." We should read this as if we are privy to Marie-Ange's wildest dreams. "Ah! she says to herself, it's not him, it's Saint Jacques. And panting, she recognized the bearing of the saint under the steel armor, the expression of his features, his conquering gestures."[60] Papa Beauville embodies the soldier spirit Ogou Feray, identified with Sen Jak Majè (St. James the Elder), the knight in the chromolithographs, but his love of women and his sexual power also link him to Dessalines in the following song:

> Ogou travaille-ô!
> Li pa mangé!
> Li séré l'agent,
> Pou-l' dômi caille bel fanm!
> Hiè au soî, Feraille dômi san soupe!
>
> (Ogou works, oh!
> He doesn't eat!
> He saves his money,
> In order to sleep with beautiful women!
> Last night, Feray slept without supper!)[61]

Papa Beauville, now Ogou, sings a battle song, and then seizes a rod of burning iron from the forge and brandishes it: "Me, Ogou, I will crush the vanquished lwa, I will skin alive the evildoers. If there are any among us, let them be saved, let them disappear." Continuing to speak, he walks up to St. Flè, who is still shivering with fever, and denounces her. He ends by gamboling like a horse, roaring:

> *Dahomey agrees*
> *The land is blessed,*
> *The devil has gone.*

Not only has Beauville accused St. Flè of killing the children, but before sinking down, spent, on the soil, he has given substance to the inexplicable longing of Marie-Ange, who from the first had recognized his incredible strength.

Obsessed with the land and seeing how the poor sell "their courage and their sweat" for nothing, Beauville angrily reminds Marie-Ange of those who "made promises to the land": "I have here, all arranged, a 'point' for this pig of a ti Fa, a 'point' that will twist him . . . like that." Beauville has inherited magic authority, but he can also turn the ancient gift into a particularly vicious spirit that can work harm when necessary. Marie-Ange decides to make the dangerous journey to Facius in order to warn him of Beauville's threat. In trying thus to evade Beauville's command, Marie-Ange must descend into the ravine "crammed with detritus" behind his hut. In this pit, she witnesses the ruin of St. Flè, who is now "the terror and the curiosity of the region. Some swore they had met her in the form of a pig; others in that of a screech owl and this screech owl, ah yes, it flew lower than the others and spoke."[62] Chauvet presents the scene as a colloquy between the spirit of love and the remnant or refuse of St. Flè. The ritualized decimation of St. Flè can be understood by looking briefly at Zora Neale Hurston's account of the zombi Felicia Felix-Mentor in *Tell My Horse*, the record of Hurston's travels to Haiti and Jamaica in the 1930s. Describing the horrific reduction of a human to "an unthinking, unknowing beast" (a recurring terror for Hurston), she writes how a once loved and cultivated person can be resurrected to work "like a beast, unclothed like a beast, and like a brute crouching in some foul den in the few hours allowed for rest and food. Then there is the helplessness of the situation."[63] Chauvet's fragment of what was once St. Flè, though not yet dead, has suffered at the hands of a zombi, perhaps the "point" (here meaning the evil spirit, or the gist of her own malevolence) sent upon or turned against her.

Marie-Ange descends into the ravine with a "protector-point" (the power of protection against magical attack) and makes the sign of the cross. As she places her foot on the wooden bridge, she hears the cry of the screech owl and falls. A heap of garbage breaks her fall. Out of a grotto comes St. Flè, "more hunchbacked than ever and so thin that she could not be recognized." St. Flè educates Marie-Ange into the other side of Beauville's heritage: the wild and unrelenting powers generated by the life of the spirit. Chauvet's drama of Marie-Ange and St. Flè in the gorge reads as if the ceremonial screen of the preceding pages has been rent. St. Flè exudes an "emptiness [that] attracted [Marie-Ange] like a lover." Slabs of dirt cake St. Flè's skin. She smells like rot; when she scratches her head, fleas leap on her neck. As she looks at the old suppliant, Marie-Ange realizes that though St. Flè urged her son Docé to steal, she is not "a criminal." St. Flè even confesses that she never killed anyone, but she has been punished by the lwa. "For a long time Petwo demanded a ceremony, he warned me in a dream, and I did not keep my obligations. This is how I pay."[64]

In the early 1970s the oungan André Pierre in Croix-des-Missions used to tell me: "Si u pa sèvi Gine, yo a kenbe" (If you don't serve Guinea [the gods], they'll make you pay). Resigned to "the will of God and the lwa," St. Flè tells Marie-Ange that the "negroes of the hills . . . must always be afraid of someone or something." Chauvet's representation of St. Flè recalls the hunting and beating of Placinette, a woman believed to be a lougawou, who was stoned and then beaten to "a wet sack of bleeding mud" in Jacques Roumain's *La Montagne ensorcelée*.[65] In a world of death, fear, and famine, women on the margins become the scapegoat. Ugly, destitute, and abandoned women, mythologized as evil, generate the multiple aspects of Ezili. Alfred Métraux lists "Ezili-mapyang, Ezili-coeur-noir [Ezili of the black heart], Ezili-bumba and Ezili Kokobe [Ezili the shriveled]," and records the song to Ezili-kanlikan, who eats the flesh of humans, or " 'two-footed goats' ":

Ezili kâlikâ elu
A la loa ki rèd
Ezilu u mâdé kochô
M'apé ba u li
Ezili mâdé kabrit dé pyé
Kòté pul'prân pu ba-li

(Ezili kanlikan elu,
Ah, what a hard loa
Ezili you ask for a pig
I will give you one
Ezili, you ask for a goat with two feet
Where could I get it, to give it to you?)[66]

Beloved Venus has become defiled Sycorax. What happened to St. Flè could, under slightly different circumstances, happen to Marie-Ange.

Marie-Ange, guided safely out of the ravine by St. Flè, recognizes that St. Flè's beliefs have "bound her hands and feet," that St. Flé has ended up in "this hole because of her beliefs." Coming out of the rut of superstition, Marie-Ange questions everything Beauville has told her and condemns this "deadly heritage that fetters its heirs like crabs in order to stop them from moving on an equal footing into progress." Here, it might seem that what I have been arguing about the intensity of Marie-Ange's attachment to Beauville and the spirits has been countermanded by her sympathy with St. Flè. Indeed, Chauvet goes so far as to describe Marie-Ange's ascent as a kind of revelation: "The dazzling light of truth redressed the distorted images and inclined her, gasping, toward the terrible reality." Yet nothing is simple in Chauvet's representation. Though Marie-Ange "feels herself liberated," and wants to fight against "the tortuous road of superstition," she returns to the yard only to doubt again.

The mysterious liberation that ends *Fonds des Nègres* generates a series of unanswered questions. Beauville, as president of the cooperative, has led the striking peasants of the hills to Miragoâne. After walking for nearly two days, they are imprisoned for having dared not to work and for demanding the return of their family lands. Chauvet subtly disturbs the climax to the peasant novel of Roumain and Alexis by drawing our attention to the make-believe quality of faith. Rumors have it that the peasants were packed into a small cell "where they were dying from suffocation." Then, so the story goes, "the papa, possessed by Ogou, had opened the door of the cell, liberated the prisoners and ran with them to the tribunal, where the judge, terrified, had been forced to listen to them . . . Many of them were dead." In this apocalyptic account, the peasants returned to Fonds-des-Nègres with Beauville, who then told a cheering crowd his final dream of lands reclaimed and roads rebuilt: "My dead came to me yesterday at night and they saluted me: hats off, they told me, hats off, oungan Beauville, you have done your duty."

If Chauvet has been pushing her readers away from belief, she suggests, in these unabashedly utopian final pages of *Fonds des Nègres,* the power of a heritage reclaimed in Haiti as a legacy of fantasy, gossip, and dream, impossible to disentangle from what we call reason or reality. To ask whether the possessed Beauville really opened the prison door to lead his followers to freedom is like asking if Dessalines was really possessed by Ogou or the Virgin at Arcahaie. In Beauville's final vision, Marie-Ange, like an apparition of bounty, offers herself to him as the generous Ezili, "borne by the land like an offering on an immense tray."[67]

Marie-Ange, Claire, and Rose

There is a kind of griffon
In this legendary country
Of the golden color of corn
Perfectly voluptuous and good.
— Isnardin Vieux, "La Griffonne"

In *Fonds des Nègres* Marie-Ange is described simply as "the *griffonne* dressed like a bourgeoise." Moreau de Saint-Méry describes the griffon, in his hierarchy of color status in *Description . . . de la partie française de l'Isle Saint-Domingue,* as three-quarters black, or 24 to 32 parts white and 104 to 96 parts black:

The griffe [or griffon] is so favored by nature, that it is very rare to see one who has not a pleasing face and is not attractive in every way. He [or she] has all the advantages of the mulatto, but there is no one among the combinations produced by the colonial mixtures who can offer a result so given over to amorous ardor as the griffe, and such is the case for both sexes. . . . The repentance spawned by pleasure is still more extreme when obtained by this category.[68]

According to Moreau, 128 gradations of "blood," in varying parts white or black, result in the possible types of skin coloring, hair, and other physical characteristics among *affranchis,* or free coloreds. The color types, especially those faded or lighter, acquired for Haitian writers a symbolic power unequaled by any other element in their descriptions of women. Offspring of a negro woman and a mulatto, the griffon was poetically rendered in shades of color named for copper, bronze, honey, amber, and even for several varieties of raisins.

In "L'Image de la femme dans la poésie haïtienne," François Hoffmann writes: "The woman who incarnates for him [the poet] the national reality is the Mulatta, the Antillean symbol of the novel individuality born of the amalgam."[69] Recall the legend of Sister Rose, the black ancestress who must be ravished in order for the color composite that is Haiti to be born. What matters in these hyperbolic celebrations of beauty is how the "calamity" or "curse" of color—colonization's harshest legacy—survives, though sugarcoated, in the images of women found in Haitian poetry and literature. Here is how Alcibiade Fleury-Battier (1841–1881) praises his muse, the ever-darkening griffon:

I am from this country where the brown-colored women flower,
Whose skin resembles ripe raisins
Where the griffonne is lively with her large black eyes,
Where the négresse has taken on the color of ebony.[70]

The "marabou," 40 to 48 parts white and 88 to 80 parts black, described by Moreau as similar to the griffon but "with more of an olive tint" and also "less inclined to pleasure," becomes the subject of one of the most popular poems in Haiti, Emile Roumer's "Marabout de mon coeur," where the woman's body is literally good enough to eat: "Marabout of my heart with mandarine orange breasts, / You're more tasty to me than the crab in eggplant."[71]

In her fictions, Chauvet literalizes the idealized Haitian history of heroes and martyrs through the bodies of women. Chauvet moves from the eve of the revolution in Saint-Domingue in *Danse sur le volcan* (1957) to the memory of the bloody week of Tonton Nord Alexis (who ruled Haiti from 1902 to 1908) in *Fonds des Nègres* to the bitter black nationalism of the mulatto Sténio Vincent in *Amour*, treated by Chauvet as precursor to her allegory of the apocalyptic terror of Duvalier's regime in *Colère* and *Folie*. In *Folie*, four poets are beaten for going through town declaiming Massillon Coicou's poem "L'Alarme":

> Do you hear the cry that resounded: To arms!
> Horror still
> Horror still! Blood still! Tears still!
> These lugubrious echoes, it is not the cannon
> Of Crête à Pierrot that thunders its fury
> To defend or avenge the rights of the Country.[72]

Haiti's national poet, Coicou was executed by Nord Alexis in 1908.

Until 1968, when Gallimard published *Amour, Colère et Folie*, Chauvet occupied a privileged position as a beautiful, light-skinned member of the Port-au-Prince bourgeoisie. The publication of this scathing analysis of Duvalier's dictatorship—more particularly, of women's place in a society crippled by color conflicts and social injustice—caused a scandal. Never before had a Haitian woman dared not only to question the nationalist assumptions of François Duvalier and the noiriste celebration of "black essence" but also to take on the burden of writing in a culture that had simultaneously praised and silenced women. The trilogy, once printed, remained in warehouses for twelve years, "blocked by the 'conciliabules' between the Haitian and French bourgeoisie."[73] Dany Lafferrière, among other Haitian critics, has discussed how *Amour, Colère et Folie* was deliberately ignored or mocked in the major papers in Port-au-Prince. Madeleine Gardiner, one of Haiti's few women literary critics, has asked: "But why this voluntary omission of the writings of a woman whose whole life has been a long quest for justice, liberty, and brotherhood, all those things that seem meanwhile to be the dream of all our men of action, poets, writers, or political men?"[74]

The suppression of Chauvet's work continues.[75] Although *Les Rapaces* (1986) was published posthumously by her children under her maiden name, Marie Vieux, stories are told about a family still embarrassed by her unremitting analyses of lust and hypocrisy under the signs of romance and authenticity. Translations of her books into English have been blocked by her descendants for reasons that remain unclear, and I have heard that the last two hundred copies of *Amour, Colère et Folie* are being held by her daughter, Régine Charlier.[76] At the time of her death in 1973, Chauvet was completing two books, which to date remain inaccessible: *Les Fils d'Ogoun* (The Sons of Ogou) and *Le Cri* (The Cry).

All of Chauvet's fictions, from *Fille d'Haïti* to *Amour, Colère et Folie,* scrutinize the idiom of color, historicized and codified as social hierarchy. The claims of sex are never far from the mechanics of power and submission correlative with this epidermic fatality. In *Amour,* Claire Clamont bears the "stain" of darkness. Her sisters Félicité and Annette are "two white-mulâtresses," but Claire is a "mixed blood," the surprise in the family heritage of lightening. This color complex is central to the story of *Amour, Colère et Folie.* If the "law of reversion," the inevitable return of blackness, was the thing most feared in colonial Saint-Domingue and independent Haiti, Claire commits herself to fulfilling the law. Instead of trying to hide or discharge the stain, she accepts this "corruption of blood," what she calls her brand of "deep-colored skin." Her mother, however, tries to pass it off as sunburn: "The sun burned her a bit, she's a pretty brown." Later in the trilogy, Chauvet mocks color prejudice when the mulatto René in *Folie* tries to define his identity by his skin: "What am I, born of a father so mulatto that he seemed white? Skin of saffron, skin of mahogany, skin of sapodilla. No, skin of a rotten coconut. 'Color of a fart,' as my mother said."[77]

Claire (the French word used in Haiti for those with light skin also evokes St. Clare, the virgin founder of the Poor Ladies of San Damiano) begins her journal in 1939, five years after the American occupation of Haiti, and during the regime of Sténio Vincent, who punished those light-skinned "aristocrats" who had never fully accepted him. My mother remembered singing "Papa Vincent, mèsi. Si gen youn moun ki renmen pèp la, se President Vincent" (Thank you, Papa Vincent. If there's anyone who loves the people, its President Vincent). In Chauvet's fiction of the rise of black nationalism, the commander Calédu (in Creole the name means someone who hits or beats hard) proves his power by violating the women of "good families," the *aristos* or "white-mulattoes." What begins as the most intimate of memoirs by an eccentric virgin ends up an allegory of Haiti as Duvalier consolidates his totalitarian state. Calédu, "a savage negro,"

Claire writes, "who had terrorized us for nearly eight years," is a figure for the dread *tontons macoutes,* Duvalier's personal henchmen who were recruited mainly from the urban poor, a group whom Claire calls "armed beggars."

Locked in her room, devouring pornographic postcards, longing for the white Frenchman Jean Luze while she obsesses about the phallus of "muscled, black, and naked" Calédu, Claire composes her narrative of compulsion. Forced for years to behave like a "good bourgeoise" who, lacking husband or child, could no longer desire or be desired, she invokes her own ceremony of knowing and abandon: "I am naked, on my bed, half-soaked in sweat, palpitating with desire. . . . Here I am possessed."[78] Claire's predicament is not only individual but collective. Even her sexual deprivation, forced upon her by the strict and hypocritical teachings of her "Parisian mulatto" father, who feared the dark and vulgar in their midst (while serving the lwa, the legacy of his black grandmother), reenacts Haiti's "history of skin." Claire was born into that history, and grew up in the shadow of disfavor: "From an early age I began to suffer because of the dark color of my skin, this mahogany color inherited from a faraway grandmother and which exploded into the close circle of whites and white-mulattoes that my parents frequented." But she adds, alluding to noirisme and the growing appeal of black nationalism, "Times have changed . . . history budges and fashion too, fortunately."[79]

Chauvet is fascinated by varying conceits of servitude. Tyrannized by a double curse, slightly dark skin and virginity, Claire relates the exaltations of her masturbatory frenzy, as well as recalling the mulatto women in her neighborhood raped or maimed by the revenge of race. Giving herself over to erotic fantasies denied by the demands of Catholic asceticism and by her public appearances as one of the twelve "Children of Mary"—she marches "in the procession in honor of the Feast of the Virgin," escorting "the statue of the Immaculate"—Claire ridicules the icon of both suffering and divinity.

In turning to *Colère,* I want briefly to demonstrate how Chauvet later distills what remained ambiguous in *Fonds des Nègres.* The mulatto daughter Rose plays to the death the game of submission, by giving herself to the embodiment of the new political dispensation in Haiti, the black thug Chauvet calls "the gorilla." All that ultimately remains of Rose is a heap of dead flesh that testifies to the efficacy of state tyranny. Her brother, at first unaware of her death, binds the reader to the specificity of her degradation in words that end the novel: "Used up, they've used her up, her also."[80] Rose's story recalls the figure of Ezili, the spirit cursed as a whore by the Church, but whose generosity knows no bounds. More than any figure, however, Rose's surrender to the "little, skinny man in a black uniform" recalls Sister Rose. If, as the legend goes, Sister Rose gave herself so the nation could be born, Chauvet questions the consequences of this idealized matriarchy.

Perhaps the greatest horror of colonization and slavery was the conversion of persons into property. Dominion over the black was extended to the bed, and the taking of black women by white men was nothing less than a ritual reenactment of the daily pattern of dominance. For Chauvet, in Duvalier's Haiti light-skinned women became the bodies upon which political power was confirmed. *Colère* begins with the appropriation of land. Duvalier's racial theories justified an authoritarian populism by claiming it was particularly suitable to those of African descent. The "men in black" stake their claim to the land owned by the Normils, who are identified as the "petite-bourgeoisie" of Turgeau, an "ultra chic" neighborhood in Port-au-Prince. Chauvet analyzes the duplicitous force of this tyranny: the conversion of color into commodity under the sign of property. Identities are constructed and histories made, but the antagonisms only perpetuate the ruses of colonialism. When the Normil house is quarantined, the inhabitants are isolated and circumscribed. The "devils" drive stakes into the ground to encircle the house, post a placard forbidding anyone to enter, and then build a wall to separate the Normils from their land. Land becomes the site for the performance of male power, but this fable of dispossession can be enacted only when that land is annexed to a woman's body, the place that *can* be entered. The desired body is Rose, the mulatto daughter. The virgin Rose assumes "martyrdom" by undergoing excruciating daily sex with the man known as "the gorilla," who confesses: "I can only be a man with these beautiful saintly heads of your kind, the beautiful head of a conquered martyr."[81]

Those who claim blackness, invade the earth, and penetrate women play a game of power in which the prizes include money and sex. Rose refigures Sister Rose, the ideally envisioned site for regenerative rape, but does not duplicate her: she willingly offers herself in exchange for land. "I will risk everything in order to save our lands." She meets with the gorilla every night for one month. The exchange both repeats and inverts the metaphoric process involved in the legend of Haitian national origins, where the submission of a mythic Rose produces the "native land." Here, however, the land precedes the lady. Chauvet's Rose is not an origin or source, but a kind of secondary benefit.

The chapter that describes her violation remains one of the most disturbing memoirs by a woman in all of Caribbean fiction. Her brother Paul, obsessed with her "error and concupiscence," reduces the once adored body to something vile and rotten, mere stench: "The odor of death is already on Rose." Yet Rose's monologue breaks out of a masculine agenda of possession, in that she turns an object of consumption—rotten merchandise—into a speaking subject. Opened by the gorilla's fist, reflected in the mirrors of his bedroom, her sex sucked bloodless by her "vampire," she admits, "My complicity has no limits." She wonders about the reductive, masculine fables of purity and impurity: "Is my fate really so terrible? Surely many husbands must behave in love like this man. Vices sanctified by the marriage sacrament."

Let the gorilla call her virgin; Rose will claim "nothing astonished me in love." She speaks of her "nauseating docility" and questions her previous celibacy: "Docile, too docile for a virgin. Am I virgin? Accomplice? Am I not getting used to him, looking to him for my pleasure?" If she could be free of the genteel constraints of her class, she thinks, with more than a hint of pride in her sexuality, "If I were liberated, he would surely find in me a partner worthy of him." Her thoughts end in a conversion ritual, with both partners turning into the "bestial couple," in which traditional sexual polarities are reversed: the gorilla becomes "a poor dog in search of tenderness," and the virgin, "lascivious and insatiable panther!" Rose's revelation of "savagery," even though marked by guilt, takes us back to the white man's most deviously manipulated fear: that of virginal white ladies mounted by dark Calibans. Chauvet spares neither Rose nor the gorilla: both are victims of what they have internalized as a racial and sexual myth.

In *Amour* Claire had said "Purity does not exist." Nowhere is the absence of purity more identifiable than in Chauvet's use of images. Two powerful emblems of male domination are compounded in the move from Claire to Rose, and both have been used against women. Claire (the dark Sycorax or old hag) and Rose (the fallen lady) both give off "an odor of death, of clotted blood and rottenness."[82] Both seize our imaginations because we assume a purity, a truth that stands firm somewhere *outside* the contingencies of history, the details of economics. Chauvet takes us through the process of idealization by giving

voice to the de-idealized, putrid body. She reanimates the corpse, the
failed icon, the dirtied ideal.

"Hallelujah for a Garden-Woman"[83]

Every woman has a karo of land between her legs.[84]

Land, women, and gods. The creation of a national
identity in Haiti has depended on the working ensemble of this metaphoric accretion. Perhaps the most revealing statement of the triad—
because it is the most sweeping in its generalities—occurs in Alexis's
Les Arbres musiciens: "The lwa were amalgamated to the body of
the nation, they fertilized the land like the male fertilizes the female!
Their breath blows everywhere, in the savannah, in the valleys, in the
plains, at the crossroads, they infiltrate everywhere."[85] When Jean-Paul
Sartre introduced the négritude poets to his French audience in "Orphée noir," the preface to an anthology of African and West Indian
poets, edited by Léopold Sédar Senghor and published in 1948, he
celebrated the new, revolutionary movement, or rather the affective,
spasmodic "being" of the black, not only by sexualizing the tropics
but by pointing to what he called "basically a sort of androgyny."
Speaking for "our black poets," he wrote, quoting Aimé Césaire: "He
is 'flesh of the flesh of this world'; he is 'porous to all its breaths,' to
all its pollens; he is both nature's female and its male."[86]

Frantz Fanon would later claim in *Black Skin, White Masks* that the
"black soul is a white man's artifact." Sartre's contrived complementarity had already demonstrated how rampant is the terminology that
controls. For, as Sartre unwittingly reveals, the construction of such
apparent opposites as male and female operates as a split or dichotomy
against which those who call themselves men can make themselves
whole. Négritude perpetuated the apparently endless making and un-
making of men carried out over the bodies of those named women. In
"Orphée noir," Sartre defined négritude as the descent of the black
man into the hell of his soul in order to retrieve his Eurydice. More
a love song between two apparent opponents—the elite black writer
and his cultivated white reader—than a means of change, the required
plunge into the depths remained a male endeavor.

In Haiti, the literary strategies employed to constitute something
called "the national soul" betray a more textured and complex narra-

tive. For the discourse of those who depend on the land, serve the spirits, and write of their lives as women is fragmented and contentious. Is there any connection between the continuous demagoguery of ever-ephemeral politicians and the particular way that "the people" (peasants and workers) and "women" get hyperbolized? Certain kinds of literary representation, even when produced by progressives on the left, allow (or encourage) the manipulation of those oversymbolized, excluded groups by individuals, factions, or parties who devise ideologies of power or "culture."

In 1938, four years after the end of the American occupation of Haiti, François Duvalier, Lorimer Denis, Carl Brouard, and Clément Magloire *fils* inaugurated their journal, *Les Griots: Revue scientifique et littéraire d'Haïti*; it was named for storytellers, chroniclers, and oral performers of West Africa. Its first editorial called for "an integral reform of Haitian mentality." For Brouard this reformation demanded a racial, religious, and social revival: "We must sing of the splendor of our peasants, . . . the beauty of our women, the exploits of our ancestors, passionately study our folklore." He further clarified the "doctrine of the new school": "With honor, we restore the *assôtor* [ritual drum] and the *ason* [sacred rattle]. Our nostalgic gaze leads us to our suffering and maternal Africa."[87]

It was Duvalier, however, who bent the sentimentalized poetics of the romantic individualist into political ideology. With the other founders of *Les Griots*, he had summoned readers down "the sacred Boulevard of the Ideal" to pursue what he called "a Thought uniquely Haitian" and proclaim "our newly discovered unity." His literary road to a "national doctrine" that brought out "the biopsychological elements of the Haitian man" was not far from the racial theories of Gobineau, and led to his effective political tyranny. For Duvalier, the transition from "totalitarian humanism" to the totalitarian state was not difficult.

As long as the symbols retained their ideological power, the actual ground of the representation could crumble, continue to disintegrate, and disappear. Duvalier's totalitarian négritude, his ideology of noirisme, like Léopold Sédar Senghor's totalizing images of glory and conquest—the "black woman" played upon like a drum, "Africa," and "black essence"—once spoken, sundered the poetic (or monumental) voice from the oppressed, both the proletarian and the peasant. It is significant that Duvalier would question the ethnographic method of Jacques Roumain in *Le Sacrifice du tambour-assotor* (1943)—a minute description of a ceremonial sacrifice to Ogou—because Roumain's concentration on the details of his peasant encounters failed to rein-force the awe Duvalier deemed necessary for the "high veneration" of vodou. In his "Etude critique sur 'Le Sacrifice du Tambour Assoto(r)' de M. Jacques Roumain," Duvalier contrasts the theoretical method of the "Historico-Cultural School of Leo Frobenius," which he fol-lows, with Roumain's attachment to the concrete facts of his observa-tion. Concluding his response to Roumain's monograph on the three drums of the Rada ritual, Duvalier laments that these "notes do not permit [him] to disengage the lofty metaphysical significance of the Assoto(r) and its cult."[88]

The "true" ethnicity advocated by Duvalier found its inspiration in the black peasantry, "the Haitian Masses," the "trustees . . . of the authentic traditions of the race." The rehabilitation of vodou as the "supreme factor of Haitian unity" led to his cynical exploitation and control of "folk" culture for political ends. The "President for Life" appeared before his followers as Baron Samedi, the chief lwa of the cemetery. Duvalier's rhetoric of redemption merely continued the distortion begun with independence in 1804: the peasants, though rec-ognized, remained voiceless, part of someone else's history, someone else's celebration.

The idea of a sensual and hieratic land, a humanization that marks early "natural histories" of the Caribbean, continues to haunt the eth-nographies, as well as the histories and romances, of Haiti. Indeed, the matter of representation, and those most compelling items of repre-sentation—natives, women, and landscapes—tend to blur genres, as Clifford Geertz has warned, either explicitly or implicitly, in all of his writings.[89] Can there be a licit or illicit representation? In Geertz's "Thick Description: Toward an Interpretive Theory of Culture," we read:

A good interpretation of anything—a poem, a person, a history, a ritual, an institution, a society—takes us into the heart of that of which it is the inter-pretation. When it does not do that, but leads us instead somewhere else—into an admiration of its own elegance, of its author's cleverness, or of the beauties of euclidean order—it may have its intrinsic charms; but it is some-thing else than what the task at hand—figuring out what all that rigamarole with the sheep is about—calls for.[90]

Using *Fonds des Nègres* as my example, I have been arguing for repre-sentations that remain incomplete, contestable, and sometimes unsat-isfactory in terms of "literary" values: order, lyricism, eloquence, or beauty. I do not, however, want to imply that my ideal is socialist realism. Chauvet's insistence on specifics, on life's most mundane and routine aspects, and her refusal to extricate these processes from their provisional locales is part of her fictional program. The hazards of ambiguity guard against the ruses of certainty: intrinsic dirt or innate quality, those made to serve and those born to master, petty details or grand ideas.

Given that myths make meaning, symbols help establish order, and metaphors overdetermine, how do these elements construe artifices of identity? Fecundity and the sweet smell of rot, exaltation and sacrifice, the sexualization of the tropics: metaphoric notions of abundance and decay typify both the language deployed in the description of the *tristes tropiques* and of the women in them. Let me recall here Rochester's vision of excess in *Wide Sargasso Sea,* Jean Rhys's reinvention of *Jane Eyre*: "Everything is too much. . . . Too much blue, too much purple, too much green. The flowers are too red, the mountains too high, the hills too near."[91]

The binaries fundamental in much of Western thought, and those compelling oppositions (virgin/whore, peasant/lady, beauty/hag) embedded in the lexicon, are difficult to break out of, especially for writers representing those places least known but most appropriated as symbols. Surely one of the most shocking and haunting passages in Hurston's *Tell My Horse* (1938) occurs in her meditation on "Women in the Caribbean," specifically the "poor black females" who are treated like "beasts of burden":

In Jamaica it is a common sight to see skinny-looking but muscular black women sitting on top of a pile of rocks with a hammer making little ones out of big ones. They look so wretched with their bare black feet all gnarled and distorted from walking barefooted over rocks. The nails on their big toes thickened like a hoof from a life time of knocking against stones. All covered over with the gray dust of the road, those feet look almost saurian and repellent. Of course their clothing is meager, cheap and ugly.[92]

Yet when Hurston turns to the mulatto Ezili, the "perfect female," the "inexorable goddess" served by more upper-class Haitians than any other spirit, she treats her readers to a rhapsody: "I looked at the little government employee . . . and with the spur of imagination, saw his common clay glow with some borrowed light and his earthiness transfigured as he mated with a goddess that night—with Ezili, the lady upon the rock whose toes are pretty and flowery."[93] From reptilian feet to beautiful toes, the transit seems irresistible.

Chauvet complicates these oppositions, which figure not only in the sensational depictions of Haitian vodou published during the American occupation—William Seabrook's *The Magic Island* (1929), John Houston Craige's *Black Bagdad* (1933) and *Cannibal Cousins* (1934), and Richard Loederer's *Voodoo Fire in Haiti* (1935)—but also in texts written by Haitians who used images of women, like those of vodou, as a means to reclaim their national history. Here is Carl Brouard in his "Hymn to Ezili," published during the occupation:

> Goddess, cannibal of Delight
> and riches,
> in robes blended with the rainbow
> Guardian
> of the sons of Yayoute.
>
> . . . .
> Ezili,
> élan,
> desire,
> cruelty,
> sweetness.
> nothingness.
> I will sing of you,
> I will glorify you,
> I will exalt you.[94]

I have suggested that the presence of Ezili in writerly reenactments transforms an erotic impulse into image. No other Haitian goddess is more often written about. In *Les Arbres musiciens,* Carles Osmin handles one of the "treasures" seized from the vodou temples during the "antisuperstition" campaign: "a perfect piece," this "statuette . . . passed from hand to hand." Continuing to fondle carvings, looking through the piled-up sacred objects—talismans, statues, drums, all kinds of sculpted iron, wood, and rock—he comes to "a statuette of polished ebony," the Venus of his dreams:

> It was woman as she had lived everywhere; the same, the only one. Kneeling down, her thighs full, gushing with an élan that enclosed a chaste and verdant sex, her stomach punctuated with a flowering navel, the piercing eye around which converged the radiant harmony of a hot, chaste, Venusian body. Her breasts were tapered and heavy like the African or Flemish art of motherhood shows us. This long and tender face with lowered eyelids sang of the eternal feminine, always prisoner of the servile needs or caprices of the male, dominating and sensual lord.[95]

Later in *Les Arbres musiciens,* the "Beautiful Venus," now explicitly identified as Ezili with "wild eyes," possesses Clémentine, a young girl "the color of honey." As the ceremony ends, she begins to weep, enacting what Maya Deren has called "a classic stage of Ezili's possession": "melted in tears, an immense distress was engraved on the pure and luminous face."[96] Chauvet, in her refiguration of the Haitian novel, urges her readers to ask difficult contextual and ethical questions. Can a particular representation of Ezili support the elaborate and usually covert metaphorizing of a masculine rhetoric of defeat, conquest, or victimization?

In *Fonds des Nègres* Chauvet demystifies the idea of Ezili as idealized love, wild passion, or unrelenting suffering, what Alexis in *Les Arbres musiciens* had iterated as "the goddess of coquetry and love, the unlucky goddess, Mistress Ezili."[97] As I have stressed, Chauvet's use of the vodou gods, whether Ogou (the warrior god who loves alcohol, politics, and women, identified with Papa Beauville) or Ezili (identified with Marie-Ange), does not depend for its effect on a contrived vodou backdrop. Instead, when she writes about those things that most tempt hyperbole, Chauvet is reticent. Nowhere do we get a full-blown, physical description of Marie-Ange as the consummate Ezili. Recall that Chauvet's footnote merely calls Ezili "wife of Ogou."

When Chauvet introduces her readers to Marie-Ange, she does not dwell upon her privileged status as a light-skinned woman or her potential for gustatory delight. Land is the issue, and Marie-Ange's character, like that of the gods, evolves out of her connection to the soil. Her sexuality is hers to use, and is not the projection of men who look, lust, and idealize. She playfully tempts Docé with a "sensuality that suffocates him," but she is acutely aware of the depth of her feelings for Facius: "my breasts hardened and my heart tumbled."[98] In *Gouverneurs de la rosée,* Manuel's "insemination" of Annaise is coordinate with his "virile labor" on the land: "It's like a woman who first struggles, but the force of man, it is right; then, she says: take your pleasure." But *Fonds des Nègres* allows for no idealization of mastery or elevation of the Haitian heterosexual couple, as in the rebel and his supportive *négresse* in Roumain or Alexis. After her first visit to Facius, the pragmatic Marie-Ange refuses his advances and makes him promise her "land and marriage."

Obsessed with his dream of serving the earth, Beauville bluntly urges Marie-Ange to trade her sex for land, first with Facius and then with the rich peasant ("le gros habitant riche"). When she doubts the meaning of Beauville's dream, communicated to Facius and to

Cherisme, Beauville reminds her: "Have you forgotten your promise to help me? . . . Cherisme is a man and you are a woman. Like a fisherman, throw out your line and catch me some men." For Beauville, the dream of possession (of the land and Marie-Ange) prophesies good fortune. Beauville's parable, his vision of Marie-Ange as "a white cow coming up the path," and his interpretation—"In dreams, aren't cows always the heads of living humans [chrétiens-vivants]"—describe a system of belief integral to the peasant's obsession with what Gerson Alexis has called the "sexualization of luck."[99] As Beauville warns:

"If you don't give welcome to whomever comes on this land, if you do not receive the cow, if you do not hear her when she calls you, if you do not care, why would she stay? The cow is the luck that wanted to visit us and that we have not helped."[100]

Marie-Ange does not accommodate herself to masculine schemes of property, possession, and propriety. What Chauvet knows, and what she uses Marie-Ange to expose (later, Claire in *Amour* and Rose in *Colère* will fulfill the same role), are the facts that undergird the metaphoric use of woman as land. The ideal of woman as property or possession, most visible in *Colère,* is a residue of that time when women, like men, were property: "movables" and "things" for use by the master. Women's bodies, violated in colonial Saint-Domingue, would become the land mistreated and recalcitrant in independent Haiti. The two would merge, and both would be played upon by the *gouverneurs de la rosée* ("masters of the dew") to take up Roumain's ideal of mastery. "The earth is like a good woman: if you mistreat her, she revolts." In *Fonds des Nègres,* Chauvet's Beauville takes up this feminization of land when he tells his followers: "The earth, it's a woman, if you love her badly, she'll spurn you, and if she spurns you, she'll leave you."[101]

Yet it is Chauvet's qualification of the most precious assumptions of her male precursors to which I now turn: her transformation of the *femme-jardin,* or garden-woman, a figure glorified by elite writers, into an illustration of the unadorned exchange relations between men and women. The garden-woman is not the lovely flower of lyric poetry, but the woman "placed" with a man in order to manage his plot of land. In contemporary Haiti, there are three kinds of unions possible between men and women: placing (*plasaj*), marriage (*mariaj*), and, finally, concubinage with or without cohabitation (known as *byen avèk,* or "keeping company"). The definition of *plasaj,* the predominant form of conjugal union in Haiti for a long time, is complex: the relationship is not one of common law marriage or concubinage.[102] It demands elaborate rituals that are often closely associated with vodou practice. Paul Moral in *Le Paysan haïtien: Etude sur la vie rurale en Haïti* notes that " 'Plaçage' comes from the colonial term 'place' (domain). To place oneself means to establish both a household and agricultural cultivation."[103] But whatever the relationship, the unions are expected to last. Chauvet's confrontation with the myth of the island woman, especially the nonliterate muse who suffers most extremely the curse of idealization, articulates itself in terms of the realities of land use, interpersonal rights, obligations, and sexual claims. Even Beauville's "dream of the cow," when examined in the context of these transactions, can be seen not as exploitation or domination but as a practice of material interdependence between men and women. Recall that after meeting Facius, Marie-Ange thinks not of the man, but "All night . . . she thought of the fields of Ti Fa."[104]

In his 1990 "Tout mounn se mounn, men tout mounn pa menm" (All people are people, but all people aren't the same), Drexel Woodson, an anthropologist doing fieldwork in northern Haiti, works against those representations, which can diminish dialogue and inhibit our understanding of cultures, literatures, and societies adamantly not our own. His examination of land tenure in Haiti suggests how reductive are mythic images of the peasantry and the silencing such mythmaking entails. But first, let me suggest a context for Woodson's reevaluation of ethnography in Bassin-Caïman, a rural section of the commune of Dondon. In order not "to fall prey to the temptations of reductionism or reification," Woodson works from the ground up, particularizing those relations and encounters in the countryside that are most often generalized or romanticized by outsiders.[105]

Woodson does not follow the new fashion of self-reflexivity in anthropological investigation, one which leads either to idealism or, more seriously, to a new kind of exoticism (often masked by the good will and liberal leanings of the writer); instead, his method remains concerned about delineating bounds. How do we capture individual human agency, the range and diversity of responses in field encounters, or the wrangling of anthropologist and respondent? Woodson aims not to speak for the silenced or disenfranchised. Resisting any theoretical framework that reduces individuals to abstractions that mean little to them in their daily lives, Woodson does not try to assign meaning, but rather tries simply to record the meaning that those frequently sentimentalized or misrepresented groups have formed for themselves.

Karen McCarthy Brown's *Mama Lola: A Vodou Priestess in Brooklyn* (1991) gives us, for the first time, a view of the gods as experienced and portrayed by the women who serve them. Instead of presenting Ezili as men's burden of dream, Brown attempts to demystify that potent image of desire. In the context of Mama Lola's selling sexual favors in order to feed her children and her repeated words—"Poor people don't have no true love. They just have affiliation"—Ezili comes to life not as Hurston's "ideal of the love bed" or Deren's "loa of the impossible perfection," but as a pragmatic response to the survival struggles of Haitian women. Brown tells "the rich and textured stories that bring Alourdes [Mama Lola] and her religion alive."[106] In her attempt to make anthropology mold itself to women's imagining, to retrieve the stories hitherto lost but regained through the communion of women, Brown preserves another kind of fiction, and her exploration of its logic is crucial to our understanding of belief.

What does "love" mean to Alourdes? In order to answer this question, Brown turns to that litmus test for appropriation and excess, Ezili Freda.

The chromolithograph of Maria Dolorosa del monte Calvario depicts the Virgin Mary with a jewel-encrusted sword plunged into her heart. Her arms, crossed over her breasts, are dripping with gold chains. Her fingers—even the thumbs—are covered in rings. On her head is a jeweled tiara, and she wears heavy gold earrings and half a dozen weighty necklaces. The wall behind her and the table in front of her are almost obscured by scores of gold, pearl, and jeweled hearts. Haitians recognize this image as Ezili Freda. . . .
Ezili Freda's connection to romance, like her light skin and her jewelry, identifies her with upper-class Haitian women. As Alourdes observed, "Poor people don't have no true love. They just have affiliation." Romance—its language, its style, its wardrobe, and its dance—belongs to the top 10 percent of the Haitian population that controls the lion's share of Haiti's wealth.[107]

Brown represents the world of humans and spirits as a complex range of transactions between high culture and low, privilege and oppression, love and labor. The ideology of romance is not only the property of elites, a special precinct of feeling unattainable by women oppressed by poverty and misogyny. For, as Brown recognizes, Alourdes's sense of "affiliation" qualifies the idea of love, and demands that the word be reinvented. Here, let me suggest that the institution of pla-saj, as still practiced for the most part in Haiti, is overlaid with elabo-rate contrivances and sentimental trappings that both sustain and call into question the presumptions of high romance. Gendered cultural identities are reembodied in the elaborate courtship rituals associated with plasaj (including "the language of flowers" or "code of flowers" between lovers; and the extremely formal "letter of proposal" that is written by a special clerk, is delivered by a messenger, and contains money for payment to a "secretary" in case the family of the woman sought cannot read), but something else happens to the cult of sen-timent in everyday practice, where men and women work out their lives in relations of complementarity that thrive under the mask of ceremony.[108]

As I have suggested, the distinctions between theory and practice, between legality and daily life, are crucial and far-reaching. For exam-ple, the laws of the capital Port-au-Prince never had much effect on a peasantry who did not read and could not know about these prolifer-ating edicts. The gap between law and custom is perhaps best demon-strated by considering that although the Toussaint's Constitution of 1801 named marriage as the only "civil and religious institution" rec-ognized by the state, and that although successive constitutions, in-cluding Boyer's adaptation of the Napoleonic Code in his Constitution of 1826, only recognized marriage, plasaj has remained the conjugal choice of the majority of Haitians. Even if plasaj is ideologically deval-ued in relation to marriage, this conceptual debasement operates like a gestural trapping, a nod to the precepts of church or state, that does not inhibit practice. Although marriage carries with it an upper-class aura, no Haitians who are "placed" see themselves as promiscuous or contemptible. In fact, many women claim to prefer plasaj to mariaj, since they believe plasaj preserves women's independence, as mariaj does not.

Ethnographers as diverse as Rémy Bastien, Sidney Mintz, Roger Bastide, and Ira P. Lowenthal have agreed that women are relatively independent because of their work as market-women, garden-women, or managers of household finances.[109] No matter how authoritarian men might appear in gestures or words (in principle), they accept the independent economic roles of women (in practice). Lowenthal's dis-sertation, " 'Marriage Is 20, Children Are 21': The Cultural Construc-tion of Conjugality and the Family in Rural Haiti" (1987), gives us a

theoretical framework for the specificities of the voices Woodson records, translates, and analyzes. Lowenthal's project is to attempt a "construction of other people's constructions." He is most concerned with
demonstrating the lived "gender complementarity" that is "infre-
quently stressed by the peasants themselves."[110] In his chapter "Sexuality," he deals with genitalia as assets, commodities that can be exchanged for other kinds of gifts. What might look like submission or
mistreatment to Anglo-European outsiders is depicted instead as part
of a sexual or economic contract agreed upon by women who do not
necessarily agree with or want monogamous marriage. Lowenthal attempts to demonstrate how bourgeois assumptions, when imposed on
the gendered roles elaborated in peasant practices, may falsify and distort complexities that are not based on notions of masculine authority
and feminine subordination. Furthermore, some fictions of female sexuality—specifically those echoing elite or Christian notions of women's
place—may have little to do with how women really see themselves.

The public ideology of sexuality differs from the private ideology in that the
former is based on a core fiction about women's sexuality. This fiction is consciously, and conscientiously, maintained by women themselves, for the "benefit" of men. Men . . . ultimately have little choice but to acquiesce in what
they, too, know to be a "false" picture of women's sexuality, and to accede to
the implications of such a view for the sexual relations that proceed from it.
Women, then, by publicly projecting an image of their own sexuality that is at
variance with their actual experience and attitudes, establish the basic ground
rules for sexual interaction.[111]

These "fictions," often gleaned from white, Western concepts of wom-
anhood—especially the ideology of "submission"—are reinterpreted,
adopted, and used by women as part of a strategy to gain relative independence. For symbolism works in different ways across the class
divide.

   Like Woodson, Lowenthal wants to demystify myths of female subordination and male domination in rural Haiti:

   Another telling aphorism solves the riddle of women's public dissimulation
concerning their own sexuality: "Every woman is born with a carreau of land
between her legs." . . . Here female sexuality is depicted as a woman's most
important economic resource, comparable in terms of its value to a relatively
large tract of land.[112]

Lowenthal then talks about how women describe their genitalia as
"*enterè-m*" ('my assets'), *lajan-m* ('my money'), or *manmanlajan-m*

('my capital'), in addition to *tè-m* ('my land')." Once placed in a context where women determine what they want or need in exchange for sexual services, we recognize how empty are the metaphors that bourgeois poets and other elite, urban writers make for and of peasant women. Intentionally or not, they press the *négresse,* eulogized as the "woman of the people" or the erotic symbol of racial recovery, into serving their myths and sanctifying their imagination.

Let us now turn to Woodson's interview with Erosmène Delva, who explains "gift-hold" (*doua onorè*) arrangements in the countryside. In a note, Woodson explains that his mode of presentation is necessitated by the desire for "ethnographic realism," his wish "to allow actors to speak for themselves and to place my observations in their proper context—encounters (formal interviews, casual conversations, etc.) with actual people who interacted with me in particular locales, and did so in real time and under specific circumstances."[113] In Haitian ethnography, this much space has never been given to a woman who calls herself a "very poor peasant" (*abitan malérè net*). So, let us listen to her for a while, since her way of talking about land and thinking about herself brings before us a range of questions and possibilities that show how much is excluded from others' fictions that celebrate female flesh and, most of all, what these exclusions mean. Though she might use her interlocutor's terms and acknowledge their significance, we learn the implications of those terms *for her.* Furthermore, what Erosmène makes of the burden of representation gives us new ways to understand and characterize the ambiguities of Chauvet's *Fonds des Nègres.*

[ED]:   In the countryside, gift-hold is something that comes from good friendship, good neighborhood, kinship, male-female relationships. A gift, I should say. An odd gift, I'd say. . . . I'm taking care of beans for the guy in La Guille I was telling you about. I'm keeping company with him—washing his feet [a reference to an act by poor peasant women that is a sign of intimacy and deference], things like that— [so] he gave me gift-hold rights and claims in his land. . . . I've been staying up there [in La Guille] for a few days pulling up beans and putting them in the sun [to dry]. It's a good walk from my house, but I eat well, I drink my fill of liquor and, then too, I'll get 2, 3 five-pound cans of beans on top of that. They're mine because the garden is on a gift-hold plot. . . .

Every gift-holder doesn't have gift-hold rights and claims in the same way. [It's the] same thing, but it doesn't work in the same way, sweetheart. A friend gives a friend [gift-hold rights and claims], a neighbor [gives them to] a neighbor because [the takers] are in a jam, that's one thing; [gift-hold arrangements based on] kinship [or relationships] between men and women, that's another. In addition to that difference, all people are people, but all people aren't the same. . . .

DGW: I don't understand.

ED: Listen carefully to what I'm going to tell you, sweetheart. You're keeping company with a guy, the two of you are together: I'm used to feeling his thing, he feels mine, too. He has land. He gives me a piece. That's gift-hold, right. It's a gift because we're together [and] getting along well. What comes from the garden is mine; I don't need to give him anything. And yet, I've already given him [something] and I'll keep on giving [something] to him. If we've been getting along well for a long time when he dies, he might leave [i.e., bequeath] the gift-hold plot to me, especially if I have a child for him.

DGW: What are you giving?

ED: Damn! What the fuck is wrong with you, Foreigner? How can you have such a big head and still be so stupid [sucks teeth]?

Your thing, right! [Stands and grabs her crotch.] This! . . .

They say every woman has a *karo* of land [between her thighs]. If I let a man feel my twat, he's got to give me land. There are women in the city of Cap-Haïtien who say it's sweetness for sweetness [i.e., a direct exchange of sexual pleasure]. That's a pretty good way to look at it. It's [just] not like that in the countryside. The man's got to *at least* give me gift-hold rights and claims [and] help me to work [the plot]. I didn't say work it for me. Help me work.[114]

Erosmène Delva's erotics have little to do with sentiment or pleasure. Instead, the way she thinks about sex says more about how she identifies or embodies herself as a woman. Erosmène is not a *plasé,* placed with one man, but a "garden-woman" (*fanm-jaden*) who works on small plots of land (gardens) that are part of gift-hold arrangements with married or placed landowners from Dondon, Bassin-Caïman, and Mathador. In describing her relations with men, she does not use words like love or desire, but defines a pragmatic exchange of services that demands different kinds of conduct: respect or deference. What is most instructive about the way Erosmène thinks through her relationship with the La Guille landowner and the other men in her life, whom she calls "'comrade friends' (*zanmi kanmarad*)," is her mode of representation. Quite artful in her own schemes of commodification, Erosmène not only confirms the metaphor of garden-woman but also embodies and particularizes it. She knows the different definition of exchange in Cap Haitien and admits that what works in the city cannot be applied to arrangements in the countryside. What this tells us, among other things, is that when a field-worker like Woodson lets his readers in on Erosmène's sense of herself in her society, we can begin to see how metaphors in literary fiction or social science—those tropes of woman as land or land as woman—obscure the intricate and distinctive experiences of women.

What bourgeois male writers have hyperbolized as their loving and sensual "garden woman" (such as René Depestre's *Hallélujah pour une femme jardin,* his *ars poetica* and diary of conquest), once placed in its actual setting, might not be seen as an idealizing term. Bastien, in *Le Paysan haïtien et sa famille,* recalls a comment he often heard during quarrels between women: "But look, I wear a ring and my marriage cost fifty dollars. You, you're nothing but a *femme-jardin!*"[115]

As I have said, what urban bourgeois writers or mimics of middle-class respectability might consider as pure or impure, modest or immodest, sacred or profane are socially loaded terms that are redefined in variable and particularized contexts. Social discrimination and low status are the rule for most Haitians, who develop responses and accommodations to those conditions that often go unnoticed by urban elites. Erosmène's matter-of-fact language relocates the ideology of sentiment in the physical act of "feeling": "I'm used to feeling his thing, he feels mine, too." Whereas the metaphoric bind of land and woman subsumes difference within generality, and traps women into an ideology of use or domination, Erosmène's delineation of the relation between land and her sex, a relation of equal exchange in which both terms are valued, discloses a way of knowing that does not collapse distinctions. Her "gift" of the "feel" of her sex exacts an exchange of equal value: she gives her lover what he desires, and he gives her land and helps her work.

The mutual arrangement Erosmène defines for her interlocutor, Woodson, leads me back to the gods. Sacred service demands money and rituals that are more effective the more they are implicated in the most ordinary aspects of life. Sexual relations between men and women often involve a liaison between men, women, and spirits in permeable relations of interdependence. The transfer of terms between spiritual and earthly matters intimates connections that remain to be studied. Land, like gods, can be either bought or inherited: *te achte/lwa achte* or *te eritaj/lwa eritaj.* The language of the gods is full of economic figurations; the language of economics is spiritualized. When we turn to sexuality and the sacred, the terms used bear looking at as evidence of something quite unsettling about vodou practice: the problems in naming, demonstrated in terms like *possession* and *mystic marriage.*

Keeping in mind the divide between rhetoric and practice, we might ask where and when the term *mystic marriage* was first used. Did some French ethnographer or priest, thinking about marriage to Christ and knowing that plasaj was the predominant form of union, describe the union of men and women with the gods in this way? Or did the terminology live on in the mouths of devotees who used it to refer to their special relation with spirits, even though it appeared to be in line with the expectations of Christian monogamy? If marriage in colonial times was viewed as the prerogative of free men and women—slaves did not marry—how did slaves see their enduring unions?

Odette Mennesson-Rigaud, in "Notes on Two Marriages with Voudoun Loa," explains that Ezili "in all her various aspects and aliases, is the divinity who most frequently—more than any other lwa—requires such a marriage with the men who serve her." She even has the right to choose the person to be married or "placed" with her "horse."[116] Marriage with a lwa can be very demanding; Ezili is so exigent that, in some cases, she demands celibacy and threatens the existence of the mortal marriage or relationship. Just how much celibacy she expects is open to question. According to Emmanuel Paul in *Panorama du folklore haïtien*, Ezili's punishment for failure to abstain from sex on her special days (he notes Tuesday, Thursday, and Saturday) is impotence for men and frigidity for women.[117] Serge-Henri Vieux in *Le Plaçage: Droit coutumier et famille en Haïti* explains:

Placing is forbidden to those who "marry" the vodou goddess, Mistress Ezili Dantò. This mystical union corresponds to a vow. One should not, however, speak of prevention, since the vow of celibacy comes from a voluntary and personal choice . . . like the celibate tied to the priesthood of the Catholic Church. The analogy applies equally to women.[118]

The anguish and early death of the Haitian painter Celestin Faustin has been linked by Haitians, both elites in the city and peasants in the countryside, with "the religious curse" of Ezili Dantò.[119]

Erosmène's story suggests that sex, like labor, involves a contractual arrangement and a reciprocal exchange of desired, valuable resources; it thrives on separate but equal possibilities. But the stories told about submission to Ezili in mystic marriage—especially those regarding recalcitrant servitors—betray vestiges of exclusivity and mastery. Unlike "possession" as experienced in vodou—the mounting by the spirit that frees the "horse" to experience an abandon consecrated most often by the community—mystic marriage exacts a service qualified by secrecy and constraint. Further, this marriage, which offers protection while simultaneously demanding proofs of submission (for example, Ezili Freda forbids drinking, swearing, and sex on her sacred days), comes closer to the delirious bondage implied by our customary use of the term *possession*. Ezili's demands of restraint and abstinence could be seen as transferring rules of conduct often applied to women—for example, devotion and fidelity—to men. But perhaps such "supernatural" domination appropriates the language and conditions of institutionalized slavery and imposes these rules of conduct on the concept of marriage. A friend of mine who claimed to be married to Ezili tried to explain what he had described as the high percentage of celibacy in rural Haiti by simply asking me, "If you can marry a god, why marry a woman?"[120] These mysteries of pleasure, possession, and servitude—as yet unmapped, unexplored, and quite possibly misleading—need the kind of study begun by Woodson in "Tout mounn se mounn, men tout mounn pa menm."

But one is always haunted by fictions. My mother used to say things that sounded like incantations. They never meant anything to me, those words said in the dark of my bedroom. Years later, I learned they were pieces of her history, not just rapt conjuring. "Je vous salue, Marie, plein de grâce" (Hail, Mary, full of grace). "Desalin pas vle oue blanc!" (Dessalines doesn't like whites!). Still later, compelled by Marie-Ange, the spirit of the virgin talking to Papa Beauville—the incarnation of Ogou Desalin—I have tried to give them the context that had been denied me. According to a folk tale recorded by George Simpson and J. B. Cinéas, who did fieldwork in the commune of Plaisance in the North of Haiti in 1937, Dessalines, "the God of War," after an impassioned speech, drew his sword from its sheath, while the people sang: "Gadé manchette à Dessalines! Li gros li longue, li pesé!" (Look out for the sword of Dessalines! It is large, long, and heavy!).[121] Given the powerful composite of angel and conquerer in Ogou, it is not surprising that oungan in various Haitian novels—whether Alexis's Bois-d'Orme and Frère Général or Chauvet's Beauville—are identified with him: they share the red handkerchief, the sword, and, of course, the sexual appetite. Yet, in making her story about Marie-Ange and Ogou, Chauvet breaks open the typology. The tempting abstraction of beauty and force is particularized and the legend retold by putting it in the context of a specific social history. Chauvet's fiction fleshes out and derails the urge to glorify. Once riddled with facts, the fiction questions the making of heroes and the ideal of love.

PART THREE

3

Last Days of Saint-Domingue

To divert oneself is to turn aside from oneself to get away from
oneself, and to forget oneself; and to forget oneself fully one must
be transported into another, put himself in the place of another,
take his mask and play his part.

—Hippolyte Adolphe Taine,
The Ancient Regime[1]

The Heat of the Climate tends so evidently to raise the Passions
to the highest Pitch, and the gratification of them being rather
looked upon as meritorious, than otherwise: all kind of female
Modesty being generally unknown [so much so] that a Man in-
clined to Libertinism finds here perhaps the largest field in the
world to gratify himself in.

—*The Haitian Journal of Lieutenant Howard,*
York Hussars, 1796–1798[2]

Those who came to Saint-Domingue in the last years of the eighteenth century came to a country where definitions were defied as they were made and categories were mixed up as more rigorous labels were invented. Describing the ambivalence of this creolizing process in Jamaica from the perspective of the subordinate majority, the Barbadian historian and poet Kamau Brathwaite writes: "'Invisible,' anxious to be 'seen' by their masters, the elite blacks and the mass of the free coloureds conceived of visibility through the lenses of their masters' already uncertain vision, as a form of 'greyness'—an imitation of an imitation."[3] Then, turning to the white colonials, he addresses not the troubled transparency of the masters' lenses, but their mirror of projection: "White attitudes to slaves and to slavery were therefore, in a subtle, intimate manner, also white attitudes and sentiments about themselves. . . . They simply looked into a black mirror of subordinate flesh."[4]

The ambivalence that threatened the codified structures of the Jamaican colonial system described by Brathwaite was exaggerated in Saint-Domingue. Regarded by European visitors and residents as the "Babylon of the Antilles," or the most beautiful colony in the Americas, Saint-Domingue was known for its splendor, profligacy, and greed. The white Creole Médéric Moreau de Saint-Méry, not easily deceived by surface glitter and high culture, described the commercial capital Cap Français (also known as Cap François and, colloquially, as Le Cap) in his *Description . . . de la partie française de l'Isle Saint-Domingue*: "There was not a moment in the day when one could not see excrement at the edge of the gutter and especially in the carriage way. In the less frequented streets there were masses of excrement. . . . The streets, alleys, and wharves are dirty and smelly; sometimes the sewers give off an unbearable odor."[5] Some one hundred years later, James Anthony Froude, Thomas Carlyle's biographer, would capture something of that gilded stench when he portrayed the young Black Republic. Arriving in what he calls the "ulcer of Port-au-Prince," he concluded: "We were in a Paris of the gutter, with boulevards and *places, fiacres* and crimson parasols." On boulevards littered with garbage, "foul as pigsties," ladies outfitted in elegant Parisian trappings pick their way through the mud.[6]

Though the society boasted castelike distinctions (*grands blancs, petits blancs,* free coloreds, slaves, and, above all, aristocrats, what one historian called "the oldest blood of France"), the overwhelming distinction seemed to be between whites and nonwhites.[7] No matter your status, distinctions disappeared if you had white skin. As Baron de Wimpffen wrote on the eve of the French Revolution:

The natural consequence of the order of things which prevails here, is, that all those titles of honour which are elsewhere, the *pabula* of emulation, of rivalry, and of discord; which inspire so much pride, and create so many claims in some; so much ambition and envy in others; shrink to nothing, and entirely disappear before the sole title of WHITE. It is by your skin, however branded it may be, and not by your parchment, however worm-eaten, that your pretensions to gentility are adjusted.[8]

Street in Cap Haïtien, 1970. Photograph by Leon Chalom.

In 1791, before what Creoles called "the troubles" began, it was estimated that of the 50,000 people residing in Cap Français about three-
fourths were slaves.[9] Throughout Saint-Domingue, in the towns and
on the plantations in the countryside, the population was predomi-
nantly in servitude. According to Moreau de Saint-Méry, who gives
figures for Saint-Domingue in 1788, there were 40,000 whites, 28,000
free coloreds, and 452,000 slaves. François Girod, in *La Vie quotidienne de la société créole,* asks, "What images of Creole society in Saint-
Domingue must we retain?" and then gives figures close to Moreau's
for 1788. He warns his readers, however, not to take these official figures too seriously:

Statistics tended to inflate the number of whites, to diminish those of "gens
de couleur," and to minimize the figures of slaves. . . . So, one might estimate
the figure for whites at approximately 32,000, that of "libres" at a number at
least equal to that of whites and probably greater. As for slaves, they were, undoubtedly, approximately 500,000.[10]

Though small in number, the white population—the descendants
of buccaneers, filibusters, and nobles—was divisive and contentious,
changing with every new influx of "French" settlers and calling into
question the meaning of national identity. The categorical exclusivity
of whiteness was riddled with qualifications. Abbé Guillaume Thomas
François Raynal, writing in 1785, had described an inchoate place
with anomalous individuals: "Ordinarily, we seek for the character of a
people in its national point of view; but, in San Domingo, there is no
real 'people'—only a mass of individuals, with common interests but
isolated viewpoints. Even the Creole is not always an American; he is a
Gascon or Provençal, if he has chanced to learn his father's dialect or
imbibe his principles."[11] The *petits blancs* ("little whites," namely, the
white middle and lower classes) hated the *grands blancs* ("big whites");
the Creole planters and the European administrators, merchants, bu-
reaucrats, and maritime bourgeoisie disdained each other; and all the
whites, no matter their tensions and rivalries, joined in degrading coloreds and slaves.[12]

The wrangling between Creole whites (those born in the colonies)
and European whites, whether aristocrats or vagabonds—what Lieutenant Thomas Phipps Howard called "a ramasse of every description"—not unlike the discord between Creole blacks and "Congo"
blacks, would determine how the French Revolution played itself out
in Saint-Domingue.[13] The conflict also infected relations between the
sexes. European ladies ridiculed Creole ladies; the latter mocked the
affectations of those polished remnants of the Old Regime; while

the men, according to many observers, unconcerned about such dis-putes, simply chose their lovers, those Baron de Wimpffen described as "black, yellow, livid complexioned mistresses."[14] Wimpffen, never mincing words, bluntly answered the question of Dominguan charac-ter: "What then, is the inhabitant of San Domingo? What every man must be who is born under a burning atmosphere, with a vicious edu-cation and a feeble government. He is born neither corrupt nor virtu-ous, neither citizen nor slave."[15]

The Paradise of the New World

In September 1791, Bryan Edwards, the Jamaican planter and historian, was in Spanish Town, Jamaica, when two gentlemen from the French part of the island of Santo Domingo informed him that negro slaves, "to the number, as was believed, of 100,000 and upwards, had revolted and were spreading death and desolation over the whole of the Northern Province."[16] Edwards had nearly completed his *History, Civil and Commercial, of the British Colonies in the West Indies,* a reasoned and, for its time, relatively moderate and humane defense of a social order based on slavery. (More characteristic of the period was Edward Long's *History of Jamaica,* which is startling in its racialist bias.) Edwards set out for Haiti and arrived in the harbor of Cap Français (after independence, renamed Cap Haitien), the colony's oldest, richest, and most densely populated city, in the evening of Sep-tember 26, 1791.[17] What he saw unleashed the horror that destroyed the veneer of moderation in his early work. When this man of prop-erty observed the conflagration of the metropolis, the symbol of what had been gained by producing sugar with slave labor, he set to work on the alarming *An Historical Survey of the French Colony in the Island of St. Domingo.*

> We arrived in the harbour of Cape François in the evening of the 26th of September, and the first object which arrested our attention as we approached, was a dreadful scene of devastation by fire. The noble plain adjoining the Cape was covered with ashes, and the surrounding hills, as far as the eye could reach, and every where presented to us ruins still smoking, and houses and plantations at that moment in flames. It was a sight more terrible than the mind of any man, unaccustomed to such a scene, can easily conceive. The in-habitants of the town being assembled on the beach, directed all their atten-tion towards us, and we landed amidst a crowd of spectators who, with up-lifted hands and streaming eyes, gave welcome to their deliverers (for such

View of Cap Français at the end of the eighteenth century. Engraving by N. Ponce, from a drawing of la Brunière. Courtesy Cabinet des estampes, Bibliothèque nationale, Paris.

they considered us) and acclamations of *vivent les Anglais* resounded from every quarter.[18]

For Edwards, like many others in Europe and the United States, the revolt of slaves that began in the North Province of Saint-Domingue, the beautiful "Plaine du Nord," was a spectacle of anarchy and blood that not only threatened the "peculiar institution" of slavery but came to symbolize the destruction of all that was best in civilization by all that was worst in savagery: the "Paris of America" overwhelmed by the horrors of Africa.

Until those ravages and devastations which I have had the painful task of recording, deformed and destroyed, with undistinguishing barbarity, both the bounties of nature, and the labours of art, the possessions of France in this noble island were considered as the garden of the West Indies, and for beautiful scenery, richness of soil, might justly be deemed *the Paradise of the New World.*[19]

But Eden would rise from the ashes, and again be consumed by flames and deserted by its white inhabitants two years later, on the night of June 22, 1793. This conflagration, incited by the slave leader Macaya and urged on by the Jacobin civil commissioner Léger-Félicité Sonthonax, marked the end of slavery and white rule in Saint-Domingue. In 1797, Toussaint Louverture was declared governor-general by Sonthonax. After five years of fighting, playing the Spanish off against the English (who had occupied most of the major seaports in the western and southern provinces by 1793) and mulattoes against blacks, Toussaint had won the colony for France. It was he, writing to Napoleon Bonaparte as "the first of the blacks to the first of the whites," who promised a return to prosperity.

By 1801, with a new constitution and with many of the exiled planters back on their plantations and productivity nearly back to normal, Saint-Domingue, though governed by a black former slave, flourished. The chief city, Cap Français, promised again to lead the West Indies in trade, opulence, and magnificence. But things had changed in France. By the time Toussaint had established himself as governor general for life and the representative of the French Republic in the New World, Napoleon had become first consul. It is hard to imagine a greater distance between Toussaint's ideal of France as the home of liberty, equality, and fraternity, and Napoleon's decision to rip every epaulette from the shoulders of the "gilded Africans" of Saint-Domingue. Not only did Napoleon send Toussaint's two sons, who had been at school in France, to their father with a false letter of praise and promise but he issued a proclamation printed in French and Creole, dated the Seventeenth Brumaire (November 8, 1802). A masterpiece of deception, the substance of this document, like its Creole, was fake: "Qui ça vous tout yé, qui couleur vous yé, qui côté papa zote vini, nous pas gardé ça: nous savé tan seleman que zote tout libe, que zote tout égal, douvant bon Dieu et dans zyé la République" (Whatever your origin and your color, you are all free and equal before God and before men).[20]

On October 24, 1801, Victor-Emmanuel Leclerc, Napoleon's brother-in-law, was named commander-in-chief of what would be the largest expeditionary army ever to sail from France: a fleet of twenty-six warships and 20,000 troops. Donatien Marie Joseph de Vimeur, vicomte de Rochambeau, was named second in command. Only thirty years old, Leclerc led troops composed of the most talented and experienced soldiers of the consular government. Once peace was established with Great Britain, Napoleon lost no time in trying to restore to France its most lucrative colony, to subdue the upstart Toussaint, and to satisfy exiled planters and mercantile speculators. General Kerversau, who had served in Saint-Domingue since 1796, returned to France in the middle of 1801, with a report that must have influenced Napoleon:

The military anarchy that Bonaparte destroyed in Egypt exists in all its force in Saint-Domingue, a restless militia that desires only disorder and does not recognize its leaders . . . a multitude brutalized and oppressed, blindly led by the strongest impulses of the moment; a crowd of merchants and travelers, nearly all transients in the island, and taking no interest in the revolutions of the Government.[21]

On February 2, 1802, with 5,000 of his 12,000 men (the remaining troops included those of Rochambeau's force of 2,000, who were ordered to capture Fort Dauphin, and General Jean Boudet with 3,500 men, who sailed on to seize Port-au-Prince), Leclerc appeared in the harbor of Le Cap and demanded that the town surrender. What has never been described adequately is the chaos that greeted the French. When they arrived, many people, no matter their color, rejoiced. Mulattoes hated their enemy Toussaint; former slaves-turned-laborers resented continued servitude on white plantations; the black population of the North could never forgive Toussaint's execution of his radical nephew Moïse; and, of course, the white Creoles of the Old Regime reveled in the opportunity to stop playing their roles in Toussaint's burlesque of enlightenment. Henry Christophe, Toussaint's general and commanding officer in the North, warned Leclerc that if he landed,

Le Cap would go up in flames, in accord with the orders of his leader. Leclerc urged Christophe to recognize that he would be responsible for the disasters to follow, and Christophe replied definitively in a letter dated February 3.

> The troops which you say are at this moment landing, I consider as so many pieces of cards, which the slightest breath of wind will dissipate.
> How can you hold me responsible for the event? You are not my chief. I know you not, and can therefore make no account of you till you are acknowledged by Governor Toussaint.
> As to the loss of your esteem, General, I assure you that I desire not to earn it at the price you set upon it, since to purchase it, I must be guilty of a breach of duty.[22]

Flames greeted Leclerc as he came in sight of Le Cap on the evening of February 4. Some described the scene as nothing but a "plain of ashes"; others say that Christophe first set fire to his own house, and of 2,000 homes in the town, only fifty-nine remained.[23] Women, children, cripples, and the wounded, taking their most precious possessions, fled the city. When Leclerc entered the town on February 6 with his wife Pauline, Napoleon's youngest sister, and their son, the city had been evacuated, the government buildings burned down, and the gunpowder factory exploded.[24] Leclerc immediately began to rebuild, hoping to return the chief city of the colony to its former splendor.

Yet once news of General Antoine Richepanse's brutal restoration of slavery in Guadeloupe (August 5, 1802) reached Saint Domingue, Leclerc realized the colony was doomed to be forever lost to the Republic. "The wretched decree of General Richepanse," Leclerc lamented to Napoleon, "which reestablished slavery in Guadeloupe, is the cause of our misfortunes."[25] Returning planters and merchants from France spoke of nothing but slaves, and Leclerc's claims to preserve freedom for all were debunked. Leclerc had reason to be alarmed. By mid-October, Jean-Jacques Dessalines and the mulatto generals Jacques Clerveaux and Alexandre Pétion revolted. Christophe soon followed their lead. These generals, who had defected to the French after the loss of the fortress Crête-à-Pierrot and their formal surrender at Le Cap, now joined the popular resistance of the black masses who had never stopped fighting for independence. By the middle of November, a large part of Saint-Domingue was again under black control. Leclerc's desperate letters to Napoleon and to the minister of the marine, from July until his death, tell how his army was being destroyed by the ravages of yellow fever; they beg for better shirts and for shoes and hats that can withstand the rains. In these letters, Leclerc also presents a plan to exterminate the blacks, whose bravery, resistance, and skill had been underestimated by the first consul: "We have in Europe a false idea of the country in which we fight and the men whom we fight against."[26] Leclerc had grown ever more ruthless in his genocidal campaign against the blacks, but by the time of his last letter to Napoleon (October 7, 1802), even he asked for deliverance:

> Since I have been here, I have seen nothing but the spectacle of fires, insurrections, assassinations, the dead and the dying. My soul is tainted, no pleasant idea can make me forget these hideous scenes. I struggle here against blacks, against whites, against misery and lack of money, against my demoralized army. When I have spent six months like this, I can ask for rest.[27]

Less than a month later, during the night of November 2, 1802, Leclerc died of yellow fever. The French army was in a shambles: out of 34,000 French soldiers, 24,000 were dead, 8,000 in hospitals, and only 2,000 wasted men remained.[28]

Locked Up in Saint-Domingue

The last years of revolution in Saint-Domingue are recognized by most historians, no matter their bias, as unparalleled in brutality. Their accounts are presented in terms worthy of the best gothic novel: the terrors of pestilence, a city become one vast charnel house, the smell of putrified corpses, black terror, white sentiment, love in the ruins, and unmitigated luxury and pleasure-seeking in the midst of blood and torture.[29] Near the end of October 1803, only Le Cap was still controlled by the French. Blockaded by the English at sea and the blacks on land, all that remained to the French on the coast was a piece of land about two miles long.[30] Literally held prisoners in their own city, no longer able to receive reinforcements or supplies, the European and Creole French and the hapless mulattoes and blacks who remained watched as Rochambeau, having centralized in Le Cap all the forces of the North, schemed to steal money and property from the Creoles, threw parties, and invented new tortures for the blacks, including feeding them to Cuban dogs. Rarely have magnificence and abjection, pleasure and atrocity been so closely allied.

Donatien Marie Joseph de Vimeur, vicomte de Rochambeau, is,

*Donatien Marie Joseph de Vimeur, vicomte de Rochambeau. Reproduced from
Michele Oriol,* Images de la Révolution à Saint-Domingue *(Port-au-Prince:
Editions Henri Deschamps, 1992).*

according to both Haitian and foreign accounts, the villain of the doomed expedition to Saint-Domingue. Napoleon chose Rochambeau because he was a career soldier who also knew blacks. Born in Paris in 1755, he accompanied his father, Jean Baptiste Donatien de Vimeur, comte de Rochambeau, to America when the elder Rochambeau commanded French naval forces during the American Revolution. The son, called "the General" to distinguish him from his father, would go to the "other America" in the Caribbean Sea and live most of his adult life in the Americas. Appointed lieutenant general in command of the French Windward Islands on July 9, 1792, he took refuge in Saint-Domingue on September 28. Returning to the Windward Islands in January, he was blockaded in Martinique and, in March 1794, surrendered to the British after the siege of Fort Royal. As a British prisoner of war, the vicomte returned to live in the United States until he could be exchanged. Once in France, he was ordered back to Saint-Domingue in January 1796 to occupy the part of the island ceded to France by the Spanish. Rochambeau, who was extremely popular with the white planters, arrived in Le Cap to serve as governor in May, but was dismissed by none other than the commissioner Sonthonax on July 18, 1796.[31]

Three days before his dismissal and his return to France, he wrote Moreau de Saint-Méry, who had been exiled from Saint-Domingue and then from the France of Robespierre. In refuge in Philadelphia, Moreau longed to return to Le Cap, where he had been a lawyer, a judge, a member of the Superior Council, and a historian.[32] Though the British had not given up on conquering Saint-Domingue, Toussaint was consolidating his power. And while the mulattoes under André Rigaud conspired against General Etienne Laveaux and Toussaint, Sonthonax had returned to a rousing welcome by thousands of blacks. Rochambeau responded to this chaos with eloquent skepticism.

We must hope that this Colony is at the end of its misfortunes. But who can positively assure it? Do you want to know in two Words where we are? Here it is. The men of color want to seize the property of the Landowners and give bad advice to the Africans who begin to distrust them. The Africans dare to believe in general liberty. They prefer the life of soldiers to that of cultivators. The small number of Whites who are not in the army are vexed and humiliated. . . . Everything has taken on a military aspect, we are making sugar with the sabre at our sides, and a musket on our shoulders.

You want to know where we are going or at least where we will go. I know nothing. What I know very well is that I am in a vile Hole.[33]

Rochambeau came back to Saint-Domingue in February 1802, during a time of greater desolation than 1796, and most important, after the remarkable Toussaint had become governor general for life and led the island's temporary return to commercial glory. By the time Rochambeau became commander-in-chief of the French army, he had seen yellow fever kill thirty to fifty French each day and Le Cap and Port-au-Prince turned into cities of the dead. In response to the courage and triumphs of those he considered unfeeling brutes, he had recourse to studied tortures, "to barbarities worse than had ever before stained the annals of any people pretending to the character of civilization. All the male negroes and mulattoes they could lay their hands on were murdered in the most shocking manner."[34] As King Christophe recalled in his "Manifesto of the King," delivered twelve years later at his palace of Sans Souci: "Gibbets were everywhere erected; drownings, burnings, the most horrible punishments, were practiced by his orders. He invented a new machine of destruction, in which victims of both sexes, heaped one upon another, were suffocated by the smoke of sulphur." Rochambeau had decided to pollute what he had called a "vile Hole" with monstrosities that far surpassed the crimes of those Christophe calls "the Pizarros, the Cortez, the Bodavillas, those early scourges of the New World."[35]

Perhaps the most haunting incidents recorded in these days of barbarity have to do with dogs. Imported dogs, starved and forced to eat black flesh and, as some accounts say, to love their white masters, ripped into blacks in the arena Rochambeau set up in the courtyard of the old Jesuit monastery. Yet sometimes these dogs refused to attack, and had to be driven to frenzy by the French. Once, the elegant General Jacques Boyer, called "le cruel" by French soldiers, leapt into the arena, slit open the stomach of his "faithful servant," and pulled out the guts in order to incite the dogs. The victim was devoured to the sound of applause, cheers, and military music.[36] In his *Etudes sur l'histoire d'Haïti*, Beaubrun Ardouin describes how a group of these dogs was sent to Petit-Goâve in the south of the island. When French soldiers landed, they were attacked by rebel forces. During the fighting the French unleashed the dogs only to be attacked by them. These dogs, according to Thomas Madiou and others, had been brought from Havana, Cuba, by the genteel aristocrat, Louis Marie, vicomte de Noailles, and sported silks, ribbons, and feathered headdresses. They would soon be eaten by starving French soldiers.[37]

To know just how excessive was the French army's quest for pleasure in 1802, we must turn to Mary Hassal's *Secret History; or, The
Horrors of St. Domingo* (1808).[38] For although Madiou (especially)
describes Leclerc's luxurious retreat on the Isle de la Tortue—where
his wife Pauline "devoted herself to every pleasure that her meridional
imagination created"—and offers his readers sordid glimpses of Rochambeau, who gave his most exceptional balls after his most horrific
tortures, no other writer recording those apocalyptic days provides as
intense or so narrowly focused a representation as Hassal.

Accustomed from my earliest infancy to wander on the delightful banks of the
Schuylkill, to meet the keen air on Kensington ridge, and to ramble over the
fields which surround Philadelphia, I feel like a prisoner in this little place,
built on a narrow strip of land between the sea and a mountain that rises per-
pendicularly behind the town. There is to be sure an opening on one side to
the plain, but the negroes are there encamped.[39]

A white woman from Philadelphia, immured in a world construed as
white, she nonetheless describes from her "prison" a society in such
detail that readers can begin to understand the contradictions, rendered even more blatant by unprecedented events, that brought an
end to "the pearl of the Antilles."

Reading Hassal, we see the glint of silver, hear the clatter of china
and the sighs of courtship amidst the cruelty of the French, the devouring pestilence and contagion. It is true that we get more information about Paris fashions and Continental coquetry than about the
daily life of the black population, but her descriptions of white Creoles
and the French, especially the women "locked up at St. Domingo"
(because of jealous husbands, Rochambeau's roving eye, or fear of
black vengeance), give us an analysis of whiteness that breaks down assumptions of homogeneity or civility, while implying much about those
she refers to as "Negroes," "revolted slaves," "slaves," "oppressed creatures," "olive beauties," "monsters," or, finally, after Rochambeau's
evacuation, "savage masters."

According to Michel-René Hilliard d'Auberteuil in *Considérations
sur l'etat présent de la colonie française de Saint-Domingue,* the city of
Le Cap in the 1770s contained as many inhabitants as all the other
towns of the colony: about 10,000 free persons (color not specified),
not including sailors, soldiers, and vagrants, and 30,000 slaves.[40] Pierre
de Vassière, in *Saint-Domingue: La Société et la vie créoles sous l'ancien
régime* (1909), writes that by 1788 there were about 3,000 whites in

Le Cap.[41] I cite these figures as background to Hassal's rendition of life in Le Cap. Though she gives us a rare look at white drama, and the battles between different classes of whites—and especially between Europeans and Creoles—the rarefied scenario was played out against a ground of color: the variations from ivory, yellow, and red to black, which accounted for the majority. The whites confined in Le Cap were surrounded by those who had been damned by Napoleon's recent decrees (reinstituting the slave trade and reducing free coloreds to their former categorical ostracism, again subjecting them to racist legislation and severe restrictions). Yet the old hierarchies were leveled by Leclerc's and especially Rochambeau's vengeance.

In spite of the lack of detailed documentation about the changing roles of mulattoes and negroes in Le Cap as Leclerc temporarily sustained his strategy of deception, we know that by the time Rochambeau took charge, everyone who could be called "colored" was subject to harassment or worse. Madiou describes the neutralizing of distinctions between men and women and between those newly freed and the former free coloreds. Prisons were filled with local women who were not accountable as wives or domestics, and when the prisons could not contain them, they were put on ships and raped.[42] When Hassal arrived in Le Cap in 1802, black officers who had fought against the English on behalf of the French were now on sentry duty, treated like inferiors by the white French officers, for how could they be treated as equals when they would soon be either deported or turned into slaves? Madiou explains:

> The system had become more horrible than that of the Old Regime. In order to buy a house you had to be European; Blacks and men of color who had been slaves before the revolution returned to the authority of masters who had rented or sold them publicly, as in the past. Meanwhile, many indigenous officers who had served under Toussaint and Rigaud, covered with wounds received in battles against the English, were still active, still decorated with their military insignia. The government, not yet daring to strike against them, humiliated them.[43]

But when Rochambeau began his flagrant war of extermination, for those *indigènes* who "remained in the cities, there was neither justice or any guarantee." They had to bear the curse Rochambeau had proclaimed on their race. Humiliation was replaced by torture and death, and no one was safe from Rochambeau's fury. In characteristically ardent detail, Madiou reminds his readers:

To be gay meant to be content with public calamity; to be sad meant to be afflicted by the defeat of the indigenous army; to write meant to correspond
with the enemy; failing to take off your hat before a White meant lack of respect for a superior. Men of color and blacks were not treated as anything but
miscreants and boors. The brave and daring *indigène* who had fought for
France was a dangerous individual; the one who declared the wish for French
triumph was a fake; gestures, sighs, smiles, silence, thinking, everything was
analyzed and could lead to death.[44]

The white world of Hassal's *Secret History* was as threatened by the
conquerors' revels as was the black majority, who appear in her book
only intermittently. Women were especially vulnerable, though tyran-
nical power was, of course, masked by sentiment. Clara, the character
she calls her "sister," whose "fate" is "to inspire great passions," is
locked up by her jealous husband, St. Louis, which leads Hassal to reflect: "But I believe Clara is not the first wife that has been locked up
at St. Domingo."[45] Husbands, themselves devoted to libertinism,
feared the inconstancy of their wives, whose time—in Hassal's rendition of life before the revolution—"was divided between the bath, the
table, the toilette and the lover."

When recalling those days, Hassal breaks into momentary raptures
similar to the exoticized pastoral of Bernardin de Saint-Pierre.[46] She
wishes the negroes "were reduced to order that I might see the so
much vaunted habitations where I should repose beneath the shade
of orange groves; walk on carpets of rose leaves and frenchipone; be
fanned to sleep by silent slaves, or have my feet tickled into extacy by
the soft hand of a female attendant." Her sentimental idyll of plantation life sounds bookish, but that is hardly surprising: imprisoned in
one area of Le Cap, never venturing out except for a risky visit to Fort
Picolet, where she and her sister meet none other than Rochambeau,
Hassal can only imagine what she does not know. Losing herself in a
cloying landscape of "voluptuous indolence," she wanders in her mind
"over flowery fields of unfading verdure, or through forests of majestic palm-trees."[47]

But as her narrative proceeds, Hassal's idealizations tend to be replaced by facts she cannot ignore: the satyr-monster Rochambeau's
tyranny and the blacks' vision of "the blessing of liberty" which no
tortures can dim. She also describes the courage, as well as the jealousy, of Sanite Belair, "a very devil," who was executed with her husband, the black general Charles Belair, on October 5, 1802; before the
sentence was carried out, she tried to console him and refused to have
her eyes bound. The execution of Sanite and Charles Belair was one of

the most publicized stories during the war for independence; accounts were published in the *Gazette officielle de Saint-Domingue,* the major journal in Le Cap.[48] What the official accounts did not chronicle—but Hassal does—is the story of Charles Belair's amorous inclinations. He had a taste for white women, who were then caught, according to Hassal, in a no-win situation: "Every white lady who was unfortunate enough to attract his notice, received an order to meet him. If she refused, she was sure of being destroyed, and if she complied she was as sure of being killed by his wife's orders, which were indisputable."[49] The sordid details Hassal supplies doubtless had their sources in gossip and the oft-suppressed rumors of white women's craving for blacks.[50] Further, of the black women rebels rarely mentioned in official histories, Sanite Belair, captured with her husband by none other than Dessalines (then still in the service of the French), is the one "heroine" who could combat the myth of the "seasoned" black women's predilections for white men. Hassal replaces the stereotypes of the "ebony queen" longing to care for her white prince with the image of the proud Sanite taking vengeance on the white man who had been her husband's secretary: "she had him bound, and stabbed him with a pen-knife till he expired!"[51]

Twice in her account of Le Cap, Hassal analyzes with care the positive transformation of blacks, who seem, in their resistance, to be the only ones who are not locked up in Saint-Domingue: "They have fought and vanquished the French troops, and their strength has increased from a knowledge of the weakness of their opposers, and the climate itself combats for them." And again, eight pages later, she describes black enlightenment through adversity in words that must have been unsettling for slave owners in the United States:

> And these negroes, notwithstanding the state of brutal subjection in which they were kept, have at length acquired a knowledge of their own strength. More than five hundred thousand broke the yoke imposed on them by a few thousand men of a different colour, and claimed the rights of which they had been so cruelly deprived. Unfortunate were those who witnessed the horrible catastrophe which accompanied the first wild transports of freedom! Dearly have they paid for the luxurious ease in which they revelled at the expense of these oppressed creatures. Yet even among these slaves, self-emancipated, and rendered furious by a desire for vengeance, examples of fidelity and attachment to their masters have been found, which do honour to human nature.[52]

White proclivities end up in Hassal's text as "intoxicating scenes" of "futile splendor," with unabashed hedonism and inane gallantry.

But the main story, perhaps more disturbing than any other, is Rochambeau's relentless attempt to conquer Clara as he carries on his usual womanizing, gluttony, and genocide. First described as a short man in a uniform "*à la hussar*" with red boots, "a Bacchus-like figure," in the course of Hassal's narrative, Rochambeau becomes evil incarnate. He dogs Clara's steps, gives her gifts, tries to get rid of her husband by assigning him to a hopeless encounter with rebels—where forty out of sixty of his men are massacred—so he can attempt to lure Clara to his bed. Clara's husband, St. Louis, locks her up, but Rochambeau sends her impassioned letters by way of his valet. Here, for the only time in her *Secret History,* Hassal describes a relationship that does not use the word *conquest* or allude to charades of sentiment, often more oppressive than amusing. If blacks are represented as liberated, while whites are increasingly confined, their relations are also described differently. The "scenes of romance" are reserved for the servants of Clara and Rochambeau.

Under the window of the little apartment in which she was confined, there is an old building standing in a court surrounded by high walls. The general informed himself of the position of Clara's chamber, and his intelligent valet, who makes love to one of her servants, found that it would not be difficult to give her a letter, which his dulcinea refused charging herself with.[53]

On May 12, 1803, the Peace of Amiens was broken by open warfare between England and France. Rochambeau returned to Le Cap from his temporary headquarters in Port-au-Prince, where he had been since March. His answer to the blockade of the ports by a British fleet, to the disintegration of his army, to the hospitals glutted with the mutilated and dying, and to Dessalines's victories was to throw a ball. Hassal describes its splendor:

The ball room had been newly furnished with regal splendor; all the chairs were removed, and long sophas with large cushions offered delightful seats. A recess at one end of the room had been fitted up *à la Turc*; the walls were entirely concealed with large looking glasses, which reached the ceiling; the floor was covered with carpets and the only seats were piles of crimson satin cushions thrown on the ground. The lustres, veiled with green silk, gave a soft light, imitating that of the moon.[54]

Perhaps Hassal did not know about another ball Rochambeau gave on his return from Port-au-Prince. Jacques Marquet de Montbreton de Norvins, who had spent three years in Saint-Domingue as the private secretary of General Leclerc, whom he called "the Bonaparte of Saint-Domingue," recounts the "cold cruelty, the violent debauchery" of Rochambeau. Norvins tells how Rochambeau, whose twisted sense of pleasure was worthy of Nero, gave a celebratory ball for *mulâtresses*: "This ball took place while Rochambeau had their fathers, brothers, and imprisoned or suspected husbands drowned in a neighboring bay; then he had these women driven home in carriages by guides on horseback carrying torches."[55]

We cannot understand the horrors realized during Rochambeau's reign of terror without understanding that Le Cap had become as circumscribed and as intimate as a drawing room of the Old Regime. Or, if we take Norvins at his word, as wanton as a harem. According to Norvins—the only historian to have recorded in detail Rochambeau's coital preoccupations—when Rochambeau initially moved from Port-au-Prince to Le Cap to take Leclerc's place, he brought with him "the old seraglio of Toussaint." This "infamous circle of fallen women" included those white women who had "prostituted themselves" to "the old negro."[56] Norvins's chronicle of Rochambeau's devotion to these "women of all colors" complicates the well-known story of Toussaint's "seduction" of white women. Rochambeau's orgies of pleasure and pain were like outré parodies of the masquerades once enjoyed by a nobility practiced in the art of diversion. He directed the changing scenes, from masked balls to naked butchery and clandestine sexual obsessions. Fastidious French egotism joined what was suspected as Creole vanity and scorned as black bestiality, and the Old Regime was replicated and transformed in the New World.

On the morning of November 30, 1803, Dessalines, at the head of 8,000 men, occupied Cap Français, renaming it Cap Haitien. By all accounts, the capitulation of Rochambeau epitomized cowardice. On November 10, Rochambeau had sailed out of Le Cap and surrendered to the British commander of the blockading squadron. About two weeks later, the French troops evacuated the Môle Saint-Nicolas. Hassal observed, "General Rochambeau, after having made a shameful capitulation with the negroes, has evacuated the Cape. . . . The English admiral would not admit the general in chief into his presence."[57] For the next seven years, Rochambeau was a prisoner in England. Exchanged in 1811 and returned to France, Rochambeau was not called up for service by Napoleon until 1813, after the Russian campaign. In command of the Fifth Corps of the Grand Armée, Rochambeau was mortally wounded in the battle of Leipzig.[58]

An American Adventure

Europeans thought of those who lived in Saint-Domingue as Americans. It is easy to forget how permeable were the borders between the young republic of the United States (which had been helped in its revolutionary struggles against the English by French and Dominguan blacks, such as Henry Christophe) and the colony of Saint-Domingue. In 1791 and again in 1793, when European and Creole planters and settlers were forced to flee from the ravages of a uniquely black revolution, they settled in the new democracy, especially in the cities of Norfolk, Baltimore, Philadelphia, New Orleans, and even New York. Médéric Moreau de Saint-Méry's *Voyage aux Etats-Unis de l'Amérique, 1793–1798* gives a Creole response to those he calls "Americans." As a Creole and not a European, he saw things in ways Charles Maurice Talleyrand-Périgord, another exile, would not. Talleyrand recorded with bewilderment the American reverence for luxury without taste: "In America luxury only serves to emphasize defects which prove that refinement does not exist in that country—either in the conduct of life or even in its incidentals."[59] The Creole Moreau de Saint-Méry, however, was used to displays of luxury for their own sake. Whereas Talleyrand—who joined Moreau in Philadelphia (November 1794–April 1795)—concentrated on making money (in a country where, he wrote, "honest people can prosper, though not as well as rogues"[60]), talked politics with Aaron Burr and Alexander Hamilton, and walked the streets with his lovely *mulâtresse*, Moreau was obsessed by the treatment of slaves and free coloreds, and wrote at length about the sexual mores of Philadelphia women: "adorable at fifteen-years old, faded at twenty-three, old at thirty-five, decrepit at forty or forty-five, they soon lose their figure, their teeth, and their hair, and are subject to fits of hysterics."[61]

Moreau responded as a Creole to a place that to him was more Creole than either Martinique or Saint-Domingue. In Virginia he described the negro's superstitious attachment to sorcerers and to Methodists: "Thus the unhappy Negro, convinced that in this life luck is not his lot, yet adopts a belief that threatens him with tasting equality with his Master only in hell." He laments that slaves "are kept in a state of degradation that even shocks an inhabitant of the Colonies. . . . The Negroes are ugly and dirty in Norfolk, where the mulattoes (and there are many) are lovely, since they are the product of

Negroes and Mulattoes. . . . The free men of color are better treated than Slaves only because no one has the right to strike them. But they are in abjection, and their relations with Whites exist only in the courtesies of women of color to white men."[62]

After fleeing Paris and Robespierre, whose hostility he incurred in the Constituent Assembly, Moreau arrived at Norfolk on March 8, 1794, at the age of forty-four.[63] There he listened to the accounts of refugees from Saint-Domingue, which convinced him that for now he should not return to the island. For a little over four years (from October 14, 1794–August 23, 1798) he remained in Philadelphia, where he opened his own bookstore and printing press, publishing two of his most important works: *Description topographique et politique de la partie espagnole de l'Isle Saint-Domingue* (1796) and *Description topographique, physique, civile, politique et historique de la partie française de l'Isle Saint-Domingue.*[64] According to Moreau, twenty-five thousand French colonists (a little over half of the number of whites in the colony before 1791) were said to have sought refuge in the United States. He does not specify how many freedmen or slaves were brought from Saint-Domingue by their masters.

These Unfortunates escaped from the disasters of their island, formerly the most celebrated of America because of its rich products, are proportionally more numerous at Norfolk than in any other place on the Continent, and because of many reasons.
The first is that the convoy that left the Cape when flames consumed this city anchored at Hampton and thus Norfolk became the first refuge. . . . The second is that most of them lacked means to go elsewhere. The third is that many of them who had brought Negroes could make them serve here because the regime in Virginia allows slavery. The fourth is that the winter so painful for inhabitants of a hot country is less palpable in Norfolk. And finally the inhabitants of this place have shown a constant affection for the French.[65]

French planters who escaped from Saint-Domingue to New York became merchants or traders and found wives or mistresses among American women. Some estimate that five thousand persons fled from Saint-Domingue to New York. Stephen Jumel, for example, was born in France around 1755 and came to Saint-Domingue as a boy. By 1791, before fleeing with thousands of others from the ravages of black insurrection, he had made a fortune in cotton, sugar, coffee, and indigo. In 1800 his warehouse on Liberty Street was known as Manhattan's leading emporium for "wines, brandies, cordials, spirits, gins and other choice fluids, including every variety of Madeira, Teneriffe,

Malaga, Jamaica, Antigua and Saint Croix, Holland Rum and York Anchor, All Fours, Metheglin, Agua Mirable, Ladies' Comfort and Double Distilled Life of Man."[66] Like many of the French refugees from Saint-Domingue, he socialized with distinguished New Yorkers, including Hamilton and Burr, and with more colorful characters as well. Eliza Brown (who was born in poverty as Betsy Bowen, took to the stage under the name Eliza Capet, married Jacques de la Croix, and after his death assumed the name of Brown) met Jumel and became his mistress. Later, hankering not only for fortune but also social standing, she tricked him into marrying her (pretending to be on her deathbed, she begged him to make her an honest woman before it was too late). Eliza Bowen Jumel would live long enough to be known as the wealthiest woman in the United States and to marry the old and bereft Burr in 1833, though their union lasted only a year.[67]

Sometimes, when things looked better for whites in Saint-Domingue, as during Toussaint's rule, they returned and brought their women with them. Louis Sansay, a French planter who had escaped from Saint-Domingue and was listed as a merchant on Bowery Lane in New York City directories from 1796 to 1798, had probably sought Aaron Burr's services as a lawyer. He also corresponded briefly with Burr, not about business but about love gone wrong.[68] By March 1802 Louis Sansay was having trouble with his wife, Leonora. She decided to visit Vice-President Burr in Washington, ostensibly to get letters of introduction for herself and her husband for their trip to Saint-Domingue. Before Leonora left and during her visit to Washington, Sansay wrote Burr, pleading for his wife's return. After not hearing from her for nine days, Sansay admitted to Burr that he feared she might leave him for another. "I tremble, that she might intend to abandon me, and I am decided rather to abandon everything, and sacrifice my life itself, rather, than have her in the possession of another." Asking Burr to convince her to go with him to the Caribbean, he also promised to give her $12,000 in case of his death.[69] On March 30, 1802, Burr wrote to Pierpont Edwards, asking that he write a letter of introduction for a woman he calls Madame Sansay ("the Lady of whom you may have heard me speak under the Name of Leonora") to General Rochambeau in Saint-Domingue.[70] Leonora returned to Louis, and they both reached Cap Français in early June 1802.

By the time Burr received what was probably his first letter from the woman he had described as having "more sense and information than all the women to be found in St. Dom.,"[71] he was a rene-gade in his own Republican administration, spurned by Republicans and Federalists alike, and embroiled in a dirty, vituperative campaign that within a year would cost him the race for governor of New York. Nearly a year later, on May 6, 1803, Leonora wrote Burr a long letter, breathlessly describing the jealousy of Leclerc, Pauline Bonaparte's dubious mourning for his death, the adventures of a woman named Clara, and Rochambeau's tortures and parties. She declared as she began her striking analysis of sexuality in the New World: "I cannot describe the effect it has had on me, the nights in particular, love-inspiring nights!—but love was never known in this desolated coun-try."[72] She must have written Burr about their departure for Santiago de Cuba, their flight from the catastrophic end of Rochambeau's the-ater of cruelty, and the beginning of Haitian Independence. For Burr wrote James Madison on December 12, 1803, asking "whether the U.S. have a Consul at St. Jago of Cuba & of his name & address," ex-plaining that "Mr. B. wishes to make a small remittance to a worthy & much distressed french refugee at that place."[73] On July 10, 1804, the night before his duel with Hamilton, Burr made special provision for Leonora in a postscript to Governor Joseph Alston, his son-in-law, say-ing: "If you can pardon and indulge a folly, I would suggest that Ma-dame—, too well known under the name of 'Leonora,' has claims on my recollection. She is now with her husband at St. Jago, of Cuba."[74]

Leonora Sansay, Aaron Burr, and the Love Letter

Secret History; or, The Horrors of St. Domingo was pre-sented as *A Series of Letters, Written by a Lady at Cape Français to Colonel Burr, Late Vice-President of the United States, Principally Dur-ing the Command of General Rochambeau.* Published anonymously in Philadelphia in 1808, the preface is signed only "The Author." Later ascribed to Mary Hassal, the book is referred to by scholars of Haiti as varied as T. Lothrop Stoddard (who refers to her as Miss Hassal), Etienne Charlier, Carolyn Fick, Robert and Nancy Heinl, and Thomas Ott.[75] The Haitian historian Horace Pauléus Sannon's introduction and translation of the majority of her letters, *Le Cap Français vu par une Américaine,* remains the most lengthy tribute to Hassal's unique brand of social history. Sannon praises her for "fine and penetrating observations, novel and little known facts, and abundant, often piquant details." While urging Haitians to turn to her book as "a first-rate source of information on Saint-Dominguan society in the last moments of French domination," he also carefully annotates her recitation of events, further contextualizing them or disclosing inaccuracies.[76] Yet historians of Haiti have never questioned the frame narrative of love and lust that she has invented: moments that seem blasted out of the continuum of history. After all, "history" and not "romance" is their concern. My concern, however, is to show how hybrid and permeable these rigid classifications truly are, and to explore their fertile borderlands. I anchor fact in the fictions too often opposed to it, and thus uncover another history.

Buried, indeed *secret,* has been the story of the woman who wrote the book, the name of the lady Burr once said was "too well known," Leonora Sansay. The author became known only as Mary Hassal. Like Eliza Bowen Jumel, Sansay might have changed names as she changed places and status. Leonora's May 6 letter, which is included in *The Papers of Aaron Burr, 1756–1836,* is reprinted only once in another, much publicized novel about Burr: Charles Burdett's *Margaret Moncrieffe; The First Love of Aaron Burr: A Romance of the Revolution* (1860). Since *Secret History* is an epistolary romance, as well as a history of the horrors of revolution in Cap Français and the expression of her longing for renewed contact with Burr, Sansay's refusal to name herself is not surprising. After all, Burr had enough problems: he had been accused of treason, forced into exile in 1808 (sailing from Falmouth, England, under the assumed name of H. E. Edwards), and still stigmatized as a debauchee and murderer (for the fatal duel with Hamilton). Although the narrator's letters tell of her going to Saint-Domingue to join her sister Clara, who has married a jealous Frenchman named St. Louis, "Clara" could be an alter ego, tempting desire in ways that her lover alone would recognize.

Hassal/Sansay in *Secret History* describes how her "sister," before leaving for Le Cap, "was less sensible to the horrors of her fate," because she enjoyed "the society of her friend," who, she implies, had urged her to marry St. Louis: "having married in compliance with his advice, she thought she would eventually be happy."[77] Could she be referring to Burr's counsel that she accompany her husband Louis to Saint-Domingue, or to the ongoing flirtation that developed into an affair but nothing more? On October 20, 1797, five years before

Leonora's visit to Burr in Washington, Burr wrote his friend William Eustis of Boston, "You talked of a Visit, for L.S. is (I am told) still in this City."[78] She had not yet become his mistress, for in July, he wrote confidentially to Eustis, complaining: "Why did you not tell me whether she had left Boston or when she would leave it—I shall certainly talk of you—there is no speaking of Boston without it—but there are Various Ways of doing the thing—and it will so be done, you may be assured, as shall not criminate you or prejudice my interests—You have excited my curiousity to an extreme—How could such an Animal be Months in my Vicinity & I not even hear of her?"[79]

Let us return to Leonora's detailed letter to Burr on May 6, 1803, since it acts as a "source" for the book of horrors and secret history to follow. Written nearly a year after she and Louis had arrived in Le Cap, a year after Toussaint's submission to Leclerc, and three months after Christophe set fire to the town, the letter dates the couple's arrival precisely as the night of June 7, 1802, when Toussaint, "general in chief of the blacks, was arrested in Gonaïves and sent to France." Even as Leonora writes, she is aware that the story of Clara, her jealous husband, and Rochambeau the "adoring general" and "military despot," set against the increasing successes of the "brigands," has "matter enough in it to form a romance." As she closes, she asks Burr if these recollections, "with many incidents which I have omitted, and some observations on all that is passing here, be written in a pretty light style, could it be printed in America in a tolerable pamphlet in french and english, & a few numbers sent here?"[80]

Writing to Burr as a lady craving for amusement and adventure (traits she will give to "Clara" in the book), but "coop'd up in the hollow bason in which the town is built," unable to go "a mile in any direction beyond it" without the risk of coming upon the marauding "brigands," Leonora Sansay devises for his benefit a witty but scathing picture of the French army in Le Cap. Leclerc is weak and jealous, duped by his officers and the black chiefs, thinking only of his escape. Then he dies. As Sansay puts it: "it was the best thing he could do, for if he had continued alive he would have liv'd dishonor'd." She portrays his wife, Pauline Bonaparte Leclerc (Napoleon's youngest and favorite sister), as small, common, undignified (an unattractive portrait that she changes in her book), uninterested in friendship with other ladies, but "far from cruel to Gen'l Boyer and all the état major." She acts her greatest role when Leclerc dies: "she cut off her hair (which was very beautiful) to put in his coffin & play'd so well the part of a disconsolate widow, that she made every body laugh."[81] No idealization for this American lady, unlike the Haitian Madiou, who celebrates Pauline Bonaparte in an ode to beauty reminiscent of Burke's apotheosis of Marie Antoinette, but moved to the tropics, where "murderous climate, the sadness of our country, the somber and monotonous aspect of our mountains" makes her languorous and takes the rosiness from her cheeks, leaving only a melancholy face girt by a bandeau ornamented with jewels.[82]

Leonora does not hide her contempt for Rochambeau and his courtship, or attempted conquest, of the one she calls "Clara," whom she identifies for Burr in this way: "That Clara you once lov'd—She came to St. domingo about the time I did, and at first liv'd tranquilly enough with her husband—but you know she never lov'd him & he was jealous, and sometimes render'd her miserable." Once Leonora turns to write her *Secret History*, this character Clara becomes the narrator's sister. Clara is no doubt Leonora, exhibited for Burr in all the theatricality of Le Cap, appearing at the numerous balls, longed for by Rochambeau and others, described like a "Venus rising from the waves," and appearing "almost naked," admired by all (to the delight of her husband, who enjoys "the splendor of what he deem'd his property"). In this text, Clara desires Rochambeau, who is described as fat with "a pretty laughing mouth, but nothing, *nothing* extraordinary."[83]

Staying true to the declaration that opened her letter—"but love was never known in this desolated country"—Leonora substitutes the facts of property, possession, and conquest for an idea of love. Vanity goads Clara on to consideration of Rochambeau, but nothing else. "Suffer me again to repeat that she was guided by vanity alone, & that not one feeling of her heart was interested. . . . 'twas power, 'twas place she aim'd at, and had she not been thwarted, she would have rul'd St. Domingue." But, as Leonora confides to Burr, "at present she has sunk back to her original nothingness," because this husband, which "she owes to you," does not have the perspicacity to "profit by her powers." The entire charade of romance sets the scene for what really seems to matter to Leonora, her exposure of the wanton and capricious Rochambeau, who does no better "in the fields of Mars than in the groves of Venus."[84]

Because of an insurrection in the southern part of the colony (probably the Darmagnac revolt in Aux Cayes in September 1802, or the general insurrection throughout the entire district of the Grande-Anse, which is to say, much of the northwestern section of southern

Saint-Domingue), Rochambeau goes to Port-au-Prince. When he returns, a ball is announced but then postponed because of the brigands' attack on the town. Rochambeau uses this crisis to try to get rid of Clara's husband: "You know that the lives of any number of citizens is a very trifling consideration when the commander-in-chief wishes to remove an incommode husband, & on this occasion they were wantonly trifled with." In the midst of reflections on fortune, fidelity, breakfasts, balls, and concerts, Leonora explains to Burr what the white "natives" think of the French and what the French are doing in Saint-Domingue. The passage is stunning, exposing the confusion of that fight to the death for the colony. The discourse of conquest that has simply opposed whites to blacks fails to recognize the intricate entanglements of white and black Creoles.

The inhabitants of this Island, that is, the creoles, regard the french army with more horror than the revolted Negroes, & with great reason. They are oppress'd beyond measure, and see daily the wreck of their fortunes torn from them by those who come to restore their property. The citizens are expos'd on every occasion to the fire of the enemy, while the troops of the line rest quietly in their forts. The people of france regard st. domingo as their peru, and each individual that embarks for it becomes fully determined to make his fortune at all events, & thus the war has been & will be continued for an indefinite time.[85]

When Leonora Sansay writes her "romance," she does not soften her critique of the French army. Just as in the letter to Burr, fictions of love are inextricable from facts of conquest.

About five years after Leonora wrote Burr the one known letter to date, she returned to America and settled in Philadelphia; there she completed *Secret History; or, The Horrors of St. Domingo,* and wrote a novel, *Laura*—by "A Lady of Philadelphia"—published in 1809 and described as "a faithful account of real occurrences."[86] In a sense, Leonora was still thinking about "the horrors," since she no doubt knew that the yellow fever in Philadelphia in 1793 was believed to have been brought by the refugees who had just fled Saint-Domingue.[87] In pestilential scenes of "terror," "agony," and "infection," like those already represented by Leonora in *Secret History,* a lonely orphan named Laura falls in love with a young medical student named Belfield, who takes her in, adores her, and catches yellow fever. Once nursed back to health by Laura's devotion, Belfield loses her, only to die in a duel when they are finally reconciled.[88] Cheated of marriage to one who was her lover as well as mentor, Laura survives, but "happiness remained a stranger to her bosom." Laura's sad story is Leonora's own, and is also the story of the narrator of *Secret History,* who laments to Burr:

You know what clouds of misfortune have obscured my life. An orphan without friends, without support, separated from my sister from my infancy, and, at an age when the heart is most alive to tenderness and affection, deprived by the unrelenting hand of death, of him who had taught me to feel all the transports of passion, and for whose loss I felt all its despair.

Could the thwarted love story also be alluding to the separation of Leonora and Burr, who appears in *Secret History* as indispensable to her life, one "whose friendship has shed a ray of light on my solitary way"?[89] In July 1812, after Burr's return from his short exile in Europe, Leonora wrote to him about life in Philadelphia (where she manufactured artificial flowers), confessing: "In August I shall give a short vacation, and will fly anywhere to meet you, though even for a moment."[90] Burr did not accept the invitation. Perhaps his memories of the adventures of "Clara" in Saint-Domingue had cooled his attachment to Leonora.

Dressed to Kill

Reading Hassal/Sansay's *Secret History,* one must wonder: what were the French doing in Saint-Domingue in 1802 and 1803 besides torturing blacks, oppressing white Creoles, flirting, philandering, and dying? As she tells stories about Leclerc's indulgence in silver dishes, while his soldiers turn into beggars, "badly cloathed, and still more badly fed, . . . asking alms in the street, and absolutely dying of want," and especially about Rochambeau's despotism, one begins to suspect that the *real* horrors in Hassal's narrative are those perpetuated by the French. Creole men lived in fear of the French officers' "attacks" on their wives. And sexual conquests seemed equal in importance to military feats. For the Europeans, Saint-Domingue was there to be conquered, and scorn for its inhabitants, black and white, justified unspeakable excesses. Hassal/Sansay notes that the island was given to Pauline as a "marriage portion" by Napoleon, and Leclerc's behavior suggests that he took quite seriously the implications of that dowry. "The Creoles complain, and they have cause; for they find in the army sent to defend them, oppressors who appear to seek their destruction. Their houses and their negroes are put under requisition, and they are daily exposed to new vexations." Hassal/Sansay talks to the Creoles and learns that many regret the end of Toussaint's reign, for "they were less vexed by the negroes than by those who have come to protect them."[91]

Another woman writing at the time corroborates Hassal/Sansay's tales of frivolity and woe experienced at the hands of the French army. In her journal, Maria Nugent, the wife of Governor George Nugent of Jamaica, worries about the troubles in Saint-Domingue, little more than a hundred miles to the windward. But her characterization of the French, especially Leclerc's officers, who turned up in Kingston seeking credit from Jamaican merchants in 1802, eloquently seconds Dessalines's judgment of the French: "blood-thirsty tigers." Writing about the vicomte de Noailles, the aristocrat who got the dogs for Rochambeau:

He told General N. [Nugent] that the French plan was, to put to death every negro who had borne arms, and to hamstring the others!—General N. then asked him, what would the colony be worth in that case; but to this he was not prepared for an answer. In short, it appears, that, though the French may have had a great deal of the monkey in their composition and character formerly, they have now more than a double proportion of the tiger. For never were there such a set of cruel heartless wretches, and I rejoiced to see them depart at eight.[92]

Later, during Rochambeau's tyranny, French deputies from Saint-Domingue visited Governor Nugent, complaining of the "rapacity and injustice," the "profligacy and misconduct" of the French troops. The inhabitants and planters, they explained, want to surrender the colony to the English, for they fear the French. Maria Nugent mentions another visit by the mulatto "Captain Dufour" (whom she describes as "not very dark," with "a pleasing countenance"), an "Aide-de-camp to one of the Brigand generals," namely, General Nicolas Geffrard. He reports the "dreadful" conduct of the French officers and their followers; she remarks that "their cruelties were not to be contemplated without horror," and then adds, "I was surprised at the good language he spoke."[93]

The French were brutal, but they had good taste. At least three times in her entries for the months between June and December 1802, Maria Nugent mentions Pauline Leclerc's gifts to her.

—I must mention, that I wore a pink and silver dress this evening, given me by Madame Le Clerc, and which was the admiration of the whole room. (June 18, 1802)

Major Pye just returned from St. Domingo, whither General N. had sent him on a mission to General Le Clerc. He brought me a second cargo of Parisian fashions from Madame Le Clerc. (August 28, 1802)

A crape dress, embroidered in silver spangles, also sent me by Madame Le Clerc, but much richer than that which I wore at the last ball. Scarcely any sleeves to my dress, but a broad silver spangled border to the shoulder straps. The body made very like a child's frock, tying behind, and the skirt round, with not much train. A turban of spangled crape, like the dress, looped with pearls, and a paradise feather; altogether looking like a *Sultana*. Diamond bandeau, cross, &c.; and a pearl necklace and bracelets, with diamond clasps. (December 30, 1802)[94]

These details form a much-needed subtext to Leclerc's desperate letters to Napoleon and to the minister of the marine begging for money. Leclerc and Rochambeau, as both Nugent and Hassal/Sansay reveal, fought a war while dressing and feeding themselves to the hilt. Imagine a burnt-out Cap Français, surrounded by "brigands," where the newly arrived French re-created for the Creoles all the excesses of the Old Regime, but transplanted in the tropics and there exaggerated. I have quoted these descriptions by Maria Nugent in order to suggest that the well-known condemnation of the Creole surrender to luxury and of their devotion to money and finery by French historians like Pierre de Vassière and Hilliard d'Auberteuil, and even the Creole Moreau de Saint-Méry, needs to be seen as a strategy of displacement. What is allowed, admired, or unquestioned in Europe becomes ludicrous in the colonies. The glories and refinements of the Old Regime, when practiced by those who did not inherit the right to do so, can be nothing but the worst kind of imitation, degraded and degrading. When does luxury become cheap? When does love become debauch? Some answered: When Paris comes to Saint-Domingue.

Hassal/Sansay's insights into the relations between castes and colors during the last days of Saint-Domingue reveal more about the kinds of mixture and erosion of boundaries that prevailed there than any other document about this period. Perhaps the right to revelation comes with what first seems to be a fault: her apparent frivolity, the easy movement from scenes of suffering to a surfeit of parties, from lopping off the head of a tempting *négresse* to having one's feet tickled by slaves. But caprice seems to sharpen her representations. For as one reads, reeling from extreme to extreme, it becomes clear that the weird oscillations themselves prove the effect of these horrors on Hassal/Sansay. Indeed, by the time we read of the intoxicating delights of Rochambeau's fêtes, we see these absurdly refined amusements as a counterpoint that only intensifies the horror.

What first seemed to be gothic commonplace—a woman's encounter with "pleasing terror" and "frivolous woe," the bacchic general who turns into a "monster," the white lady's trembling at approaching black brigands, the wife locked up by a jealous husband—ends up a deeply disturbing inquiry. It is as if Edgar Allan Poe's "Masque of the Red Death" had been rewritten by Madame de Staël. Hassal/Sansay's letters from Le Cap demand that we make the journey with her to a place where words and events no longer mean what we thought. By shifting back and forth from black brigand to sable beauties to white Creole and French ladies to French generals and jealous husbands, she undercuts customary representations in surprising ways. No hierarchy can stand firm in the violence of this text. Words like *charming, splendor, pleasures,* or *romance* contribute not only to making fiction but become indices of an unsettling social history that follows the injunction of Elsa Goveia, more than a century later, in *Historiography of the British West Indies*: "to seek, beyond the narrative of events, a wider understanding of the thoughts, habits, and institutions of a whole society. In the society itself, in its purpose and in its adaptive processes, will be found the true genesis of its history."[95]

The most telling habits of the society observed by Hassal/Sansay are disclosed in matters of dress. When Pauline Leclerc arrives, the ladies of Le Cap do not greet her "because having lost their cloaths they could not dazzle her with their finery." But after a few months, Pauline dresses and acts like a Creole: "She has a voluptuous mouth, and is rendered interesting by an air of languor which spreads itself over her whole frame. She was dressed in a muslin morning gown, with a Madras handkerchief on her head."[96] Note that the silly game Pauline plays with General Jacques Boyer, "letting her slipper fall continually, which he respectfully put on as often as it fell," described by Hassal as part of her first impression, sets the stage for a surfeit of coquetry. "There is no lack of *beaux* here; but the gallantry of the French officers is fatiguing from its sameness. They think their appearance alone sufficient to secure a conquest. . . . In three days a love-affair is begun and finished and forgotten; the first is for the declaration, the second is the day of triumph if it is deferred so long, and the third is for the adieu."[97] Sometimes flirting leads to possession, and then things get more serious, as with her "sister," Clara, "that form so vilely bartered."[98] The game of Boyer, whose "form and face," according to Hassal/Sansay, "are models of masculine perfection," becomes especially unsettling for the reader who recalls his other game of disemboweling blacks and tempting Rochambeau's dogs to feast.

The madras handkerchief adopted by Pauline Leclerc is a detail that tells us a great deal about the functions of dress and women's experiences in Le Cap. Lieutenant Thomas Phipps Howard of the York Hussars noted in his journal of 1796 to 1798, the last two years of the five-year British occupation of Saint-Domingue:

The mode of wearing Handkerchiefs about the Head is in universal Practice Amongst the people of Colour. Those that can possibly get them wear *Madrass Handkerchi[e]fs*, the beautiful Colours of which contrast in a very lively Manner with the Teint [tint] of their different Complections; & those who are really Handsome are generally coquets Enough to chuse those [which are] the most becoming. The manner of putting them on also is another Circumstance by which the pretty Black or Mulattoss shews her taste in a very eminent Degree.

He reminds his readers that though these handkerchiefs are forbidden in England and France, in Saint-Domingue they amount to a "Considerable Branch of Commerce."[99] Numerous European accounts of the mulatto women dwell, in particular, on their exquisite taste, their love of finery, and their special attachment to lace, linen, silks, and gold. They are objects ready for possession, marked by their possessions. "Dress is the reigning Passion of these Sable Beauties," as Lieutenant Howard puts it, who grants these women, some of whom cared for him when sick, "the full Tribute of my Praise." Returning again to the issue of color, he hints that the very idea of "mixed Blood" is never certain, thus confounding the most rigorous and categorical designations in the colonies: "For I have seen many Mulâttresses as white, if not whiter, than the generality of European women."[100] Baron de Wimpffen, in *A Voyage to Saint Domingo in the Years 1788, 1789, and 1790,* also praises them; and, like Howard, he says that education would make them honorable, for they would know how "to turn to the advantage of the genius and the heart, that excess of sensibility which they abuse." In concluding his observations, he also turns to their dress: "Their favourite coiffure is an India handkerchief, which is bound round the head: the advantages they derive from this simple ornament are inconceivable; they are the envy and despair of the white ladies, who aspire to imitate them, and who do not see that it is impossible for strong and glaring colours, calculated to animate the monotonous and livid hue of the mulatto, to harmonize with the alabaster and the rose of Europe!"[101]

This picture of white ladies imitating women of color recurs in many accounts of the Caribbean, but for a Jamaican planter like Edward Long, the whites' gradual taking on of the traits of blacks was seen not as imitation but infection. They insensibly adopt the "drawling, dissonant gibberish" of their domestics; and in the countryside the effects of climate and poor habits are most apparent. "We may see, in some of these places, a very fine young woman awkwardly dangling her arms with the air of a Negroe-servant, lolling almost the whole day upon beds or settees, her head muffled up with two or three handkerchiefs, her dress loose, and without stays."[102] Even Maria Nugent notes the "incredible" fact that many ladies take on the Creole of the negroes, "speak a sort of broken English, with an indolent drawling out of their words, that is very tiresome if not disgusting."[103] Henry Breen, in *St. Lucia: Historical, Statistical and Descriptive* (1844), gives a fascinating account of linguistic cross-fertilization: he not only depicts Creole as an adulteration, but stresses its allure for the "pure" speakers of French. Lamenting that French is corrupted once in the mouths of the black population, he admits that this "unintelligible" travesty of the French language—an effeminate "gibberish" best suited for "children and toothless old women"—has spread to "the highest circles of colonial society." When he is confronted with this "corruption of the language," he decides to speak only his "best French." But the negroes continue to pretend that they cannot understand French in order to tempt others to descend into this slough of linguistic deformity: "They often pretend ignorance in order to allure you into their own soft, silly dialect, whose accents are always flattering to their ears, however imperfectly it may be spoken."[104]

The crucial distinction most colonial historians make between those whites who adopt black style and the blacks who imitate white behavior establishes difference where uneasy similarities abound. While blacks are represented (for example, by Long, Edwards, Nugent, and Lewis in the West Indies) as consciously and conscientiously trying to assimilate white ways (but never transforming what they observe), white Creoles—especially those women "creolizing" or lounging indolently—

The Barbados Mulatto Girl, *from a color engraving by A. Brunias. Courtesy Cabinet des estampes, Bibliothèque nationale, Paris.*

The West India Flower Girl, *from a color engraving by A. Brunias. Courtesy Cabinet des estampes, Bibliothèque nationale, Paris.*

appear in their descriptions to have caught a disease, as if they were too weak-willed or amoral to resist the contagious attractions of loose living, scanty dress, and languorous talk. Black people mimic. White Creoles yield to the ambient atmosphere.[105] Unbearable heat and numerous blacks contributed to the inevitable pollution of civility and grace.

But accounts of Saint-Domingue, especially those of Moreau de Saint-Méry, show that Creole whites take on masks as deliberately as do blacks. He represents life in Saint-Domingue as an intriguing mix of things usually kept separate. Furthermore, mimicry, thought to be a propensity of the black Creoles, flourishes among white Creoles. Refusing to oversimplify a complex situation, Moreau gives a detailed account of dancing in Saint-Domingue that involves both groups in reciprocities usually ignored.[106] Africans and Creole blacks dance the *calenda, chica,* and *vaudoux.* Vaudoux, first described by Moreau de Saint-Méry as an electrifying dance, combines song, "superstition," and "bizarre practices." Performed with wild and "convulsive" abandon by slaves (but also by occasional, unidentified whites), leading to a kind of "fit," vaudoux has its no less intense analogy in the "excited dancing" of white Creole women: "They give themselves to it unreservedly, in spite of the hot climate and the weakness of their health. . . . Such, by the end, is the sort of delirium into which the dance plunges them that a visiting stranger would think that this pleasure monopolized their souls." Household slaves are great imitators of their white masters: "they love to dance minuets and quadrilles and do so with the most serious faces," and they introduce "bizarre changes" in European dances, which are sometimes "really grotesque." Creole whites and blacks shared experiences often discounted by reactionary colonial accounts: something like double possessions. Describing the white Creole passion for dress balls at the theater—a "voluptuous exercise" and "the most delicious spectacle"—Moreau conflates Creole passion and Old World splendor: "The prettiest faces, the most seductive grace and elegant outfits, completely ravishing; and at the end of these charming fetes, the soul is in a kind of delirium."[107]

How, then, can we understand the goal of adornment, or the uses of imitation by white women in Saint-Domingue? In *The Ancient Regime,* Hippolyte Taine presents the Duchesse de Bourbon "attired as a voluptuous Naiad" as she guides the Comte du Nord "in a gilded gondola, across the grand canal to the island of Love."[108] Without pushing the analogy too far, perhaps we see in Pauline Leclerc's performance of the languorous Creole a spectacle not of love but of seduction, the flip side of Rochambeau's Creole tyrant. As Hassal/ Sansay observes, "the French appear to understand less than any other people the delights arising from an union of hearts. They seek only the gratification of their sensual appetites. They gather the flowers, but taste not the fruits of love."[109] The game has little to do with sentiment and everything to do with conquest. Something like Jean-Jacques Rousseau's good, native simplicity of heart, for Hassal/Sansay, "is borne away by the torrent of fashion and dissipation."[110]

But this story of polished and fitful excess "without the glow of passion," like Pauline's indolent pose, has little to do with the daily Creole competition between white wives and mulatto favorites, those Hassal/Sansay portrays as "the hated but successful rivals of the Creole ladies."[111] White Creole women took on some of the traits of their opponents. They preferred Creole, conversed indelicately, and moved suggestively, according to Justin Girod de Chantrans, writing *Voyage d'un Suisse* in 1782. In one of his letters from Saint-Domingue, he opines: "Instead of imitating the indecency of the *filles de joie,* let them take for their models our gracious Europeans."[112] But a white Creole, Madame Laurette Aimée Mozard Nicodami Ravinet, writing her memoirs of Port-au-Prince in the early years of the revolution, recalls the heady contest between Creole ladies, who felt "humiliated in their claims by mulâtresses, *femmes publiques,*" and women of color. Desiring a distinguishing mark that would place them on a higher level than these courtesans, the white women presented their woes to the Superior Council of Le Cap. "At the Cap they issued an order that forbade this degraded class from wearing shoes. They then appeared in sandles, with diamonds on the toes of their feet."[113]

The rigorous codifier of colonial law, Moreau de Saint-Méry, noted that since 1770 women of color displayed riches startling in their splendor. The cities, especially Le Cap, were the sites for a "luxury" that "consists, nearly entirely, in a single object, dress."[114] In 1775 the attorney general of Le Cap endeavored to "restrain the excessively dazzling luxury of the *filles publiques* [prostitutes, though male visitors and even Moreau warned they are *not* what that European term denotes]." A statute in 1779 determined the dress of all people of color for "the purpose of morals."[115] By regulating what could be worn, or what could be purchased, on moral or religious grounds, the mask of virtue disguised the necessity for racist segregation. Nevertheless, dress, supposedly the surest proof of either privilege or debasement, was always being subtly undermined. Furthermore, we must remember that white women, by adopting the "immoral" dress and carriage of mulatto women, contributed to making futile the laws of perceptible difference.

The stereotype of the luxurious *mulâtresse,* a necessary prop in the colonial fantasy of Saint-Domingue, operates as a dream of whiteness against the fact of blackness. The obsession with the light-skinned mistress obscured the presence of black women, who, in a few accounts, appear as well dressed, as beautiful—and, though unsaid, as desirable—as the mulatta with thin lips and aquiline nose. With all the attention paid to the *mulâtresse* and her finery, it is easy to forget that the handkerchief was first used as a headdress by slave women, who took a sign of servitude and adroitly turned it to their own advantage. Their inventiveness and the ever-changing precepts of style made sumptuary laws ineffective. As Moreau de Saint-Méry reminds his readers, "coquetry comes in all colors." Black Creole women, he writes, even slaves, are "very well dressed," wearing in the most capricious, gracious, or bizarre fashion their kerchiefs around their heads or necks, ornamenting themselves with "fine gold earrings of all shapes, necklaces of gold beads mingled with garnets," and displaying a variety of costumes, "from the heavy linen of Vitré in Brittany, the *Brin* and the *Ginga,* to the toile of Flanders and the baptismal dress!"[116] Moreau generalizes a plenitude of dress that was for most slaves, as Gabriel Debien notes, limited to holidays and to the one day of rest, Sunday, "the general day of coquetry,"[117] or reserved for servants, in some accounts, decked out with jewels and diamonds to display the wealth of their owners.

Hassal/Sansay, always interested in specifics—even if, like other white women writers, she hides the black woman's vexing desirability under the image of the alluring mulatto—tells a story from before the revolution. The extravagant charms of those taught "to express in every look and gesture all the refinements of voluptuousness" so threatened the white ladies, whose jealousy knew no bounds, that they complained to the Superior Council of Le Cap. In a vain attempt to put a stop to "their influence over the men, and the fortunes lavished on them by their infatuated lovers," the council issued a decree restricting their dress: "No woman of color was to wear silk, which was then universally worn, nor to appear in public without a handkerchief on her head." Unlike the terrible rules delimiting the dress and comportment of mulatto men, this decree had a happy ending. The mulatto women answered the legal ploy with a display of their economic power: they stayed in their houses, and the merchants "represented so forcibly the injury the decree did to commerce, that it was reversed, and the olive beauties triumphed."[118] As did their handkerchiefs.

Moreau de Saint-Méry had described Creole white women as morbidly sensitive and so jealous that "they are ready . . . to bear more easily the death of a loved one than the loss of his love." Scenes of terrible vengeance, once rare, Moreau wrote, "are becoming daily occurrences."[119] Indeed, during Rochambeau's bloody spectacles, Madiou noted that the general never stopped his debauching, favoring young and beautiful white Creoles who, "animated with the most violent jealousy against black women and women of color whom the Europeans generally preferred, . . . supported his system of extermination and perpetually incited him to new cruelties. Most of the indigenous women delivered up to unspeakable torture were sacrificed in these instances."[120] Hassal/Sansay dwells on white ladies' rage and infidelities rather than the pain and suffering of their socially subordinate rivals; and she concludes that "the influence" of these mulatto women, who "breathe nothing but affection and love," could not be outmaneuvered.

What is even more interesting, when compared with her admiration for the nuanced women of color, is Hassal/Sansay's rather grisly, if ambivalent, depiction of the Saint-Domingue of Creole ladies. Her acquaintances lament the island as a lost Eden, where everyone lived "like a Sovereign ruling his slaves with despotic sway, enjoying all that luxury could invent, or fortune procure. . . . Gaming knew no bounds, and libertinism, called love, was without restraint." Hassal/Sansay then moralizes a little: "The Creole is generous, hospitable, magnificent, but vain, inconstant, and incapable of serious application; and in this abode of pleasure and luxurious ease vices have reigned at which humanity must shudder." She will soon counter that momentary *frisson* with stock phrases of praise for her friends' "voluptuous languor," despotic charms, and their "indolent" but agreeable "drawling accent." Some of their other characteristics are more memorable, and refuse to lend themselves to the usual clichés.

Hassal/Sansay gives an example of what she means by "jealousy."

A lady, enraged by "some symptoms of *tendresse* in the eyes of her husband," decides to do away with the "beautiful negro girl" who is the cause.

> She ordered one of her slaves to cut off the head of the unfortunate victim, which was instantly done. At dinner her husband said he felt no disposition to eat, to which his wife, with the air of a demon, replied, perhaps I can give you something that will excite your appetite; it has at least had that effect before. She rose and drew from a closet the head of Coomba. The husband, shocked beyond expression, left the house and sailed immediately for France, in order never again to behold such a monster.

Hassal/Sansay assures us that her Creole friends have told her "similar anecdotes," but chooses instead another kind of story. In a place where libertinism could be called love, madras handkerchiefs are valued more than family. One of the women recalls how "her husband was stabbed in her arms by a slave whom he had always treated as his brother." She saw her children killed and her house burned. A faithful slave saves her life and, "after incredible sufferings" and "innumerable dangers," takes her to Le Cap. But most important of all—"and the idea seemed to console her for every other loss"—the slave (knowing well what mattered) "saved all my madrass handkerchiefs."[121]

A New World Theater

In 1764 the theater at Cap Français, the oldest and most glorious in Saint-Domingue, became a public theater, opening on the night of October 13 with a performance of *Le Misanthrope* and *Les Trois Gascons*. Two years later, the theater was relocated between Espagnole and Sainte-Marie streets; it ran the entire length of a city block and had its entrance on the north side of Montarcher Place. Moreau de Saint-Méry was often puzzled by the oddities of Le Cap, with bizarre street names like "Lion Street, Bear Street, Cat Street, Street of the Devil's Fart." Before getting to the theater, he paused to describe the fountain at Montarcher Place: "A pedestal shaped like an abacus, on which four Ionic columns were erected, was girded with a strip sculpted with the arms of France and those of the Chevalier de Vallière and Montarcher who were Administrators in 1772." Then, with his usual appreciation of the telling detail, Moreau notes, describing the theater: "Two busts of gigantic satyrs, positioned by the forestage, seemed to sustain the edifice. On the frontispiece are the arms of France."[122]

The hall, 120 feet long by 40 feet wide, was divided into three parts. In the first two boxes of the first row near the stage sat the governor-general and his guests, the officers of the garrison, the intendant, and the officers of the colonial administration. Of the ten third-row boxes, farthest from the stage, seven seated mulatto women and three seated *négresses*. Hilliard d'Auberteuil, the Breton lawyer and historian, resident in the colony for about twenty years, warns against this habit of allowing blacks to watch white drama in Le Cap:

In vain did one point out that if it is a privilege for free coloreds to enjoy spectacles made for Whites, the right must be restricted not extended, and not offered to slaves: that it was more reasonable to leave this privilege to the Mulattoes and Mulâtresses than to make them share it with Negroes and Négresses, because the Mulattoes make up the smallest number, are more attached to the Whites, richer and better bred.

Furthermore, he warns, when blacks try to dress for the occasion, they not only look ridiculous but may end up stealing: a free negro and négresse who make their living selling chickens, and make a sufficient amount to dress modestly, would be tempted to steal in order to dress in pearls and lace.[123] The Creole Moreau de Saint-Méry, ever the more cautious historian, as well as incisive ethnographer and lawyer, tells another kind of story that shows how the valuation of color prejudice had penetrated even to the family:

Since the month of June, 1775, free négresses have obtained entry into the theater, to which one had admitted lighter-skinned persons of both sexes since 1766, at the further end of the passage of the amphitheater. They chose me to draw up their request, and I said only a word; this was to demand *that they would be able to sit next to their daughters*. But these girls threatened to yield them the entire place, if this *confusion* [mingling] had taken place, and it was necessary to put them in separate boxes. So, when a négresse and her mulatto daughter come to the theater, they separate; the ebony to the left, the copper to the right.[124]

Both Hilliard d'Auberteuil and Moreau de Saint-Méry agree that the performances were often annoying. Hilliard d'Auberteuil insists that the theater was often deserted and that "Tragedies, Dramas, Comedies, Opera were poorly, imprecisely, and falsely performed."[125] Moreau describes how the theater presented a hodgepodge of amateurs, foreign actors, and tightrope dancers. Not only was boulevard theater sometimes indistinguishable from high theater, but Moreau notes that "as in provincial cities, tragedy and comedy are confounded, tragedy and comedy have at Le Cap a common temple and common disciples, and it is not unusual to see Melpomene take on the tone of a comic muse. What is most singular, is the eagerness, I nearly said the furor, of Creoles to see tragedies, whose grotesque character repels persons of taste."[126] Yet what was perhaps vulgar to Moreau de Saint-Méry or Hilliard d'Auberteuil might, to a later Haitian historian like Jean Fouchard, be fascinating proof of an increasingly vital and innovative Creole culture on the eve of revolution.

A new form of theater was in the making. We can only begin to reconstruct details that could tell us how altered French culture in Saint-Domingue had become before the revolution. Fouchard suggests striking similarities in the predilections of whites and blacks: a cultural intermingling that extended into the United States. Artists from Saint-Domingue performed in New Orleans, Boston, Philadelphia, and New York. The theater in Saint-Domingue performed local pieces in Creole mixed with "negro dances" and introduced accomplished mulatto artists "of color," like the famed Lise and Minette of the Theater of Port-au-Prince.[127] Louis-François (César) Ribier, an actor of the Paris Variétés, a libertine and also a hero of the Bastille, created an ensemble or a "company" especially for Le Cap, called Troupe des Comédiens de Paris. On July 14, 1787, he performed in his own play, L'Héroïne Américaine, which he had adapted from the Abbé Raynal's Histoire philosophique des deux Indes.[128] Our source for this information is Ribier himself; his defense of his play, printed in the Feuille du Cap on July 28, was unearthed by Fouchard:

It has been reported to us that a public fuss brews, suggesting our intent was to delude by the title of Heroine, while travestying the American Hero, a pantomime that we had the honor of presenting three times with success. Such a fraud is far from our intent; the subject we present is absolutely new and is taken from the Histoire philosophique et politique des établissemens et du commerce des Européens dans les deux Indes; we followed as closely as possible this historical subject and made changes only when necessary to the theatrical action.[129]

We do not know whether this play dealt with Raynal's critique of slavery, or concentrated more on the Europeans' discovery of the New World and their reactions to the customs and values of the inhabitants of the islands.

Many of the spectacles of life in Le Cap were impassioned—if somewhat crude—trivial pursuits. Not only did Creoles crave for tragedies in the theater, they probably spent more time watching executions in "La place-d'armes" (the Parade Ground). There, blacks as well as whites could see the execution of whites. (Until 1766, when the Negro Market in Clugny Square was installed, *both* blacks and whites had been executed on the Parade Ground.)[130] Moreau describes an execution in 1777 that made this place "the theater of extraordinary circumstances." A young officer on a ship from Bordeaux was condemned to the gallows for burglary. The rope broke when the trap beneath his feet was sprung by the hangman. The victim jumped up, went down on his knees, and shouted "Mercy!" As the hangman tried to make him ascend the scaffold again, the condemned man put his legs through the rungs of the ladder and blocked the executioner's efforts. The spectators went wild. Someone hit the hangman with a club, others followed. Constables tried to surround the guilty man and the executioner, but a storm of rocks forced the constables to flee. Two sailors seized the hangman and freed the young thief. Negroes pursued the hangman as he attempted to get back into the prison. They stoned him dead in front of the gallows.[131]

Moreau de Saint-Méry described Le Cap as a place where blacks frequented taverns, where slaves went armed with clubs, gambled, and broke "all the regulations" while the police did nothing. Noting that the slaves of important masters were never arrested for misconduct, he adds that the only blacks jailed were "some negroes of the plain, whom they accuse of having no passes" or city blacks not valued by their masters and therefore not exempt from punishment. He complains about the inadequate police force and the masters' assumption that they gain dignity by obtaining immunity for their slaves.[132] Reading Moreau de Saint-Méry's account of this city, where slaves accounted for two-thirds of the population, it becomes clear that slaves in the towns lived differently from those on the plantations. Life at Le Cap was an experience riddled with ambiguities, a fact too often masked in records that oversimplify the intricate social relations between masters and slaves, between whites and blacks.[133]

Once Toussaint became governor of Saint-Domingue, the theater at Le Cap, "destroyed in the conflagration of 1793, was rebuilt on No. 145 Pantheon Street, at the corner of Commerce Street, facing the house of the American merchant Mayer."[134] New and stunning pieces were put on there—plays adapted, according to Fouchard, to the social and political transformations of the colony. On May 29, 1797, a pantomime in three acts set in the Congo and called *Héros africain* was performed. The play has been lost, so we can only wonder how Toussaint's "theater of Africa" played in the New World.[135] The "African Hero," a work no doubt more earnest than Ribier's "American Heroine," might well have been the first literary reinvention of Africa by black rebels. It was perhaps a corrective to the denigrating portraits of racist historians, but we can only guess at the play's treatment of Africa: no longer a landscape occupied by "savages," but a place romanticized to suit new Creole sensibilities.

But as we have seen, the events following Leclerc's arrival and the more diabolic accession of Rochambeau shattered the hybrid delights of this makeshift Paris in the New World. The white spectators (including women, colonists, and numerous officers, according to Madiou) were as avid for spectacles of torture as they had been for Molière. The French army that occupied Le Cap brought a kind of monstrous order to an anomalous world that had been rendered no less confused by eleven years of revolution. The "gilded negroes" scorned by Napoleon would endure and conquer those who had stooped to inhuman acts, like the appalling murder of Jacques Maurepas, one of the first black generals to join the French. In front of his wife and daughter, he was dragged on board the French admiral's ship in the bay and bound to the mainmast. Then, his epaulettes hammered into his shoulders with long nails, a cocked hat was nailed on his head, and he was savagely whipped. He died without a word, tears flowing down his face. They threw him into an Atlantic that already reeked of corpses.

Years later, Jonathan Brown, in his *History and Present Condition of St. Domingo* (1837), blames blacks for a country caught in a comical replication of French custom: "The customs of the ancient regime became thus perpetuated or burlesqued under the dominion of the blacks, and the national politesse of the French was superadded to the more barbarous propensities of the African slave." Though Brown condemns Haitians for their donning of masks, "servilely imitating the French in all qualities, good and evil," his account more accurately describes what happened when white terror came to Saint-Domingue.[136] For nothing they would do could surpass the horrors exhibited by their "civilized" French models, performed for all to see on the stage of colonial violence.

4

Gothic Americas

And to hold a man or to rob him of his liberty is a greater sin, than to steal his property, or to take it by violence. And to hold a man in a state of slavery, who has a right to his liberty, is to be every day guilty of robbing him of his liberty, or of manstealing. The consequence is inevitable, that other things being the same, to hold a negro slave unless he have forfeited his liberty, is a greater sin in the sight of God, than concubinage or fornication.
—Jonathan Edwards, September 15, 1791[1]

Because of the inhabitants' conduct, we cannot count on the return of any prosperity for Saint-Domingue, since the terrible lesson the men have received has not been corrected. Everyone has their mulâtresse that they have brought up or just found, and with whom they are going to produce a new generation of mulattoes and quarterons destined to butcher our children. Here is what must happen: . . . prescribe the destruction or the deportation of every free man and woman of color, after branding them on their two cheeks with an "L" which will mean Libre.
—The Marquise de Rouvray, in exile from Le Cap, Saint-Domingue, writing from New York to her daughter, Madame de Lostanges, August 13, 1793, *Une Correspondance familiale*[2]

In the chapter "Results" in *Uncle Tom's Cabin*, the mulatto George, presented by Harriet Beecher Stowe as spokesman for "the oppressed, enslaved African race," wonders where to look for "an African *nationality*." He dismisses Haiti, for "in Hayti they had nothing to start with. A stream cannot rise above its fountain. The race that formed the character of the Haytiens was a worn-out, effeminate one; and, of course, the subject race will be centuries in rising to anything." Although George probably means the French, he does not say who formed the race that formed the Haitian character, or what that character is. For in George's quest romance, precision is not necessary. All he has to do is turn to the shores of Africa, where he envisions "a republic formed of picked men" and "acknowledged by both France and England." He will go to this Liberia, he says, and "find myself a people."[3]

The problem of where to put blacks, or how gradually to remove them from the southern United States, had been debated some fifty years before Stowe's book was published. The revolt in Saint-Domingue left Southerners in fear of insurrection. "Over ten thousand émigrés from that island fled to the Southern States, bringing with them new elements of fear of slave uprisings."[4] In 1800 the slave rebel General Gabriel's conspiracy to kill the inhabitants of Richmond was discovered, moving the Virginia legislature to find a "receptacle" to contain emancipated slaves and free negroes.

In 1801 Thomas Jefferson wrote a letter to James Monroe, the governor of Virginia, first referring to the "conspiracy, insurgency, treason, rebellion, among that description of persons who brought on us the alarm, and on themselves the tragedy, of 1800"—and then considering where they might be sent. For the first two pages of this letter Jefferson never identifies those he calls "these people," "that race of men," "the persons under consideration," until he finally turns to Saint-Domingue—at that time still under Toussaint Louverture's leadership—as the most "probable and practicable retreat for them." Only then does he mention the word *blacks*. Of course, the unsaid itself carries great weight; for there can be no doubt whom he means. There is no need to designate in any detail who this mass of people is, for, according to Jefferson, they would not be welcome anywhere within the limits of the United States or on its northern boundary or on its western and southern frontiers.

Even contact with such a colony, he implies, would be undesirable. Jefferson speaks a language of limits, even as he anticipates that "our rapid multiplication will expand itself beyond those limits and cover the whole northern, if not the southern continent" (the British and Spanish frontiers of the United States). As he thinks about the expansion of the nation, he sees its citizens as "a people speaking the same language, governed in similar forms, & by similar laws." Jefferson wants the nation kept pure, with no "blot or mixture on that surface." But Saint-Domingue is mixed and ready to receive blacks, for there "the blacks [and he includes mulattoes in that racial category] are established into a sovereignty *de facto,* & have organized themselves under regular laws & government." Further, the one he merely calls "the present ruler"—meaning Toussaint, though he does not name him—would probably welcome those exiled for acts we call "criminal," for he would perhaps deem them "meritorious."[5] Given such suspicions, it should not be surprising that when Napoleon decided to attack Toussaint's government, destroy those he called "rebels," and reinstitute slavery, Jefferson's newly elected government in Washington abruptly changed U.S. policy and refused to support Toussaint. In March 1802 President Jefferson assured the French minister Louis Pichon that the United States would do everything possible to support Napoleon's agenda for Saint-Domingue: the reconquest of the island and the reestablishment of slavery.

On February 4, 1824, Jefferson, now thinking about emancipation, wrote to Jared Sparks, explaining how best "people of color" can be colonized at the least cost to their owners. How, he wonders, can "the getting rid of them" be cheaply done when the possessors of them must be paid for their property? He advises that newborns be left with their mothers "until a proper age for deportation." He reminds his reader that some forty years ago in his *Notes on the State of Virginia,* he had already projected the great savings to be had in deporting children. At that time, he recalls, no place of asylum could be named. But now Saint-Domingue is independent, has "a population of that color only," and President Alexandre Pétion has offered "to pay their passage, to receive them as free citizens, and to provide them employment." He concludes by admitting that the "separation of infants from their mothers, too, would produce some scruples of humanity." "But," he reflects, "this would be straining at a gnat, and swallowing a camel."[6]

Romance and Race

The development of romance in the Americas was linked in unsettling ways to the business of race. Out of the ground of bondage came a twisted sentimentality, a cruel analytic of "love" in the New World: a conceit or counterfeit of intimacy. As we have seen, something happens to romance when we turn to those places where everything was allowed because thousands were enslaved, where the fact of slavery—the conversion of person into thing for the ends of capital—turned all previous orders upside down. If racial mixing threatened to contaminate, the masters had to conjure purity out of phantasmal impurity. This sanitizing ritual engendered remarkable racial fictions.

One of the thorny problems in justifications of slavery, the place where the argument for black bestiality foundered, was the possibility of human sentiment in the slave. Could a thing, a piece of property, feel? Writing about the Caribs in his 1793 *History, Civil and Commercial, of the British Colonies in the West Indies,* Bryan Edwards stressed their "insensibility towards their women" and judged their choice of combat over "Love itself" as a mark of savagery.

But brutality toward their wives was not peculiar to the Charaibes. It has prevailed in all ages and countries among the uncivilized part of mankind; and the first visible proof that a people is emerging from savage manners, is a display of tenderness towards the female sex.[7]

The Caribs, once replaced by the transplanted African, were then idealized as the "golden Carib," to be contrasted with the black slave, whom Edward Long, a Jamaican planter and the most severe of colonial historians, compared to the orangutan.

If the Caribs were a repository of Antillean innocence, then the Africans became the exemplum of waste, treachery, and barbarism. When turning to what he called "the contemplation of human nature in its most debased and abject state," Edwards discusses at length what happens to "the best affections of the human heart" in a state of slavery. He turns to what he knows, the enslaved "Africans" he has observed in Jamaica. What he had only suggested in his meditation on the Caribs he now particularizes. Negroes are brutal to their animals, who suffer from their "caprice and cruelty." The unfortunate animal which finds itself the property of a negro takes on "the cowardly, thievish, and sullen disposition of his African tyrant." Implied here, if we follow the analogy, is the promise that the black who becomes the property of whites can acquire some of the attributes of civilization. But when Edwards turns to "Love," he concludes that though some argue otherwise, Africans cannot experience it. Turning to those who idealize natural desire or tender passion as alleviating the horrors of slavery, claiming that "Love" is a balm to affliction, Edwards astutely dismisses their surmises as "the language of poetry and the visions of romance."

The poor Negro has no leisure in a state of slavery to indulge a passion, which, however descended, is nourished by idleness. If by love, is meant the tender attachment to one individual object, which, in civilized life, is desire heightened by sentiment, and refined by delicacy, I doubt if it ever found a place in an African bosom.

A lack or incapability that first seemed to be imposed by slavery is then elided by Edwards into generality, an all-encompassing and innate failure of feeling shared by all Africans. Those who need more than one woman are therefore judged guilty of "licentious and dissolute manners." Edwards concludes by qualifying African passion—too often "dignified by the name of Love"—as "mere animal desire." Lust alone perpetuates the species. Sex is enjoyed without the artifices of "ceremony," and fidelity comes by default, when old age diminishes ardor and encourages "attachments, which, strengthened by habit, and endeared by the consciousness of mutual imbecility, produce a union for life."[8]

Racialist arguments foundered on the fact of feeling.[9] Though proslavery ideology depended on the negro's lack of *proper* "love" or refined feeling for the brute underpinning that could justify subjugation, a certain kind of feeling, defined variously as "attachment," "fidelity," and "devotion," became central to the apotheosis of the master and slave relation: here could be found an intimacy deeper than that between whites. In these writings, especially those written by ideologues in the southern United States, the word *love* takes on bizarre connotations: in its most intense manifestations, the idea of love depends on a relation of domination that is enacted best in bondage. Even after the Nat Turner rebellion, when slavery—its nature, continuation, or redefinition—was being debated in the Virginia legislature during January and February of 1832, some polemicists defended servitude by appealing to special precincts of feeling reserved for masters and slaves. Love is made better when what you love is what you own, whether slave or wife. Here is George Fitzhugh, writing in 1850 what would become part of his acclaimed *Sociology for the South*; he gives his readers some sense of the tight weave of dependency invoked by women, children, and blacks:

A state of dependence is the only condition in which reciprocal affection can exist among human beings. . . . A man loves his children because they are weak, helpless and dependent. He loves his wife for similar reasons. When his children grow up and assert their independence, he is apt to transfer his attention to his grandchildren. He ceases to love his wife when she becomes masculine or rebellious; but slaves are always dependent, never the rivals of their master.[10]

Being master or mistress was so addictive a pleasure that the slave as ultimate possession became a necessary part of the master's or mistress's identity, but the very terms of exclusivity or control, once proclaimed and repeated, were further confounded by the facts of slavery. The myth of affectionate service, whether domestic affection or domesticized servitude, what Edgar Allan Poe called "affectionate appropriation" ("the habitual use of the word 'my'"), undergirds much of nineteenth-century literature: "That is an easy transition by which he who is taught to call the little negro 'his,' in this sense and *because he loves him,* shall love him *because he is his.*"[11] Not only do you love most what you own, but you own what you love. Poe, unlike his fellow Southerners George Fitzhugh, Thomas Dew, or Beverley Tucker, is not simply speaking of desirable submission; he is busy making convertible love and possession.

Fictions of sentiment and idealizations of love are linked in unsettling ways to the social realities of property and possession. From Caleb Williams's anguished and ambiguous declaration to Falkland, "Sir, I could die to serve you!" to Jane Eyre's "I'd give my life to serve you," to the paradoxical Bartleby, who quite literally dies to serve while refusing to, readers who thought they could escape into fictions found themselves treated to historically accurate scenes of mastery and servitude. Even the supernatural in many gothic tales had its real basis in the language of slavery and colonization, put forth as the most natural thing in the world. One has only to read the 1685 *Code Noir* (Black Code) to understand how what first seems phantasmagoric is locked into a nature mangled and relived as a spectacle of servitude. As I will argue, its surreal precisions in human reduction (how best to turn a man into a thing), like Edward Long's anatomical permutations on monkey, man, horse, and negro in his *History of Jamaica* (1774), demonstrate how unnatural the claims to right and property had to be.

The most compelling nineteenth-century fictions—for example, Poe's "love" stories, the Brontës' *Wuthering Heights* and *Jane Eyre,* and Herman Melville's *Pierre*—are bent on proving how the language of romance can animate and sustain utter servility. What Beverley Tucker called "the law of love" depended absolutely on the existence of human property. The rare and special love between slave and master, based on the bond of property, becomes the medium by which perfect submission becomes equivalent to a pure (if perverse) love. And sentiment, as Poe confirmed in "The Black Cat," is not only coercive but despotic. A slave, a black pet, a white wife, once loved in the proper domestic setting, exacts a bond that, as Captain Delano in Melville's *Benito Cereno* confessed, is not possible between two equals.

If we begin to reread unnatural fictions as bound to the natural histories that were so much a part of their origination, inexplicable fantasies (or supernatural events) become quite intelligible. Conversely, local historiography—like Hassal/Sansay's *Secret History; or, The Horrors of St. Domingo*—becomes a harrowing myth of the Americas. There is a curious way in which women, animals, and blacks work together in these histories to foment an unsettling ambiguity in what these writers have claimed is perfectly clear. I have turned briefly to literary conflations of romance and service, since the natural histories of the Caribbean, like gothic romances, are most jarring when love is invoked or sentiment is addressed in terms of or because of enslavement.

For some writers, the "nature" of the black depended for its clarification on the difference between being a *feeling* and a *thinking* thing. Buffon describes blacks as "naturally compassionate and tender," and Long discusses at length the "courteous, tender disposition" of the orangutan, the animal in his scale of being—a scale that runs from brute matter ("a lump of dirt") to man—that most closely resembles the black.[12] Some settler-historians—for example, William Beckford, Jr. (not the Beckford of Fonthill, author of *Vathek*)—granted the black feeling, but only in the present tense. As he writes in his 1788 *Remarks upon the Situation of the Negroes in Jamaica,* arguing against emancipation in the West Indies: "A slave has no feeling beyond the present hour, no anticipation of what may come, no dejection at what may ensue: these privileges are reserved for the enlightened."[13]

Yet even those who granted feeling and a peculiarly sensuous spiritual dispensation to blacks became mired in contradictions when they tried to explain the nature or depth of feeling in slaves. The rigors of classification became blurred when turned upon humans who had to remain things if they were to continue as subjects of legal bondage. Jefferson, who considered Saint-Domingue the appropriate place to send southern blacks (describing it as a sinkhole fit to receive the contaminants of his America), in his *Notes on the State of Virginia* (1785) demonstrated how perplexing enlightened discourse can become when trying to separate humanity from animality, civility from barbarism.

In *Notes,* Jefferson explains the permutations of romance and race.

Blacks "are more ardent after their female: but love seems with them to be more an eager desire, than a tender delicate mixture of sentiment and sensation." In his manuscript the phrase originally read: "but love is with them only an eager desire, not a tender delicate excitement, not a delicious foment of the soul." He has substituted a general, more abstract definition for what was before an expression dangerously close to what he had construed as specifically black ardor. The more rarefied composite of sentiment and sensation replaces what had implied a source for assumptions of white refinement in a masking or misrepresenting of what has no color: "excitement" and "delicious foment of the soul."[14] The artificial demarcations of color and character slide perilously into indistinctness. So, when Jefferson turns again to love, it is to prove that blacks like Phyllis Wheatley cannot write poetry. Explaining that "love is the peculiar œstrum of the poet," he grants blacks love, but then redefines it, in order to show, as did Bryan Edwards, that they love differently from whites. "Their love is ardent, but it kindles the senses only, not the imagination." When Jefferson considers Ignatius Sancho's letters, he grants him more heart than head, but he does grant him imagination, though he is careful to stress its limitations: "his imagination is wild and extravagant . . . we find him always substituting sentiment for demonstration."[15]

For Long, in his *History of Jamaica,* blacks, excluded from the rest of mankind, were the signal for a particular kind of exaltation. From degradation, from "mere inert matter" we ascend "into the animal and vegetable kingdoms," until finally we proceed "from analogy" to "matter endued with thought and reason!" What is most striking and most infamous in Long's meditation is that the word *negro* calls up a minute analysis of body parts and "infinitely graduated" differences in "animate beings," until finally he draws an analogy between the negro and the orangutan, whose brain is "meer matter alone," unanimated with a thinking principle.[16] But what has not been examined is how black women and monkeys are used by Long further to debase the black man. Sex is the issue.

Elsa Goveia has eloquently argued that Long attempted to create an Africa he had never before seen, "to elaborate a 'pseudo-Africa'": "this was the Africa of pro-slavery apologists, a country of unspeakable barbarity and terror, by contrast with which the West Indies could be represented as a virtual Paradise."[17] In order to make this false Paradise out of the plantation Hell, Long would create hypothetical scenes of forbidden coupling situated somewhere in Africa. Long tells his readers that orangutans "sometimes endeavour to surprize and carry off Negroe women into their woody retreats, in order to enjoy them." A few pages later, he reflects, "Ludicrous as the opinion may seem, I do not think that an oran-outang husband would be any dishonour to an Hottentot female." Who are the Hottentots? They are "a people certainly very stupid, and very brutal . . . more like beasts than men . . . short and thick-set; their noses flat, like those of a Dutch dog."

From the tenderness and attachment of the orangutan for his orangutan mate, who, "dejected in captivity," in "heart-felt affliction" does not survive the death of a loved one, to Hottentot lust, Long moves unerringly toward "the negro," who *might* rise in the scale of intellect to the degree that he moves beyond "brute creation." But in these pages, Long never grants the black race feeling or attachment. As with Jefferson's straying into the murky precincts of romance, what is unsaid carries a great deal of weight, for all that remains in the portrait is "corporeal sensation," until Long gets back to the scene of sex: "they are libidinous and shameless as monkies, or baboons." Women, described now as negro, not Hottentot, again carry the burden of lasciviousness. No longer asking whether or not the female would accept an ape for a husband, Long assures us that these "hot" negro women frequently seek out these animals to "embrace":

An example of this intercourse once happened, I think, in England; and if lust can prompt to such excesses in that Northern region, and in despight of all the checks which national politeness and refined sentiments impose, how freely may it not operate in the more genial soil of Afric, that parent of every thing that is monstrous in nature, where these creatures are frequent and familiar; where the passions rage without any controul; and the retired wilderness presents opportunity to gratify them without fear of detection![18]

In his *Notes on the State of Virginia*, Jefferson suggests how blacks, given the chance, would choose the white race, here offered as the blushing belle, as preferable to "that immoveable veil of black which covers all the emotions of the other race." Then, reasoning by analogy, he states "the preference of the Oran-ootan for the black women over those of his own species."[19] Whereas Jefferson suggests that black men long for white women (though he only implies, never states, the sexual myth), as orangutan males long for black women, Long never allows the white race to figure in his fantasy of brutalization. For Long, such provocative bestiality was off limits when conjuring representations of white masters and mistresses.

But in Saint-Domingue, however, the lusts and lapses of whites appear as often in discussions of sexuality, pleasure, and abandon as in antebellum writings of the South. *Love* becomes as hazardous a term to apply to whites as it was when used for blacks in Long and Edwards. Recall Hassal/Sansay's accounts of women driven mad by jealousy, of unfaithful wives and despised husbands. Debauched masters, "cloyed with Possession," freed their female slaves; thinking about what to call this relation between master and servant, Lieutenant Thomas Phipps Howard definitively concludes: "I'll not say Love, for that would be disgracing the Passion, but all powerful Passion itself frequently leads a Master to Emancipate his handsome female Slaves."[20]

Pierre de Vassière laments in *Saint-Domingue: La Société et la vie créoles sous l'ancien régime* that women married too often: "Even among honorable women themselves, the frequency of second marriages attests to the imperious necessity of love. Second marriage? I should say third, fourth, fifth, sixth, seventh."[21] Others complained that among townsmen and planters, there were too few marriages, since there were so few "white" women. When men did marry, they made bizarre unions. Old colonists, worn out from debauchery, took into their beds less-moneyed young girls, offering them luxury and a blasé heart. Love came in all different guises: scorned as lust, passed over as libertinage, or dismissed as an impossibility. We get glimpses of black and mulatto women who nursed French soldiers dying of yellow fever in the last years of Saint-Domingue; black women rebels who did not hesitate to die for liberty; mulatto beauties who lived for pleasure (while, according to Moreau de Saint-Méry, avenging their degradation in the arms of their white lovers); jealous white Creole women whose fury knew no bounds.

The greed of those who came to make quick fortunes in Saint-Domingue and then return to France ended up making all experience, even amatory, subordinate to the lure of money and property. Baron de Wimpffen, shocked by the conflation of avarice and pleasure, suggests that colonists not only turned blacks into property, but commodified all relations, whether black or white.

Avarice has even extended its power over the pleasures of love; for just as a servant-maid in Europe asks her mistress's permission to walk out, so a negro woman here, asks leave to go and sleep with such or such a white: and she is obliged, in many houses, to pay her mistress a certain sum out of the produce of her nocturnal labours.

He adds that if, out of "decency," a white mistress refused permission, she would be accused of being a "bad economist."[22]

The pursuit of luxury and pleasure, as Moreau de Saint-Méry

had demonstrated in *Description . . . de la partie française de l'Isle Saint-Domingue,* infected white Creole men and women, and free coloreds, especially the mulatto courtesan, whose consummate sensuality knew no bounds. For Moreau, the lack of morality made the word *love* nothing more than a glittering husk, a cliché that masked the transactions that really mattered in the colony: money, sexual intrigue, and despotic display.

Wimpffen devotes one letter in his *Voyage to Saint Domingo,* written on the eve of the French Revolution, to the way avarice works in the colony to reduce everyone, regardless of color, to the same level. He begins by comparing "the inhabitants of our colonies" to the soldiers with whom Alexander overran Persia: "The conquerors have assumed the manners of the conquered. The colonists have preferred the disgrace of adopting those of the slaves to the merit of giving them better." When conquerors turn into their conquered, conquest is a dubious proposition. Wimpffen suggests the perils of domination that nineteenth-century tales of terror and conversion would make clear. The forbidden complicities portrayed in most gothic fiction find their source in enslavement or bondage. In a bind of covert mutuality, where masters become slaves and slaves, masters—the reversible world Hegel would later describe—the proprietor becomes possessed by his possession.

The overweening desire for property turned whites into nothing but procurers. Calling the white colonists "Rivals of the son of Alcmene" (rivals, that is, of Hercules), Wimpffen advises them to imitate the hero's labors or to show industry like that which "gave the good old Danaus fifty grand-children!" Danaus's daughters, persuaded to marry their cousins, the sons of Aegyptus, become for Wimpffen metaphors for the women of color sold to white Dominguans. Yet, implicit in this complex analogy is a story of revenge. On the wedding night, each daughter lopped off her husband's head. After that, Danaus had a hard time finding them new husbands, so he offered them as prizes in a footrace.[23] Legend has it that the daughters slept with their husbands before killing them, and the heirs were part of Danaus's domain. Could Wimpffen be implying that sexual rapacity in Saint-Domingue will put an end to whites, as the mulatto heirs endure? (This color conquest will be echoed by Shreve in the conclusion of William Faulkner's *Absalom, Absalom!*)

Although comments on the "peculiar nature" of blacks were well known during this time of brutality in the service of economic gain, the unnatural nature of the whites who dabbled in human flesh and lived off protracted dehumanization rarely got the attention Wimpffen grants. Wimpffen describes "girls" (usually black women) with "the smallest pretensions to beauty" who can "excite, amongst the unmarried whites, an admiration which assures them a price impossible to ascertain, since it is love, and what is more, self-love, which determines it." In Le Cap and the other port towns, he adds, whites and free coloreds "make a great deal of money, merely by letting out their male or female negroes."[24] Wimpffen does not say whether these negroes are rented to white women, to white men, or to both. The sexual needs of white women are silenced in natural histories that depend for their acceptability on representations of pairings of white men and black women; other, more forbidden arrangements are kept hidden: for example, generally speaking, white women and black men, white women and black women.

For a moment, let us reflect on Wimpffen's move from love to self-love, for it is crucial to the dehumanization exacted by the colonial enterprise, in which reproduction is capital gain, love is self-promotion, and bastardy is a lucrative speculation. Wimpffen is most shocked by the way the "Genius of commerce" has somehow become synonymous with, even dependent upon sexual pleasure. To my earlier query about how a slave, a piece of property, becomes an object of love, Wimpffen suggests a response. If whites sell or "let out" their black men and women to other whites for purposes of pleasure, then the relationship that matters is that between the whites: their exchange of money over the black body. Love becomes self-love when the seller makes money from his object and the buyer pays for his pleasure. Both get something from the transaction, but not without some attachment to the human property. As women are bought they become valuable; but the real power and self-recognition belongs to the white who owns the property and sells it to another white who desires the property.

In *The Philosophy of Money* (1900), Georg Simmel gets at the additive, and addictive, power of possession:

It has been stated that possession universally engenders love of possessing. One not only makes sacrifices for what one loves, but also one loves that for which one has made sacrifices.[25]

We are talking about an accumulative relation whereby the beloved piece of property accrues value as the lover sacrifices for it. Simmel refers to the love of a husband for his wife, but Wimpffen focuses on the way self-love depends on ownership, which validates not only the owner, but—if he chooses, say, to sell what he owns in the flesh market of Saint-Domingue—also validates the buyer. In a Swiftian parable of commodification and lust, Wimpffen pushes further the possibilities of sex for profit, the collective reproduction of humans of color. He expresses surprise that with all these resources no "ingenious speculator" has thought to "monopolize, under the name of *Etalon Banal,* Colonial Stallion, the fabrication of all the people of colour at so much a head"; and he concludes with a swipe at metropolitan cupidity, the imperial *Exclusif,* and the economic subordination it entailed:

Perhaps they are afraid lest the Chamber of Commerce should take advantage of the luminous idea, and add to their other *exclusive privileges,* that of manufacturing the human race. I do not think their fears are altogether without foundation, for there would be no more injustice in preventing the colonists from begetting their own children, than in prohibiting them from refining their own sugar, or spinning their own cotton![26]

The Black Code

In one of his last letters from Saint-Domingue, Wimpffen envisions his departure from Saint-Domingue for Philadelphia as a passage from "the flames of purgatory to the joys of Paradise."[27] Not only did he lament the greed, waste, and sham luxury of the society, but he was shocked by its dubious claims of white supremacy, its vilification of color, and, most of all, by the overwhelming presence of living capital: blacks. The letters that deal exclusively with slaves betray a racism that seems to emerge from his discomfort at the sight of so much flesh, even though black, reduced to so much matter. In a world so fallen, so contrary to nature, his only way out of the rampant perversion of "universal reason" was to assume that there was some justification for the subordination of blacks, some flaw in *their* nature. Eventually he converts blacks into a new kind of demon. The transformation is significant, for it demonstrates the inescapable logic he called upon when confronted with blacks and not, as in his references to Danaus's daughters or the "Colonial Stallion," the behavior of whites. Wimpffen's slaves are rendered as if curiously devoid of will, and their servility becomes, in his fabrication, tantamount to a cardinal sin—a sin not of pride but of passivity.

The legal and actual embodying of the black as merely material—

as the body that has no mind—disconcerted some outside observers, who did not like to acknowledge the source of metropolitan polish and prosperity to be the colonies and chattels they had themselves ordained. Wimpffen's discomfort leads him to two bizarre meditations on the nature of blacks. Thinking that the striking number of slave deaths represents a substantial capital loss for planters, he develops a theory. Some kind of inner contamination, a rottenness of blood, causes disease and keeps wounds from healing. He surmises that the black is an infected vessel, ripe for degeneration. What he calls "this original vice" overshadows the masters' tortures, overwork, lack of nourishment, and the other possible external cause he mentions, "change of climate."

Owing either to a habit of body, naturally bad, or to an unwholesome regimen, the mass of their blood is so corrupt, that the slightest scratch soon degenerates into a most dangerous wound. If to this original vice, we add the infirmities they necessarily contract in the middle passage; where they are crowded for months together, like sheep at a fair . . . we shall not be astonished to find that, cruelly treated at the slightest symptom of impatience, wretchedly fed, wasted by chagrin, and devoured by rage, whole cargoes of these unhappy beings perish before they reach the shores where they are doomed to be sold; and where the greatest part of them, persuaded that they would not be bought like flesh in a market, if they were not intended to serve for the same use, firmly believe they are destined to be eaten.[28]

Bad blood, a tinge of Calvinist innate depravity, and a fable of cannibalism combine to offer an explanation for the shocking fact, mentioned by most observers, that in spite of the increasing import of slaves in the late eighteenth century, their numbers in Saint-Domingue steadily declined. Since 1680, according to Hilliard d'Auberteuil, more than 800,000 negroes were brought to Saint-Domingue; by 1776 there were only 290,000. For him, the death of more than one-third of the Africans brought to the colony in their first few years was caused not by illness within, but by the tyranny of masters.[29]

In his version of the myth of the lazy native, Wimpffen diverts the reader from the degradation of slaves, who "contract," as Hilliard d'Auberteuil puts it, "an infinity of vices because of servitude that they did not have in their natural state."[30]

When the negro has eaten his banana he goes to sleep—and though a hurricane destroy the hopes of the planter; though fire consume the buildings erected at a vast expense; though subterraneous commotions engulf whole cities; though the scourge of war spread devastation over our plains, or strew the ocean with the wrecks of our scattered fleets—what is all this to him! Enveloped in his blanket, and tranquilly seated on the ruins, he sees with the same eye, the smoke which exhales from his pipe, and the torrents of flame which devour the prospects of a whole generation![31]

This focus on the easy pleasures of eating a banana will be carried further in Thomas Carlyle's "The Nigger Question," where the banana is replaced by a surfeit of pumpkins.[32] Wimpffen's fantasy of the negro calmly surveying a sequence of calamities ignores the effects of coercion. What meaning could these events have for the black bought and sold as property, who owns nothing, not his body or his labor? Why should this slave, reduced by terror and regulated by force, feel sorrow for the hopes, buildings, cities, or plains of the planter?

But let us consider the most exalted commerce, not Wimpffen's selling the services of the Colonial Stallion, but the slave trade that made the French West Indies so lucrative that pro-slavery ideologues could claim that to interfere with slavery or the trade was to threaten the prosperity of France, if not to destroy the fortunes of cities like Nantes and Boston. As a merchant in Nantes declared: "What commerce could be compared to one which results in obtaining men in exchange for merchandise?"[33] He could have argued conversely and had the best of both worlds: what could be better than getting goods in exchange for men? Saint-Domingue was the unsurpassed "market of the New World." By 1787 the colony produced 131,000,000 pounds of sugar and 70,000 pounds of indigo, and in 1788 it legally imported 29,506 slaves.[34]

In March 1685 at Versailles, Louis XIV, the Sun King, presided over the completion of what would be his minister Jean-Baptiste Colbert's greatest creation: the *Code Noir* or *Edict Regarding the Government and the Administration of the French Islands of America, and the Discipline and the Commerce of Blacks and Slaves in the Said Countries.* Twenty years earlier, Colbert had formed the Compagnie des Indes (Company of the West Indies), which sent French slavers into Africa, shipped Africans to the Americas, and returned to France with coffee, sugar, and tobacco. The Black Code, the most barbaric product of the Enlightenment, was ignored by the philosophes and later forgotten— or, more precisely, never mentioned. This discourse on methodical dispossession, a logic of conversion more horrific than the threat of damnation, has been relegated to the bowels of white thought, like the Furies hidden beneath Athens so that the city could be born. The

Black Code provides the context for understanding the "humanitarianism" of the "Amis des noirs" and of Montesquieu and Rousseau. Had they allowed this French code of laws into their reflections on servitude, slavery, and nature, it would have made a mockery of their highest truths.[35]

In three hundred years the Black Code has never been published in English, but, more significant, as Louis Sala-Molins reminds his French readers, "the worst refinement in wickedness, the most glacial technicality in the commerce of human flesh and in genocide" remains so difficult to find that it has vanished from historiography. "One knows about the slave trade. Also of its 'abolition' in 1794. Of its 'restoration' in 1802, somewhat less. But of the existence of a specific codification of what was abolished, then restored, not a trace in the common mind."[36] Yet the Code existed as a puzzle, an anomaly, even in the colonies for which it had been especially constructed. Though Colbert was influenced to some extent by the concepts of Roman canon law, he based most of the Code on existing local slave laws and on consultations with French colonial authorities. The Code granted official recognition to an institution that had functioned for half a century without the king's seal; and while it was ostensibly written to protect the planter's property, while denying the slaves' humanity, the Creole whites conspired to make it a dead letter from the moment of its emergence. Wimpffen goes so far as to claim that the royal authorities (governor and intendant), as well as the local councils, "have not, to this day, succeeded in causing a single article of the CODE NOIR to be put in force."[37]

Planters cooperated with the king's ordinances only if they did not oppose the planters' customs and interests. Any slave who availed himself of the Code's legal protection was summarily punished for his presumption. Numerous accounts—including those by Vassière and Hilliard d'Auberteuil, and especially Moreau de Saint-Méry's six-volume *Lois et constitutions des colonies françaises de l'Amérique sous le Vent, de 1550 à 1785* (1784–1790) and Lucien Peytraud's monumental *L'Esclavage aux Antilles françaises avant 1789* (1897)—testify that in no instance was a black slave in Saint-Domingue helped by laws or regulations emanating from France.[38] Hilliard d'Auberteuil complains of this divorce of law from historical reality, the gap between legal prescriptions and practice:

The Negroes of the French colonies are bound by the penal Code, and judged according to criminal regulations; the Edict of 1685 regulates the punishment that their masters can inflict on them, and establishes a kind of ratio between offense and punishment; but that does not stop Negroes from dying daily in chains, or under the whip; from being starved, smothered, burned without ceremony: so much cruelty always remains unpunished, and those who exercise it are ordinarily scoundrels or persons born in the gutter of European cities; the vilest men are also the most barbarous.[39]

Hilliard d'Auberteuil, however, would find that in Saint-Domingue whites knew when and whom to punish. Suspected of planning to write a report in favor of the *sang-mêlés* (mixed-bloods), he was arrested and imprisoned for two months in Port-au-Prince sometime in 1786, and then released to die. As radical critic of the colonial regime and liberal supporter of slavery (with reservations), Hilliard d'Auberteuil blamed inefficient government on metropolitan greed and protectionism, as well as Creole ruthlessness and irresponsibility. As hated and feared by authorities in Paris as in the colony, he was suspected of discrediting authority and was pursued by officers of the king. His *Considérations sur l'état présent de la colonie française de Saint-Domingue* was suppressed by an edict of Louis XVI.[40]

The Black Code is a document of limits. Unlike the racist disquisitions that point to blacks as lacking the finer feelings of a tender heart, the Code is not concerned with the tangled semantics of charitable servitude, lurking debauchery, or the blacks' proclivities that come perilously close to romance. We read instead sixty articles that take us into a chilling series of qualifications: prohibitions that permit, limitations that invite excess, and a king's grandiloquence that ensures divestment. There is no time in the Code for discussions of innate inferiority, natural difference, or nightmares of contamination. The blacks and slaves in French America are introduced not as persons but as a special kind of property: a "thing," according to Roman law, juridically deprived of all rights. Legally, their being was "a being-for-others," and their civil status, that of things.[41]

Slaves, legally divested of their selfhood and removed from their land, became the possessions of the planters who bought them. Alternately defined as chattel and as real property, they were sometimes movable assets (part of the planter's personal estate) and sometimes immovable, disposed of as if real estate, or in some especially macabre cases, as if garbage. What is remarkable about this text is its language. Existing only as precepts and never in practice, the Black Code can be read as a philosophy of denaturalization or, to put it another way, the natural successor to René Descartes's *Discourse on Method* and

Meditations concerning First Philosophy. It is the nasty belch that follows a meal of pure thought.[42]

The thinker of Descartes' *Meditations* in 1640 sets the stage for the 1685 edict of Louis XIV. These two texts show how the making of enlightenment man led to the demolition of the unenlightened brute, how the thinking mind's destructive or generative proclivities dominated a passive nature or servile body. Descartes sits by the fire. He dismembers himself. He plays with asking what remains if he takes off his ears, his arms, removes all his senses in his urgency to know what constitutes his identity. "Although the whole mind seems to be united to the whole body, I recognize that if a foot or arm or any other part of the body is cut off, nothing has thereby been taken away from the mind."[43] The mutilation only aggrandizes this *I* that needs no senses and no body. Listen to Descartes's elation: "Thinking? At last I have discovered it—thought; this alone is inseparable from me. . . . I am, then, in the strict sense only a thing that thinks; that is, I am a mind, or intelligence, or intellect, or reason—words whose meaning I have been ignorant of until now. But for all that I am a thing which is real and which truly exists. But what kind of a thing? As I have just said—a thinking thing." Descartes sloughs off surfeit matter to get at essential mind. What, then, does this thing do? The answer will be crucial to the assumptions that underlie the judicial regulation of blacks in the colonies. "It is a thing which doubts, understands, conceives, affirms, denies, wills, refuses, which also imagines and feels."[44]

Once you establish who is rational man, you can ascertain what is not. Descartes's methodical but metaphoric dispossession becomes the basis for the literal expropriation and dehumanization necessary to turn a man into a thing. What is this thing that does *not* think or feel, and *cannot* will, refuse, deny, or imagine? The Black Code responds by inventing the slave, whose only rights and duties—except for the terribly ambiguous liberation of the soul in baptism—are those shared in society by beasts and objects. They are the reclaimed remnants of what Descartes has cast off: the "pieces of the Indies" or "ebony wood" found in Africa, bought, bartered, and sold, and then figured as heads of cattle, coins, parcels of land, pieces of furniture. Think about the legality of dismemberment. Since slaves are construed as things without thought, then no amount of amputation, torture, or disfiguring can matter. The rules for controlling slaves in the colonies depended on the enlightenment strategy by which humans ruled the universe of things, including, through a fantasy of reification, slaves. Descartes's experiment with himself to establish the idea of the white universal subject is thus recovered as a collective experiment to legally produce black nonpersons in the New World.

The passage out of Africa and into the islands of America called for two kinds of stories: first, those that would create a servile body, unfit, incapable, and destitute; and then, those that would promise salvation through conversion to Christianity, which liberated the soul and gave the true God to the blacks. Degenerate but redeemable, brutalized but perfectible, blacks were afforded the boon of baptism along with the judicial destitution of the Black Code. The slave is recognized as having a will only insofar as it is perverted. The king, in his godlike reason, declares his concern for infinite perversion, for "all the people which Divine Providence has under our obedience." The first eight articles of the Code establish the only true religion to be "Apostolic, Roman, and Catholic," demand that slaves must be baptized and instructed in this religion, and forbid the practice of any other religion. In addition, they expel all Jews from the French islands and validate only the marriages of Catholics (all others will be considered to be living in "true concubinage," and their children bastards).

Like other regulations in the Black Code, the gracious dispensation of baptism and conversion was a theory that did not change practice. Though the period prior to 1685 was the most active for missionaries, by 1758 the Church was in obvious decline. Numerous are the accounts of the way the needs of the market and the dependence on enslaved bodies replaced the desire to evangelize souls.[45] Even in 1685, because of the mix of Saint-Domingue society—a few regular planters, plus buccaneers, noblemen, filibusters, adventurers, indentured white workers, and slaves—the various orders (Carmelites, Dominicans, Capuchins, and Jesuits), as well as the secular clergy, were not as successful as they had been on the other French islands. Furthermore, note that when the Code was issued, Saint-Domingue had not yet been officially recognized as French territory; French claims were authenticated with the Treaty of Ryswick in 1697. Few planters arranged for the religious instruction of their slaves, and the "conversion" of many adults consisted only of baptism and renaming. The provisions calling for baptism and instruction of slaves that begin the Code did not in any way alter the condition of slavery. As slave populations increased, along with the profits from sugar, coffee, and cotton, anticlerical opinions intensified, leading to the expulsion of the Jesuits in

1763. Vassière gives us a sense of the religiosity prevailing among whites in Le Cap: "The sacraments were ignored, and parents left their children unchristened or mockingly baptized them in a punch-bowl."[46]

Père Jean-Baptiste Labat, a missionary to the Antilles in the service of Louis XIV, caught a black from a neighboring plantation calling upon an idol for another slave who had fallen ill. Here is Labat's description of penitential discipline: "I tied up the sorcerer, and I dealt out around three hundred lashes of the whip that flayed him from the shoulders to the knees. He cried out in despair, and our negroes asked me to have mercy on him, but I told them that sorcerers did not feel pain, and that he cried in order to mock me."[47] Because slaves were legally "things," they needed to be protected by the same magisterial and pious code that legitimated that degradation; because they were also human, slaves must be cared for; and because, individually, they had will and tenacity, they had to be terrorized, or "contained," as numerous judgments put it, if the society were to survive.

Père Labat's flagellation of the "sorcerer" exemplifies the horrendous care visited upon slaves. What should concern us more than the whip is the dreadful "cure": After once again flogging the "devil," Labat puts him in irons, but not until he has washed him with a *pimentade,* a "pickling brine in which you crush red pepper and citrons." Labat explains that it caused "a horrible pain to the places that the whip had flayed, but it is a certain cure for gangrene that inevitably comes from these wounds."[48] Some accounts that focus on the application of salt, pepper, cinders, or lemon juice to open wounds maintain that it was done, in one historian's words, "under the pretext of cauterizing the skin, while at the same time increasing the torture."[49] Though torture was no doubt the effect of these remedies, they were absolutely necessary in order to preserve the human merchandise that brought such profits to masters. This specific kind of concern, and the reasons for it, are themselves more telling than any mere punishment, however horrible. In the specific kind of reduction and evisceration of humans outlined in the Code, nothing, not even "kindness," can alleviate the slave's condition. This is the terror.

You harm, and then you alleviate the harm you have caused: the executioner also gets to be the savior; the benevolence continues the brutalization, while claiming otherwise. Nowhere does this disempowering become so clear as in the articles concerning manumission (*affranchisement*). The white man gives in order to take away. First, freed slaves are granted "the advantages of our natural subjects in our kingdom, lands, and countries paying us obeissance" (article 57), then the obedience is qualified and made unique:

We commend all freed persons of color to carry a singular respect toward their former Masters and their Children so that should the freed persons of color cause them any injury they shall be punished more gravely than if the injury were done to someone else or by someone else. (article 58)

The Code thus sets up quite clearly what will be spelled out in the later edicts concerning the rights of those persons wearing the tag of "acquired liberty." The more you appear to get ("the advantages of our natural subjects"), the more you must be reduced (even after you are freed, you are still a denatured object of judicial largesse and liable to be punished with special severity if you "cause any injury" to your master or his family). At least as far as the Code intends, the gift and goodwill of the master simply ensures his continued mastery.[50]

Bryan Edwards understood the kind of order the institution of slavery demanded: "In countries where slavery is established, the leading principle on which the government is supported is fear: or a sense of that absolute coercive necessity which, leaving no choice of action, supersedes all questions of right. It is vain to deny that such actually is, and necessarily must be, the case in all countries where slavery is allowed."[51] Though the official policy of the Code was to set limits to brutality, to curb tortures, its strange logic not only allowed planters to hide behind legality, but, as I will demonstrate, its gradation of sufferings and, most of all, its guise of care are themselves a fiction. Let us now see how the Code's most rational language makes no sense, how the commitment to protection becomes a guarantee of tyranny.

Deprivation and exclusion are the basis of the Black Code: an abandonment or removal ever more severe in those articles (22–29) that "oblige" the master to feed, house, and clothe his slaves. Excessive rigor and excessive kindness work together to reduce more surely what is most "human" about the slave. First, however, let us examine articles 18 through 21. These rules set up the fundamental distinction between "subject" and "slave." As strategies for circumscribing the details of the slave's daily life, they limited movement and prohibited access to products, earnings, or savings. Though usually unsuccessful, these laws were designed to destroy the slave's initiative.

At the time the Code was written, sugar from Saint-Domingue was not yet the extraordinary commodity for export it would become. Though plantations had been established in Martinique and

Guadeloupe, no cane plantation would exist in Saint-Domingue until 1690. By 1789, however, eight hundred plantations produced 143,000,000 pounds of sugar, nearly as much as all the British Caribbean islands.[52] According to the 1687 census, two years after the royal edict, there were only 3,358 slaves to 4,411 whites in Saint-Domingue.[53] As we have seen, the number of slaves would increase in the last years of the Old Regime to about 500,000, as opposed to 40,000 whites. To control this far from servile black majority, the planters demanded more blatant policing and prohibitive measures. Yet the Code of 1685 already provides the machinery by which rational French law, through a series of exceptions, could decree both servile animality and the despotism necessary to enforce it.

Though their labor produced the sugarcane, slaves were prohibited from selling it for any reason or at any time (article 18). To make sure that slaves had no access to what they produced and could not intervene in the commerce that was the reason for their enslavement, they could not even "display for sale at a market or . . . carry to specified houses with a view to selling any kind of commodity, either fruits, vegetables, wood, fodder for the feeding of animals, and manufactured items without the express permission of their Masters" (article 19). Since most planters gave their slaves small plots of land, called provision grounds, which they could work on their own time, this prohibition means that slaves can earn nothing masters do not give them.[54] Produce and merchandise had to be examined by officers at the market, and slaves were to be issued passes when they went to market or to be given other visible proofs by their master showing that they transported the items they carried with their master's permission (articles 19–20). Lacking the latter, "subjects" could seize the items carried by "slaves" (article 21).

The meaning of emptying commodities of their exchange value when in the hands of slaves becomes clearer if we reflect on the relation between production and denial. The master can deny the slave control of his body, owning him physically, affectively, and even nutritionally. If the slave must be hungry, let him at least hunger within limits. The weekly nourishment prescribed for slaves between the ages of ten and sixty amounted to "two and a half pots of manioc flour, or three cassavas each, weighing at least two and one-half pounds, or other equivalent staples, with two pounds of salted beef or three pounds of fish or other items in similar amounts" (article 22). The master then gets the most out of the human he has deprived in order to get him to produce things for the white subjects of French law. Having no right to buy and sell what they produce for themselves, and in many cases deprived of sufficient food by their master, slaves were given alcohol made from the very sugarcane they could not sell. The rum produced by the labor of slaves becomes a way for the colonist to subjugate the slave under the pretext of magnanimity. And magisterial law steps in again. "We prohibit the Masters from giving the Slaves alcohol made from sugarcane [rum, called *rossoli* or *guildives*], which is supposed to take the place of the items mentioned in article 22" (article 23).

Not only are masters enjoined to feed and house their slaves, but they must also clothe them. Given the emphasis on colonial luxury and ostentation in most accounts by outsiders, this article reveals how deprivation is recast as sustenance, or how literally divesting blacks guarantees the investment in slaves. The more miserable and derelict slaves appeared, the more they reflected the white symbolic system. "The Masters shall be required to provide each Slave annually, two outfits of linen or four bolts of cloth at the convenience of the Masters" (article 25). As descriptions of slaves in Saint-Domingue in the 1780s revealed, there were many variations in slave dress, depending on whether one was a field slave or held a more privileged position as an artisan (carpenter, mason, logger, or keeper of animals) or a domestic. Indeed, domestics were often turned into objects that displayed their master's extravagance; their embellishment signaled the glut of wealth on the plantation. In dress, as in food, slaves exercised ingenuity within these limits, acquiring clothes even though they were prohibited from having any savings, or possessing anything that did not belong to their master (article 28).

The Black Code designates slaves only to negate them. Its rigorous logic does not permit the slave to play any role in the arena of law and right. Slaves exist legally only insofar as they disobey: no juridical mention is made of obedience. Recognition is granted only as a prohibition or corrective for insubordination. What about the slave's right to complain? In article 26, surely one of the strangest moments in the Code, the "thing" suddenly becomes a "subject" who can deposit his written testimony (*mémoire*) with a lawyer ("our general procurator"), a privilege which was "observed for crimes and barbarous and inhumane treatment by the masters toward their slaves." Coming as it does after the rules for clothing, food, and housing, it would seem at this point in the Code that the only "crimes" or "barbarous and inhumane treatment" of slaves involved neglect or stinginess. But no article in the Code has meaning in itself, since the subterfuge of this regulatory benevolence depends on how the articles are interrelated, how what is granted in one place is qualified in another. The concession of article 26 is undone in articles 30 and 31. Slaves can complain (article 26), but "their testimony shall only be used as a *mémoire* to help the judges clarify the matter under investigation without any presumption or conjecture or admission of proof" (article 30); "neither may they be civil parties in a criminal matter, except if their Masters act and defend them in a civil matter and prosecute them in a criminal matter" (article 31).

The Black Code was heralded as defining and prohibiting brutality. Even a perceptive historian like Sir James Barskett, whose *History of the Island of St. Domingo* (1818) was one of the most unprejudiced nineteenth-century accounts of the Haitian Revolution, praised Louis's "celebrated edict" for having "breathed a spirit of tenderness and philanthropy highly honourable to the memory of its author."[55] In the restrictions of articles 32 through 43, the power to exceed what might be considered humane lies in the unsaid—in those places where the law falls silent—or where the language is deliberately vague or hypothetical. No limits are invoked for the number of lashes a slave can receive, or for the number of hours of work that can be imposed on him. Phrases like "corporeal punishment, even death" and "let them be severely punished, even with death" were general enough to permit the severing of ears. What, then, are the kinds of punishment allowed and under what circumstances? Death for the slave who strikes his master, mistress, or the husband of his mistress (article 33). Assault and battery against free persons are "severely punished even by death if the person struck falls to the ground" (article 34). Masters were allowed to use a rod to beat or a cord to lash the slave, but they sometimes chose to use whips not authorized by the Code: the *rigoise* (a thick rope of cowhide) or *des lianes souples* (local reeds as pliant as whalebone). Masters took flagellation (dubbed *tailler nègre*, to carve or cut up a nigger) quite seriously, and numerous accounts preserve the names for the different decor or props that went along with whipping and the positions the slave to be whipped could assume: *quatre piquets* (hands and arms tied to four posts on the ground); *echelle* (tied to a ladder); *hamac* (suspended by four limbs as if on a hammock).[56]

Only Masters shall be able, when they believe their Slaves have deserved it, to chain them up and beat them with cords and rods. It is forbidden to torture or to mutilate any part of their bodies, upon pain of confiscation of the said Slaves with charges brought against the Masters under such extraordinary circumstances. (article 42)

Supposedly, quartering, hanging, burning alive, and other kinds of mutilation and torture were left to the courts. But the two articles concerning theft demonstrate how blurred or indecipherable were the Code's touted distinctions. Here, their difference is supposed to hinge on the "seriousness" of the deed.

Serious thefts, including those involving horses, mares, mules, bulls, or cows which may have been perpetrated by Slaves or Free Persons, shall be punished with personal or bodily punishment, even death if the case requires it. (article 35)

Thefts of sheep, kids, poultry, sugarcane, peas, meal, manioc, or other vegetables [or animals] kept by Slaves, shall be punished according to the quality of the theft by Judges who shall be able, if they so regard it, to condemn them to be beaten with a stick by the Executioner of High Justice and be branded with a fleur-de-lis. (article 36)

The hypothetical *if* that occurs in many of the articles also promotes the ominous leeway that is a salient feature of the Code. The laws are precarious; their interpretation and enforcement often depend on the will or whim of an often erratic master. As we saw in Moreau de Saint-Méry's account of diversions in Le Cap, some masters showed their power by bribing the police not to arrest their slaves when they were caught drinking and gambling in Le Cap.

I have been suggesting that during the Old Regime the excessive tortures and mutilations of slaves by masters, mistresses, and overseers were so frequent in spite of the Code's restrictions that, as Lucien Peytraud explains in *L'Esclavage aux Antilles françaises avant 1789,* only the most scandalous cases prompted sanctions.[57] Yet I direct us again to the Black Code, since its apparent beneficence is belied by those few places when its language becomes precise. Here, for example, is the punishment for *marronage,* or escape from servitude:

A fugitive Slave who shall have escaped for a month, counting from the day his Master denounced him to Justice, shall have his ears cut off and be branded with a fleur-de-lis on one shoulder; and if he repeats the offense for another month, counting from the first days of report to the authorities, he shall be hamstrung, and branded with a fleur-de-lis on the other shoulder; and for the third time, he shall be punished by death. (article 38)

The greatest threat to the planter's property, other than overwork, starvation, torture, and sickness, was the increasing number of runaway slaves, called *maroons,* fugitives whose flight repudiated their juridical identity as "socially dead persons" deprived of freedom.[58] And when it came to the economics of slavery, the Code is unambiguous: "We declare Slaves to be chattel and as such do they enter into the community having no consequence other than that of something mortgaged" (article 44). There is no generality in this discourse on property. The securing of profit for the metropole and assuring a supply of servile "pieces of the Indies"—bodies intact, healthy, and young enough to labor—account for the restrictions on gratuitous and excessive tortures. Torture, often a mere diversion for bored masters, was considered as destruction of property in the eyes of the law. Slaves, like animals on a farm or furniture in a house, must remain in colonies that are in turn defined as the property of France.

Sade, Lejeune, and the Manual

Shortly before July 2, 1789, the Marquis de Sade rolled up the manuscript he called *Les Cent Vingt Journées de Sodome,* written during his thirteen years in the Bastille, and hid it in a hole in the wall of his cell. We can read Sade as a literalization of the Black Code and a record of those practices that exceeded its regulations. Like Descartes's thought experiment, Sade's exercises in coercion and coition push to the limits the idea of the human. At the same time that Sade attacked the humanitarian idealism of Rousseau and the noble pathos of the whitewashed "noble savage," he revealed the truth at the heart of the traffic in slaves: not only economic gain, but the tempting and pleasurable reduction of human into thing.[59] The one living model for *The Hundred and Twenty Days of Sodom* was slavery in the French Antilles, a fact ignored by all critics of Sade. It is no accident that Sade's introduction begins with "the reign of Louis XIV," who promulgated the Black Code for the slave owners of the French Antilles: "The end of this so very sublime reign was perhaps one of the periods in the history of the French Empire when one saw the emergence of the greatest number of these mysterious fortunes whose origins are as obscure as the lust and debauchery that accompany them."[60]

Where did these mysterious fortunes originate? Where did profligate consumption reign supreme? In *Etudes sur l'histoire d'Haïti,* Beaubrun Ardouin recalled Hilliard d'Auberteuil's judgment on Saint-

Domingue: "a second Sodom, which the fires of heaven must destroy."[61] A new class of wealthy Creoles, usually absentee colonial planters, descendants perhaps of criminals, pirates, and buccaneers, ended up in France with new identities; they formed what some observers called a "Creole court" at the Versailles of Louis XVI—Marie Antoinette was wearing her loose white cotton, linen, or muslin dresses, Creole style—while the French nobility, who had been divested of power by Louis XIV and his absolute monarchy, went to Saint-Domingue to recover their fortunes and their masterly presumption.[62] Sade knew French history and was determined to strip it of glory. He was harassed and imprisoned not only for his intimate sexual acts and the pornographic outrages his fictions celebrated but because his fables also threatened to expose the dark side of "the age of lights" without the inevitable softening of humanitarian sentiment. His stories also uncovered the new blood and new profits in a doddering Old Regime. Sade brought the plantation hell and its excesses into enlightenment Europe. He no doubt read Charles de Rochefort, Père Jean Baptiste Du Tertre, Père Labat, Hilliard d'Auberteuil, and, most important, the Black Code, which was readily available in the Paris of the 1770s.

In *Juliette* (1797), the minister Saint-Fond (the name could be translated as Saint-Bottom, or rendered homonymically as Saint-Property) explains how best "the elite in substance and mind" can "load further and heavier chains upon the captive masses." It seems that Sade is writing an apologia for absolute despotism. But if we consider how Sade's cruelties carry fantasies of superiority to unspeakable extremes, we begin to appreciate the lesson of his codified inequalities, tortures, and erotics. "The common herd will be kept in a state of subservience, of prostrate bondage, which will render them powerless even to strike for, let alone attain to, domination."[63] Saint-Fond's regulations for order and lubricity echo the language of both planters and governmental ordinances that understood the brute despotism necessary for control. In 1771, the Crown delivered instructions to one of its colonial representatives which clarify the necessary reduction of humans to proprietary objects.

It is only by leaving to the masters a power that is nearly absolute, that it will be possible to keep so large a number of men in that state of submission which is made necessary by their numerical superiority over the whites. If some masters abuse their power, they must be reproved in secret, so that the slaves may always be kept in the belief that the master can do no wrong in his dealings with them.[64]

Saint-Fond's regulations for order and lubricity also depend for their logic on attitudes similar to the natural historian's gradations, from barbaric to civilized, from monkey to man, or to that popular sequence of images: chimpanzee, slave, Hottentot. Here, then, is Saint-Fond's retelling of Buffon's *Histoire naturelle,* which he seems to combine with Rousseau's *Discours sur l'inégalité.*[65]

Now perform the same study upon the animal resembling man the closest, upon, for example, the chimpanzee; let me, I say, compare this animal to some representative of the slave caste; what a host of similarities I find! The man of the people is simply the species that stands next above the chimpanzee on the ladder. . . . And why should Nature, who so assiduously observes these gradations in all her works, have neglected them here? . . . You should certainly never lump Voltaire and Fréron in the same class, any more than you would the virile Prussian grenadier and the debilitated Hottentot.[66]

Sade not only imported the plantation into the metropole, but he carried the Enlightenment, its patterns of thought, and the consequences of that reasonable uplifting (for example, the lumping together of the slave and *le peuple*) to places undreamed of by the philosophes. He then turned again to the colonies, taking the justifications of slavery in the Americas and applying them to the masses back in France. The colonial masters were embodied by dubious French aristocrats; and the plantations of the colonies were narrowed to the space of a bedroom or torture chamber. But even in Saint-Fond's blunt cruelty, distinctions between beast and human were not necessary. What mattered was the division between the powerful and the victimized. The lists of tortures Sade narrated—the dismemberment, castration, roasting, cauterizing of wounds with a red-hot iron, and, of course, flogging, all those things apparently so scandalous to readers—are no more severe (even if more elaborate) and no less Cartesian than the Black Code.

The Hundred and Twenty Days of Sodom (stolen from Sade's room in the Bastille and never returned to him), what Sade called his "impure tale," ends with a chronicle of "The 150 Complex Passions," "The 150 Criminal Passions," and "The 150 Murderous Passions," statutes that compound the particulars of the Black Code. The debauchery and unbridled tyranny of Sade's libertines have their sources in the emblematic Creole planters, dedicated to the heady interests of pleasure, greed, and abandon. To read the Black Code along with *The Hundred and Twenty Days of Sodom* is to understand that the strategies for degrading a body into mere matter—whether contained in "a novel" or "the law"—are elements of fictions that must be read as histories. Obviously, the facts disclosed in both texts are so troublesome as to have been either dismissed as pornography or, as in the case of the Black Code, simply forgotten.

Though the Code urged planters "to govern slaves as good fathers of the family," in Saint-Domingue the later royal edicts and police regulations were concerned with maintaining subordination, cracking down on slave gatherings, and punishing those free coloreds who helped escaped slaves. Previously, the *affranchi* who concealed an escaped slave on his property had to pay the slave's master a fine of three hundred pounds of sugar for each day the slave remained on the premises; now, offending free coloreds would be declared "'deprived of their freedom, and . . . sold, with their family residing with them.'"[67] As we will see in the next section of this chapter, this increased severity was accompanied by other restrictions on the increasingly wealthy and influential mulattoes. Some historians note that the terrors of slavery had somewhat ameliorated by the 1780s, but they refer to Louis XVI's interventions of 1784, 1785, and 1786 concerning the proper treatments of slaves, rather than to actual practice.[68]

"How empty was the policy of prudence, as distinct from the reality of that policy of terror," writes Gordon Lewis in *Main Currents in Caribbean Thought*. Lewis argues that, despite the supposed existence of a much-vaunted "spirit of pity" in Saint-Domingue, very few members of these enlightened or "moderate" elements could bring themselves to repudiate the system of slavery. In order to clinch his argument, he discusses the well-known trial of Nicolas Lejeune at the Superior Council of Le Cap.[69] For historians as diverse as Moreau de Saint-Méry, Pierre de Vassière, Lucien Peytraud, Antoine Gisler, C. L. R. James, and Gabriel Debien, this story is the quintessence of justice in Saint-Domingue. On the eve of the revolution in Saint-Domingue, Debien writes, the Lejeune affair demonstrated the impotence of justice in dealing with the colonial mind.[70] Flogging and burning, excessive tortures required by the thankless task of controlling the enslaved black majority, came to sound like gratuitous cruelty, an addictive pleasure. Lejeune's crimes not only gratified the perverse tastes of those guilty of such crimes, but functioned practically to distinguish masters from slaves. Moreover, Lejeune's words to the council, like the Sadean libertine's contracts, make a pact with his white listeners that makes them his accomplices: "My cause in this matter becomes the cause of every colonist."

Sometime in the middle of March 1788, Seigneur Nicolas Lejeune, a coffee planter in Plaisance—a mountainous region about twenty-nine miles from Cap Français—suspected that the death of many of his slaves had been caused by poison. To elicit a confession, he killed four slaves and tortured two other women. According to the judicial records, Lejeune and a so-called surgeon named Magre killed the four by burning them "with torches of resinous pine, their feet, legs, and thighs, torments which made them 'confess to anything.' "[71] Though Lejeune had a history of barbaric tortures and slave retaliation that had been known to the courts for at least six or seven years, he had never been restrained. On this occasion, when Lejeune began to torture the two women by roasting their feet, legs, and elbows, and threatened any French-speaking slave that denounced him, fourteen slaves went to Le Cap and charged Lejeune before the court. The documents record that they were " 'full of moderation, submission,' " an accord with the law " 'all the more surprising since their master had violated everything with regard to them.' "[72] The judges appointed a commission, led by M. de Montarand, to investigate the charges. On their visit to Lejeune's plantation, they found two women in irons. Their elbows and legs were already rotting. When they died, Lejeune, assuming that prosecution was inevitable, escaped with the help of white neighbors.[73]

What then ensued—the total inversion of protection and blame, in the name not of justice but of control—provoked numerous debates and conflicting testimonies that swelled the colonial files. More important, it established, once and for all, the law of terror in Saint-Domingue. Slaves had to be "contained," and no amount of torture and mutilation could be allowed to outweigh that precept. White planters of Plaisance petitioned the governor and the intendant on Lejeune's behalf; around seventy other planters from Le Cap presented a petition for acquittal. Many who were morally opposed to his crimes nevertheless knew that the security of the colony depended on slaves having no recourse to the law, since slaves might take their right to complain as an invitation to rebel against "the privileged species." The official investigators, sickened by the demand that innocent slaves be punished with fifty lashes for having denounced their tormentor, wrote: " 'We could not see without deep sadness such a mighty scheme to stop the efforts of justice and governance.' "[74]

Lejeune's testimony is stunning in its matter-of-factness. That a man of such unabashed cruelty could not only defend his actions but articulate a Creole code that was unnerving in its cool, blunt analysis of the effects of slavery, makes it one of the most compelling of colonial texts. He builds his defense by invoking images of bondage, fear, and revenge, and concludes with a black stabbing his master. Yet the power of his words lies in *what* he grants the slave, *how* he removes the myth of natural servility so dear to charitable individuals. There is no place for "Uncle Tom" in Lejeune's Saint-Domingue. Instead, we hear another version of Abbé Raynal's words as supposedly read by Toussaint: "A courageous chief only is wanted. Where is he?" In this version, the French priest's desire for the hero's appearance is replaced by the planter Lejeune's anxiety about the inevitable:[75]

"There is not one planter who has not seen with concern the daring walk of my negroes. . . . What safety will three or four whites have among one or two hundred men, whose courage will be strengthened by the support you give them? My cause in this case becomes the cause of every colonist. . . . The wretched state of the negro naturally makes him detest us. It is only by force and violence that we subjugate him; he must nourish in his heart an implacable hatred, and if he does not commit against us every evil that he could, it is only because his will is enchained by terror: so, if we do not weigh down his chains proportionate to the dangers that we risk with him, if we draw out his hatred from its state of numbness, what can stop him from trying to break these chains? The bird locked in his cage profits from the slightest negligence to escape. I dare to say that our negroes lack only sufficient courage or resolution to buy their freedom with the blood of their masters. Just one step can enlighten them about what they have the power to undertake, . . . it is not the fear and equity of the law that forbids the negro from stabbing his master, it is the consciousness of absolute power that he has over his person. Remove this bit, he will dare everything."[76]

In spite of the accumulated evidence of Lejeune's odious crimes and his signed confession, the judges were intimidated; Lejeune was acquitted by the Superior Council. M. de Montarand, the lawyer who had recorded the slaves' oral testimony, was denounced; and the slaves were punished. The rules Lejeune had articulated were upheld; but in just three years, the slaves, whose courage he had foreseen, revolted. Louis XVI's royal ordinances had initially prohibited masters' cruelty to slaves (slaves could receive no more than fifty lashes of the whip; they were not to be mutilated or killed; and killing a slave was punishable by execution), but he then undid these regulations in a series of royal mémoires. His administration warned: " 'So, there remains to the slaves no other means except revenge and no other feeling except despair.' "[77]

Ten years before the Lejeune case and its narrative of domination, revenge, and revolution, Hilliard d'Auberteuil had published his *Considérations sur l'état présent de la colonie française de Saint-Domingue.* Let us return briefly to the history he tells of masters and slaves, since it provides an uncanny gloss on Lejeune's argument and its Sadean debunking of nature and convention.

We are alienated from nature and we are not free; we are reduced to maintaining an inhuman politics, by a course of cruel actions . . . and dragged along by a host of passions that we want to satisfy: not being able to break so many chains, we want to polish them and make them shine, and, in this work, we use thousands of arms that nature has made for liberty.[78]

For Hilliard d'Auberteuil, both master and slave are trapped in Lejeune's bird cage: chains bind them together in reciprocal brutalization. Like the chains of Sade's most rigorous libertines, their use on select victims also ensnares the torturers in the glut of labor, duress, and debilitation.

Sade and Lejeune are not mere hedonists. Instead, they are committed to a job well done, whether it be the seriatim sodomy of a Juliette or Lejeune's regulated system of burning and confession. Although titillation might be the effect, it is *never* the rationale. In the library of Edmond Mangonès, a Haitian bibliophile and scholar whose collection was catalogued by Drexel Woodson and Ira Lowenthal in 1974, there is a book called *Manuel théorique et pratique de la flagellation des femmes esclaves.*[79] Purporting to be the translation of an unpublished manuscript of an eighteenth-century Spanish planter in Cuba, it was published anonymously and without a date by Librairie Franco-Anglaise, 54, rue Bonaparte in Paris. Like the Black Code that it no doubt mocks, the manual begins with the author's presumption of "the protection of the Heavens" and praise of the "All-Powerful," recognition of his duty "toward the Eternal, source of all authority, and toward the King (whom God keeps from harm)," and a prayer that his life as a planter helps "uphold divine morals and public good."[80] Then, like the Black Code, the writer descends from God to slaves, from celestial concerns to the sticks and whips used to correct "their preferred sins of laziness or insubordination."

What first seemed to be a methodical exposition of what is called "the royalty of the whip"—which was, after all, defined in the Code as the unique prerogative of the master—turns out to be nothing other than an impressionistic, and pornographic, lesson in what this planter calls "the ideal of the proprietor of black flesh: absolute submission . . .

to all his wishes."[81] What was only suggested in the Black Code—or, in some sense, oozed out of its cracks—this writer decides to make the stuff of his story. The "things" most silenced in the Code and, according to most accounts, most abused by the system—that is, the unnamed women slaves—here get preferential treatment. The author's professed aim is to record everything about the control of the "feminine sex," down to the places and positions for whipping, the different kinds of whips chosen for distinct anatomical parts, and a veritable codification of sufferings, tears, and their redemptive results. Moreover, the language of this text is that of the nineteenth century, as if someone wrote for a French pornography series at a time when the government was cracking down on dangerous fictions, even stories like Gustave Flaubert's *Madame Bovary* (1856). So, this discourse on method (more than three hundred pages long) is nothing but a fake, masquerading as an authentic document: authenticity and translation being the only way that such a text could stay on the shelves in Second Empire Paris. A fiction with historical import—Emma Bovary in Louis Napoleon's France—had to be taken to court, but a pseudohistory with no matter except feminine flesh prodded, opened, gashed, and violated did not threaten the status quo.

This fiction of an "authentic" manuscript—like any good gothic tale, it is claimed to have been lost and then resurrected—nonetheless gives another kind of history to texts like the Black Code: it documents the kind of thoughts no planter in Saint-Domingue would have recorded. Though exaggerated scenes of uppity female mulatto slaves (they must be light-skinned) being taught their place by randy male black slaves utterly obedient to the white planter—who, meanwhile, keeps calling on God—retain none of the terrible (because so reasonable) logic of the Code, the document proves how right Sade had been. Whether in eighteenth- or nineteenth-century France, whether Louis XIV, Louis XVI, Napoleon Bonaparte, or Louis Napoleon is in power, the beating of women of color, as long as it appears empirical, remains a permissible pleasure.

Taxonomies of Enlightenment

On January 26, 1766, the "Negro Market" was established in the Place Clugny (which had once been a marsh) in Cap

Français. At first it was open only on the slaves' "free" days—holidays and Sundays—but by 1768 the market was held daily. Moreau de Saint-Méry's journey through this center of Creole life in his *Description* calls into question the regulations of the 1685 Black Code: particularly the prohibition of slaves' bartering, exchanging, or selling their goods, and the requirement that products be marketed only with their masters' passes or letters of approval. By the eighteenth century, an amalgam of classes, castes, and colors had begun to threaten the rules for order in slave society. Marketing was one of the institutions that allowed independent transactions that contradicted the divestiture and subordination demanded by slavery.[82]

Moreau celebrates the rich and varied products of "the colonial soil" displayed at the "Negro Market" at Clugny. Each section of the market was reserved for the sale of different products: vegetables, herbs, and other plants were sold on the east side; meat (lamb, pork, and sausage) on the south; live poultry on the west, and behind the poultry dealers were sellers of millet, "Guinea grass," and "Scotland grass"; and fish and shellfish (clams, oysters, and *lambi,* or conch) on the north side. The Place Clugny, crosscut by several streets, formed intersections or *carrés.* On either side of these intersections, harmoniously laid out, were stalls for different grains and legumes—for example, peas (twenty different kinds), lentils, corn, and a number of other substances that, according to Moreau, replaced bread for negroes and even for white Creoles: cassava, sweet potato, yam, or cabbage. Flowers and fruits—including oranges, lemons, pineapple, *corossol* (custard apples), papaya, and "the monstrous apricot, the insipid coco-plum"—were sold by slave cultivators from both the city and the countryside on Sundays and by retailers (*revendeuses*) on weekdays. Mixed among an "army of symmetrically disposed vendors" were throngs of buyers and traders, or higglers.

Moreau's catalogues reveal the wondrous "species" of plants, animals, and vegetables available for consumption. He delights in describing "an infinity of things": the fruit of the calabash tree or gourds carved in "an ingenious or bizarre way"; the truffle's perfume stunning the gourmand from afar; two cocks making war with their sharp beaks even though their feet are bound; the "inviting smile" of the marketwoman. The frequent rains in Le Cap, Moreau adds, make it nearly impossible to move in the mud; he then prods readers to consider the rains, the muck, and the 15,000 blacks who come to the market on Sundays. He does not say whether slaves are sold in Clugny

Market. If we assume that not only city and country slaves (cultivators) but also free coloreds and even *petits blancs* frequented this place, the crowds on Sundays might well have surpassed Moreau's surprising estimate. Moreau concludes: "Everything that the island can produce for nourishing its inhabitants or for perfuming the air they breathe, is in the Clugny Market, except for the commodities of colonial manufacturing." Administrators in Le Cap cared about this market, for by 1784, about twenty years after its construction, the Negro Market at Clugny was paved.[83]

In 1773 the "White Market" on the Parade Ground in Le Cap was closed. Between 1735 and 1773 this market had supplied whites with imported items, mostly from France—dry goods and foods, pottery, haberdashery, china, jewels, shoes, parakeets, and monkeys—instead of the necessities and the local foodstuffs of Clugny. The White Market boasted European luxuries, but it is generally far less fascinating to Moreau's ethnographic eye than Clugny, although, he tells us, the market was known as the place for the stylish promenade. There the fashionable went to be seen, not necessarily to buy. Women of color, especially, "cannot abide the thought of not going and showing off their luxury."[84] It is unclear why the White Market shut down, or how segregated were personnel and shoppers in the two—at least in name—racially distinct markets. Perhaps the native products of colonial soil, these Creole women, most often dubbed *mulâtresses,* called into question the racial exclusivity reserved for such a market. By 1773, the number of *gens de couleur,* especially free women of color, had steadily increased. Administrators doubtless hoped to circumscribe the places these *libres* could display themselves, since public opinion deemed their liberty to be the telltale sign of libertinage.[85] Yet, in spite of the numerous rules, ordinances, and judgments meant to redefine and restrict liberty, habitual behavior continued, as did the proliferation of irregular freedoms.

The necessity to separate materially what had been constituted as two races—and, in some extreme cases, fantasized as two species—even as they mixed, meant that the very idea of *free* or *freed* had to be qualified and transformed. This "systematic abasement" worked, according to Yvan Debbasch in *Couleur et liberté* (1967), by power of association, a succession of images and ideas: "Whoever says *libre* in white society continues instinctively to think of concubinage, of deep-seated immorality . . . the spectacle of the great city, with the mulâtresse-courtesan and the tandem species of free-slave . . . it was convenient to reduce every person of color to this kind of robot-portrait."[86] The European ideal of beauty, once exported to the colonies, began to seem as misplaced as outmoded Parisian goods in a Creole market. The imported ideal ran up against the fact of "misalliances" that debunked the myth of the repugnant black: the physical deformity so necessary to the invention of a servile soul.[87] In 1770 there were about 6,000 emancipated people of color; in 1780, 12,000; and by 1789, 28,000.[88] The geometric increase doubtless reminded white ideologues of what they kept trying to conceal or constrain in their laws, statutes, and memoirs.

Moreau records the words of a traveler to Le Cap, who overheard an upper-class white lady exclaim, when she saw three *mulâtresses* in muslin skirts, garnished with lace: " 'Look at these rotten pieces of meat! They deserve to have their lace cut flush with their buttocks and to be sold on the fish table in the Clugny Market!' "[89] Yet when Marianne and Françoise, two women of color, spoke sharply about a white woman, their chastisement is chronicled, though their words are not. Their punishment—its form and the place chosen for this display—would demonstrate to such women where (and to whom) they belonged. On June 9, 1780, the Superior Council of Le Cap condemned them to be shown in the Clugny Market, affixed to a pole by iron collars placed around their necks. They were to remain there from seven in the morning until ten at night, with a placard in front of them bearing these words: "Mulâtresses insolent toward white women."[90] The spectacle doubtless was intended to exemplify the precarious status of the "free" products of colonial mixing. The council's order proved the power of white justice to denude what some deemed objects of luxury. Not only were people of color forever excluded from becoming white, but these women, like the thousands of slaves in Clugny, would be forced to relive the shame of their origins as flesh for sale in the marketplace. But once again, ingenuity outsmarted the law. Marianne and Françoise went into hiding, and the council had to be satisfied with carrying out their sentence in effigy.[91]

Other *affranchis* who lacked respect for whites were not so lucky. In 1775 a new legal offense was invented by the authorities, based, as Michel-Rolph Trouillot aptly puts it, "on a dubious interpretation of the 1685 *Code Noir*—disrespect!"[92] In a bold misinterpretation of article 58 of the Black Code—freed persons of color must "bear a singular respect toward their former masters and their children"—unique deference to the liberating master was now transferred to all whites, no matter their class, and no matter how they offended, threatened, or stole from the free coloreds. Any dispute between a white and a person of color could be settled—meaning whites would be exonerated—if the white simply said: "Le mulâtre m'a manqué" (The mulatto has been disrespectful to me).[93] In 1767, a freed person of color who beat a white was whipped, fitted with irons, and sold as a slave.[94] Selling a wealthy mulatto coffee planter into slavery doubtless became a way for whites—many of whom had borrowed money from these freedmen—to cancel their debts, or simply to take over lucrative coffee plantations that mulattoes had established and sustained.

As early as 1733 the division between black and white was substituted for that of free and slave, which had been instituted by the Code (articles 55–59). After 1760, free coloreds were treated more harshly than ever before. What Debbasch has called "racist systematization" continued as royal ordinances were passed (between 1784 and 1786), threatening masters who overworked, neglected, or killed their slaves.[95] As long as persons were clearly slaves, they deserved protection as property. But the intermediate class of persons, who had been freed and were "lightened" by interbreeding, threatened the cause of white supremacy. New laws were needed to regulate their behavior and thus redefine their status as *libres*. The privilege of whiteness had to hold fast.

In less than a century the promise of "same rights, privileges, and immunities as persons born free" had been perverted. Louis XIV had expressed in the Black Code the wish "that the merit of acquired liberty" would "produce . . . the same effects that the happiness of natural liberty produces in our other subjects" (article 59). That such happiness would be impossible, that the boon of "natural liberty" would become the doom of "acquired liberty," would be the story of the *libres* of Saint-Domingue. So numerous were the restrictions and vexations accorded free coloreds that the term itself would become meaningless or, as C. L. R. James put it, "a cross between a nightmare and a bad joke."

The Mulattoes were forbidden to wear swords and sabres and European dress. They were forbidden to buy ammunition except by special permission with the exact quantity stated. They were forbidden to meet together "on the pretext" of weddings, feasts or dances, under penalty of a fine for the first offence, imprisonment for the next, and worse to follow. They were forbidden to stay in France. They were forbidden to play European games. The priests were forbidden to draw up any documents for them. In 1781, eight years before the revolution, they were forbidden to take the titles of Monsieur and Madame. Up to 1791, if a white man ate in their house, they could not sit at table with him. The only privilege the whites allowed them was the privilege of lending white men money.[96]

In Saint-Domingue the term *gens de couleur* (people of color) was used interchangeably with *sang-mêlés* (mixed blood) and *affranchis* or *libres* (emancipated or free). Of the *gens de couleur*, only one-third were black, so the term became synonymous with *mulatto*, though like *affranchi*, it actually applied indistinctly to the mulatto born free and the freed slave, thus to every member of the category called *libres*.[97] Though in France and sometimes in the colonies *mulatto* was used to denote all persons neither black nor white (like *sang-mêlés* or *métis*), in Saint-Domingue, it most often referred specifically to the offspring of a white or a *négresse* in a genealogical scale of minute gradations of blood and nuances of color. Moreau de Saint-Méry clarified these trials of definition: "The Affranchis are more generally known under the name of *Gens de Couleur* or *Sang-mêlés*, although this denomination, taken strictly, also designates negro slaves. As soon as the Colony had slaves, she did not delay in producing Affranchis, and many reasons joined in producing this intermediate class between master and slave." Moreau then qualifies his usage: "*Gens de couleur* and *Sang-mêlés* in order to designate those who are neither Black nor White," and "*Affranchis*, whomever is neither White nor Slave."[98]

The free coloreds in Saint-Domingue were three times more numerous than those in the remaining islands of the French Antilles. By 1789, they owned one-third of the plantation property, one-quarter of the slaves, and one-quarter of the real estate property in Saint-Domingue; they were also competing vigorously in commerce and trade.[99] The cities were "less colored" (had fewer *libres*) than the countryside: for example, in 1789 Moreau estimated that there were only 1,400 *libres* to 3,600 whites in Le Cap.[100] But Gabriel Debien in *Les Esclaves aux Antilles françaises* also singles out a distinctly urban situation: the cultivation of a category called courtesans or *mulâtresses*, either name referring to these women of pleasure. In the rural areas the majority of those freed were devoted slaves, especially women domestics emancipated by their masters (*affranchissements de grâce*). These women continued to produce people of color, increasing fear, as well as jealousy, among whites.[101]

White women envied women of color; petits blancs despised the free coloreds, whose sobriety and talent made them tough competitors; the established sugar planters were threatened by the extraordinary boom in coffee plantations, mostly owned by enterprising mulattoes; and the metropole kept trying to restrict emancipation, since the mulatto's links with enslaved maternal relatives could erode white racial hegemony and thus threaten slavery itself. Little did the king's lawmakers suspect that some of their fiercest allies and most devoted followers of the style and taste of the Old Regime would be mulattoes. Nor did it stop there: the aristocratic Marquise de Rouvray of Le Cap, writing to her daughter, called them wretches and scoundrels, "a race truly so abominable that it is urgent we annihilate it."[102] The colonists had always disdained the pretenses of those they named "suspects," and the mulattoes, whom they had earlier scorned for their stinginess and restraint, were soon blamed for ostentation, greed, and debauchery.

Since "concubinage" with slaves had created the "discoloration" of blacks so feared by whites, in 1733 a royal edict modified article 9 of the Black Code, which had legalized marriage for interracial couples (if the white man was unmarried). Not only did this revision forbid marriage with a person of color, but it abolished the emancipation that could follow from such an alliance. Also, since there were numerous cases of whites marrying women of color (about three hundred white planters had married women of color by 1763),[103] those whites guilty of *mésalliance* (misalliance) had to suffer the curse of color and descend into the purgatory assigned to *affranchis*. These "degenerated" whites, who formed yet another intermediate category between whites and people of color, were evicted from public life. King Louis XV declared that anyone "who married a négresse or mulâtresse could not be an officer, or have any profession in the colonies."[104] Hilliard d'Auberteuil explains the reasoning behind this judgment of indelible contagion:

A white who legitimately marries a mulâtresse descends from the rank of whites, and becomes the equal of the affranchis; even they consider him their inferior: in effect this man is despicable. Anyone who is so low as to fail himself, is even more sure to fail the laws of society, and one is right not only to scorn, but furthermore, to suspect the probity of those who by interest or by thoughtlessness, descends so low as to misally himself.[105]

No gift of liberty could remove the contamination of blood, that "ineradicable stain," as Hilliard d'Auberteuil called it. "Libres" were free, as Moreau de Saint-Méry explained, "but different, and of course, contemptible."[106] Strict reminders of the stain became ever more necessary as people of color began to lose the visible mark of inequality and fade gradually into areas reserved only for whites. Justin Girod de Chantrans, writing from Saint-Domingue in 1782, caustically observed:

> It is necessary at least to give up selling all those gens de couleur less black than mulattoes. It is now time to declare them free; since nature often enjoys flinging ridicule in these kinds of dealings by producing a slave much whiter than the Provençal who buys him, although the difference between white and black had been the primitive claim on which our decent fellows of Europe had established slavery.[107]

The "new whites" had to be recolored, inventively darkened; and the resulting "onomastics of color" depended on a fiction of whiteness threatened by what you could not always see, but must learn to fear, and always suspect: a spot of black blood.[108]

The techniques of degradation depended on social segregation and judicial inequality, all of which read as if they were castigation for the sin of blurring the "demarcation line" between castes (that is, between colors) in Saint-Domingue. Those believed to be passing as white were called "suspects" and, once exposed, suffered an excommunication so extreme that a fiction of whiteness became a cult of purity. The compulsive ritual of naming, so central to enslavement, was now brought to bear upon the free people of color. Let us recall that names condensed a history of outrage and loss but also preserved a history that might later be reclaimed. Debien, in *Les Esclaves aux Antilles françaises*, explains that the slave had two or three names: a historical or mythological name; the African name that was also used in the course of the Middle Passage and adopted by the crew; and, once on the plantation, a surname that emphasized physical traits or place of origin, which would be added to or would replace these names. Once baptized, the slave received another name, often the name of a saint.[109] Yet names also maintained the choices of those who reclaimed their identity by choosing the very labels that might seem to deny or thwart it. It was through naming, as Jean Fouchard has demonstrated, that the slaves, in later taking the names of French colonists as their own, would record the presence of the masters in independent Haiti.[110] Names, then, acted as specters of the past in a locale where repetition became reinvention.

Administrators and planters were ignorant of such transformative possibilities. For them, the logic behind the new system of naming free coloreds was simple: if naming slaves confirmed them as white property while symbolically stripping them of their past identity, the new onomastics reminded *libres* of their origins. Not only could they no longer be called Monsieur or Madame, but any member of this intermediate class could only be referred to as *le nommé* or *la nommée* (as in "a man called——" or "a woman called——"). In July 1773, the administrators in Saint-Domingue forbade *sang-mêlés* from taking the name of a white, whether of their natural father or the person who freed them: "The name of a white race usurped can cast doubt on the status of persons, throw confusion into the order of inheritance, and ultimately destroy this insurmountable barrier between Whites and people of color that public opinion has established, and the wisdom of government maintains."[111] Further, no longer owned but free, they were now to bear names that referred to another kind of freedom, forever distinct from that enjoyed by European subjects: that of their past in Africa. Mothers were forced by law to remind their newborn children of their heritage of servitude by giving "them a surname drawn from African idiom, or from their trade and color, but never can it be that of any white family in the colony." The same practice applied to masters who requested manumission for their slaves.[112] Free coloreds usually turned away from Africa and toward classical mythology or toward Greek, Roman, or French history for their names, for example: César, Vénus, Voltaire, Hector, or Brutus.[113]

The law requiring that names show no trace of mastery but instead metonymize servitude was matched by directives intended to strip away the trappings of acquired taste. The number of ordinances concerned with removing external embellishment were plainly intended to signal a fundamental inferiority that was only masked by finery. "The luxury of mulâtresses," lamented Moreau de Saint-Méry, "has gone beyond the limits. . . . It is always in the cities that one must observe it in order to get an exact idea of it. Luxury consists, nearly entirely, in a single object, dress."[114] To remind these ladies of their servile origins and to restrain their "insolence," various laws were passed to coerce "simplicity," "decency," and "respect." They were to be stripped of their finery and reduced to an appearance that signaled submission. Provisions against lace, silk, and jewels were intended to correct affectation. Yet, as we have seen, women of color staked their reputation on evading these strictures; and even when they acceded to the denuding strategies of the courts (simple coiffure, unadorned dress), this supposed lack became the style imitated by their white rivals. Minimalism became the mode.

How could one tell if a "suspect" was colored? Could an expert eye apprehend the stages of discoloration? The attempt to categorize, name, label, and classify the degrees of color between the extremes of black and white resulted in fantastic taxonomies of a uniquely Antillean enlightenment. Once it became necessary to classify the amount of blood that determined racial identity, as well as to give a name to an appearance of color, the system of differentiation generated phantasms of color, spectral members of a new species. The naturalist Georges Louis Leclerc, comte de Buffon dedicated his *Histoire naturelle* to Louis XV, as intriguing a connection as Sade's reference to the reign of Louis XIV at the beginning of *The Hundred and Twenty Days of Sodom*. If Sade's fiction referred to Louis XIV and his formulation of a Black Code for the Antilles, Buffon's natural history, read carefully by the next Louis, might well have resulted in the king's decision formally to issue his 1771 *Instructions to Administrators* in the colonies, a new code of restrictions and repressions meant especially for the *gens de couleur*. Buffon recognized a "first truth . . . perhaps humiliating to man: that he must rank himself in the class of animals, which he resembles in everything that he possesses that is material." If Buffon complained about the difficulty in separating men from animals—especially from the orangutans Linnaeus named *nocturnal men*—and called for more rigorous categorization, the administrators of the Old Regime saw the naturalist's theoretical problem literalized when their symbolically loaded hierarchies began to break down.

Buffon's descent "by nearly insensible gradations from the most perfect creature to the most unformed matter, from the best organized animal to the most brute mineral," and his celebration of these "imperceptible nuances" as "the great work of nature," once applied to the successive generations of blacks with the traits and colors of whites, required a new typology. Buffon recognized that the "arbitrary" must enter into any "general system" or "perfect method." But this way of thinking, once exported to the Antilles and tested on persons in the colonial laboratory, resolutely ignored Buffon's caveat: "But nature proceeds by unknown gradations, and thus she cannot lend herself totally to these divisions, since she passes from one species to another species, and often from one genus to another genus, by imperceptible nuances . . . so that one does not know where to place himself."[115] Instead, the project of certifying place, position, and rank in a chaos of contradictions became a colonial obsession; and, as the visible, economic, and traditional proofs of distinction vanished, systems of classification, backed up by repressive laws, became both more stringent and more necessary.

An artificially induced regression to blackness was summoned in order to take away from the *gens de couleur* everything that made them appear white. A taxonomy was invented that was scientifically spurious, but mathematically exacting. No longer was it necessary to prove that certain people were beasts in order to justify slavery. Instead, one only had to demonstrate how these people, even if freed, were still slaves with a damning defect: black blood. As time passed, with each new generation, with successive "misalliances," those who used to be closer in appearance to apes—or so the ideology of natural bestiality went—looked more and more like apparitions of men. These appearances haunted whites. People of color were generally reclassified as mulatto or mule, the sterile product of the cross between a horse and a donkey. The mongrel name reminded them that they were hybrid: the offspring of two species, black and white. As skin colors faded, and hair texture, eye color, and other arbitrarily selected traits entered the schema, new divisions had to be made and other names invented that would refer to any category, class, or genus *except* human.

The epistemology of whiteness, which was absolutely dependent for its effect on the detection of blackness, resulted in fantasies about secret histories and hidden taints that would then be backed up by physical, explicit codes of law. Such a system not only displaced the human element from the hybrid offspring of colonial coupling, but became a desperate attempt to redefine whiteness. Moreau de Saint-Méry's taxonomy of color in his *Description . . . de la partie française de l'Isle Saint-Domingue* is crucial to this analysis. Not only was he Saint-Domingue's most acute ethnographer and historian—observing traditions, behavior, and rituals in detail unsurpassed by any other eighteenth-century writer on Saint-Domingue—but he was also an untiring codifier of French colonial law, whose six-volume collection, *Lois et constitutions des colonies françaises de l'Amérique sous le Vent, de 1550 à 1785,* was published in Paris between 1784 and 1790.[116] He traveled throughout Saint-Domingue, Martinique, Guadeloupe, and St. Lucia, rescuing the colonial records from neglect and ruin. "What weariness, what expenses in the voyages I must undertake in order to discover what I want. What searching and what time it takes to find them [these records] in the public repositories, where they are terribly out of order. What disgust to endure, what obstacles to surmount!"[117]

Moreau's hierarchy of color status—complete with combinatory tables of varying mixtures between the poles of white and black, and charts showing how generations of interbreeding produce new combinations and nuances—occupies most of the pages in the section called "*Des Affranchis*," that follows the sections "*Des Blancs*" and "*Des Esclaves*." For Moreau, Saint-Domingue is a "colored locality," and he reproduces ghosts of the place, a fable of enlightenment that would not only be used by those who called themselves whites, but internalized by the *clairs* or light-skinned residents of the Antilles.[118] Moreau's color distinctions in Saint-Domingue have analogues in other places in the Americas, especially in the Spanish and Portuguese colonies, where terminological distinctions for racial identification were as elaborate.

If we take Moreau's text as the first attempt to theorize color as part of a peculiarly colonial enlightenment, we can go further. In 1796 in Philadelphia, Moreau published his *Description topographique et politique de la partie espagnole de l'Isle Saint-Domingue*. Whereas he developed complex racial hierarchies for his treatment of the French part of Saint-Domingue, when discussing the Spanish part of the island, he simply divides the population into "three classes of individuals": whites, freedmen, and slaves.[119] Just as the slave laws in the Spanish colonies of the Caribbean were less severe than in the English and French colonies, the facts of color, at least as Moreau presents them, had less oppressive consequences.[120] In Santo Domingo, Moreau notes that freed persons, though not as numerous as whites, far outnumbered slaves. Since this society was less dependent on black slavery, he concludes that "color prejudice, so powerful in other nations, where it established a barrier between whites and freed coloreds or their descendants, scarcely exists in the Spanish part. Also, the laws of the Spanish Indies concerning freed coloreds, have fallen completely into disuse."[121] Moreau describes color prejudice as "null," since "most of the Spanish colonists are mixed bloods"—a fact which "more than one African trait sometimes reveals." The religious life also accommodates principle and practice: "Men of color are admitted to the priesthood," which, he adds, accords with "the principles of equality that are the basis of Christianity." Moreover, slaves are as well fed as their masters "and treated with a mildness (*douceur*) unknown to other peoples who possess colonies."[122] In a colony that does not depend on plantation slavery and where colonists have not made the most of their "possessions," Moreau does not need to reassure his readers with a rationalist-mathematical foundation for systemic prejudice.

Let us turn to Moreau's systematizing of the conundrum of color in Saint-Domingue, which constitutes the Creole answer to Buffon.[123] Moreau's taxonomy operates on two fronts: color and blood, what ostensibly can be observed and what is invisible. Something like a racialized body and soul dichotomy, the distinctions brought forth are chimerical, as fantastic as the "superstitions" Moreau had ridiculed when talking about the spiritual beliefs of Creole and African slaves. He presents eleven categories of 110 combinations ranked from absolute white (128 parts white blood) to absolute black (128 parts black blood), pushing the invisibility of color differentiation to such extremes that even he must admit defeat. In spite of his exhaustive classifications and endless combinations, he ultimately confesses, as did Buffon, that "the arbitrary influences all classifications, and that one can only approximate what I have established."[124]

In Saint-Domingue, it took a universally applicable concept of blackness, and as it turned out a fairly rarefied one, to underpin both a sense of white racial superiority and the privileges or arrogations that were supposed to stem from it. The people of color might *appear* white, might have been educated in France, might possess great wealth and even own slaves. But though white in skin and cultivated in manner, they housed inferior blood. What became known as "the law of reversion" certified the futility of trying to remove blackness—even "the least molecules of black blood"—by successive alliances with whites. "In a word, one can say that a colored population, left to itself, is fatally destined again to become black at the end of a small number of generations."[125] In Moreau's system, the concept of blackness (like that of bestiality in other natural histories) had to be reinforced, made absolute and ultimately unchangeable against the prima facie evidence of fading color. The strategy was to call this idea "blood." As a metaphysical attribute, blood provided a rational system for the classification and distribution of a mythical essence: blood = race. Once the connection is made, color can be referred to, but now it denotes blood. Finally, the word *color,* like *blood,* is fictitious, signaling—especially in extreme cases, like Moreau's example of "8,191 parts white opposed to one part black"—what is not observable: not fact, but ideology.

Stranger than any supernatural fiction, the radical irrationality of Moreau's method demonstrates to what lengths the imagination can go if driven by racial prejudice. What is most shocking about Moreau's fantastic system are the names he uses. For this is not Columbus renaming places in the New World, nor the legal onomastics ordained for *affranchis*. Ostensibly these names designate a type of human, but in reality they remind those who seek identification in these terms that they are anything but human. Some of the names sound like scientific taxonomy; others are borrowed from birds, sorcerers, or mythical beasts. For example, *marabou* is the name of a bird, and also of Muslim priests or sorcerers in West Africa. In the abstract of the Jamaican *Code Noir*—which Edward Long published as a section of his *History of Jamaica*—*obeah-men,* those he called "pretended conjurors, or priests," are identified (in a note) as "incendiaries, called marabuts or marabouts, on the coast of Guiney . . . banished from their own country for malpractices."[126] *Mamelouque* (Mameluke) denotes a fighting slave or, according to the *Oxford English Dictionary,* "an enslaved depredator in Mahommedan countries." *Griffon* has numerous meanings: a coarse-haired dog; a fabulous animal with the head and wings of an eagle and hindquarters of a lion; or, according to Buffon, as quoted in Littré, a type of mulatto.

To know how we might seek out the sense of these names and their sources would be to write a new history of colonial Saint-Domingue. For the figures of blackness imagined by the white colonialist exposed how unnatural became the attempt to sustain "natural" distinctions between races of men. This kingdom of grotesques would resonate in later supernatural "fictions" that were rooted quite naturally in the need for racist territoriality: Emily Brontë's Heathcliff, not "a regular black"; the blood taint lurking in Dracula's not-quite-right white skin; or Stéphane Mallarmé's "femme stérile," his Hérodiade. The gothic obsession with identity and origins, for example, the indeterminacy of Isabella in Herman Melville's *Pierre*—even more than in such obvious tales about miscegenation as Lydia Maria Child's "The Quadroons" or *A Romance of the Republic*—gets its metaphors and the myth of its ambiguities from the mottled discourse of racial identity: the metaphor of blood taint that unveils the most hidden genetic history.

How does the color continuum work? If one wants to know what happens when a mamelouque sleeps with a mulatto, or a pure-blooded negro with a *sacatra,* or a mulatto with a *négresse,* Moreau gives the result, figured mathematically in eleven tables with titles like "Combinations of White," "Combinations of Negro," "Combinations of Mulatto," "Combinations of Quarteron," and so on through "Marabou." (The twelfth and thirteenth set of combinations with, respectively, "Savages and Caribs of America, or Western Indians" and "Oriental Indians" does not concern me here.) The "misallied" couple is the foundation for Moreau's combinatorial romance: a father and a mother of different colors (unequal in degree of "blood") appear in each operation, or "combination," as Moreau terms it. Here, then, is his first example of one of the eleven lists of possible "nuances," based on a common denominator, the white man:

Combinations of the White

From a White and a	Négresse, comes	a Mulatto.
"	Mulâtresse	Quarteron.
"	Quarteron	Métis.
"	Métis	Mamelouque.
"	Mamelouque	Quarteronné.
"	Quarteronné	Sang-mêlé.
"	Sang-mêlé	Sang-mêlé,
		that continually approaches White.
"	Marabou	Quarteron.
"	Griffonne	Quarteron.
"	Sacatra	Quarteron.[127]

In order to get the color of the offspring, you must always divide by two the additive color obtained by two parents. For example, one white + one *mulâtresse* = 0 + 1/2 divided by 2 = 1/4, a *quarteron,* or one quarter black. The stable figure in every combinatorial sequence is the male (whether white, negro, mulatto, quarteron, métis, mamelouque, et cetera), and he chooses from among the supply of female specimens, as shown in the table above. Note that even though the example comes from the table "Combinations of the white [father]," the child is articulated in terms of blackness—that which is feared in oneself and treated with contempt in others—rather than in terms of the desirable white. No matter how many kinds of blackness can be named and claimed, whiteness remains a supernal ideal. As in Zeno's paradox, one can keep combining and approaching zero without ever being able to attain it.

After these charts of what Moreau calls "distinct classes, as regards the nuance of skin in individuals who form the population of the [French] part of Saint-Domingue," Moreau describes a few of the types in terms of physiognomic traits (skin color, hair texture, and facial features), as well as explaining how many different ways you can produce mulattoes (twelve ways), quarterons (twenty ways), métis (called octoroons in Louisiana and other islands of the Americas, the product of six combinations), and so on. "Of all the combinations of White and negro, it is the Mulatto who unites the most physical advantages; of all these crossings of races it is he who retains the strongest constitution, the most appropriate to the climate of Saint-Domingue."[128]

Yet it is Moreau's attempt to define an invisible distinction that creates the greatest oddities. How do you distinguish the whiteness in coloreds from the whiteness in whites? The quarteron "has white skin, but tarnished by a shade of very weak yellow. . . . There are Quarteronnes whose whiteness is such that you must have very expert eyes to distinguish them from Whites." The métis (one-eighth black) has "markedly white skin and long hair, but this whiteness is not at all animated"; and the mamelouque "can never be confused with the White [even though one-sixteenth black], precisely because he has a dull, faded whiteness, where one untangles something of a yellowish tint. This skin is still more opposed to the drying effects of the sun than that of the Métis, and it seems to lack elasticity."[129] To counteract the illusions of those who appear white, or have more parts white blood than black, Moreau targets those *gens de couleur* who are lighter in his ranking than quarterons as symbols of "degeneration." Since it is not always possible to discern false whites, Moreau suggests that they may manifest traits such as effeteness, weakness, or debilitation. In some cases, the white skin might be a bit dark, unpleasantly wan, or sallow; in others, a lighter shade of white, or as Vincent Marie Viennot, comte de Vaublanc later put it, "white, *but pale.*"[130]

This "colored nomenclature" presents problems as one travels from Saint-Domingue to Europe. Lest anyone worry, even though there are quarterons who look twice as white as Spaniards or Italians, Moreau assures his readers, "*no one would confound them.*" In Saint-Domingue itself, Moreau conceded that observation alone could not distinguish the "last mixtures from pure whites . . . and generally, there are not many oral or written traditions that serve as guides in this regard." Yet opinion, rumor, and suspicion would support

Moreau's maxim, which stood firm even with those *sang-mêlés* who had in their veins only 1/512 part African blood: "Besides, whatever whiteness the mixed race possesses, it never takes on the tone of the skin of pure white and that assists eyes accustomed to the comparison."

In order to make himself "more intelligible" in this habitat of "denominations drawn from color," Moreau turns to rigorous mathematical calculations, giving numerically the *possible* range of combinations, figured with the exact parts black to white, for example, "the 20 combinations of the Quarteron offer from 71 to 96 parts white and from 32 to 57 parts black." There are always new admixtures and changing nuances, though the names themselves do not denote the yellows, reds, browns, whites, or blacks of Saint-Domingue. The differences are, after all, *insensible* in a climate where even "the skin of the European . . . takes on a yellowish [or sallow] tone" or, as some noted, a brown tint.[131] Moreau thus returns to the rigor of numbers in order to define what was rapidly becoming indefinable. These numbers tell a very different story than Moreau's less than precise representations. The person named is an amalgam of "white parts and black parts," the product of an illicit mixture of blood quanta:

	White	Black
. . . .	0	128
The Sacatra	16	112
The Griffe	32	96
The Marabou	48	80
The Mulâtre	64	64
The Quarteron	96	32
The Métis	112	16
The Mamelouque	120	8
The Quarteronné	124	4
The Sang-mêlé	126	2 [132]

When Dessalines drafted his constitution in 1805, recall that he took the most crucial ideological configuration of Saint-Domingue and annihilated it. Instead of the tripartite division of whites, people of color, and blacks, he created one category for Haitian identity that absorbed all other distinctions: Haitians, no matter their color, would henceforth be referred to "only by the generic word black" (article 14). Returning to the Black Code, Dessalines took the signs of illegality—concubinage, bastardy, religious practices other than Catholic—and legalized them. Turning them into proofs of a new citizenry, he took what France had supposedly granted, only to take away in the years following the Black Code in order to subordinate the *affranchis,* and he tossed it all to the winds. The Black Republic, at least as Dessalines envisioned it, would recognize only one cursed color, *blanc.* No nuanced subtleties for him.

But like the colonial taxonomist, Dessalines intended the idea of whiteness to mean many other things besides color. Indeed, color mattered little, since Poles and other friends of Haiti were called *noir* or *nègre.* To be white meant to be an outsider, an enemy of the nation, or, in some cases, simply one whose origins were French. Unfortunately, many of those mulatto elites, who had been lightened and then debased under French rule, disavowed Dessalines's new classification. Calling upon Africa as a trope for nation, they still considered themselves different from the black masses and feared what one planter called "the drums in the night."

But what about this majority, the slaves in Moreau's *Description?* Immediately after his section on the white population of Saint-Domingue and before discussing the *affranchis,* he turns to negro slaves, both African and Creole. After describing the individual nations and their traits, as well as what he calls "the negro character" and "magic and sorcery," he turns to the overwhelming preference of African women for black men over white. "Neither their behavior with whites, nor the advantages which that brings them, even the possible freedom, for themselves or for their children, can hold them back. . . . Nor can their concern about the punishment that white pride and jealousy can make so severe." Even if they "more or less happily hide this inclination, their preference for black men wins in the end." Though Moreau seeks the cause in commonality of thought and language, their "perfect equality" and "familiarity," he also adds that several *négresses* have avowed that the negro's "physical agent of love" has been graced both by nature and by the use of palm wine.[133]

The production of variously shaded and "lightened" people of color, Moreau implies, was less a habit acquired by choice than a response to coercion which slavery made possible and sustained. Whiteness, therefore, meant something very different to those he calls "slaves from Africa." But even slaves born in America retained their sensitivity to color and to those whose skins and ways of thinking suggested either privilege or perversion. Blacks also invented names for whites who were not-quite-right whites, not in terms of color but in status: *nègres blancs* (white niggers), and petits blancs or *blanchets* (little whites), as opposed to the true whites, the wealthy grands blancs or *blancs-blancs* (meaning something like "whiter than white").[134]

Discussing the "legends and superstitions" of Creole slaves, Moreau records two of their own stories about their origins. Both have to do with conversion. The cosmologies are racialized, as if God quite efficiently worked the world into black and white.

According to them, God made man and he made him white; the devil who spied on him made another being just the same; but when he finished, the devil found him black, by a punishment of God, who did not want his work to be confounded with that of the Evil Spirit. The latter was so irritated by this distinction, that he slapped the copy and made him fall on his face, which flattened his nose and swelled his lips. Other less modest negroes say that the first man came out black from the hands of the Creator and that the White is only a negro whose color has degenerated.[135]

In a world where identities wavered between colors, where signs of whitening and darkening were quickly apprehended by all inhabitants, enlightenment depended on shadows. They were never fully exorcised, no matter how many stories were told. The gods, monsters, and ghosts spawned by racial terminology redefined the supernatural. What colonists called sorcery was, rather, an alternative philosophy. The most horrific spirits of the Americas came out of the perverse logic of the master, reinterpreted by slaves who had been mediated to their bones by the colonial myths.

Tools of Terror

In "Varieties in the Human Species," along with giants, dwarfs, and porcupine-men, Buffon tells the story of Geneviève, a "white négresse," born to "perfectly black" parents on the island of Dominica in 1759, though Buffon assures his readers that such curiosities could be found in Cuba or Saint-Domingue as well. Geneviève exemplifies those "deviations," variously called *blafards* (pale-colored or wan), albinos, *dondos,* or white negroes, typed by Buffon as "sterile branches of degeneration" rather than "a stock or true race in the human species." Using the same argument as that applied to mulattoes, he then turns to sterility, the lack of generative possibilities in males, as further proof of what he calls this "degradation of nature." When the female, fertile specimens reproduce, however, their children return to "the primitive color from which their fathers or mothers have degenerated." The curse of blackness, when denatured into whiteness, can only be made intelligible in terms of defilement, rot, or imbecility, a ghastly bestiality: hands so poorly formed that "one must call them paws"; hair described as wool, fur, or down. Buffon implies what Moreau and other theorists of color will emphasize: mulattoes (and the different nuances "degenerated" from whiteness) are as weird or monstrous as the blafards, who have issued from blackness.[136]

Buffon met Geneviève in April 1777, when she was about 18 years old. Well-proportioned and totally white, she had the same features as "black négresses." Though Geneviève's lips and mouth were negroid, they were as white as the rest of her body. But as we saw with Moreau, language gets most intense when dealing with skin color. The locale for identifying vice always resides in its texture or hue. Her whiteness was "a white like tallow that has not been purified, or if you prefer, like a matte-white, wan and lifeless; meanwhile a light tint of rosiness could be seen on her cheeks when she approached the fire, or when she was roused with shame at being seen naked."[137]

Such corporeal surprises, Buffon concludes, "do not form a real race." Like the anomalous Geneviève, they can never be part of "the race of blacks and whites," with their generic characteristics passed on from generation to generation. Instead, this figure of reproductive variety is never specific, but more like a trick of nature or, as Buffon puts it, a "monster by default." What matters here is that Buffon's elucidation of the proliferating changes possible, in terms of the "nuances and limits of these different varieties," resembles the nearly infinite rarifications of color and appearance in Moreau's taxonomy.

Uncontrollable concubinage and licentiousness, as we have seen, were considered by some as producing unholy mixtures—what the superior of the missions, writing to the governor and intendant of Martinique in 1722, called a "criminal conjunction of men and women of a different species," giving birth to "a fruit that is a monster of nature."[138] One offshoot of coital combination—in fact, what could be seen as a literalization of the trope of crossbreeding—is the "pied negro," dappled in spots or stains of white and black. M. Taverne of Dunkerque sent Buffon his account of a pied négresse, Marie Sabina, born in October 1736 in Matuna, "a plantation belonging to the Jesuits of Carthagène in America." M. Taverne explains that, in spite of the English legend at the bottom of her portrait, which claims her

Geneviève, as she appears in Buffon's Histoire naturelle, *published by Th. Lejeune. Photograph courtesy Special Collections, University of Arizona, Tucson.*

to be the offspring of two negro slaves, he suspects that she issued from "the union of a white and a négresse," and a question of honor (according to Taverne, the mother's) resulted in the false genealogy. Buffon answers Taverne's letter with his astonishment at the portrait, a marvel of nature, but focuses on proving that she has negroes for parents. The proof lies again in expelling *real* whiteness from anything faintly redolent of black blood. Buffon supposes that there might have originally been negroes who were white or blafard, "that is to say of a whiteness absolutely different from that of other white men, because these white negroes . . . have wool instead of hair, and all other attributes of true negroes, with the exception of the color of the skin, and the weak configuration of their eyes." Yet, whiteness, whether "true" or "sham," sustains itself, here reappearing in this child in these pieces or parts of white scattered over her body.[139]

Moreau refers to Buffon when he discusses "*Albinos* or *White Negroes*," but it is to Buffon's example of the pied or piebald *négresse* that he specifically turns. The spots of white are dead, like paper or muslin. Stains of black, sometimes in the middle of a white spot, or larger black spots on which are smaller, blacker marks, cover her body. Buffon had described the form of Marie Sabina's irregular splotches as if gray, streaked, or striped, with "the black and white joined by imperceptible shades to the color of mulattoes."[140] Moreau doubtless appreciated the link between Buffon's peculiar specimen and his own account of the indiscernible, secret, and strange color variations in mulattoes. "The whole world knows," Moreau writes, "what Buffon published about a pied négresse, and about the near symmetry of these spots, which is a very rare phenomenon; one often sees negroes so marked, be it over the entire body, or a part, and sometimes on only a member."[141]

If whites were threatened with moral deformation when they misallied with blacks, and even risked transmitting not only darkened skin, but black blood "that would attack in France the very heart of the nation,"[142] blacks also found themselves surprised into whiteness. Not only might offspring after many generations revert to blackness, but "White Negroes" could issue from the loins of very dark-skinned mothers. What did it mean when the skin started to alter, sometimes in "marks" or "stains" large or small, "and with nuances that varied from reddish to a milky white"? How did blacks—aware, as Moreau implies, that "the deep black of the skin is a beauty"—react to getting stained white?

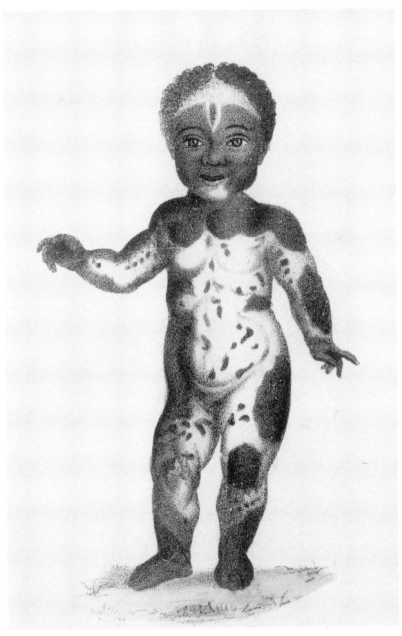

The "Pied Négresse," as she appears in Buffon's Histoire naturelle, *published by Th. Lejeune. Photograph courtesy Special Collections, University of Arizona, Tucson.*

All the attention to bodies—to skin tones, like copper or bronze, or dull and chalky, or pale and grayish yellow like ivory—must have pre-occupied the vision of blacks as well as whites in Saint-Domingue. Some blacks feared lightening in much the same way as whites did the black stain; it was invisible, but *sensed* as degeneration. Yet what whites feared as an internal transformation, a demonic lapse, was physically, externally visited on blacks, described in passages on white negroes, pied negroes, and albinos, as literally breaking out in spots, splotches, stains, or blemishes. White "natural historians" were obsessed with these wonders. The bodily change signified something much more subtle than the stories about Hottentot females and orang-utans. White and black skin combined—nature wronged—generates monsters. (Derek Walcott, much later, would call them "prodigies of the wrong age and color.") Or so an ideologue might reflect. These figures might seem fantastic, but no matter how strange they appear, they are natural products. As Buffon warned, "the prejudice with respect to spectres, therefore, originates from nature; and such appearances depend not, as philosophers have supposed, solely upon the imagination."143

But what about those reactions that did not get written down? What were the thoughts of Frances, "the Negro cook of Colonel Barnet of Virginia," when at "about the age of fifteen years, she observed that those parts of her skin which were near her nails and her fingers gradually became white"? How did she feel when "a short time after, her mouth underwent the same change; and from that period to her fortieth year, the white has been gradually extending over her whole body"?144 Ghosts, creatures of the night, and other spirits, alternately embodied and disembodied, skinned or colored, became part of the population of Saint-Domingue. These seductive, troubling inhabitants revealed what white enlightenment was really about. Out of what white priests or planters projected onto blacks, blacks created stories, sometimes shaped by their own legends, but always reinvented in the New World.

In trying to bring into history the life of the spirit in colonial Saint-Domingue, we must attend to the risks involved in such a reconstruction. As noted, in rereading early accounts of vodou, whether French or Haitian, one is introduced to narratives that repeat formulas for belief. Colonists, missionaries, and the first chroniclers of Saint-Domingue, for example, speak of any faith or inspiration associated with blacks as "magic," "sorcery," or "superstition." Moreau de Saint-Méry's famous

Danbala and Ayida Wèdo, snake gods, painted on the side of a house, with their veve in the center. Port-au-Prince, Haiti, 1974.

description of the "cult of the snake," with its hierarchies of queen, king, and devotees "dominated" by "the *Vaudoux*," the snake, in a box on an altar, is retained with variations in numerous later accounts. Moreau emphasizes what he calls "blind submission"; and when he turns to what we now call "possession," he describes it as an acting of the "Spirit." The vodou queen, as soon as she stands on the box containing the snake,

becomes a new female python, she is penetrated by the God. She becomes nervous and her whole body goes into convulsions. Then the oracle speaks through her mouth; now she flatters and promises happiness, then she calls out in deep tones and screams reproaches. . . . All this is spoken in the name of the snake before this imbecilic troop which hasn't even the slightest doubt about the most monstrous absurdity. They only obey whatever is so despotically prescribed![145]

Moreau's account of vodou (meaning, in his narrative, the God, the sacred dance, and the participants) and the violent *danse à Dom Pèdro*—which terrified the colonists—are far too complex to be considered here. Note, however, that Moreau's rigorously stylized kingdom of belief is distinct from what we now know about serving the spirits in Haiti, even though his account of spirit possession, what he called "a kind of crisis," resembles what we have come to understand as the unequal but reciprocal relationship between humans and gods. Instead of treating as frozen memorials what some allude to as African retentions in the New World, repeated as if in homage to an authentic heritage, I want to suggest instead how the mission of conversion to the Apostolic, Catholic, and Roman churches might well have goaded the amorphous, Dahomean nature spirits into the powerful, anthropomorphized embodiments we now call *lwa*. What is important to note here is that although some contemporary writers on Haiti write as if spirituality in the last half of the eighteenth century can be gleaned from twentieth-century observations, the subversive strategies of Christianity as practiced and reinterpreted in the colony might well offer more insight into the peculiarities of vodou as we know it.

For outside observers of black practices in Saint-Domingue, especially in the last years of the colony, religious gatherings of slaves and free coloreds increasingly became identified with marronage, poison, and conjuring. All kinds of deaths and illnesses—whether tetanus in slave children or tropical infections and chronic illnesses among whites—were seen as the consequences of sorcery. "We attributed to the black slaves the effects of all illnesses including those which had entirely other causes and with which people throughout the island are usually afflicted."[146] Hilliard d'Auberteuil condemns the cult of poison and the whites who teach their negroes its uses. "Poison, which for twenty years has been fatal to many men in the dependency of Le Cap," he argues, "is not composed of plants; it is not a secret, a spell [*ouanga*], as the people of the Colony so foolishly believe." Except in rare cases, white surgeons who teach their blacks to practice pharmacy and the "one hundred Druggist shops" in Le Cap are to blame for the "deadly science," rather than blacks, "who do not possess the atrocious character that ignorance and fear has attributed to them."[147] Yet, the burnings of blacks, alleged to be poisoners or sorcerers, intensified, especially after the poisoning scares of the 1750s. The panic resulted in accounts that treated even the most devoted Catholic worship as a cover for deadly magic.

More intriguing than these tales of terror is the way that whatever remained powerful in the minds of both African-born and Creole slaves and free coloreds in Saint-Domingue had a great deal to do with

Catholicism, even if deformed by abortive, neglectful, or hypocritical missionary efforts. In the towns, certain ritual words and songs, the life of Christ, stories of the saints, and the ornate accoutrements of Catholic ritual were eagerly adopted by those forbidden the opportunity to become familiar with Christian doctrine. Perhaps the less carefully instructed the believer was in the lives of the saints and the sacraments, the more these empty relics could contain the powerful substance of other beliefs. The saints, often named and portrayed inconsistently by the priests, served as convenient vessels for the new gods. What was considered to be only a superficial attempt at religious education gave the black inhabitants of Saint-Domingue what they needed to revitalize dead forms and hollow rituals.

Recall that from the time of Haitian Independence in 1804 to the Concordat in 1860, the Catholic Church had nothing to do with Haiti. During those years, religious forms and rituals developed that had been either forbidden or masked before the revolution. But even though the priests were gone, practitioners of what became known as vodou remembered and retained Catholicism, just as before they had preserved the pasts of Rada, Congo, Ibo, or Nago spirits in Africa.[148] Yet, as Jean Price-Mars has demonstrated in his reflections on "Le Sentiment et le phenomène religieux chez les nègres de St.-Domingue" (1926), even this diversity of African cultures and religions must be further qualified. Not only were many of the first arrivals from the upper west coast of Africa Islamic but many of those from the kingdoms of the Congo, Angola, and Mozambique had been both affected by "Islamic propaganda" and "inculcated with ideas of catholicity by the Portuguese, the first explorers of the African coasts, around the fifteenth century." Referring to Moreau de Saint-Méry's account of this "'rather monstrous assemblage,'" Price-Mars concludes that quite possibly "the large majority of negroes torn from different places in Africa and brought to Saint-Domingue were pious peoples attached simultaneously to the Muslim and Dahomean faith, and even slightly Catholic."[149]

In the twentieth century the Church would condemn what it called *le mélange,* the mixture of vodou and Catholicism (for example, vodou lwa identified with Catholic saints and absorption of the festivals of the Roman calendar by vodou adherents). But what if those disdained as "fetichists" (even, Price-Mars notes, by Haitian historians) brought with them to Saint-Domingue a confluence of beliefs? If the "mixture" existed before the passage to the New World, then what characterized

Christ Crucified. *Iron sculpture by Jean Brierre. Collection of Leon Chalom.*

the relationship between the "infidels" or "pagans" and their Christian proprietors? In colonial Saint-Domingue, it was not syncretism, but rather the use of the sacred to conceal prohibited practices, that concerned secular power.

The dualistic opposition between divine power and sorcery seems to have been much more fragile and vulnerable to reversal than standard accounts suggest. Let us consider how threatening religious practices, whether those executed by slaves and free coloreds who called themselves Christians or by the priests themselves, had become. More telling than the narratives of "abominable orgies," "infernal bacchanals," and "indefatigable Corybantes" (as Leclerc's secretary Norvins described a dance performed for Madame Pauline Leclerc at Isle de la Tortue in 1802) are the legal and administrative responses to blacks too inspired by Catholic practices and to Jesuits too zealous in their duties. The confusing similarity between divine and magical forces characteristic of Catholicism was doubtless sensed by the secular powers of Saint-Domingue. The superstitions, demons, and witches of pre-Reformation Europe, transported to the island by provincial priests, intensified a nightmare atmosphere that was no doubt as terrifying to whites as it was to the numerous blacks accused of curses, spells, and poisons. White terror—fear of evil spirits, hauntings, and magic—resulted in narratives at least as bizarre and horrifying as the zombi spirits and revenants purported to be part of the spiritual surround of what later became identified as black folk belief.

How did whites externalize images of power by devising monsters? What I want briefly to consider is how the bodily tortures and incarnate terrors necessary to sustain the institution of slavery were projected onto the victims by their oppressors. Numerous are the accounts of slaves committing suicide, especially the *bosals* (African-born and "unseasoned"), who had not yet been integrated into the slave community. Believing they would return to Africa after death, they hanged themselves one by one, ate dirt, and swallowed their tongues. In order to prevent what was judged a criminal destruction of property (and to derail what Moreau de Saint-Méry called a "Pythagorean voyage"), planters contrived mutilations that would discourage such attempts to return home. Here is Moreau's description of how planters dissuaded the Ibos from suicide: "They cut off the head of the first one who killed himself, or only his nose and ears that they keep on top of a pole; then the others, convinced that no one would ever dare reappear in his native land thus dishonored in the opinion of his compatriots, and, fearing the same treatment, renounce their ghastly plan of emigration."[150] This gruesome bodily deformation shows how profoundly whites both understood and perverted the mysteries of the spirit.

The tense, unwieldy, and silenced dialogue between spirits straddling both white and black worlds produced unlikely reversals. The worst imaginings of the whites, afraid of the increasing numbers and daring of slaves and free coloreds, doubtless added to uneasiness, if not guilt, about the tortures they had forced humans to endure. They projected their unquiet phantasms onto blacks. Anything diabolical, irrational, or superstitious became materialized as the spirit of blackness, but not without another inversion. Established orthodoxy, the conversion to Christianity that the Black Code had ordained in order to justify the slave trade, once practiced by blacks, had to be shunted aside, condemned as illegality or sacrilege. Note that it was not the ecclesiastical authorities who denounced vodou ceremonies but, according to Gabriel Debien, "the magistrates and administrators, further confounding vodou, sorcery and African dances."[151] Yet, what if this negative triad had not only infiltrated but been transformed by Catholic practices? If impressive rituals and ostentatious trappings were condemned as proof of the corruption of the Church in Saint-Domingue, this deformation of sacred calling ended up accelerating the religious beliefs and practices of blacks, who took up the task of giving meaning to the ceremonial scraps and putting spirit back in the letter.

Later laws for the policing of slaves and the regulation of free coloreds did not, as we have seen, proceed a priori, as did the Black Code, but responded to practice. These edicts tell us much about the daily lives of slaves, the increasing difficulty of distinguishing slaves from those who were reputed to be or who passed themselves off as emancipated, and those actions imagined to be the greatest threats to law and order in the colony. "Slaves who try to pass themselves as free persons must be stopped. We have seen how incapable the police are at collecting all the phony free persons in the colony. Those blacks have a thousand ways of escaping detection."[152] A subtle variation on the camps of maroon bands in the mountains or hidden forest recesses, and difficult to combat, was the flight into the cities by those crowds of coloreds, who blended easily with the inhabitants of those sections of town called "Little Guinea":

The slaves, especially the Creoles, would escape from the plantations and gather in the obscure and hidden places of the quarter. They sometimes carried arms so as to appear the same as free men simply living by expediency. Not only men, but women could also be found at those meetings. In fact, some slave women escaped with the idea of trying to have families of their own far from the plantations.[153]

What is most astonishing in rethinking the proliferation of ordinances, decrees, and laws issued in the last years of Saint-Domingue is how rarely these orders were obeyed. Legal prescriptions, no matter how severe, were increasingly transgressed. Not only were the rigors of law often tempered by the tolerance, generosity, or insouciance of masters, but slaves and free coloreds generated ways of skirting prohibitions. Sometimes these strategies became new rituals, appreciated for their spiritual or symbolic force, but also for their practicality. Saint's days and religious processions offered slaves a respite from work; ceremonies gave them a chance to assemble, and churches even became a sanctuary for escaped slaves. Yet, prejudiced accounts that refused to see blacks as anything but impressionable and unthinking evangelical subjects revealed more about the wayward practices of the clergy than the backward beliefs of slaves. According to one priest in a town in the North, confessions revealed to him what he considered to be the basis of black spirituality:

"Every day I would be consulted by a lover about what he would have to do to be in the good graces of a particular black woman he desired. Or they would come to ask me to get rid of a rival or to engage a *zomby* to come and do the work that he had been charged to do. . . . Oh, sir, I have been afraid to profane our sacred mysteries. These unhappy creatures always ask to be in communication with the saints. I have trembled before some of them, half drunk with tafia who dare to present themselves at the church. . . . These and other monstrous disorders are found only among the blacks in the cities."[154]

But in trying to fit abstract dogma into their daily lives, were these blacks not understanding and assuming that if anyone could influence spirits, bodies, love affairs, and luck, it might well be these clerics, many of whom were known for their promiscuity, greed for gold, dramatic handling of sacred relics, or display of ceremonial attire.

In critical ways, colonial Catholicism was far more materialistic, more dependent on the extremes of awesome incomprehensibility as well as corporeal representation, than the spiritual brotherhoods of the African nations. Pierre Pluchon has described the two-way configuration of magic and materialism as a "Creole Catholicism" that took root in "the shadow of apostolic truth."[155] It is no accident that on

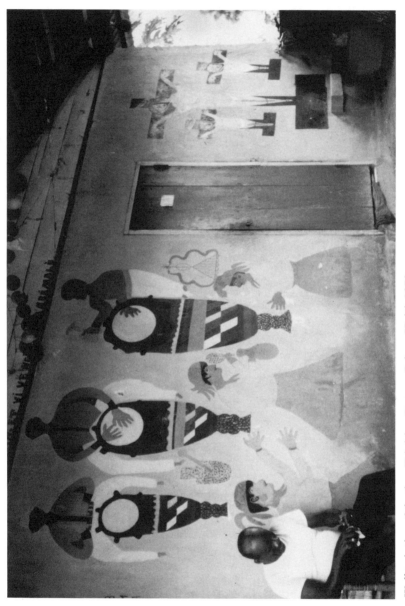

Wall painting of the three Trinities. Port-au-Prince, Haiti, 1970.

the eve of the revolution in Saint-Domingue, a *mulâtresse* recognized as the best student in the educational order for young girls, the Communauté des Religieuses Filles de Notre Dame du Cap Français, had joined "the cult of Voodoo, a sort of religious and dancing masonry introduced into Saint-Domingue by Arada negroes."[156] She attracted a number of students (color not specified) into the sect, and was later known as "the princess Amethyst."[157] Originally founded in Bordeaux by Mère Jeanne Lestonnac, the niece of Michel de Montaigne, and established at Le Cap in November 1731, the nuns in this order had connections with the Jesuits and were known initially in Saint-Domingue as *jésuitines*. A sister described the interior of the new choir "as similar to that in Bordeaux. The statue of the Holy Virgin is most beautiful. Eight candles continually burn before her."[158]

In Le Cap during the years before the conflagration in 1791, the rituals of freemasonry had infiltrated the Church. Vodou assemblies were not the only hieratic sites. Women and young Creole girls joined secret societies, and political meetings gained influence as they manipulated cryptic scenarios. One priest praised a dead nun by assuring his audience that she had not died but had been sent "'on the seraphic wings of cherubs, in the Elysium where philanthropists rest in the breast of the Great Architect!'" Remarking on these details from notes published by the nuns of the Communauté des Religieuses Filles de Notre Dame, Father Pierre Adolphe Cabon suggests that blacks might well have found white "confabulations" to have much in common with vodou: "Somewhat before the events of the month of August 1791, one was prompted to see a sort of freemasonry of blacks in certain manifestations of their activities. Among the young black girls, former students of the nuns, their dances were marked by a strange effervescence, by unusual refrains that one supposed to be negro chants."[159]

When clandestine Catholic traditions joined with the no less powerful attractions of African beliefs and cult practices, the colonial taxonomies were stunned into a vital ambiguity. These kinds of slippages confounded the artificial and legal divisions of Saint-Domingue. Not only did people of color pass for white, and slaves for emancipated blacks, but, according to some accounts, "sorcerers" posed as Christians, and Jesuits encouraged "crime" and threatened the institution of slavery. Churches in the cities, religious dances in the countryside, and holidays or weddings provided the occasion for the promiscuity so feared by the colonial administration. Moreau de Saint-Méry, for example, ends his description of the *danse Vaudoux* with a collective delirium, shared even by the white spectators, who, when "touched" by one of the devotees, began to dance in a frenzy. Moreau explained that though practitioners pretended to dance in public to the noise of drums and clapping hands, as if merely partying, such antics were intended "to escape the vigilance of the magistrates, and in order to assure the success of shadowy secret meetings, which are not a place of entertainment and pleasure, but rather a school where fragile souls surrender to domination, which a thousand circumstances can turn deadly."[160]

Let us return to Cap Français as locale for forbidden spectacles of religiosity. The following regulation, passed in Le Cap in April 1758, demonstrates how threatening had become religious practices, especially those that appeared Christian or were executed by those who called themselves Christians. It seemed as if the more Christian you claimed to be, the more certainly you could be accused of conniving with the devil. The decree forbade "all inhabitants to allow meetings and superstitious ceremonies that certain slaves have the habit of holding at the death of one of them, and which they incorrectly term prayers."[161] But these gatherings were soon revealed to include free persons as well as slaves; and what whites called "evil spells" and "charms" were evidenced by all colors and all ranks. Another decree, passed in 1758, for example, prohibited both free coloreds and slaves "from composing, selling, distributing, or buying *garde-corps* or *makandals*." Moreau de Saint-Méry describes *garde-corps* as "little, coarse figures, of wood or rock, representing men or animals" and thought to possess supernatural powers.[162] The term for the amulets or packets (containing incense, holy water, little crucifixes, and wax from the Easter candle, as argued in the trial of a black accused of *maleficium* or occult malevolence in 1755) invokes the famous priest, prophet, and maroon revolutionary François Makandal, from the northern province of Saint-Domingue, who was convicted in 1758 for the composition and distribution of poisons during what became known as "the great fear of 1757," during and just after which the figures for those poisoned reached more than six thousand.[163]

Using Christian words for demonic acts, illicit reunions in churches, public penitence that infringed on secular justice, and priestly solicitude for the souls of black folk resulted in another distinctive statute made by the Council of Le Cap in February 1761. A long preamble reproduced the complaints made by the procurer general:

In spite of prohibitions . . . slaves cover their meetings "with the veil of obscurity and religion," by meeting at night in the churches, which then become the refuge for fugitives and even places of prostitution. Since we have tried to put an end to these nightly gatherings, the very numerous domestics and workers in Le Cap devote themselves to assembling from noon to two o'clock, and it is difficult to stop them from doing this. Moreover, the Jesuit charged with the religious instructions of negroes alone performs "all the priestly functions" in regard to these same free negroes and slaves. . . . They see themselves as forming "a distinctive body of adherents": some of them have become cantors, vergers, churchwardens, and pretend to copy the practices of a Church council; when they assemble, there is one who usually catechizes or preaches to the others; in their zeal, they are also catechizing in houses and plantations of the parish.[164]

Who were these blacks who took the sacraments seriously enough to adapt them to their own needs, mingling holy utensils with their own sacred objects? Apparently, they were groups of slaves and free coloreds in Le Cap: artisans, domestics, courtesans, and unskilled laborers working as street cleaners, in the warehouses, and on the docks.[165] In the towns, unlike on plantations in the countryside, blacks often had an opportunity to see parish priests and, most important, to share in the observance of religious processions and saint's days, which because of the planters' demands were legally reduced to ten by 1787.[166]

What apparently outraged colonial administrators and other whites who were themselves far from religious was the "indecent" noise and lingering of slaves who appeared at the Jesuit church for daily public prayer, their "contamination" of sacred relics with "idolatrous" and "profane" things, and, of course, their "vanity" in daring to think they had the right to be anything but beasts or heathens. Far more menacing, I suspect, was a subtext of invention and commitment that unsettled racist assumptions. In the colony, blacks (of all colors), whether slave or emancipated, were more attracted to the demands of religious observance than most whites. Their willingness to combine European prayers and relics with African practices generated a belief system of unprecedented resilience. A group of black students, listening to the recitation of Christ's passion, after hearing the preacher pronounce the fifth word of the dying Jesus—*Sitio* (I thirst)—cried out: "'—Bon Dié [God] is thirsty! Give Bon Dié some tafia [rum] with lemon, that's

St. Martin. *Son of a Spanish knight and a free woman of color from Panama, St. Martin was known for his charity toward animals, especially rats, mice, cats, and dogs. Iron sculpture by George Liautaud. Collection of Leon Chalom.*

good!' The preacher continued: 'No, gall and vinegar.' "[167] These devotees had, at least momentarily, put into question the Catholic obsession with mortification and suffering, responding to the enigma of sacrifice with renewed and ardent service.

Mère de Combalas, known as "the good mother of blacks" or "the *daughter of Miracles*" in the Communauté des Religieuses Filles de Notre Dame, began teaching young *négresses*, though white residents tried to stop her.[168] Mère Recoudert, who had succeeded Mère de Combalas, wrote to the vicar-general of Limoges: " 'Our Order is so necessary in the Colony! Our children are the edification of everyone. The students are extremely attached to us,' " and speaking of the devotion of the *négresses,* she concluded: " 'The whites do not equal them.' "[169] Further, even though the Jesuit church in Le Cap was finally closed from noon to two o'clock, blacks held ceremonies and preaching sessions among themselves, during which, as the Council of Le Cap put it in the 1761 decree, "the truths and dogmas of our religion could be altered in the mouth of a missionary of this type."[170]

How do we understand this "type" of practitioner so threatening to the colonial administrators? The Haitian ethnographer Jean Price-Mars, who responded to the occupation of Haiti by U.S. marines by writing *Ainsi parla l'oncle* (1928), sought to demonstrate that blacks are not "the refuse of humanity, without history, without morality, without religion." In order to prod the assimilated elites—those he called "des Français colorés" (colored Frenchmen)—to appreciate their African origins, most concretely preserved in vodou, he turned to the dichotomy between what he called "forced Christianization" and the deep-rooted power of ancestral belief, which would coalesce in time as "the product of a long process of affective accumulation." What he called a "camouflage" or "caricature of conversion," Catholicism (at best practiced as an opportunity for a respite from hard work or a promise of fun), was nothing more than dissimulation.[171] These hollow rites Price-Mars opposed to the secret, authentic, undying "mysteries" and "time-honored sentiment" observed deep in the woods where the black multitudes turned to Africa and its gods.

Tenacious belief is opposed to superficial and official conversion. But the laws and edicts of Saint-Domingue reveal that something happened to join what Price-Mars kept separate: official and unofficial, mimicry and belief. Though he claimed that conversion was "a simple formality which did not at all engage their consciousness," that made no impression on their minds, we need to consider other possibilities: Is it not possible, and probable, that blacks could remain attached to their "original" religion, their "interior god," and still be affected by surface sacraments or changed by the new? Mimicry can be transformative when accomplished by those who do not adhere to sharp divisions between matter and spirit, outside and in. How long can one wear a mask before the mask becomes an integral part of one's identity? Do not stereotypes and repetitive gestures, banal in their imitativeness, get at the innards of feeling, and tacitly engage belief?

On November 24, 1763, the Superior Council of Le Cap delivered the definitive decree expelling the Jesuits from the colony that they had served for nearly sixty years. According to the procurer general, the doctrine and moral practices of the Jesuits resulted in "the enormous crimes, particularly the desecrations and poisonings" committed by slaves.[172] The "condemnation of the morals and doctrine of the so-called Jesuits" had more to do with their religious teachings, which had influenced most of the Catholic slaves of Le Cap, than any alleged criminal activity.[173] Girod de Chantrans, in writing about his travels in Saint-Domingue in 1782, reported what he had heard about the Jesuits: "They worked hard to earn the confidence of the negroes, by instructing them carefully in their religion, by making them know the sublimity of their being, the majesty of man and his hopes for the future. With such consoling subjects they did not have any trouble enticing them: also the negroes at this time were quite greedy for masses, sermons, catechisms, and all the ceremonies of the church."[174]

Once the Jesuits had been expelled, the church, no longer a refuge of salvation, became an extension of the slave-based Old Regime. Dogma was to be directed toward the containing of slaves and increasing the wealth of the planters. Right of sanctuary was forbidden slaves. From Versailles came a mandate titled *Regulation of Discipline for Blacks, Addressed to the Priests in the French Islands of America*. Several of these regulations were posted on the church doors and read aloud. They prescribed that on Holy Saturday slaves who had been denounced as runaways and evildoers, slave women who had prevented pregnancy by abortion or miscarriage, and poisoners were all to be brought before the priest and made to kneel and hear a sermon pronounced in Creole about their "evil," "frenzy," "abomination," and "atrociousness."

For those women who aborted their children rather than give birth to slaves, the admonition of the Church was cruel in its incarnation of perverse and wanton intent. This holy blame becomes even more horrible when we consider that many slave women, even when giving birth, could not escape punishment. In Saint-Domingue, until around 1788, the disease of tetanus (commonly called *mal de mâchoire,* or lockjaw) "annually killed more than 20,000 negro infants within eight days of birth." The white population, convinced that this illness was a negro curse, inflicted "revolting atrocities" on mothers "who had the misfortune of losing their children." To choose abortion, in this case, thus became a way to avoid the torture or mutilation that threatened those who became mothers.[175]

Abominable creature, you who have only wanted to become a mother so as to destroy yourself and the fruit of your own insides and cause the flesh of your flesh to perish, the blood of your blood, the blackness of your outrage cries out for vengeance before God and man, and deserves the gallows and death. But as the Holy Church does not reject those who sincerely want to repent and correct themselves, we must condemn you by the authority of our ministry to live in penitence for the period [to be supplied by the authorities]. We declare that if you do not give certain proofs of having changed your ways and if you ever commit such an atrocity again you shall be removed from the list of Christians, forbidden to enter the church and abandoned to death without the assistance of sacrament or grave![176]

How many "sinners" answered the call and came to church for their holy denunciation is not known, but these words, the threat of the gallows, the promise of penitence, and, most of all, the curse of an unquiet death and incomplete burial doubtless worked on slaves in ways the authorities could not have anticipated. Some lamented that with the Jesuits gone, the parish priests exhibited such "indecent conduct, that the inhabitants and the negroes have lost all the religious sentiments the Jesuits had given them."[177] Yet the life of the spirit had not come to blacks with the arrival of the Jesuits, nor did it disappear with their expulsion. Instead, slaves and free coloreds adapted the language of blood, vengeance, and death as another modality in implementing their own subversions and revolts.

When the slaves revolted in 1791, their already syncretic religious practices converged with the blood of a new covenant. Two years later, after flames destroyed most of Le Cap, including the church, services were held in the chapel of the nuns of the Communauté des Religieuses Filles de Notre Dame, while the two or three thousand blacks who still followed the Jesuit tradition of public prayer gathered together in the Champ de Mars and prayed in unison.[178] As the black revolution took hold in Saint-Domingue, some of the "missionaries" followed the slaves. Whether because of greed or fear, Jacobin ideals or Christian communion, some priests joined the slave insurrection, and their names appeared in parish records. Although one observer called the priests "angels of peace," others recorded the ferocity of these "brigands." Five weeks before Léger-Félicité Sonthonax's general emancipation decree in August 1793, for example, Delahaye, the former parish priest of Dondon, according to the *Feuille du Jour,* struck "terror and fright in the soul of the proprietors who could not tell whether his fiery expression and instructive style designated the general emancipation of the slaves or the total carnage of those who possessed them."[179]

The Long Road to Guinea

It's the long road to Guinea
Where your fathers await you without impatience.
Along the way, they talk,
They wait.
This is the hour when the streams rattle like beads of bone.

—Jacques Roumain, "Guinée,"
translated by Langston Hughes

The relics and scraps of bodies, variously called "ebony wood," "pieces of the Indies," "heads of cattle," buried indiscriminately in the savannah and fields, returned as zombi spirits, baka, or lougawou, condemned to wander the earth in the form of cats, dogs, pigs, or cows. What links these evil spirits is the capacity for transformation into things that are not human. Whether *zobops, kochons gri* (gray pigs), or identified with secret, horrific sects known as *san pwèl* or *san po* (hairless or skinless), or *bizango,* the spirits are known by their hunger for humans, usually children (called *kabri san kòn,* or hornless goats), and their incessant disguises. These "monsters" are the surfeit or remnants of an institution that turned humans into things, beasts, or mongrels. In this regenerative, reinterpreted, and vengeful history, dislocated bodies return to find their place. What whites called "superstition" and "fetishism" turned out to be something more akin to the journeys of bodies that relocalize themselves as spirits and consumers, taking up space, greedy for goods, services, and attention.

Wall painting of a baka (on left) "walking" with machann, or market woman. Bainet, Haiti, 1986.

Let me recall the story of the Ibo slave, who, longing to return to his native land, committed suicide but, instead of being resurrected in Africa, was mutilated in Saint-Domingue. Turned into an example of imperfect, stunted rebirth, he became a spectacle of failure offered to those slaves who might have cherished this desperate escape from slavery. Saint-Domingue was a country obsessed with death. As we have seen, slaves, especially, died in great numbers. Slaves were ordained to be suspended between the promise of sanctified earth and the curse

Veve of Gede. Port-au-Prince, Haiti, 1986.

of defilement, which meant an unquiet wandering, a state of unrelenting restlessness. As early as the Black Code, the rite of exclusion was
specified. Deceased slaves who had been baptized would be buried in
"Sacred-Ground, in cemeteries designated for this purpose. In regard
to those who die without having received Baptism, they shall be in-
terred at night in some field near where they have died" (article 14).
Numerous are the stories of unbaptized blacks, denied last rites, un-
ceremoniously buried in unconsecrated earth. If whites feared blacks,
who in one way or another began to threaten the stability of a society
based on artificially induced servitude, the blacks no doubt feared the

dead more than the living: the revenants, angry ancestors, and zombis who roamed the soil of Saint-Domingue.

In contemporary Haiti there are many forms of death and perpetual rites for the dead. Still, after the 1991 coup that sent Aristide into exile in the United States, the heaps of bodies found with skinned faces and limbs trussed up like animals for sacrifice carried a new message to believers. Instead of curtailing the possibility of sorcery and the return of the unhappy dead, the military government decided to make a spectacle of sacrilege. Though the traditions tied to land, memory, and family are disintegrating, the ceremonies connected to the dead and the dying remain vital and obligatory. As Roger Bastide once wrote, "the dead remain hidden in us." We can only imagine what the sight of numerous bodies treated like sacrificial beasts and then turned into skinless demons meant to a population already victimized by terror.

The ritual of *degrade* (degradation, in the North) or *desounen* (to stun or put into a stupor, in the West) remains the most critical ceremony for the dead. It harkens back to the Ibo, whose longed-for return to Africa was thwarted by white masters who desecrated the body so it could not travel. The degradation of the body of the slave in colonial Saint-Domingue, like the degeneration (or deterioration) of color, has been preserved and recuperated only to be reinterpreted. In cases of unnatural death, where the fact or threat of evil magic is sensed, some oungan literalize the ritual prayers of dispossession by cutting off the head of the deceased in order to prevent the guardian spirit or lwa in the head (*lwa mèt tèt*) from holding fast to the corpse of its devotee or, in some accounts, from angrily tearing itself free from the body only to be tempted and stolen by a sorcerer. But usually the oungan calls the spirit, or in some cases the name of the dead, then removes the lwa and puts it in a pitcher or bottle, called a *govi*.[180] In death, the link between the spirit and its human vessel must be broken, so that the individual's spirit can move beyond death, and beyond revenge, joining the ancestors under the waters in the mythical place called *Ginen* (Guinea). The violence of this gesture has been captured in the ethnologist J.B. Romain's account of the ceremony in Milot, not far from Le Cap. The oungan "places the corpse facing west. Near the head, he sets out a pottery jug filled with water, with a rock in the bottom that can serve for the refuge of the *pitit bon anj* [little good angel]. He pronounces the words *Iku Kato Ko Kami*,

"Brave Guede" (on left) and Danbala and Ayida Wèdo (on right), painted on the walls of a sanctuary consecrated to the lwa of the Gede family. Bainet, Haiti, 1986.

Bagi or altar for Gede and Ezili-nwa-kè (Ezili black heart). Port-au-Prince, Haiti, 1974.

while commanding the dead to get up from his place. He must explode gunpowder so that the pitit bon anj escapes by the mouth of the dead."[181] At the moment of the spirit's passage, however, a sorcerer's magic can steal it, leaving the *zombi kadav* (the zombi in flesh and bones).

For the Haitian who serves the spirits there is no "beyond" in the Christian sense, no redemptive surcease of sorrow, but rather an uncertain realm of obligation, of broken but obstinate communion between the living and the dead. In a country obsessed with death, the tombs (*kav*) of the dead are elaborate, crosses are the objects of devotion, and burial obligations are costly. Cemeteries, presided over by Gede Nibo, Baron Samedi, and his partner Manman (Mama) Brijit, are the center of "the cult of the ancestors." Here "the living speak with the dead," and "kneeling, holding a candle," they address the "invisibles." In a chant that shifts from spirits speaking to the servitor praying, from sensory power and infinite knowledge to suffering and surrender, it seems as if the one sung about and the singer merge in an identity collusion common in vodou song.

'Cé nous qui tendé,
Cé nous qui ouè,
Nous qui connin toute tribulation, toute misère m'ap passé
Sitou m'lagué toute lan main nous'

(It is we who hear,
It is we who see,
We who know every tribulation, I'm going through every misery
Above all, I leave everything in your hands)[182]

If the disposal of dead slaves was a careless deed that marked ir-
revocable inhumanity, funeral rites in independent Haiti became central to both the living and the dead.[183] The deceased do not worry
about their future life but fear they might not be properly served by
the living. And for those who live, the dead threaten to become objects of sorcery or catalysts of revenge. If not served, fed, or remembered, they can become evil and unpredictable. As Alfred Métraux has
explained, suggesting how permeable is the divide between vigilant
ancestor and dread zombi: "A dead person is spoken of as though
he had survived himself in the form of a disembodied soul."[184] Besides being given a wake, a funeral, and a nine-night (a nine-night
prayer cycle, known as *chante kantik,* or "singing canticles," usually presided over by the *pè savann,* a nonordained holy man, once the slave
preacher who substituted for priests and now called "bush priest"),
the dead ancestor must be sent under the waters. After a few years,
they long to return to earth. They are called back, and, no longer
silent, they speak from their watery abode in a ritual of retrieval or
reclamation, known as *wete mò nan dlo.*[185]

The landscape of Haiti is filled not only with spirits of the dead
seeking rest and recognition but with other corporeal spirits who recall the terrors of slavery and the monstrous, institutionalized magic
of turning humans into pieces of prized and sexualized matter. Most
of the spirits called "evil," whether lougawou (vampires), djablès (she-
devils), or *soucriant, sucettes,* or *soucougnan* (suckers), are women. Consider these witches, whether called lougawou or soucriant, who must
first get out of their skin in order to "eat" their victims, which usually
means sucking their blood. The stories are usually told in three parts:
the shedding of skin; the empty skin put in a cool place so that it fits
when the witch puts it back on after her nightly roaming; and, finally,
the destruction of the witch by putting salt, pepper, or lemon on the
skin so that she cannot get back into her human envelope.[186] It is only
by assuming a nonhuman form (taking off the skin) that she can commit evil. A story told by Bertrand Velbrun, born in the Artibonite but

a resident of Cap Haitien for many years when he told this story to George Simpson, emphasizes the drama of taking off and putting on skin. Suspecting that his wife had become a lougawou, a man pretended to fall asleep so that he could watch her nightly doings.

He saw her take a bottle from its hiding place and bathe herself with its contents. At once her skin slipped off and the *loup garou* left the house by going through the roof. The man took the skin which his wife had left in the room and proceeded to spice it with salt, red peppers, and lemons. About three o'clock the next morning the loup garou returned through the roof and tried to get into her skin again. Her attempt was unsuccessful because of the spices, and later that morning her husband found her dead without her skin.[187]

Let us recall the most popular form of torture in colonial Saint-Domingue, sanctioned and recognized by the Black Code: the whip. Once the skin was flayed, pepper, salt, lemon, and ashes were applied to the wounds. This inhuman refinement on bodily punishment is reimagined in the mysteries surrounding the skin-shedding spirits who drain the living of blood. I am suggesting that we connect remembered torture with oppressive magic. Phantoms of domination and scenes of the past return, transmogrified and reinvested with new meanings. Once reconsidered in the context of slavery, the meaning of that figure, human in form but monstrous in spirit, confounds the so-called natural order of things.

In popular belief, people-turned-spirits shed skin, but people also become white by shedding skin. The Haitian colonel Jean-Claude Delbeau, in *Société, culture et médecine populaire traditionnelle* (1990), after describing "the color of the skin as the measure of everything" and explaining the desire for lightening, what Fanon had called "lactification," concludes: "Nothing is more difficult to deny than skin color." He lists the names for different shades—distinctions that still remain important to Haitians—including white, mulatto, griffon, marabou, red-brown, brown, black, albino. Then, he moves from these physical attributes to legends: the san pwèl who shed their skin before committing their nightly atrocities, and the blacks who turn white. He recalls the story of a man turning white during the American occupation of Haiti: "An inhabitant of Marigot, known in his village as a very dark black, suddenly changed skin and became completely white. His terrified parents took him to Port-au-Prince where he was admitted to the general hospital."[188]

How does the judgment about skin color (too dark, not white enough, too white) produce these representations of skinless and unexpectedly whitened figures? What interests me here is the displacement

of white racism and its classification mania onto evil spirits or hapless victims. These skin transformations suggest both monstrosity and
whitening: dark flesh peeled white. Consider this logic: to be without
skin is to be white and to be white is to be a devil. Although none
of the tales of demon spirits ever mentions the color underneath the
skin, I am concerned with the insistence on the absence of skin in
accounts of baka, san pwèl, or lougawou. I am influenced in my interpretation by Toni Morrison's "men without skin" in Beloved's
monologue remembering the crush of violation, by Derek Walcott's
supplication in his autobiographical long poem, *Another Life*, as he
looks at the moon in St. Lucia—"he had prayed / nightly for his flesh
to change, / his dun flesh peeled white by her [the moon's] lightning
strokes!"—and by Topsy's unsettling confession in Harriet Beecher
Stowe's *Uncle Tom's Cabin*: "Couldn't never be nothin' but a nigger,
if I was ever so good. . . . If I could be skinned, and come white, I'd
try then." Though I recognize the danger in moving from assorted
literary renditions of folk belief (especially a text as destructive in its
sentimental beneficence as Stowe's), I believe the images occurring in
written texts and oral traditions might sometimes be mutually adaptable. The Haitian poet René Depestre, who had been raised in Jacmel
by a mother who served the gods, returned to the folk beliefs of his
childhood in his best writings. Here is Depestre's rendition of the evil
baka as a lyric fantasy combining legends of the Ku Klux Klan, the
lougawou (here made male), and Dracula from his epic *A Rainbow
for the Christian West*. In the drama called "Cantata for Seven Voices,"
the female lwa join in telling history and making prophesy:

EZILI
I'll wash his white face
With seven kinds of pepper!

SIMBI
When he goes off to hunt
The black race
He sheds his white skin
And leaves it to keep cool
In an electric jar
Or in a coffin-shaped pitcher.

GUEDE MAZAKA
If one night I find
His baka-skin
I will give him
A brine bath!

. . . .

CARIDAD
And putting on his skin again
Will be as vain for him
As threading a needle without an eye!

GRANDE BRIGITTE
The sunrise
Will surprise him
With his flesh laid bare
And he will die
Far from his skin![189]

What happened to women in this contentious, reversible space? Whether nuns in Cap Français, mulatto courtesans, black slaves, or white Creole wives, women in Saint-Domingue were vessels for the taxonomic vocations of white male supremacy. Alternately etherealized and brutalized, represented as angels, virgins, furies, or wenches, they carried the symbolic weight necessary to the learned discourse on race and the justifications of slavery. In a world where purity was never simply metaphysical but physical as well, where a bodily trait (whiteness or blackness) became spiritual truth (purity or impurity, angel or demon), such divisions were confounded and then reborn.

One of the most feared ghosts is the djablès, known in the English West Indies as *jablesse,* and in Martinique and Guadeloupe as *guiablesse* or *diablesse.* She can be seen near a bridge or a river. Men are warned that if they follow a seductive woman, they might disappear, never to be seen again. As Jamaica Kincaid warned in *At the Bottom of the River*: "Take good care when you see a beautiful woman. A jablesse always tries to look like a beautiful woman."[190] Haitians tell a unique version of this tale of a reembodied woman, substituting dispossession for temptation. The djablès, so their story goes, is condemned to walk for a number of years for the sin of having died a virgin. Could the memories of chastity, penitence, and mutilation, urged by the Catholic Church as the way to salvation, have produced a ghost that proves celestial promise is a dirty trick? If we recall the meaninglessness of virginity in the promiscuities and forced intimacies of colonial Saint-Domingue, and appreciate it as only a metaphor for what did not exist, then we can imagine how those thought to have no history took the idea—and even the cult of the Virgin—fleshed it out, and, in some sense, finally gave it its proper burial.

Chronology

The chronology that follows provides connections for events in Haiti and France, and also lists a few events in the United States that help frame and articulate my narrative. In the United States, the terms *Saint-Domingue, Santo Domingo, San Domingo,* and *St. Domingo* were often used interchangeably when referring to the French colony. Writing about the term *San Domingo,* Ludwell Lee Montague explains that "before 1844 the term suggested *La partie française de Saint Domingue,* or Haiti, with which the United States had important relations, rather than *La partie espagnole,* in which there was little American interest; thereafter it came to apply more particularly to the Dominican Republic, to the exclusion of Haiti" (*Haiti and the United States: 1714–1938* [Durham, N.C.: Duke University Press, 1940], x). To avoid confusion, throughout the chronology the French part of the island is referred to as Saint-Domingue and the Spanish part is referred to as Santo Domingo.

The most comprehensive recent narratives in English concerning military and political events in Saint-Domingue and the Haitian Revolution are Carolyn E. Fick, *The Making of Haiti: The Saint Domingue Revolution from Below* (Knoxville: University of Tennessee Press, 1990), and Thomas O. Ott, *The Haitian Revolution, 1789–1804* (Knoxville: University of Tennessee Press, 1993).

Year	Haiti/USA	France
1492	6 December Columbus lands at Môle St. Nicholas, names island Hispaniola.	
1685		March Louis XIV issues Colbert's *Code Noir*.
1697	20 September Treaty of Ryswick. Spain officially recognizes French presence and cedes western third of island to France, henceforth referred to as Saint-Domingue.	
1758	March Execution of François Makandal.	
1763	24 November Jesuits expelled from Saint-Domingue.	
1771		May Louis XV decrees *Instructions to Administrators*, a new code of restrictions and prejudices designed specifically to oppose *gens de couleur*.
1777		17 December France recognizes the independence of the United States of America.
1789		17 June The Third Estate proclaims itself the National Assembly. 4 July The National Assembly votes to seat six delegates from Saint-Domingue.

9 July
The National Assembly becomes the National Constituent Assembly.

14 July
French Revolution officially begins with the fall of the Bastille.

20 August
Colonists in Paris found Club Massiac to oppose colonial participation in the French Revolution.

26 August
Declaration of the Rights of Man and Citizens adopted by National Assembly.

5 October
Louis XVI assents to the Declaration of the Rights of Man and Citizens: "granted to all men by natural justice."

22 October
National Assembly accepts petition of rights of "free citizens of color" from Saint-Domingue.

October
Formation of Colonial Assembly in order to combat actions of National Assembly on behalf of *gens de couleur*. Mulatto leaders, including Vincent Ogé, Jean-Baptiste Chavannes, and Julien Raymond, ally themselves with the Amis des Noirs, while white deputies from Saint-Domingue seek colonial representation.

1790

8 March
Decree grants full legislative powers to the Colonial Assembly in Saint Marc. The ambiguous article 4 gives political rights to persons aged twenty-five years or older who own property or pay taxes and have resided for two years in the colony.

Year	Haiti/USA	France
	May News of 8 March decree reaches Saint-Domingue. Constitutional Assembly in Saint Marc issues radical decrees and reforms, pushing colony toward independence from the dictates of the metropole and resulting in the colonial conflict between the *pompons blancs* (the royalists) and the *pompons rouges* (the patriots). The Colonial Assembly at Saint Marc declares the royal governor Comte de Peynier a traitor, while the Provincial Assembly at Le Cap sides with governor. Both sides exclude mulattoes from the provisions of article 4.	12 October National Assembly dissolves Assembly at Saint Marc, reaffirming the colonists' right to legislate the future of free persons of color.
	23–28 October Ogé lands in Saint-Domingue, fails in petition to Peynier demanding mulatto rights and begins rebellion.	15 May National Assembly declares a limited number of free-born persons of color eligible to be seated in future assemblies, with "the rights of voting citizens."
1791	9 March Chavannes and Ogé executed at Le Cap.	
	14 August Ceremony of Bois Caïman.	
	22–23 August Slave insurrection in the North.	

24 September
National Assembly revokes 15 May decree.

26 September
Cap Français, the oldest, richest, and most densely populated city of the colony, burned to the ground by rebelling slaves.

1792

4 April
Louis XVI affirms Jacobin decree granting equal political rights to all persons of color and free blacks in Saint-Domingue.

9 July
Rochambeau appointed lieutenant general in command of the French Windward Islands. Fights against British in West Indies until besieged in Martinque in 1794. Surrenders and is allowed to reside in United States as British prisoner until exchanged.

18 September
Jacobin commissioners Polverel, Sonthonax, Ailhaud, and General Laveaux arrive in Le Cap with troops.

21 September
Monarchy abolished. National Convention elected. The Republic declared.

10–13 March
Royalist uprisings in La Vendée and military reverses lead to a Reign of Terror in which tens of thousands of opponents of the Revolution and criminals are executed.

1793

Year	Haiti/USA	France
		21 January Louis XVI beheaded.
		1 February France declares war on Great Britain and Holland.
	February While Spain, Britain, and France fight for Saint-Domingue, Toussaint, Jean-François, and Biassou join Spanish forces.	
	20–21 June Cap Français again consumed by flames and deserted by the white inhabitants. 10,000 refugees arrive in the United States.	
	29 August Sonthonax issues a General Emancipation decree abolishing slavery in the North.	September 1793–October 1795. National reforms include the abolition of colonial slavery, economic measures to aid the poor, support for public education, and a short-lived de-Christianization.
	20 September The British invasion of Saint-Domingue begins.	16 October Marie Antoinette beheaded.
1794		4 February The Convention officially abolishes slavery in France and French territories, including Saint-Domingue.
		5 February Mixed delegation from Saint-Domingue seated at National Convention.

24 March
Rochambeau, having returned to the Windward Islands on 30 January, surrenders to the British at Fort Royal in Martinique.

6 May
Toussaint turns on the Spanish and joins Republicans under Laveaux.

4 June
The British take Port-au-Prince. British troops occupy most of major seaports in western and southern provinces; Spanish troops and a number of former slaves occupy western provinces.

25 June
The French legislature recalls commissioners Polverel and Sonthonax.

28 July
Robespierre, Saint-Just, and 19 adherents executed.

22 July
France signs peace treaty with Spain that cedes Santo Domingo to France.

26 October
National Convention dissolved. Directory established.

1795

Year	Haiti/USA	France
1796		January Rochambeau returns to France but is ordered back to Saint-Domingue to occupy the part of the island ceded to France by Spain.
	11 May Rochambeau arrives in Le Cap as governor with new civil commissioners, including Sonthonax, and republican reinforcements.	
	June Final withdrawal of Spanish forces.	
	18 July Rochambeau clashes with Sonthonax; is dismissed as governor and returns to France.	
		September Laveaux and Sonthonax elected delegates from Saint-Domingue to Legislative Assembly under Directory.
1797	2 May Sonthonax appoints Toussaint governor general.	
	25 August Toussaint forces Sonthonax to return to France.	
1798	March British general Maitland arrives to negotiate peace.	

April
Commissioner Hédouville arrives in Le Cap.

13 June
Congress suspends commercial trade with France and her possessions.

October
British forces evacuated from Saint-Domingue.

23 October
Toussaint forces Hédouville to return to France.

1799 June
Civil war between mulatto André Rigaud and Toussaint breaks out.

26 June
President Adams issues proclamation lifting embargo imposed on Saint-Domingue and promises cooperation with Toussaint.

9 November
As part of a planned coup d'état General Bonaparte is illegally named commander of the troops in Paris. The Directory is officially ended.

1800 25 July
Dessalines defeats Rigaud with help of American vessels at port of Jacmel.

Year	Haiti/USA	France
1801	*30 August* *In Richmond, Virginia, General Gabriel's plan for slave insurrection revealed.*	
	8 July New Constitution proclaimed. Toussaint declared governor general for life.	
	19 July *Jefferson assures French minister Pichon that he opposes independence of Saint-Domingue and supports Napoleon's agenda.*	
		24 October Victor-Emmanuel Leclerc named commander in chief of the largest expeditionary army ever to sail from France. Rochambeau named second in command and returns for the third time to the Caribbean.
	24 November *Thomas Jefferson writes to Virginia Governor James Monroe regarding relocation of emancipated slaves and free negroes to Saint-Domingue.*	
1802	4 February General Christophe, following Toussaint's orders, sets fire to Le Cap.	

6 February
Leclerc enters Le Cap.

24 March
Loss of Battle of Crête-à-Pierrot.

25 March
Treaty of Amiens between England and France.

26 April
Christophe meets with and joins Leclerc's forces.

27 April
Bonaparte approves decree reestablishing slavery and the slave trade.

6 May
Toussaint agrees to surrender to Leclerc.

23 May
At Saint Marc, Dessalines assumes command of the Artibonite under Leclerc.

7 June
Toussaint tricked, taken prisoner, and deported to Fort de Joux in the Jura mountains.

13–14 October
Dessalines, Pétion, and Clerveaux defect from the French. Christophe then joins them.

Year	Haiti/USA	France
	2 November Leclerc dies of yellow fever. Rochambeau takes command as capitaine général de la colonie.	
1803		7 April Toussaint dies at Fort de Joux.
		18 May War declared between England and France.
	18 May Dessalines rips white from French tricolor at Arcahaie, and Haitian flag is born. Black and mulatto generals swear allegiance to Dessalines.	
	18 November Battle of Vertières. French evacuate Le Cap.	
	19 November Rochambeau sails from Le Cap and surrenders to the British admiral who had offered Dessalines naval support.	
	28 November Môle-Saint-Nicolas evacuated by French troops.	
	29 November 8,000 survivors of 43,000 men sent by Napoleon surrender to the British.	

30 November
Dessalines, at the head of 8,000 men, takes possession of Cap Français and renames it Cap Haïtien. Rochambeau capitulates and flees.

1804
1 January
In Gonaïves, Dessalines proclaims independence for the first black republic.

February–April
Dessalines orders the slaughter of the remaining French after promising them protection.

8 October
Dessalines crowned Emperor Jacques I of Haiti.

2 December
Napoleon Bonaparte crowns himself emperor.

1805
20 May
Dessalines ratifies Haiti's first constitution as independent nation and the first Black Republic in the New World.

1806
17 October
Dessalines betrayed and murdered in an ambush at Pont-Rouge.

1807
17 February
Christophe proclaimed president of newly created state of Haiti in the North.

Year	Haiti/USA	France
	11 March Alexandre Sabès Pétion elected president of republic of Haiti in Port-au-Prince. The struggle between the *noirs* of the North and the *jaunes* of the South and West results in a divided Haiti.	
1811	2 June Christophe crowned King Henry I.	
1816	2 June Pétion declared president for life.	
1818	29 March Pétion's death.	
	30 March Jean-Pierre Boyer elected president for life.	
1820	30 April President Boyer offers blacks emigrating from the United States land for homesteads in Haiti.	
	8 October Christophe commits suicide.	
	26 October Boyer enters Le Cap. Haiti reunited.	

1822　9 February
Boyer enters the city of Santo Domingo.

30 May
In Charleston, South Carolina, Denmark Vesey's plot for a
massive slave uprising exposed.

1824　*4 February*
Thomas Jefferson writes to Jared Sparks with an emancipation
plan that calls for "colonization" of U.S. blacks to Haiti.

1825　17 March
Charles X recognizes independence of Haiti, and conveys his
royal recognition to Port-au-Prince with two admirals and the
494 guns of 14 warships.

April
Haitian government abandons program of U.S. black
emigration.

1826　6 May
Boyer signs into effect the *Code Rural,* consigning most
Haitians, especially rural cultivators, to severe laws, amounting
to nothing less than compulsory labor and curtailed freedom
of movement.

1831　*28 August*
Nat Turner revolt in Southampton, Virginia.

Year	Haiti/USA	France
1832	July Thirty-two black slaves arrive in Port-au-Prince from New Orleans under the auspices of Miss Frances Wright, a Scottish inhabitant of the United States.	
1843	13 March Boyer abdicates and leaves for Jamaica.	
1844	3 April During provisional government of Charles Rivière-Hérard, Piquet uprising begins in the South, led by Louis Jean-Jacques Acaau. 3 May Rivière-Hérard deposed. Philippe Guerrier becomes president.	
1845	16 April Council of State elects Jean-Louis Pierrot president.	
1846	1 March Pierrot deposed. Jean-Baptiste Riché declared president.	
1847	1 March General Faustin Soulouque becomes president.	
1848		24 February The Second Republic proclaimed after popular insurrection, leading to massacre of the June days and defeat of working-class struggle.

4 March
The provisional government of the Second Republic decrees the emancipation of the slaves in Guadeloupe and Martinique.

2 December
Louis Napoleon announces coup d'état and becomes president in token election.

20 November
Louis Napoleon proclaims himself Emperor Napoleon III.

1849   16 April
President Faustin Soulouque begins massacre of mulattoes suspected as conspirators in Port-au-Prince.
25 August
President Soulouque declares himself Emperor Faustin I.

1851

1852

1859   15 January
Soulouque abdicates and leaves for Jamaica.
18 January
Fabre Nicholas Geffrard becomes president.

1860   28 March
Concordat between Haiti and the Vatican.

Year	Haiti/USA	France
1861	*May* *Reverend James Theodore Holly, black Episcopalian priest, and nearly 2,000 blacks emigrate to Haiti from New Haven, Connecticut.*	
1862	*5 June* *U.S. government recognizes Haiti.*	
	22–24 September *"Preliminary Emancipation Proclamation" contains a plan "to colonize persons of African descent," which would not appear in the final Proclamation.*	
	31 December *Lincoln signs a contract to pay the adventurer Bernard Kock $250,000 for the colonization of 5,000 freed men at Ile-à-Vache.*	
1915	28 July Admiral Caperton and U.S. marines land in Haiti, occupying Haiti until 1934.	

Notes

Chapter 1. Rituals of History

1. M. Chauvet, *Chant lyrique* (Paris: Chez Delaforest, Libraire, 1825), 9. All French and Creole texts are my translations except where otherwise indicated.

2. Aimé Césaire, interviewed by René Depestre, in Depestre's *Pour la révolution, pour la poésie* (Montréal: Editions Leméac Inc., 1974), 166.

3. Quoted in Timoléon Brutus, *L'Homme d'airain: Etude monographique sur Jean-Jacques Dessalines Fondateur de la nation haïtienne* (Port-au-Prince: Imp. N.A. Theodore, 1946), vol. 1: 264.

4. Thomas Madiou, *Histoire d'Haïti* (1492–1846), 8 vols. (Port-au-Prince: Editions Henri Deschamps, 1989), vol. 3: 149. The first three volumes of Madiou, published in Port-au-Prince with l'Imprimerie Joseph Courtois (1847–1848), began with the arrival of Columbus and ended with the struggles between Christophe and Pétion in a divided Haiti. In 1904 on the 100th anniversary of independence, Madiou's descendants published a volume dealing with the events of 1843–1846; and in 1988 Editions Henri Deschamps undertook the publication of Madiou's complete works. Though Madiou would later be claimed by Haitian ideologues as the *noiriste* historian of Haiti, it should be recalled that though Madiou was born in Port-au-Prince in 1814, he lived and was educated in France from the age of ten until he was twenty-one. After receiving his diploma of "Bachelor of letters," he remained in Paris and returned to Haiti in 1835, where he died in 1884.

5. Madiou, *Histoire,* vol. 3: 179, 147, 180.

6. See Michel de Certeau, Dominique Julia, and Jacques Revel, *Une politique de la langue: La Révolution francaise et les patois* (Paris: Gallimard, 1975) for a discussion of Abbé Grégoire's decision to inquire into patois and

customs in the French countryside in 1790. The correspondences between a political and linguistic revolution are examined in Jean Bernabé's "Les Proclamations en Créole de Sonthonax et Bonaparte: Graphie, histoire et glottopolitique," *De la Révolution francaise aux révolutions créoles et nègres* (Paris: Editions caribéennes, 1989), 135–150. See also Hénock Trouillot, *Les Limites du créole dans notre enseignement* (Port-au-Prince: Imprimerie des Antilles, 1980).

7. *Vodou* is a word used by the Fon tribe of southern Dahomey to mean "spirit," "god," or "image." In his *Description topographique, physique, civile, politique et historique de la partie française de l'Isle Saint-Domingue,* Moreau de Saint-Méry depicts in detail, for the first time, the rites and religious practices of the slaves in colonial Saint-Domingue. He explains that "Vaudoux means an all-powerful and supernatural being upon whom depends all of the events that come to pass on earth." I use the term *vodou* to describe the belief system of the Haitian majority, though I realize that devotees, when asked about their traditional practices, simply say: "I serve the gods."

8. Janvier published his first responses to Cochinat in the Port-au-Prince journal *l'Oeil.* Other articles appeared in Haiti in the journal *Perseverant.* The 636-page *La République d'Haïti et ses visiteurs (1840–1882)* (Paris: Marpon et Flammarion, 1883) was reprinted in Haiti in 1979 by Ateliers Fardin, with the added title, *Un Peuple noir devant les peuples blancs (Etude de politique et de sociologie comparées).*

9. Janvier, *La République d'Haïti,* 319.

10. Ibid.

11. Edward Long, *The History of Jamaica, or General Survey of the Antient and Modern State of That Island* (London, 1774; reprint, New York: Arno Press, 1972), vol. 2, book 3, chapter 3, 476.

12. Ibid., 483.

13. Beaubrun Ardouin, *Etudes sur l'histoire d'Haïti, suivies de la vie du Général J.-M. Borgella,* 2d ed. (1853–1860; reprint, Port-au-Prince: Chez l'éditeur François Dalencour, 1958), introduction, 5; and vol. 11: 75. For many Haitian critics, Ardouin represented exactitude and verifiability, studying documents in the archives of the Haitian Senate and in the French Colonial Archives, and completing his archival research while in exile in Paris. Although some mulatto elite considered Ardouin a necessary corrective to Madiou, who they felt relied too heavily on oral testimony, Madiou had consulted written documents. Since most of those who lived during the Haitian Revolution did not know how to write—and those who did, like Baron de Vastey or Juste Chanlatte, had a political axe to grind—Madiou's interest in preserving the stories told by those who had not been educated in French, who did not share in the mastery of the text, results in those contradictions for which he has been condemned, but which help us to get closer to a history shot through with ambiguity. Ardouin had access to volumes 1–3 of Madiou (published 1847–1848).

14. The first three volumes of Madiou's *Histoire* appeared in Imprimerie Joseph Courtois, Port-au-Prince. As Gordon Lewis notes in *Main Currents in Caribbean Thought* (Baltimore: Johns Hopkins University Press, 1983), 257, "in a long passage of his preface, suppressed by the Haitian Ministry of

Education in the second edition, Madiou perceives the national history of his country as a logical outcome of the great principles of 1789." See *Histoire d'Haïti,* ed. Départment de l'Instruction Public (Port-au-Prince: Edmond Chenet, 1922). Madiou's ardent republicanism disconcerted some Haitians. According to Dantès Bellegarde in his "Notice" in the book he edited, titled *Ecrivains haïtiens: Notices biographiques et pages choisies* (Port-au-Prince: Société d'Editions et de Librairie, 1947), 51, the first volumes became *introuvables* (unobtainable) when the "Minister of Public Instruction" decided to produce a "popular" second edition in 1922. Such censorship was doubtless expedient, occurring as it did during the American occupation of Haiti (1915–1934). When the light-skinned Louis Borno became president in 1922, he denied the populace the right to free elections, since he claimed they were "incapable of exercising the right to vote." Further, in 1918 a new constitution was drafted by Franklin D. Roosevelt, then assistant Secretary of the Navy, which contained an article that permitted foreigners to own land in the country, annulling article 12 of Dessalines's 1805 constitution, which forbade whites to set foot in Haiti as "master" or "proprietor."

15. For an examination of the problematic social and historical construction of that totalizing category called *race* in Haiti, see Michel-Rolph Trouillot, *Haiti: State Against Nation* (New York: Monthly Review Press, 1990), 110–113.

16. Spenser St. John, *Hayti, or the Black Republic* (1884; reprint, London: Frank Cass and Company, Limited, 1971), 95–96.

17. Ardouin, *Etudes,* "Avertissement," 4.

18. Madiou, *Histoire,* xiii.

19. Spenser St. John, *Hayti, or the Black Republic,* 95–96.

20. Karl Marx, *The Eighteenth Brumaire of Louis Bonaparte* (1851; reprint, New York: International Publishers, 1972), 134.

21. Gustave d'Alaux, *L'Empereur Soulouque et son empire* (Paris: Michel Lévy Frères, Librairies-Editeurs, 1856), 1.

22. Wendell Phillips, *Speeches, Lectures, and Letters* (Boston: Lee and Shepard, 1892), 482.

23. Dantès Bellegarde, *La Nation haïtienne* (Paris: J. DeGirord, 1938), 119.

24. Retrieving details of the publication history of Ardouin's *Etudes* necessitates further research. Dantès Bellegarde, in *Ecrivains haïtiens,* 19, notes that the first edition of Ardouin's "monumental work in eleven volumes" appeared in 1855 "at Dezoby et E. Magdeleine, libraires, 1, rue des Maçons-Sorbonne," in Paris. After its great success, a second edition appeared in 1860 at "l'Imprimerie Donnand, 9, rue Cassette."

25. According to Ardouin, *Etudes,* vol. 10: 90, later negotiations in 1838 resulted in two French treaties that decreed unconditional recognition of the sovereignty and independence of Haiti and reduced the remaining indemnity to sixty million francs, payable over a thirty-year period.

26. Jonathan Brown, *The History and Present Condition of St. Domingo,* 2 vols. (1837; reprint, London: Frank Cass and Co., 1971), vol. 2: 259.

27. *The Rural Code of Haiti; in French and English,* with a prefatory letter to the Right Hon. The Earl Bathurst, K. G. (London: sold by James Ridgway,

169, Piccadilly, printed by B. McMillan, Bow-Street, Covent-Garden, 1817), reprinted in *West Indian Slavery: Selected Pamphlets* (Westport, Conn.: Negro Universities Press, 1970), 2.

28. Salomon's speech is reprinted in the appendix of Leslie Manigat's *Un Fait historique: L'Avènement à la présidence d'Haïti du Général Salomon: Essai d'application d'un point de théorie d'histoïre* (Port-au-Prince: Imprimerie de l'Etat, 1957), 73–78.

29. For a superb analysis of Ardouin's work, see Hénock Trouillot, *Beaubrun Ardouin: Homme politique et l'historien,* Publicación número 106 (Port-au-Prince: Instituto Pan Americano de Geografia e História, 1950).

30. Ardouin, *Etudes,* vol. 6: 74.

31. Madiou, *Histoire,* vol. 3: 405.

32. Jean Price-Mars, "Jean-Jacques Dessalines," in *Silhouettes nègres* (1938; reprint, Paris: Présence Africaine, 1960), 43.

33. Horace Pauléus Sannon, "Dessalines et Pétion," in Dantès Bellegarde, ed., *Ecrivains haïtiens,* 206.

34. Madiou, *Histoire,* vol. 1: 105.

35. The gruesome details of Dessalines's life in servitude are described in Timoléon Brutus's *L'Homme d'airain,* vol. 1: 27–57.

36. Ardouin, *Etudes,* vol. 6: 45–46.

37. Madiou, *Histoire,* vol. 3: 156.

38. Spenser St. John, *Hayti, or the Black Republic,* 79.

39. Derek Walcott, "What the Twilight Says," *Dream on Monkey Mountain and Other Plays* (New York: Farrar, Straus and Giroux, 1970), 11–12.

40. See Jean Fouchard, *La Méringue: Danse nationale d'Haïti* (Montréal: Editions Leméac, Inc., 1974), 68–72 for his account of Couloute, Dessalines, and the *carabinier.*

41. In *Aperçu sur la formation historique de la nation haïtienne* (Port-au-Prince: Les Presses Libres, 1954), Etienne Charlier, Secretary-General of the Haitian Communist Party in 1954, condemns historians who concentrate on the actions of "a few great men" and ignore the masses he calls "the only great midwives," p. 284. Carolyn E. Fick, in *The Making of Haiti: The Saint Domingue Revolution from Below* (Knoxville: University of Tennessee Press, 1990), demonstrates how *marronage,* fugitive slave resistance by the individuals history has obscured, was crucial to the course of the revolution in Saint-Domingue. See also Jean Fouchard, *Les Marrons de la liberté* (Paris: L'Ecole, 1972; Port-au-Prince: Editions Henri Deschamps, 1988).

42. Michel Étienne Descourtilz, *Voyages d'un naturaliste,* 3 vols. (Paris: Dufart, 1809), 212, cited in Carolyn Fick, *The Making of Haiti,* 211–212.

43. Hénock Trouillot, "Dessalines, Général en Chef de l'armée des Indépendants," *Le Nouvelliste,* 13 August 1971, 5.

44. Ibid.

45. Hénock Trouillot, *Les Limites du créole dans notre enseignement* (Port-au-Prince: Imprimerie des Antilles, 1980), 67.

46. Etienne D. Charlier, *Aperçu sur la formation historique de la nation haïtienne* (Port-au-Prince: Les Presses Libres, 1954), 307.

47. George E. Simpson and Jean-Baptiste Cinéas, "Folk Tales of Haitian Heroes," *Journal of American Folklore* 54, nos. 213–214: 185.

48. Madiou, *Histoire,* vol. 2: 112.

49. Gustave d'Alaux, *L'Empereur Soulouque,* 239–240.

50. Although most accounts record Toussaint, Christophe, and Dessalines's attempts to eradicate "vodou," they ignore how this persecution of "African superstitions" and "sorcerers" could well result from belief. In an especially revealing note, Madiou explains that "Toussaint was horrified by anything to do with vodou. He often said that he spoke through the nose only because 'the vaudoux' [practitioners] had set evil spells on him." When Césaire and Glissant wrote their respective dramas of Christophe and Toussaint, they both presented their heroes haunted by the ancestors or revenants from a Guinea they had tried to ignore.

51. Zora Neal Hurston, *Tell My Horse: Voodoo and Life in Haiti and Jamaica* (1938; reprint, New York: Harper & Row, 1990), 114.

52. félix morisseau-leroy, *Dyakout 1, 2, 3, 4* (Jamaica and New York: Haïtiana Publications, 1990), 24–28.

53. Janvier, *Les Constitutions d'Haïti (1801–1885)* (Paris: Marpon et Flammarion, 1886), 31–32.

54. Pierre de Vassière, *Saint-Domingue: La Société et la vie créoles sous l'ancien régime, 1629–1789* (Paris: Perrin et Cⁱᵉ, 1909), 219.

55. See Yvan Debbasch, *Couleur et liberté: Le Jeu du critère ethnique dans un ordre juridique esclavagiste* (Paris: Librairie Dalloz, 1967), vol. 1: 55, for his argument that such distinctions were the "ideological arsenal" of slavery: "Without segregation, no peaceable, or even possible, domination over the servile masses."

56. Moreau de Saint-Méry, *Description topographique, physique, civile, politique et historique de la partie française de l'Isle Saint-Domingue,* 3 vols. (Philadelphia: Chez l'auteur, 1797; new edition by B. Maurel and E. Taillemite, Paris: Société de l'histoire des colonies françaises, 1958), vol. 1: 71–87.

57. Madiou, *Histoire,* vol. 3: 409.

58. Madiou, *Histoire,* vol. 3: 270; Louis Janvier, *Les Constitutions d'Haïti,* vol. 1: 43.

59. Catts Pressoir, Ernst Trouillot, and Hénock Trouillot, *Historiographie d'Haïti,* Publicación número 168 (Mexico: Instituto Panamericano de Geografía e História, 1953), 190.

60. In a footnote to *Les Arbres musiciens,* Alexis writes: "Dessalines developed the struggle against slavery by infusing it with a ferocious spirit of political independence, equality, and social revolution." Gallimard, in their biographical note to Alexis's novel *Compère Général Soleil,* names Alexis as "a descendant of the Emperor Jacques I, Dessalines, the founder of Haitian independence." See René Depestre's homage in *Bonjour et adieu à la négritude* (Paris: Robert Laffont, 1980), 117.

61. Anténor Firmin, *De l'égalité des races humaines (anthropologie positive)* (Paris: F. Pichon, 1885), 544.

62. Madiou, *Histoire,* vol. 8: 77.

63. See Brutus, *L'Homme d'airain: Etude monographique sur Jean-Jacques Dessalines Fondateur de la nation haïtienne* (Port-au-Prince: Imprimerie de l'Etat, 1947), vol. 2: 246–265, for details about the succession of monuments to Dessalines.

64. David P. Geggus, *Slavery, War, and Revolution: The British Occupation of Saint Domingue, 1793–1798* (Oxford: Clarendon Press, 1982), 40. See also François Hoffmann's "Histoire, mythe et idéologie: La Cérémonie du Bois-Caïman," *Études créoles: Culture, langue, société* 13, no. 1 (1990): 9–34, for his analysis of what he believes are the French sources of the legend, and of the stylized Haitian renditions of the story, which were then reabsorbed into oral tradition as national myth. Most recently, Geggus has responded to Hoffmann and deconstructed the "exaggerated" mythologizing of "the insurrection of August" in "La Cérémonie du Bois-Caïman," *Chemins Critiques* 2, no. 3 (May 1992): 59–78.

65. Madiou, *Histoire,* vol. 1: 96.

66. Ardouin, *Etudes,* vol. 1: 50–51.

67. Michel Etienne Descourtilz, *Voyages d'un naturaliste* (Paris: Dufart Père, 1809), cited in Alfred Métraux, *Voodoo in Haiti,* trans. Hugo Chartiris, with a new introduction by Sidney Mintz (New York: Schocken Books, 1972), 48–50.

68. Duverneau Trouillot, *Le Vaudoun: Aperçu historique et evolutions* (Port-au-Prince: Imprimerie R. Ethéart, 1885), 26, 30–31, 37.

69. See Odette Mennesson-Rigaud and Lorimer Denis, "Cérémonie en l'honneur de Marinette," in *Bulletin du Bureau d'Ethnologie,* no. 3 (Port-au-Prince: Imprimerie de l'Etat, 1947), 21. Alfred Métraux, in *Voodoo in Haiti,* 49, gives the following transcription of the song: "Pito muri pasé m'kuri / Désalin Désalin démânbré / Viv la libèté."

70. Mennesson-Rigaud and Denis, "Cérémonie," note, 21. The belligerent Petwo nation of lwa (as distinct from the Rada family, the lwa-Guinin-Daomen, as Legba or Damballah, known to be more benevolent and predictable) was historicized as violent and revolutionary. The "danse à don Pétro," described by Moreau de Saint-Méry in his *Description,* sends its participants into "convulsions" and "horrible distortions." Some Haitians say "Petwo" are "plus raide" (hard or stiff). In practice, however, the division between Petwo and Rada does not always hold. As I suggest in my analysis of Ezili Freda, something else happens to the ideal of "love" on the soil of Haiti. The luxuriant coquette often defies the very love or eloquence she suggests. In ceremony she can behave like Ezili-je-wouj or Ezili Mapian of the Petwo group, who disdain the trappings of culture and inspired the revolutionary soldiers: "Me, Ezili Freda Dahomey / I will thunder the canons." See Dayan, "Caribbean Cannibals and Whores," *Raritan* (Fall 1989): 45–67.

71. Métraux explains that the Creole word *nanm* corresponds with the idea of "spiritual essence" or "power," or simply "what is sacred," p. 153. Jean Price-Mars, in his little known "Le Sentiment et le phénomène religieux chez les nègres de St.-Domingue," in *Une Étape de l'évolution haïtienne* (Port-au-Prince: Imprimerie "La Presse," 1930), 129, cites Maurice Delafosse's description of black "animism": "in every being containing a visible or latent life,

there exists a spiritual power or dynamic or efficacious spirit (niama in mandingo), which can act by itself."

72. Serge Larose, "The Meaning of Africa in Haitian Vodu," in *Symbols and Sentiments: Cross-Cultural Studies in Symbolism,* ed. Ioan M. Lewis (London: Academic Press, 1977), 97.

73. See Serge Larose, "The Haitian Lakou, Land, Family, and Ritual," in *Family and Kinship in Middle America and the Caribbean,* ed. Arnaud F. Marks and René A. Romer (Curaçao, Netherlands Antilles: Institute of Higher Studies; Leiden: Royal Institute of Linguistics and Anthropology, 1978), 482–511; and Jean Maxius Bernard, "'Démanbré' et croyances populaires," *Bulletin du Bureau National d'Ethnologie,* no. 2 (1984): 35–42.

74. Letter from Le Cap, October 6, 1803, quoted in C. L. R. James, *The Black Jacobins: Toussaint Louverture and the San Domingo Revolution* (1938; revised ed., London: Allison & Busby, 1980), 360.

75. Madiou, *Histoire,* vol. 3: 168–169.

76. Milo Rigaud, *La Tradition voudoo et le voudoo haïtien* (Paris: Editions Niclaus, 1953), 67.

77. Melville J. Herskovits, *Dahomey, an Ancient West African Kingdom* (New York: J. J. Augustin, Publisher, 1938), 243.

78. Moreau de Saint-Méry, *Description de la partie française,* vol. 1: 70.

79. Maya Deren, *Divine Horsemen: The Living Gods of Haiti* (1953; reprint, Kingston, New York: Documentext, McPherson & Company, 1989), 42.

80. René Depestre, *A Rainbow for the Christian West,* translated and with an introduction by Joan Dayan (Amherst: University of Massachusetts Press, 1977), 147.

81. Rigaud, *La Tradition voudoo,* 41.

82. Deren, *Divine Horsemen,* 249.

83. Brutus, *L'Homme d'airain,* vol. 1: 288–289.

84. The most complete story about Défilée is that preserved by Jean Fouchard in *La Meringue,* 77–80, where he recounts the stories of Didi Condol, a survivor of Défilée's family, in 1916, and Joseph Jérémie.

85. Hénock Trouillot, *Dessalines ou le sang du Pont-Rouge* (Port-au-Prince: Imprimerie des Antilles, 1967), act 5, scene 8, p. 121.

86. Madiou, *Histoire,* vol. 3: 406.

87. Ardouin, *Etudes,* vol. 6, fn. 1, 74.

88. Massillon Coicou, *L'Empereur Dessalines: Drame en deux actes, en vers* (Port-au-Prince: Imprimerie Edmond Chenet, 1906), iv. The unpublished second act, which contains the murder and apotheosis of Dessalines through the medium of Défilée is now lost, though writers, including Duraciné Vaval, *Histoire de la litterature haïtienne ou "l'âme noire,"* Ghislain Gouraige, *Histoire de la litterature haïtienne (de l'indépendance à nos jours)* (Port-au-Prince: Editions de l'Action Sociale, 1982), and Dessalines's biographer, Timoléon Brutus, *L'Homme d'airain,* vol. 2, focus on the drama of Défilée's devotion.

89. Coicou, *L'Empereur Dessalines,* v.

90. Quoted in Brutus, *L'Homme d'airain,* vol. 2: 245. Brutus thanks Victor Coicou, son of Massillon, who loaned him the original manuscript of the

second act of the play. Note that the pronoun shifting in this quotation (from third to first person) and identity collusion between the one sung about and the singer is customary in vodou song, when the spirit sings through the body of his/her horse.

91. Trouillot, *Dessalines ou le sang du Pont-Rouge,* act 5, scene 12, p. 129.

92. Windsor Bellegarde, "Les Héroines de notre histoire," in Dantès Bellegard, ed., *Ecrivains haïtiens,* 218–219.

93. Edgar La Selve, *Le Pays de nègres* (Paris: Librairie Hachette, 1881), 166.

94. Quoted in Rigaud, *La Tradition voudoo,* 62, and in Fouchard, *La Meringue,* 77–78.

95. Fouchard, *La Meringue,* 77.

96. Ertha Pascal-Trouillot, *Retrospectives . . . Horizons* (Port-au-Prince: Imprimerie des Antilles, 1980), 392–393.

97. See Lelia J. Lherisson, *Manuel de litterature haïtienne: Textes expliqués* (Port-au-Prince, 1955), published under the auspices of the government and adopted by the Department of National Education, for a discussion of Jérémie, born in Port-au-Prince 21 March 1858, 200–201.

98. Fouchard, *La Meringue,* 79–80.

99. For the most incisive history of the conflations and confusions of the Marys, see Marina Warner, *Alone of All Her Sex: The Myth and the Cult of the Virgin Mary* (New York: Vintage Books, 1983), 227–229.

100. Caroline Bynum's work on fragmented corpses and improbable resurrections, her emphasis on the radical and often distasteful changes the body must undergo in order to rise again incorruptible is essential to any understanding of the operations of deification. See "Material Continuity, Personal Survival, and the Resurrection of the Body: A Scholastic Discussion in Its Medieval and Modern Contexts," *History of Religions* 30 (1990): 51–85, reprinted in *Fragmentation and Redemption: Essays on Gender and the Human Body in Medieval Religion* (New York: Zone Books, 1991), 239–297.

101. Deren, *Divine Horsemen,* 43.

102. Fouchard, *La Meringue,* 80.

103. Although I have translated *Tignan* as "Ti Jean," the word *Tignan,* according to Drexel Woodson, is a phrase used when marketing, meaning "a little more." For example, the marketwoman is asked to add extra grain, filling the can above its rim. He adds that when a man asks for *Tignan,* he means something like "a piece of ass." See also Woodson, "Tout mounn se mounn, men tout mounn pa menm: Microlevel Sociocultural Aspects of Land Tenure in a Northern Haitian Locality" (Ph.D. dissertation, 3 vols., University of Chicago, 1990), vol. 1: 521, where one of his informants in Dondon, speaking about *afè tè* (land transactions), here sharecropping, explains that "*Tiyon* [*tinyon* or *chinyon,* as pronounced by some speakers] means to add a little more to his share" (Woodson's transcription and translation). See also Sidney Mintz, "Standards of Value and Units of Measure in the Fond-des-Nègres Market Place Haiti," *The Journal of the Royal Anthropological Institute* 91, part 1 (1961): 29, and 37, note 13, for a discussion of substances being measured, with *tiyô* meaning "extra," but Mintz also notes that the verb "*tiyóné*

means 'to raise the feathers of the neck and head, to bristle,' and is used literally for fighting cocks, figuratively for human beings." Spenser St. John in *Hayti, or the Black Republic,* 154, mentions the "tignon, or handkerchief tied gracefully round the head," and concludes: "A white tignon is a sign of mourning."

104. Fouchard, *La Meringue,* 78.

105. J. B. Romain, *Quelques moeurs et coutumes des paysans haïtiens* (Port-au-Prince: Imprimerie de l'Etat, 1959), 59. Carolyn Fick in her work of historical reconstruction, *The Making of Haiti,* discusses the presence of the mulatto Cécile Fatiman in the Bois-Caïman ceremony, 93–94, 242, 265, and notes the first reference in the Haitian historian Etienne D. Charlier's *Aperçu sur la formation historique de la nation haïtienne* (Port-au-Prince: Les Presses Libres, 1954), 49.

106. Arlette Gautier, *Les Soeurs de solitude: La Condition féminine dans l'esclavage aux Antilles du XVIIe au XIXe siècle* (Paris: Editions Caribéennes, 1985), 221. Three significant books reconsider the forms women's resistance took in the Caribbean. Lucille Mathurin, *The Rebel Woman in the British West Indies During Slavery* (Kingston: Institute of Jamaica, 1975); Barbara Bush, *Slave Women in Caribbean Society: 1650–1838* (Kingston, Bloomington, and London: Heinemann, Indiana University Press and James Currey, 1990); and Marietta Morrissey, *Slave Women in the New World: Gender Stratification in the Caribbean* (Lawrence: University Press of Kansas, 1989).

107. For the most complete account of this heroine's life see Joseph Eveillard, "Marie Claire Félicité Guillaume Bonheur," *Revue de la Société d'Histoire et de Géographie d'Haïti* 5, no. 14 (Port-au-Prince, April 1934): 1–19.

108. Charlier, *Aperçu,* 49, note. As the first to reveal this information, Charlier notes that General Pierrot Benoit Rameau, the grandson of Cécile, allowed him to make it public.

109. Jacques-Stephen Alexis, *Compère Général Soleil* (Paris: Gallimard, 1955), 7–8.

110. Rigaud, *La Tradition voudoo,* 66.

111. Dominique Hippolyte, with Placide David, *Le Torrent: Drame historique en 3 actes* (Port-au-Prince: Presses Nationales d'Haïti, 1965).

112. Hénock Trouillot, *Dessalines ou le sang du Pont-Rouge,* 6–7.

113. Jean Price-Mars, J. C. Dorsainville, and François Mathon, "Report of the Jury Examining Manuscripts" (6 April 1940), *Le Torrent,* 12.

114. Hippolyte, *Le Torrent,* act 3, scene 7, p. 99.

115. Jules Michelet, *La Femme* (1859; reprint, Paris: Flammarion, 1981), 184.

116. Ibid., 180–181.

117. Janvier, *La République d'Haïti,* vol. 1: 248.

118. Horace Pauléus Sannon, "Création du drapeau national," in Dantès Bellegarde, *Ecrivains haïtiens,* 208.

119. Luc Grimard, "La Légende du premier drapeau," in Lelia Justin Lherisson, *Manuel de littérature haïtienne,* 256.

120. Brutus, *L'Homme d'airain,* vol. 1: 264. In a note that explains why the Virgin is protector of blacks, Brutus reveals that for many Haitians the

Virgin Mary is black, quoting what he believes to be her words from the Song of Solomon: "I am black, but comely." Images of the Black Madonna of Czestochowa, who reigns from the Basilica in the Jasua Gora monastery, were brought to Saint-Domingue with the Polish Legion, who had been sent by Napoleon to fight under Leclerc. Many deserted the French to fight with the *indigènes,* so the cult of the Black Virgin could have been passed on to Haitians. Catholic chromolithographs of the Black Madonna of Czestochowa, who has three scars on her right cheek, are identified in contemporary Haiti as Ezili Dantò.

121. Gustave d'Alaux, *L'Empereur Soulouque,* 112–113. See also Pierre-Adolphe Cabon, *Notes sur l'histoire religieuse d'Haïti: De la révolution au Concordat (1789–1860)* (Port-au-Prince: Petit Seminaire Collège Saint-Martial, 1933); Dantès Bellegarde, *Histoire du peuple haïtien 1942–1952* (Port-au-Prince: Collection Tricinquantenaire de l'Indépendance d'Haïti, 1953), 150; and Michel-Rolph Trouillot, *Haiti: State Against Nation* (New York: Review Press, 1990), 234–235, note 7.

122. The slogan is most often known as "nèg rich se milat, milat pòv se nèg" (A rich negro is mulatto, a poor mulatto is a negro).

123. D'Alaux, *L'Empereur Soulouque,* 111–115.

124. Madiou, *Histoire,* vol. 8: 318–319. See also Dantès Bellegarde, *Histoire du peuple haïtien,* 150, for a discussion of Pierrot's anarchy caused by the spread of superstitious practices.

125. Duverneau Trouillot, *Le Vaudoun,* 31–32.

126. Thomas Jefferson, *Notes on the State of Virginia,* ed. William Peden (New York: Norton & Company, Inc.), 162.

127. Moreau de Saint-Méry, *Description de la partie française,* vol. 1: 104.

128. C. L. R. James, *The Black Jacobins,* 32.

129. Pierre de Vassière, *Saint-Domingue (1729–1789): La Société et la vie créoles sous l'ancien régime* (Paris: Perrin et Cⁱᵉ, 1909), 281.

130. Ibid., 280–281. Note that cocotte means both "darling" and "tart." This example of complicitous comradery should not be taken too far, lest the brutal and unalleviated domination of the plantation mistress be ignored. It would be instructive to analyze how women's bonds differ from the much-touted "devotion" of the black slave for his male master.

131. Jean Fouchard, *The Haitian Maroons: Liberty or Death,* trans. from the 1972 French edition by A. Faulkner Watts, with preface by C. L. R. James (New York: Edward W. Blyden), 43.

132. For a discussion of what could be seen as a Haitian trinity that includes Ezili Dantò, Ezili Freda, and Lasyrenn (the mermaid and water mama) and substitutes a "human drama" for the "impossible ideal of perfectly submissive (and virginal) motherhood," see Karen McCarthy Brown, *Mama Lola: A Vodou Priestess in Brooklyn* (Berkeley and Los Angeles: University of California Press, 1991), 220–257.

133. Henry H. Breen, *St. Lucia: Historical Statistical and Descriptive* (London: Longman, Brown, Green, and Longmans, 1844; London: Frank Cass and Company Limited, 1970), 183.

134. Milo Marcelin, *Mythologie vodou* (Port-au-Prince: Les Editions Haïtiennes, 1949), 77–78.

135. Deren, *Divine Horsemen,* 143.

136. Justin Girod de Chantrans, *Voyage d'un Suisse dans différentes colonies d'Amérique,* ed. Pierre Pluchon (Paris: Librairie Jules Tallandier, 1980), 138–154.

137. Deren, *Divine Horsemen,* 144, 138.

138. Moreau de Saint-Méry, *Description de la partie française,* vol. 1: 42–43.

139. Herskovits, *Life in a Haitian Valley,* with introduction by Edward Brathwaite (Garden City, New York: Doubleday & Company, Inc., 1971), 299.

140. Ibid., 301.

141. Note that Erika Bourguignon, in "Haïti et l'ambivalence socialisée: Une Reconsidération," *Journal de la Société des Américanistes* (Paris: Au Siège de la Société Musée de l'homme, 1969), argues that this incomplete combination of divergent traditions is more applicable to the Haitian elite than to the masses. Being unaware of the existence of "diverse origins" and the "resultant possible incongruity" thus faciliates "the process of reinterpretation and syncretism," 174–191.

142. Lorimer Denis, "Le Cimetière," *Bulletin du Bureau d'Ethnologie,* series 2, no. 13 (Port-au-Prince: Imprimerie de l'État, 1956), 2.

143. For the differing accounts (in English) of "possession" in Haiti, see Maya Deren, *Divine Horsemen,* 247–262, and 320–321, note; Alfred Métraux, *Voodoo in Haiti,* 120–141; Erika Bourguignon, *Possession* (San Francisco: Chandler and Sharp, 1976); Bourguignon, "Spirit Possession and Altered States of Consciousness: The Evolution of an Inquiry," in *The Making of Psychological Anthropology,* ed. George Spindler (Berkeley: University of California Press, 1978), 479–515; and most recently, Karen McCarthy Brown, *Mama Lola.* More generally, see especially Vincent Crapanzano, *The Hamadsha: A Study in Moroccan Ethnopsychiatry* (Berkeley: University of California Press, 1973); and his "Introduction" and "Mohammed and Dawia: Possession in Morocco," in *Case Studies in Spirit Possession,* ed. Vincent Crapanzano and V. Garrison (New York: John Wiley & Sons, Inc., 1976).

144. Derek Walcott, *The Muse of History,* in *Carifesta Forum: An Anthology of 20 Caribbean Voices,* ed. John Hearne (Kingston: Institute of Jamaica and *Jamaica Journal,* 1976), 118–119.

145. Gabriel Debien, *Les Esclaves aux Antilles françaises (XVIIᵉ–XVIIIᵉ siècles)* (Basse Terre: Société d'histoire de la Guadeloupe et Fort-de-France: Société d'Histoire de la Martinique, 1974), 8.

146. Orlando Patterson, *Slavery and Social Death: A Comparative Study* (Cambridge, Mass.: Harvard University Press, 1982), 100.

147. See Patterson, *Slavery and Social Death,* 54–58. In his *Les Esclaves aux Antilles françaises,* 72, Gabriel Debien explains how the slave would have two or three names: historical, mythological, or religious.

148. For two important accounts of Jesuit activities in Saint-Domingue and the colonists' distrust of the Jesuit influence on slaves, see Lucien Peytraud, *L'Esclavage aux Antilles françaises avant 1789,* vol. 1 (1897; reprinted as *Histoire de l'esclavage,* Edition et Diffusion de la Culture Antillaise, Paris: E. Kolodziej, 1984), 234–235; and Debien, *Les Esclaves aux Antilles françaises,* 282–287. Debien notes that *serviteurs* was also the name previously used for *engagés* (indentured whites).

149. Moreau de Saint-Méry, *Description de la partie française,* vol. 1: 35.

Chapter 2. Fictions of Haiti

1. Hippolyte Adolphe Taine, *The Ancient Regime,* trans. John Durand (1875; translation, New York: Henry Holt and Company, 1896), 374–375.

2. Adeline Moravia, *Aude et ses fantômes* (Port-au-Prince: Editions Caraïbes, 1977), 34.

3. Jacques Roumain, *Gouverneurs de la rosée* (1944; reprint, Paris: Editions Messidor, 1988), 11.

4. Louis-Joseph Janvier, *La République d'Haïti et ses visiteurs (1840–1882)* (Paris: Marpon et Flammarion, 1883), 47.

5. Louis-Joseph Janvier, *Les Affaires d'Haïti,* quoted in Pradel Pompilus, *Louis-Joseph Janvier: Le Patriote et le champion de la négritude* (Port-au-Prince: Imprimerie des Antilles, 1976), 38.

6. Glenn Smucker, "Peasants and Development Politics: A Study in Haitian Class and Culture" (Ph.D. dissertation, New School for Social Research, 1983), 64.

7. Colonel Jean-Claude Delbeau, *Société, culture et médicine populaire traditionelle* (Port-au-Prince: Imprimerie Henri Deschamps, 1990), 90.

8. Léon Vieux, "Au Printemps," in Louis Morpeau, ed., *Anthologie d'un siècle de poésie haïtienne: 1817–1925* (Paris: Editions Bossard, 1925), 330.

9. For the most astute discussion of the symbolism of land for the Haitian peasantry and the binding relations between the gods and those who serve them, see Ira P. Lowenthal, "'Marriage Is 20, Children Are 21': The Cultural Construction of Conjugality and the Family in Rural Haiti" (Ph.D. dissertation, Johns Hopkins University, 1987), 212–222.

10. Marie Vieux Chauvet's first published work, written for the stage under the pseudonym Colibri, was *La Légende des fleurs* (Port-au-Prince: Editions Deschamps, 1950). *Fille d'Haïti* (Paris: Fasquelle Editeurs, 1954) won the *Prix de l'Alliance française* in Haiti; *La Danse sur le volcan* (Paris: Librairie Plon, 1957) was translated into English by Salvator Attanasio as *Dance on the Volcano* (New York: William Sloan Associates, 1959); and *Fonds des Nègres* (Port-au-Prince: Editions Deschamps, 1960) won the *Prix France-Antilles* in Paris. *Amour, Colère et Folie* (Paris: Gallimard, 1968), once published, caused a scandal in Port-au-Prince, and Chauvet was forced into exile in New York.

In New York, she wrote *Les Rapaces* (1986), published posthumously by Editions Deschamps in Haiti.

11. Jacques Barros, *Haïti de 1804 à nos jours* (Paris: L'Harmattan, 1984), vol. 1: 404.

12. Chauvet, *Fonds des Nègres*, 1.

13. Antoine Innocent, *Mimola, ou l'histoire d'une cassette* (Port-au-Prince: Imprimerie E. Malval, 1906), 7.

14. Frantz Fanon, *Black Skin, White Masks*, trans. Charles Lam Markmann (New York: Grove Press, Inc., 1967), 41; originally published as *Peau noire, masques blancs* (Paris: Editions de Seuil, 1952).

15. Roumain, *Gouverneurs*, 34, 75, 60, 84, 65, 158.

16. François Hoffmann, *Le Roman haïtien: Idéologie et structure* (Sherbrooke, Québec: Editions Naaman, 1982), 241.

17. Paul Moral, *Le Paysan haïtien: Étude sur la vie rurale en Haïti* (1961; reprint, Port-au-Prince: Les Editions Fardin, 1978), 7.

18. Michel-Rolph Trouillot, *Nation, State and Society in Haiti, 1804–1984* (Washington, D.C.: The Wilson Center, 1985), 12–13.

19. Roumain, *Gouverneurs*, 13.

20. Rémy Bastien, *Le Paysan haïtien et sa famille* (1951; reprint, Paris: Editions Karthala, 1985), 159.

21. Chauvet, *Amour, Colère et Folie*, 4.

22. Jacques Stephen Alexis, *Les Arbres musiciens* (Paris: Gallimard, 1957), 140, 61, 82, 83.

23. Ibid., 343–344.

24. Jean Price-Mars, *So Spoke the Uncle*, trans. Magdaline W. Shannon (1928; first English ed., Washington, D.C.: Three Continents Press, 1983), 105; originally published as *Ainsi parla l'oncle* (Compiègne, France: Imprimerie de Compiègne, 1928), 105.

25. Alfred Métraux, *Voodoo in Haiti*, trans. Hugo Charteris, with new introduction by Sidney Mintz (1959; reprint, New York: Schocken Books, 1971), 350.

26. Bastien, *Le Paysan*, 142.

27. Chauvet, *Fonds*, 131.

28. Alexis, *Les Arbres*, 270, 178.

29. Roumain, *A propos de la campagne "anti-superstitieuse"* (Port-au-Prince: Imprimerie de l'Etat, 1942), 11, 12.

30. Jean-Baptiste Cinéas, *L'Héritage sacré* (Port-au-Prince: Editions Henri Deschamps, 1945), 12–13.

31. Chauvet, *Fonds*, 26, 219.

32. Ibid., 81–82, 83.

33. Téo St.-Jacques in Drexel Woodson, "Tout mounn se mounn, men tout mounn pa menm: Microlevel Sociocultural Aspects of Land Tenure in a Northern Haitian Locality" (Ph.D. dissertation, 3 vols., University of Chicago, 1990), vol. 3: 558.

34. I use *lakou* to mean "yard" or "compound," as Serge Larose defines it in "The Haitian Lakou, Land, Family and Ritual," in *Family and Kinship in*

Middle America and the Caribbean, ed. Arnold F. Marks and René A. Romer (Curacao, Netherlands Antilles: Institute of Higher Studies, and Leiden: Royal Institute of Linguistics and Anthropology, 1978), 482–512. "Though it [the lakou] is sometimes extended to the whole undivided family property, it is usually restricted to the household grouped together in a vague circle all around the cult house, or the 'démembré.' In both cases, 'lakou' and family land are more or less identified and the emphasis is put on land as a family patrimony: 'land is for all of us,'" 494.

35. Chauvet, *Fonds,* 4. Serge Larose distinguishes between "Guinea and Magic, the ancestors and the 'points,'" in "The Meaning of Africa in Haitian Vodu," in *Symbols and Sentiments: Cross-Cultural Studies in Symbolism,* ed. Ioan M. Lewis (London: Academic Press, 1977), 110. The latter, he claims, are "specific powers which can be bought at the hands of a *houngan.*" For Larose, doing fieldwork in Léogane, they are a sign of evil practice: "All 'points' are means by which an individual tries to manipulate his environment to his own individual profit, usually at the expense of others," 106. Unlike Frère Général in Jacques Stephen Alexis's *Compère Général Soleil* (Paris: Gallimard, 1955), rich from doing magic for politicians and the military, Beauville remains poor, even though he could have sold his points to the powerful who consult him. Instead, Beauville offers his inherited points to Marie-Ange as a gift, albeit a somewhat sexually loaded proposition.

36. Chauvet, *Fonds,* 7, 10.

37. Larose, "The Meaning of Africa," 110. Note, however, that the symbolic good of the calabash tree is not as absolute as it might first appear. In "Cérémonie en l'honneur de Marinette," *Bulletin du Bureau d'Ethnologie,* no. 3 (Port-au-Prince: Imprimerie de l'Etat, 1947), 15, Odette Menneson-Rigaud identifies the calabash tree as the *reposoi* (habitat) of the evil spirit Marinèt.

38. Chauvet, *Fonds,* 102.

39. Ibid., 15.

40. Smucker, "Peasants and Development Politics," 65.

41. Chauvet, *Fonds,* 179–180, 181–182.

42. Ibid., 134, 80, 85, 92, 163.

43. Ibid., 144, 126, 168.

44. Maya Deren, *Divine Horsemen: The Living Gods of Haiti* (1953; reprint, Kingston, N.Y.: Documentext, McPherson & Company, 1989), 155.

45. Chauvet, *Fonds,* 168.

46. Louis Maximilien, *Le Vodou haïtien: Rite radas-canzo* (Port-au-Prince: Imprimerie Henri Deschamps, 1945), 79. Maximilien quotes here from A. Besant's *La Sagesse antique.*

47. Chauvet, *Fonds,* 205–206, 79, 125.

48. Louis Mars, "La Crise de possession et la personnalité humaine en Haïti: Leçon d'Ethno-Psychiatrie," *Revue de la Faculté d'Ethnologie,* no. 8 (Port-au-Prince: Imprimerie de l'Etat, 1964), 46.

49. Erna Brodber, *Jane and Louisa Will Soon Come Home* (London and Port of Spain: New Beacon Books, 1980), 112. In *Mama Lola: A Vodou*

Priestess in Brooklyn (Berkeley and London: University of California Press, 1991), 6, Karen McCarthy Brown warns against applying some static and restrictive idea of morality to vodou: "The Vodou spirits are not models of the well-lived life; rather, they mirror the full range of possibilities inherent in the particular slice of life over which they preside."

50. See my earlier rendition of Beatrice St. Jean's story in "Vodoun, or the Voice of the Gods," *Raritan* (Winter 1991): 32–58.

51. Chauvet, *Fonds,* 162.

52. For a fascinating analysis of how "nations" of spirits evolved as ancestors of the newly arrived Africans, whose ethnic traits were codified by planters and traders and then passed on to slaves, see Larose, "The Meaning of Africa in Haitian Vodou," 100–103.

53. Chauvet, *Fonds,* 96.

54. Alexis, *Compère Général Soleil,* 121–127.

55. Chauvet, *Fonds,* 144–145.

56. Deren, *Divine Horsemen,* 250–262.

57. Sidney Mintz, introduction to Alfred Métraux, *Voodoo in Haiti,* 12.

58. Chauvet, *Fonds,* 150–151. See Milo Marcelin, *Mythologie vodou,* 2 vols. (Port-au-Prince: Les Editions Haïtiennes, 1950), vol. 1: 109.

59. Chauvet, *Fonds,* 153–154.

60. Ibid., 155, 157–159.

61. Marcelin, *Mythologie vodou,* vol. 2: 60–61.

62. Chauvet, *Fonds,* 160, 186, 162.

63. Zora Neale Hurston, *Tell My Horse: Voodoo and Life in Haiti and Jamaica* (1938; reprint, New York: Harper & Row Publishers, 1990), 181.

64. Chauvet, *Fonds,* 189–192.

65. Jacques Roumain, *La Montagne ensorcelée* (1931; reprint, Paris: Editions Messidor, 1987), 112.

66. Métraux, *Voodoo in Haiti,* 116–117.

67. Chauvet, *Fonds,* 194, 223–224, 226.

68. Moreau de Saint-Méry, *Description topographique, physique, civile, politique et historique de la partie française de l'Isle Saint-Domingue,* 3 vols. (Philadelphia: Chez l'auteur; new edition by B. Maurel and E. Taillemite, Paris: Société de l'histoire des colonies françaises, 1958), vol. 1: 94.

69. François Hoffmann, "L'Image de la femme dans la poésie haïtienne," *Présence Africaine* 34–35 (1960–1961): 201–215.

70. Alcibiade Fleury-Battier, "Mon Pays! . . . ," in *Panorama de la poésie haïtienne,* ed. Carlos Saint-Louis and Maurice Lubin (Port-au-Prince: Henri Deschamps, 1950), 56.

71. Emile Roumer, "Marabout de mon coeur," *Panorama de la poésie haïtienne,* 364.

72. Chauvet, *Amour, Colère et Folie,* 362.

73. Dany Laferrière, "Marie Chauvet: *Amour, Colère, Folie,*" *Littérature haïtienne,* ed. Jean Jonassaint, special issue of *Mot pour Mot* 11 (July 1983): 7–10.

74. Madeleine Gardiner, *Visages de femmes: Portraits d'écrivains* (Port-au-Prince: Editions Henri Deschamps, 1981), 11–111. See also Pierre-Raymond

Dumas, "Chauvet: 'Amour, Colère et Folie,'" *Conjonction* 167 (1985): 17–19; Franck Laraque, "Violence et sexualité dans *Amour, Colère et Folie,*" *Présence Haïtienne* 2 (1975): 53–56; "Marie Chauvet (1916–1973): Notice biographique et littéraire," *La Nouvelle Haïti Tribune* (New York), 16–23 June 1982, 8; Madeleine Cottenet-Hage, "Violence libératoire/Violence mutilatoire dans *Amour* de Marie Chauvet," *Francofonia* 4, 6 (1984): 17–28; and Maximilien Laroche, *Trois études sur Folie de Marie Chauvet* (Montréal: GRELCA, 1984).

75. Though uncomfortable about putting gossip in the service of elucidation, I suspect that a bit of Chauvet's personal history might help us to understand how Haiti's greatest writer has suffered the curse of near oblivion. Chauvet's attachments were much discussed in Port-au-Prince: her literary fictions were no doubt consumed by her legendary beauty and by that unfortunate invention of men, "the fatal woman." As a Haitian friend of hers revealed to me, she followed an "itinerary of color" from "black" to "brown" to "mulatto" to "white." Before marrying, Marie Vieux had a romance with the black Haitian Sylvio Cator; her first husband, Aymé Charlier, was brown; her second husband, Pierre Chauvet, light-skinned mulatto; and her third husband, Ted Proudfort, a white American.

76. CARAF Books at the University of Virginia Press had hoped to publish a translation of *Amour, Colère et Folie*, but this project failed due to the family's insistence that they were not ready to release the rights to the book. Patricia Francis of "La Petite Boutique" in New York, one of the finest Haitian bookstores, where I used to order copies of *Amour, Colère et Folie* for my classes, has informed me that she no longer has access to the last copies because Chauvet's daughter has them "under lock and key" (personal communication, October 18, 1993).

77. Chauvet, *Amour, Colère et Folie*, 340.

78. Ibid, 49. For a full discussion of this work, see my "Reading Women in the Caribbean: Marie Chauvet's *Love, Anger, and Madness,*" in *Displacements: Women, Tradition, Literatures in French*, ed. Joan Dejean and Nancy K. Miller (Baltimore and London: Johns Hopkins University Press, 1991), 228–254.

79. Chauvet, *Amour, Colère et Folie*, 12.

80. Ibid., 330.

81. Ibid., 284.

82. Ibid., 285, 291, 288, 289–290, 293, 292.

83. I refer to Depestre's *Alléluia pour une femme-jardin*, first published in Cuba in 1973—bringing with it accusations of vain eroticism and bourgeois individualism—and then reprinted in France in 1981, where Gallimard touted it as "a celebration of woman." Depestre's search for a lost Eden or ellusive lyricism manifests itself in the pursuit and conquest of women. See my "Hallelujah for a Garden-Woman: The Caribbean Adam and His Pretext," *The French Review* 59, no. 4 (March 1986): 581–596.

84. A *karo* is approximately three and one-third acres.

85. Alexis, *Les Arbres*, 174.

86. Jean-Paul Sartre, "Orphée noir," preface to Léopold Sédar Senghor,

ed., *Anthologie de la nouvelle poésie nègre et malgache de langue française* (Paris: Presses Universitaires de France, 1948), xxxiii.

87. Carl Brouard, *Les Griots: Revue scientifique et littéraire d'Haïti* (April–September 1939), cited in Roger Gaillard, *La Destinée de Carl Brouard* (Port-au-Prince: Editions Henri Deschamps), 36.

88. François Duvalier, "Etude critique sur 'Le Sacrifice du Tambour Assoto(r)' de M. Jacques Roumain," in *Eléments d'une doctrine,* in the multivolume work, *Oeuvres essentielles* (Port-au-Prince: Presses Nationales d'Haïti, 1966–1967), vol. 1: 178.

89. See Clifford Geertz's essay, "Blurred Genres: The Refiguration of Social Thought," in *Local Knowledge: Further Essays in Interpretive Anthropology* (New York: Basic Books, Inc., 1983), 19–35, for his interpretive anthropology that cautions against the traps of representation.

90. Geertz, "Thick Description: Toward an Interpretive Theory of Culture," *The Interpretation of Cultures* (New York: Basic Books, Inc., 1973), 18.

91. Jean Rhys, *Wide Sargasso Sea* (1966; reprint, New York and London: Norton, 1982), 70.

92. Hurston, *Tell My Horse,* 59.

93. Ibid., 128.

94. Carl Brouard, *Pages retrouvées: Oeuvres en prose et en vers* (Port-au-Prince: Editions Panorama, 1963), 23. This collection was published with the support of François Duvalier, "Honorary President of the 'Sixtieth Anniversary Committee of Carl Brouard.'"

95. Alexis, *Les Arbres,* 241–242.

96. Ibid., 316–317.

97. Ibid., 240.

98. Chauvet, *Fonds,* 60.

99. Ibid., 140, 138. For an explanation of the "sexualization of luck," see Gerson Alexis, "Le Concept de chance dans la culture populaire haïtienne," in *Lecture en anthropologie haïtienne* (Port-au-Prince: Presses nationales d'Haïti, 1970). Alexis also notes that "certain lwa and saints of the Catholic Church are seen as holders of the keys of luck [or good fortune]: Saint Nicholas, Ezili, Loko, Sen Jak Majè [chief of the Ogou family], Saint Antoine are some examples," 64. I thank Drexel Woodson for alerting me to Gerson Alexis's text and I refer the reader to "Tout mounn se mounn," vol. 1: 576–588, for Woodson's discussion with Gabi Bonjean and the sex-marking of good luck.

100. Chauvet, *Fonds,* 44.

101. Roumain, *Gouverneurs de la rosée,* 37; Chauvet, *Fonds,* 106.

102. See the fine analyses of *plasaj* in Bastien, *Le Paysan haïtien et sa famille,* 91–116, and Serge-Henri Vieux, *Le Plaçage: Droit coutumier et famille en Haïti* (Paris: Agence de Cooperation Culturelle et Technique, 1989).

103. Paul Moral, *Le Paysan haïtien,* 172, note. The meaning of plasaj for Anglo-European outsiders is difficult to grasp, and Haitians themselves suggest differing ways of looking at plasaj as opposed to marriage. The conceptual debasement of plasaj, for example, has little to do with the practices of daily life. For even though ideologically devalued in terms of marriage, plasaj is practiced by at least 80 percent of the population. Deren, in *Divine*

Horsemen, refers to Simpson's list of four possible relationships between men and women. In considering Deren, we should note the difference from Moral's or Woodson's categories: "'femme caille' or the woman of the house (which would be a common-law wife); 'mamans petits,' who, as mother of a man's children outside his house, has certain rights and privileges; 'femme placée,' a woman who is taken to live with a man but is not the mother of his children; and 'bien avec,' who might be a man's mistress," 155, note.

104. Chauvet, *Fonds,* 65.

105. Woodson, "Tout mounn se mounn," vol. 1: 7.

106. Karen McCarthy Brown, *Mama Lola,* 14. See my review in *The Women's Review of Books* (September 1991): 24–25.

107. Brown, *Mama Lola,* 246–247.

108. What we need to remember, especially in reading someone like Jacques Barros, in *Haïti de 1804 à nos jours* (Paris: l'Harmattan, 1984), is that what might look like submission or mistreatment (in his opinion, the "sad" fact that men have more than one woman), may well be part of a sexual or economic contract agreed upon by women who do not agree with or want to adhere to Catholic ideals of monogamy. Martine Segalen, in *Mari et femme dans la société paysanne* (Paris: Flammarion, 1980), deciphers the folkloric assumptions of bourgeois ethnographers at the end of the nineteenth century in France. "The central hypothesis of this book," she explains, "is that the relation husband-wife in peasant society is not founded on the absolute authority of one over the other, but on the complementarity of the two," 15–16. Her chapter, "L'Autorité masculine, un discours de folkloristes," is especially critical for understanding how a rhetoric of male superiority does not necessarily diminish female agency and independence.

109. On women, economics, and power in Haiti, see Sidney Mintz, "The Employment of Capital by Haitian Market Women," in *Capital, Saving and Credit in Peasant Society,* ed. R. Firth and B. Yamey (Chicago: Aldine, 1964); Mintz, "Men, Women, and Trade," *Comparative Studies in Society and History* 13, no. 3 (1971): 247–269; Ira P. Lowenthal, "Labor, Sexuality, and the Conjugal Contract in Rural Haiti," in *Haiti—Today and Tomorrow: An Interdisciplinary Study,* ed. Charles R. Foster and Albert Valdman (New York: University Press of America, 1984), 15–33; Roger Bastide, ed., *La Femme du couleur en Amérique Latine* (Paris: Editions Anthropos, 1974), which includes Mintz's "Les Rôles économiques et la tradition culturelle" and another essay that contradicts Mintz by the Haitian anthropologist, Suzanne-Sylvain Comhaire, "La Paysanne de la région de Kenscoff."

110. Lowenthal, "'Marriage Is 20, Children Are 21,'" 57.

111. Ibid., 70.

112. Ibid., 74.

113. Woodson, "Tout mounn se mounn," vol. 3: 604.

114. Erosmène Delva in Woodson, "Tout mounn se mounn," vol. 3: 588–597.

115. Bastien, *Le Paysan haïtien,* 100.

116. Odette Mennesson-Rigaud, "Notes on Two Marriages with Vou-

doun Loa," in Appendix A, to Deren's *Divine Horsemen*, 263. Rigaud's descriptions of marriage ceremonies for Ezili and Gede are still unsurpassed.

117. Emmanuel C. Paul, *Panorama du folklore haïtien* (Port-au-Prince: Imprimerie de l'Etat, 1962), 274–275.

118. Serge-Henri Vieux, *Le Plaçage*, 105.

119. An issue of the Haitian journal, *Conjunction: Revue franco-haïtienne* 156 (January 1983), was devoted to Faustin. A homosexual, and convinced that he was *réclamé* (summoned or demanded) by Ezili Dantò, he was made her future "mystic husband" by his grandmother. His painting, *The Dream of Ezili Dantò*, portrays a hieratic, aloof Ezili, who presides over Faustin's torments.

120. See Paul Moral, *Le Paysan haïtien*, for a discussion of the high percentage of those who neither marry nor place themselves (in the countryside as well as the cities): "Between twenty and fifty years old, one counts actually six times more 'placés' than 'mariés':—placed—60%; married—10%; celibate and others—30%," 172.

121. George Simpson and J. B. Cinéas, "Folk Tales of Haitian Heroes," *Journal of American Folklore* 54, nos. 213–214 (1941): 176–185.

Chapter 3. Last Days of Saint-Domingue

1. Hippolyte Adolphe Taine, *The Ancient Regime*, trans. John Durand (New York: Henry Holt and Company, 1896), 152.

2. *The Haitian Journal of Lieutenant Howard, York Hussars, 1796–1798*, ed. Roger Norman Buckley (Knoxville: University of Tennessee Press, 1985), 101.

3. Kamau Brathwaite, *Contradictory Omens: Cultural Diversity and Integration in the Caribbean* (1974; reprint, Mona, Kingston, Jamaica: Savacou Publications, 1985), 22.

4. Kamau Brathwaite, *The Development of Creole Society in Jamaica 1770–1820* (Oxford: Clarendon Press, 1971), 179.

5. Médéric Louis-Elie Moreau de Saint-Méry, *Description topographique, physique, civile, politique et historique de la partie française de l'Isle Saint-Domingue*, 3 vols. (Philadelphia: Chez l'auteur, 1797; new edition by B. Maurel and E. Taillemite, Paris: Société de l'histoire des colonies françaises, 1958), vol. 1: 474–475. After two hundred years of no English-language edition, Moreau's work was translated, heavily abridged, and edited by Ivor D. Spencer. Spencer titled his translation (only about 280 pages of the original work of over 1,500 pages): *A Civilization that Perished: The Last Years of White Colonial Rule in Haiti* (Lanham, New York, and London: University Press of America, 1985).

6. James Anthony Froude, *The English in the West Indies, or the Bow of Ulysses* (New York: Charles Scribner's Sons, 1888), 343.

7. The diversity in terms of class and social status is much more complex than I can analyze here. Charles Frostin, in *Les révoltes blanches à Saint-Domingue aux XVIIe et XVIIIe siècles (Haiti avant 1789)* (Paris: Editions de l'Ecole, 1975), has begun the necessary work in reconceiving such divisions as *petits blancs, grands blancs,* slaves, and free coloreds. As he demonstrates through exhaustive research, the categories of whiteness were themselves more vexed than has been allowed, especially in the 1770s, as more white workers, adventurers, and individuals of ill-defined and varied activities left France for Saint-Domingue.

8. Francis Alexander Stanislaus, Baron de Wimpffen, *A Voyage to Saint Domingo, in the Years 1788, 1789, and 1790,* trans. from unpublished manuscript by J. Wright (London: printed for T. Cadell, Jr., and W. Davies; Successors to Mr. Cadell in the Strand; and J. Wright, opposite old Bond Street, Picadilly, 1797), 63.

9. Figures from Baltimore *Daily Repository* (November 19, 1791), in Thomas O. Ott, *The Haitian Revolution: 1789–1804* (Knoxville: University of Tennessee Press, 1973), 7.

10. Moreau de Saint-Méry, *Description de la partie française,* vol. 1: 28. François Girod, *La Vie quotidienne de la société créole: Saint-Domingue au 18e siècle* (Paris: Librairie Hachette, 1972), 10, and 227, note.

11. Abbé Raynal, *Essai sur l'administration de la colonie de Saint-Domingue,* quoted in T. Lothrop Stoddard, *The French Revolution in San Domingo* (1914; reprint, Westport, Conn.: Negro Universities Press, 1970), 20.

12. Yet David Geggus, in *Slavery, War, and Revolution: The British Occupation of Saint Domingue, 1793–1798* (Oxford: Clarendon Press, 1982), 8–10, has argued that although "the petits blancs were the most racist element in colonial society," they also "spent their days and nights in close proximity to the slaves and the poorer mulattoes," intermarrying and even fighting or collaborating with mulattoes and slaves.

13. *The Haitian Journal of Lieutenant Howard,* 101.

14. Baron de Wimpffen, *A Voyage,* 49. In *La Danse sur le volcan* (Paris: Librairie Plon, 1957), trans. by Salvator Attanasio as *Dance on the Volcano* (New York: William Sloan Associates, 1959), 2, Marie Vieux Chauvet describes the rivalry between women—especially between white and mulatto women—in Saint-Domingue as "a fight to the death that pervaded at that time into the heart of everything." She then turns to "the rivalry between the white colonists and 'the little whites,' between the officers and the Government; between the nouveau riche without names or titles and those of the grand nobility of France; rivalry between white planters and freedmen planters, between house slaves and field slaves."

15. Baron de Wimpffen, *A Voyage,* 264.

16. Bryan Edwards, *An Historical Survey of the French Colony in the Island of St. Domingo* (London: printed for John Stockdale, Piccadilly, 1797), preface.

17. Edward Long, *The History of Jamaica, or General Survey of the Antient and Modern State of That Island* (London, 1774; reprint, New York: Arno Press, 1972), vol. 2, book 3, chap. 1, 351–383. Bryan Edwards, *History, Civil and Commercial, of the British Colonies in the West Indies* (Dublin,

1793–1794; reprint, New York: Arno Press, 1972). As Edwards notes in his preface to the 1793 first edition of *The History,* xviii, "the first part of the work was written before his Return to the West Indies in the beginning of 1787;—a considerable part while he was there, and the remainder, with most of the notes, since his return to Great Britain, in the autumn of 1792."

18. Edwards, *An Historical Survey,* preface.

19. Ibid., 123.

20. For the Creole text of Bonaparte's proclamation, see Jean Bernabe, "Les Proclamations en Créole de Sonthonax et Bonaparte: Graphie, histoire et glottopolitique," in *De la Révolution française aux révolutions créoles et nègres,* ed. Michael L. Martin and Alain Yacou (Paris: Editions Caribéennes, 1989), 149–150.

21. Quoted in Paul Roussier, *Lettres du Général Leclerc: Commandant en Chef de l'Armée de Saint-Domingue en 1802* (Paris: Société de l'Histoire des Colonies Françaises et Librairie Ernest Leroux, 1937), 23–24.

22. Quoted in Sir James Barskett's powerful account of the last months of the French in Haiti, *History of the Island of St. Domingo: From Its First Discovery by Columbus to the Present Period* (1818; reprint, London: Frank Cass, 1972), 222. See also Madiou's account of the letters between Leclerc and Christophe in *Histoire d'Haïti* (1492–1846), 8 vols. (Port-au-Prince: Editions Henri Deschamps, 1989), vol. 2: 171–173.

23. Thomas Madiou, *Histoire,* vol. 2: 174–176; C.L.R. James, *The Black Jacobins: Toussaint l'Ouverture and the San Domingo Revolution* (1938, revised ed., London: Allison & Busby, 1980), 295–296.

24. Madiou, *Histoire,* 176–177.

25. Roussier, *Lettres du Général Leclerc,* 243.

26. Ibid., 251.

27. Ibid., 260.

28. These are the figures of C.L.R. James in *The Black Jacobins,* 355. According to Jacques Marquet de Montbreton de Norvins, private secretary to Leclerc, of the 34,000 men who embarked for Saint-Domingue, 24,000 had died, 7,000 were dying in hospitals, and 3,000 "discouraged fighters" remained. See *Souvenirs d'un historien de Napoléon: Mémorial de J. de Norvins,* 3 vols., ed. L. de Lanzac de Laborie (Paris: Libraire Plon, 1896), vol. 3: 41. General Pamphile de Lacroix, who took part in the expedition and published in 1819 his *Mémoires pour servir à l'histoire de la révolution de Saint-Domingue,* counted those dead from combat and illness, and included blacks and men of color, and women and children, as well as soldiers. According to Lacroix, about 62,000 people died during Leclerc's command. See Roussier, *Lettres du Général Leclerc,* 8.

29. For the most revealing documents of increasing French frenzy during Leclerc's last feverish days, see Roussier, *Lettres du Général Leclerc.*

30. Jonathan Brown, *The History and Present Condition of St. Domingo,* 2 vols. (1837; reprint, London: Frank Cass & Co., Ltd., 1971), vol. 2: 132.

31. See chronology in *A Calendar of Rochambeau Papers at the University of Florida Libraries,* compiled by Laura V. Monti (Gainesville: University of Florida Libraries, 1972), 3.

32. The Superior Council for the northern province was at Cap Fran-çais, and that for the western and southern provinces at Port-au-Prince. According to Sir James Barskett in *History of the Island of St. Domingo,* 109, these councils were composed of the governor-general, the intendant, the deputy-governors, the king's lieutenants, a president, twelve counsellors, four *assesseurs,* or assistant judges, together with the attorney-general and registers. In these courts of supreme jurisdiction, the king's edicts, and those of the governor and intendant, were registered. In 1786, the Superior Council of Saint-Domingue replaced the two courts.

33. Letter cited in Moreau de Saint-Méry, *Voyage aux Etats-Unis de l'Amérique, 1793–1798,* ed. Stewart L. Mims (New Haven: Yale University Press, 1913), 327–328.

34. W.W. Harvey, *Sketches of Hayti: From the Expulsion of the French to the Death of Christophe* (1827; reprint, London: Frank Cass & Co., Ltd., 1971), 15.

35. "Manifesto of the King," delivered by Christophe at Sans Souci on September 18, 1814, appendix in Barsket, *History of the Island of St. Domingo,* 438.

36. Beaubrun Ardouin, *Etudes sur l'histoire d'Haïti,* 2d ed. (1853–1860; Port-au-Prince: Chez l'éditeur, François Dalencour, 1958), vol. 5: 84–85; and Madiou, *Histoire,* vol. 2: 506.

37. For the account of the dogs' arrival in Le Cap, see Madiou, especially, *Histoire,* vol. 2: 506. Like Henry Christophe, the black *affranchi* from Saint-Domingue, Louis Marie de Noailles had served with Lafayette in the American war for independence, and later emigrated to the United States, where he profited in banking, and then rejoined the French army in Saint-Domingue. See Sir James Barskett, *History of the Island of St. Domingo,* for his account of the bloodhounds the French were forced to eat in the last months of 1803.

38. Mary Hassal [Leonora Sansay], *Secret History; or, The Horrors of St. Domingo, in a Series of Letters, Written by a Lady at Cape François to Colonel Burr, Late Vice-President of the United States, Principally During the Command of General Rochambeau* (Philadelphia: Bradford & Inskeep, 1808).

39. Ibid., 35.

40. Michel-René Hilliard d'Auberteuil, *Considérations sur l'état présent de la colonie française de Saint-Domingue,* 2 vols. (Paris: Grangé, 1776–1777), vol. 1: 75–76.

41. Pierre de Vassière, *Saint-Domingue: La Société et la vie créoles sous l'Ancien Régime (1629–1789)* (Paris: Perrin et Cie, Libraires-Editeurs, 1909), 327.

42. Madiou, *Histoire,* vol. 2: 502–503.

43. Ibid., 503.

44. Ibid., 509.

45. Hassal, *Secret History,* 53.

46. For the most detailed literary analysis of the representation of the colonial "negro," the sentimentalized "slave," and the metropolitan "white" in eighteenth- and nineteenth-century drama, fiction, and poetry, see François

Hoffmann, *Le Nègre romantique: Personnage littéraire et obsession collective* (Paris: Payot, 1973).

47. Hassal, *Secret History*, 25.
48. Madiou, *Histoire*, vol. 2: 404–405.
49. Hassal, *Secret History*, 69–70.
50. Surely one of the most problematic uses of women by abolitionists was their supposed conversion of the racist portrayal of a demonic and lascivious ape-woman into the sentimental heroine, later processed as the refined, potentially salvageable but ever fallen "tragic mulatta." For two differing accounts that work together in important ways, see Barbara Bush, *Slave Women in Caribbean Society: 1650–1838* (Kingston, Jamaica: Heinemann Publishers; Bloomington: Indiana University Press, 1990), 11–22, and Mary Louise Pratt, *Imperial Eyes: Travel Writing and Transculturation* (London and New York: Routledge, 1992), 86–102.
51. See also Hassal, *Secret History*, 70. Horace Pauléus Sannon's account in his translation of Hassal, *Le Cap Français vu par une Américaine* (Port-au-Prince: Imprimerie Aug. A. Heraux, 1936), 73–75, notes, for his enlightening discussion of Hassal's rendition of the Belair affair.
52. Hassal, *Secret History*, 25–26, 34–35.
53. Ibid., 60.
54. Ibid., 89.
55. *Souvenirs d'un historien de Napoléon: Mémorial de J. de Norvins*, vol. 3: 80–81. Beaubrun Ardouin's account of this "spectacle" is more detailed and gruesome. Rochambeau invited the principal black and colored families to a ball. After dancing until midnight, the guests were taken to another room faintly lit and "hung with draperies of mourning bearing death's heads represented on white canvas." Sacred funeral hymns, coming as if from nowhere, were sung by lugubrious voices. In the middle of the boisterous laughter of the white women present, Rochambeau said to the terrified indigenous women: "You just assisted in the funerals of your husbands and your fathers!" See Fernand Hibbert's article, "Le Néronisme de Rochambeau," *La Ronde*, September 1901, cited in Dantès Bellegarde, ed., *Ecrivains haïtiens: Notices biographiques et pages choisies* (Port-au-Prince: Société d'Editions et de Librairie, 1947), 246–249.
56. Norvins, *Mémorial de J. de Norvins*, vol. 3: 47. According to C.L.R. James, in *Black Jacobins*, 293, "Bonaparte ordered that all white women who had 'prostituted themselves' to Negroes, were to be sent to Europe, whatever their rank." Norvins claims to have discovered with General Boudet "the secret documents" of Toussaint, as well as "love letters, tresses of every color hair, rings, and hearts with arrows from white Creole women distinguished by their breeding and beauty." According to Norvins, he and Boudet did not follow the instructions of Napoleon and Leclerc, but instead burned the letters. Norvins concludes with Bonaparte's commendation, later passed on to him by Leclerc, for having "annihilated 'these shameful proofs of the prostitution of white women,'" vol. 2: 376–377.
57. Hassal, *Secret History*, 143.

58. Arnold Whitridge, *Rochambeau* (New York: The Macmillan Company, 1965), 316.

59. J.F. Bernard, *Talleyrand: A Biography* (New York: G.P. Putnam's Sons, 1973), 158.

60. Letter to Madame de Genlis, in Michel Poniatowski, *Talleyrand aux Etats-Unis, 1794–1796* (Paris: Presses de la Cité, 1967), 156.

61. Moreau de Saint-Méry, *Voyage aux Etats-Unis, de l'Amérique, 1793–1798*, ed. Steward L. Mims (New Haven: Yale University Press, 1913), 302–303. Note how similar is his description of Creole white women in Saint-Domingue in *Description de la partie française*. The climate and inherited faults have made their nervous systems too irritable to nurse their own children, and too many diversions, overwrought emotions, and bad food "make their charms wither. As brilliant as flowers, they are also as short-lived," 39–40.

62. Moreau de Saint-Méry, *Voyage*, 55–56.

63. As a member of the *Musée de Paris*, Moreau was chosen its secretary in 1784 and became president in 1787. Moreau received the keys of the Bastille when it fell, helping to organize the Parisian militia and distributing arms and ammunitions on July 14. During his exile, he would quip that he had been "King of Paris for three days." He resigned from the Commune on October 10, but remained in Paris as a member of the *Constituante* as deputy from Martinique.

64. Among the 128 original subscribers to the two-volume set of Moreau's *Description de la partie française* were "Colonel Burr, at New York" and "S.E. (*Son Excellence*) Thomas Jefferson, Vice-President of the United States."

65. Moreau de Saint-Méry, *Voyage aux Etats-Unis*, 55–56.

66. William Cary Duncan, *The Amazing Madame Jumel* (New York and Chicago: A.L. Burt Company, Publishers, 1935), 94.

67. See details of the failed marriage in Milton Lomask, *Aaron Burr, The Conspiracy and Years of Exile, 1805–1836* (New York: Farrar, Straus & Giroux, 1982), 395–403.

68. *Political Correspondence and Public Papers of Aaron Burr*, ed. Mary-Jo Kline et al., 2 vols. (Princeton: Princeton University Press, 1983), 703.

69. Letter of April 2, 1802, in *The Papers of Aaron Burr, 1756–1836* (New York Historical Society; Glenrock, N.J.: Microfilming Corporation of America, 1957), cited and discussed in a note in *Political Correspondence and Public Papers of Aaron Burr*, 703.

70. Letter quoted in *Political Correspondence and Public Papers of Aaron Burr*, 702.

71. Ibid.

72. "Letter from Leonora to Aaron Burr," in Charles Burdett, *Margaret Moncrieffe; The First Love of Aaron Burr: A Romance of the Revolution* (New York: Derby & Jackson, 1860), 428–437.

73. *Political Correspondence and Public Papers of Aaron Burr*, 808.

74. Quoted before Leonora's letter in appendix, in Burdett, *Margaret Moncrieffe*, 428.

75. See T. Lothrop Stoddard, *The French Revolution in San Domingo* (1914; reprint, Westport, Conn.: Negro Universities Press), for his bibliographical note: "Miss Hassal arrived at Le Cap in May 1802, and remained until shortly before Rochambeau's evacuation in November 1803. Interesting viewpoint, though so gossipy and personal in tone as to be generally unavailable for exact quotation in this connection," 401. Etienne D. Charlier, in *Aperçu sur la formation historique de la nation haïtienne* (Port-au-Prince: Les Presses Libres, 1954), 274–276, quotes from Sannon's edition of these letters, along with other documents concerning the last days of Leclerc and the arrival of Rochambeau at Le Cap. Carolyn E. Fick, in *The Making of Haiti: The Saint-Domingue Revolution from Below* (Knoxville: University of Tennessee Press, 1990), 221, cites Hassal to demonstrate Rochambeau's brutality, while Heinl and Heinl turn to her *Secret History* as evidence for Pauline Leclerc's "kindnesses" to the French General Boyer, which Heinl and Heinl surmise were "arrangements" not unfamiliar to Hassal, "a close friend of Aaron Burr," 109. Thomas O. Ott, *The Haitian Revolution: 1789–1804* (Knoxville: University of Tennessee Press, 1973), 170, refers to Hassal as authority for Leclerc's desperate need for reinforcements by mid-July 1802. Ott refers to American sources as "generally the most objective accounts of the Haitian Revolution," singling out Samuel Perkins's *Reminiscences* and Mary Hassal's *Secret History,* 204. The only previous notice I have discovered connecting Leonora Sansay to Hassal is tentative, and accepts as true what I question: a sister Clara. "Sansay, Leonora, perhaps *née* Hassal, novelist writing as 'a Lady of Philadelphia,' who says she grew up an orphan and went to Santo Domingo, 1802, with a sister married to a Frenchman." See Virginia Blain, Patricia Clements, and Isabel Grundy, *The Feminist Companion to Literature in English: Women Writers from the Middle Ages to the Present* (New Haven: Yale University Press, 1990), 946–947. As this book goes to press, Phil Lapsansky shared with me his revelatory "Afro-Americana: Rediscovering Leonora Sansay," in *Annual Report* (Philadelphia: Library Company, 1992), 29–36.

76. Sannon, *Le Cap Français vu par une Américaine,* v.

77. Hassal, *Secret History,* 6.

78. Letter in *Political Correspondence and Public Papers of Aaron Burr,* 316.

79. Note in *Political Correspondence and Public Papers of Aaron Burr,* 317.

80. Letter in "Appendix" to Burdett, *Margaret Moncrieffe,* 436.

81. Ibid., 428–429.

82. Madiou, *Histoire,* vol. 2: 307.

83. Letter in "Appendix" to Burdett, *Margaret Moncrieffe,* 430–431. Note, however, that the famous statue of Pauline by Canova represents her as Venus, which Hassal might have known, thus transferring the French monument to her American fiction of Clara.

84. Ibid., 432–433.

85. Ibid., 435.

86. *Laura,* by A Lady of Philadelphia (Philadelphia: Bradford & Inskeep, 1809). In "Literary Intelligence" for *Portfolio* 1 (1809), the reviewer explains

the "moral of the story" in terms that recall, though with far more sobriety, the adventures of *Secret History*: "It affords an impressive lesson to the imprudent female; and speaks home to the heart of the libertine," 275.

87. See Alfred N. Hunt, *Haiti's Influence in Antebellum America: Slumbering Volcano in the Caribbean* (Baton Rouge and London: Louisiana State University Press, 1988), 63–64.

88. Charles Brockden Brown's *Arthur Mervyn, or Memoirs of the Year 1793,* the gruesome narrative of the horrors of yellow fever in Philadelphia, when nearly 2,500 people died in the summer of 1793, was no doubt in Leonora's mind as she composed her stories of Philadelphia and Saint-Domingue. Note that at this time many of those who had fled the ravages of revolution in Saint-Domingue found themselves in another city in ruins. According to one eyewitness, wives and daughters supported themselves by prostitution, and he uses the French term, *filles de joie,* heard so often in Saint-Domingue, to describe these prostitutes, who were supposedly less immune to the disease than proper citizens. See Norman S. Grabo, ed., "Historical Essay," in *Arthur Mervyn, or Memoirs of the Year 1793* (1799–1800; reprint, Kent, Ohio: Kent State University Press, 1980).

89. Hassal, *Secret History,* 39–40.

90. Cited in note, *Political Correspondence and Public Papers of Aaron Burr,* 703.

91. See Hassal, *Secret History,* 33–36.

92. *Lady Nugent's Journal of Her Residence in Jamaica from 1801 to 1805,* new and revised edition, ed. Philip Wright (Kingston, Jamaica: Institute of Jamaica, 1966), 137–138.

93. Ibid., 170, 173.

94. Ibid., 106, 112, 132–133.

95. Elsa Goveia, *Historiography of the British West Indies* (Washington, D.C.: Howard University Press, 1980), 177.

96. Hassal, *Secret History,* 8. For descriptions of the voluptuous languor and indolence of the white Creole, see *Lady Nugent's Journal,* 98, and especially the note from John McLeod's *Narrative of a Voyage in His Majesty's Late Ship Alceste, to the Yellow Sea,* 1817, in *Lady Nugent's Jamaica Journal,* 117: " 'Creolizing is an easy and elegant mode of lounging in a warm climate; so called, because much in fashion among the ladies of the West Indies: that is, reclining back in one arm-chair, with their feet upon another, and sometimes upon the table.' " In *History of the West Indies,* Edwards describes Creole women as if "just risen from the bed of sickness. Their voice is soft and spiritless, and every step betrays languor and lassitude." As Edwards moves from the pallor of white women to the variegated colors of persons of mixed blood to blacks, he sets up a sequence of Creole coloration that links Creoles to each other in their departure from the norm of blushing Anglo-European ladies. See also for Saint-Domingue, Moreau de Saint-Méry, *Description de la partie française,* on the sweet languor" of "large spiritual eyes" and the "voluptuousness" and "nonchalance" that characterize their actions.

97. Hassal, *Secret History,* 35–36.

98. Ibid., 6.

99. *The Haitian Journal of Lieutenant Howard,* 104.

100. Ibid., 104, 105.

101. Baron de Wimpffen, *A Voyage,* 113, 114.

102. Long, *The History of Jamaica,* vol. 2, book 2, chap. 13, 279.

103. *Lady Nugent's Journal,* 98.

104. Henry H. Breen, *St. Lucia: Historical, Statistical and Descriptive* (1844; reprint, London: Frank Cass & Co., Ltd., 1970), 185–186.

105. Note that Edouard Glissant, writing his *Caribbean Discourse: Selected Essays,* trans. Michael Dash (Charlottesville: University of Virginia Press, 1989), 46, laments not contamination, but the "dispossession" and "dislocation" that came with "cultural contact." Distinguishing between "self-destructive imitation" and what he calls "the process of Creolization" and "cultural cross-fertilization," he uses theater as his metaphor. For him "the pressure to imitate is . . . the most extreme form of violence that anyone can inflict on a people; even more so when it assumes the agreement (and even, the pleasure) of the mimetic society. This dialectic, in fact, suppresses this form of violence under the guise of pleasure." Yet, Glissant's "reductive power of imitation," conceived of as copying the mere externals of "dominant" society, plays the same role as does "lactification" or "whitening" for Frantz Fanon in *Black Skin, White Masks,* trans. Charles Lam Markmann (New York: Grove Press, Inc., 1967), 41; originally published as *Peau noire, masques blancs* (Paris: Editions de Seuil, 1952). For Kamau Brathwaite, however, the either/or distinction (imitation vs. creation; acculturation vs. "indigenization") does not work. In *Contradictory Omens: Cultural Diversity and Integration in the Caribbean* (Mona, Kingston, Jamaica: Savacou Publications, 1974; reprinted 1985), 15–16, he argues that "our real/apparent imitation involves at the same time a significant element of creativity, while our creativity in turn involves a significant element of imitation." See also Homi Bhaba, whose "Of Mimicry and Man: The Ambivalence of Colonial Discourse," *October* 28 (Spring 1984), 125–133, takes issue with "the familiar exercise of *dependent* colonial relations through narcissistic identification, as exemplified for him by Fanon and Césaire's emptying out of "presence" or "identity," leaving only a husk. What Bhaba calls mimicry's "*menace*" is its "*double* vision which in disclosing the ambivalence of colonial discourse also disrupts its authority." Somewhere between mimicry and mockery lies the possibility that the "civilizing mission" itself can be "displaced" by what Bhaba calls "its disciplinary double." Bhaba captures here the doubling that also ruptures, the power of apparent capitulation to subvert.

106. Moreau de Saint-Méry's *Danse,* published as part of *Répertoire des notions coloniales* in Philadelphia in 1796, was unavailable until Jean Fouchard published it as appendix to his *La Meringue: Danse nationale d'Haïti* (Montréal: Editions Leméac, Inc., 1973), 159–198.

107. Moreau de Saint-Méry, *Description de la partie française,* vol. 1: 66–68, 41.

108. Hippolyte Adolphe Taine, *The Ancient Regime,* 152.

109. Hassal, *Secret History,* 79.

110. Ibid., 80.

111. Ibid., 77–78.

112. Justin Girod de Chantrans, *Voyage d'un Suisse dans différentes colonies d'Amérique,* presented by Pierre Pluchon (Paris: Librairie Jules Tallandier, 1980), 188.

113. Madame Laurette Aimée Mozard Nicodami Ravinet (1788–1864), *Mémoires d'une Créole du Port-au-Prince (île St.-Domingue)* (1844; reprint, Paris: A la Librairie-Papeterie . . . et Chez l'auteur, 1973), 24. The story of the prohibition against wearing shoes and the revenge of "these creatures" by insolently wearing jewels on their feet, begins Marie Chauvet's *La Danse sur le volcan,* 2.

114. Moreau de Saint-Méry, *Description de la partie française,* vol. 1: 105.

115. Yvan Debbasch, *Couleur et liberté: Le Jeu du critère ethnique dans un ordre juridique esclavagiste* (Paris: Librairie Dalloz, 1967), vol. 1: 96, cites Moreau de Saint-Méry, *Loix et constitutions,* vol. 5: 855–856 (ruling of February 9), in *Lois et constitutions des Colonies Françaises de l'Amérique sous le vent de 1550 à 1785* (Paris: Quileau, Méquignon jeune, 1784–1790).

116. Moreau de Saint-Méry, *Description de la partie française,* vol. 1: 75, 76. See also *The Haitian Journal of Lieutenant Howard,* 107, and the memoirs of Justin Girod de Chantrans.

117. Gabriel Debien, in *Les Esclaves aux Antilles françaises (XVIIe– XVIIIe siècles)* (Basse-Terre: Société d'Histoire de la Guadeloupe; Fort-de-France: Société d'Histoire de la Martinique, 1974), 243, distinguishes between the weekday dress of the working slave, "the clothing of submission," and the glorious clothes reserved for Sunday. In great detail, he also describes differences in dress—type of linen, head covering, and jewelry—between field slaves and domestic.

118. Hassal, *Secret History,* 78.

119. Moreau de Saint-Méry, *Description de la partie française,* vol. 1: 41.

120. Madiou, *Histoire,* vol. 2: 508.

121. Hassal, *Secret History,* 18–19.

122. Moreau de Saint-Méry, *Description de la partie française,* vol. 1: 358.

123. Michel-René Hilliard d'Auberteuil, *Considérations sur l'etat present de la colonie Française de Saint-Domingue,* 2 vols. (Paris: Grangé, 1776– 1777), vol. 1: 111.

124. Moreau de Saint-Méry, *Description de la partie française,* vol. 1: 362. Note than Jean Fouchard, in *Le Théâtre à Saint-Domingue* (Port-au-Prince: Imprimerie de l'Etat, 1955), 187, wonders about Moreau's story about a contest between mothers and daughters, ebony and copper, since in Port-au-Prince, Saint-Marc, and Léogane, blacks and mulattoes of all shades of color were seated together, "mixed without distinction, usually in the back of the amphitheater or upper gallery or in the pit." Did Moreau, Fouchard wonders, "sacrifice truth to the cruelty of a whim" that masked other realities of social life in the colony?

125. Hilliard d'Auberteuil, *Considérations,* vol. 1: 109.

126. Moreau de Saint-Méry, *Description de la partie française,* vol. 1: 360.

127. Fouchard, *Le Théâtre,* 279–283. Fouchard in his notes refers to the

need to get to boxes of archival material as yet uncatalogued in Haiti, for further research could show that many of the "facts" recorded in a certain way because of a "colonial mentality" might well be revised. For example, there might well have been "nearly equal numbers of free blacks and free mulattoes," though the obsession with color on the part of the authorities might have equated freedom with lightness, "parodying," as Fouchard puts it, "Acaau's formula, free negroes are christened gens de couleur, while mulatto slaves are declared negro," 182, note.

128. Fouchard, *Le Théâtre*, 251.

129. Ibid., 251–252.

130. Note that Foucault's world of public torture ("the great spectacle of physical punishment") in *Discipline and Punish: The Birth of the Prison*, trans. Alan Sheridan (New York: Pantheon Books, 1977)—originally published as *Surveillir et punir; Naissance de la prison* (Paris: Editions Gallimard, 1975)—died out by the end of the eighteenth and the beginning of the nineteenth century. Could this disappearance have been possible because of its transfer to the colonies? According to Foucault, "modern" codes were planned or drawn up in France in 1791. By 1801 torture would resurface, represented as theater in the French army's antics in Saint-Domingue. Of course, the inventive ceremonies of cruelty had always been part of planter practice, especially as the number of slaves grew and profits to be made increased. Perhaps sobriety is possible in the metropole because the colonies act as receptacles for what is no longer allowed or legal in those places called "civilized." See Césaire's telling condemnation in *Discourse in Colonialism*, trans. Joan Pinkham (New York: Monthly Review Press, 1972), 19–20—originally published as *Discours sur le colonialisme* (Paris: Editions Présence Africainé, 1955)—of how colonies served as a "safety valve" for modern society. The ghosts of old metropolitan practices thrived in the colonies.

131. Moreau de Saint-Méry, *Description de la partie française,* vol. 1: 329.

132. Ibid., 475–476.

133. Gabriel Debien, in "Le Marronage aux Antilles Françaises au XVIIIᵉ siècle," *Caribbean Studies* 6, no. 3 (October 1966): 34, specifies that it was the unacclimated *bosals* who filled the jails, while "the Creole slave rarely found himself in the colonial prisons."

134. Fouchard, *La Théâtre*, 33.

135. Ibid.

136. Jonathan Brown, *The History and Present Condition of St. Domingo,* vol. 2: 276–277.

Chapter 4. Gothic Americas

1. Jonathan Edwards, *The Injustice and Impolicy of the Slave Trade, and the Slavery of the Africans,* illustrated in a Sermon Preached before the Connecticut Society for the Promotion of Freedom, and for the Relief of Persons

Unlawfully Holden in Bondage, at their Annual Meeting in New Haven, September 15, 1791 (New Haven: New Haven Anti-Slavery Society, Press of Whitmore & Buckingham, 1833), 32.

2. *Une Correspondance familiale au temps des troubles de Saint-Domingue: Lettres du Marquis et de la Marquise de Rouvray à leur fille, Saint-Domingue— Etats-Unis, 1791–1796*, published by M. E. McIntosh and B. C. Weber (Paris: Société de l'histoire des colonies françaises et Libraire Larose, 1959), 106.

3. One of the oddest traces of the vexed dialogue between Haiti and the United States is the Haitian historian St. Rémy's homage to Harriet Beecher Stowe as a "daughter of heaven" in the preface to his *Mémoires du Général Toussaint-L'Ouverture* (Paris: Pagnerre, Libraire-Editeur, 1852). Had St. Rémy read Stowe's final judgment on Haiti—a condemnation of black rule, ignored by recent critics as well—he might not have so readily claimed Stowe as his muse. Note that *Uncle Tom's Cabin* was reviewed in Paris in *Revue des Deux Mondes* 16, "Le Roman Abolitioniste en Amérique," 1852.

4. Clement Eaton, *The Freedom of Thought Struggle in the Old South* (1940; reprint, New York: Harper & Row, 1964), 90.

5. *Thomas Jefferson: Writings,* ed. Merrill D. Peterson (New York: The Library of America, 1984), 1096–1098.

6. Ibid., 1484–1487.

7. Bryan Edwards, *The History, Civil and Commercial, of the British Colonies in the West Indies,* 2 vols. (Dublin, 1793–1794; reprint, New York: Arno Press, 1972), vol. 1, book 1, chap. 2, 39.

8. Ibid., vol. 2, book 4, chap. 3, 74–76.

9. If racialist arguments foundered on the fact of feeling, abolitionist fictions thrived on the costs of sentiment, though such charitable pathos was costly only to those who were not white.

10. Originally published as *Slavery Justified by a Southerner,* later included in *Sociology for the South, or The Failure of Free Society* (1850) in *Slavery Defended: The Views of the Old South,* ed. Eric L. McKitrick (Englewood Cliffs, N.J.: Prentice-Hall, 1962), 45.

11. Edgar Allan Poe, "Review of J. K. Paulding's *Slavery in the United States* and William Drayton's *The South Vindicated from the Treason and Fanaticism of the Northern Abolitionists,*" *Southern Literary Messenger,* April 1836. See my previous discussions of this much disputed review: "Romance and Race," in *The Columbia History of the American Novel,* ed. Emory Elliott (New York: Columbia University Press, 1991), 94–102; and "Amorous Bondage: Poe, Ladies, and Slaves," *American Literature* 66 (June 1994): 239–273.

12. Georges Louis Leclerc, comte de Buffon, *A Natural History of the Globe, of Man, of Beasts, Birds, Fishes, Reptiles, Insects, and Plants,* ed. John Wright, trans. W. Kendrick, 3 vols., new edition with improvements from Geoffrey, Griffith, Richardson, Lewis, Clark, Long, and Wilson (Boston: Gray and Brown, 1831), vol. 1: 163. Edward Long, *The History of Jamaica, or General Survey of the Antient and Modern State of That Island* (London, 1774; reprint, New York: Arno Press, 1972), vol. 2, book 3, chap. 1, 356, 372.

13. William Beckford, Jr., *Remarks upon the Situation of the Negroes in Jamaica* (London: T. and J. Egerton, Military Library, 1788), 84.

14. Thomas Jefferson, *Notes on the State of Virginia,* ed. William Peden (1787; reprint, New York: W.W. Norton & Company, Inc., 1972), 139 and 288, note.

15. Ibid., 140–141.

16. Long, *History of Jamaica,* vol. 2, book 3, chap. 1, 356, 363.

17. Elsa V. Goveia, *Historiography of the British West Indies* (Washington, D.C.: Howard University Press, 1980), 61.

18. Long, *History of Jamaica,* vol. 2, book 3, chap. 1, 360, 364, 361, 383.

19. Jefferson, *Notes,* 138. See Winthrop Jordan, *White over Black: American Attitudes toward the Negro, 1550–1812* (New York and London: W.W. Norton & Company, Inc., 1977), 457–461, for an incisive analysis of Jefferson on beauty, blacks, and passion.

20. *The Haitian Journal of Lieutenant Howard, York Hussars, 1796–1798,* ed. Roger Norman Buckley (Knoxville: University of Tennessee Press, 1985), 104.

21. Pierre de Vassière, *Saint-Domingue (1629–1789): La Société et la vie créoles sous l'ancien régime* (Paris: Perrin et Cⁱᶜ, Libraires-Éditeurs, 1909), 311.

22. Francis Alexander Stanislaus, the Baron de Wimpffen, *A Voyage to Saint Domingo, in the Years 1788, 1789, and 1790,* trans. from unpublished manuscript by J. Wright (London: printed for T. Cadell, Jr., and W. Davies; Successors to Mr. Cadell in the Strand; and J. Wright, opposite Old Bond Street, Picadilly, 1797), 277–278.

23. Baron de Wimpffen, *A Voyage,* 275–276. Story adapted from Edward Tripp's *Crowell's Handbook of Classical Mythology* (New York: Thomas Y. Crowell Company, 1970), 189.

24. Baron de Wimpffen, *A Voyage,* 277.

25. Georg Simmel, *The Philosophy of Money,* trans. Tom Bottomore and David Frisby (London, Henley, and Boston: Routledge & Kegan Paul, 1978), 372.

26. Baron de Wimpffen, *A Voyage,* 276–277.

27. Ibid., 308.

28. Ibid., 225–256.

29. Michel-René Hilliard d'Auberteuil, *Considérations sur l'etat présent de la colonie française de Saint-Domingue,* 2 vols. (Paris: Grangé, 1776–1777), vol. 2: 63.

30. Ibid., vol. 1: 130.

31. Baron de Wimpffen, *A Voyage,* 245–246.

32. Thomas Carlyle's "The Nigger Question," first printed in *Frazer's Magazine,* December 1849, laments that "Philanthropic Liberalism" has merely "'emancipated' the West Indies into a *Black Ireland*; 'free' indeed, but an Ireland and Black!"; but Carlyle's real obsession is with the abundance of pumpkins in the West Indies, so satisfying to what he calls the idle Quashee,

"sunk to the ears in pumpkin, imbibing saccharine juices," that he need never work.

33. Quoted in Pierre Pluchon, *La Route des esclaves: Négriers et bois d'ébene au XVIIIᵉ siècle* (Paris: Hachette, 1980), 19.

34. Thomas O. Ott, *The Haitian Revolution: 1789–1804* (Knoxville: University of Tennessee Press, 1973), 6.

35. I refer the reader to the stunning argument of Louis Sala-Molins in *Le Code Noir, ou le calvaire de Canaan* (Paris: Presses Universitaires de France, 1987), especially the section, "Le Code Noir à l'ombre des Lumières," 206–280. Nowhere in Montesquieu's sections on slavery in *L'Esprit des lois* is the Code Noir mentioned. Though Rousseau solemnly expels slavery from his *Contrat social*, condemning for all time slavery as contrary to human dignity, he never deals with the French institution of slavery in Africa and America: "The Black of the Black Code gets none of Rousseau's attention. . . . The only slave in the juridical sense of the term spoken of in a French code of laws at this time, Rousseau does not care about," 241. See also *La Traite des noirs au siècle des lumières*, ed. Isabelle and Jean-Louis Vissière (Paris: Editions A. M. Métailié, 1982) for the accounts of slave-traders, who deal with the traffic in humans not only as legal but honorable. In the introduction, the editors note that were you to read only Montesquieu and Voltaire, you would assume that "this abuse was, in the 18th century, universally condemned," so they will attend to the "scandalous paradox" that "Christian, Humanist Europe, which considered slavery like a defect of pagan antiquity, resurrected in the colonies an institution contrary to right, morals, and religion," 7.

36. Louis Sala-Molins, *Le Code Noir.* Confronting what he takes to be a neglect nearly as pernicious as the Code itself, Sala-Molins introduces the Code to his readers as if a fairy tale in six parts, told for the pleasure of the "little Frenchman grown big." Note that the only English translation I have found is in an appendix in Howard Justin Sosis, "The Colonial Environment and Religion in Haiti" (Ph.D. dissertation, Columbia University, 1971). Sala-Molins demonstrates its inaccessibility by noting how, were you so inclined, you might locate and read the unreadable. Fully transcribed in Labat, evoked in Raynal, and listed in the *Encyclopédie* under "Code," it is otherwise ignored. See pages 82–84 for his exhaustive recovery of this text and its traces. I first read the Code in a collection that included all the king's added rulings and edicts, 1699–1742: *Recueils de règlements, édits, déclarations et arrêts . . . concernant le commerce, l'administration de la justice, la police des colonies françaises de l'Amérique . . . avec Le Code Noir et l'addition au dit Code* (Paris: Chez les libraires associés, 1745), 220 pages. Note that the 1685 Code was only a dozen pages, while its 1770 edition, though it contained the same number of articles, required more than four hundred pages in the same size print; see Sosis, 111–112.

37. Baron de Wimpffen, *A Voyage*, 55.

38. See two more recent works that are marvels of historiographic research: Antoine Gisler, *L'Esclavage aux Antilles françaises (XVII–XIXᵉ siècle): Contribution au problème de l'esclavage* (Fribourg: Editions Universitaires Fri-

bourg Suisse, 1965); and Gabriel Debien, *Les Esclaves aux Antilles françaises* (*XVII*ᵉ*–XVIII*ᵉ *siècles*) (Basse-Terre: Société d'histoire de la Guadeloupe; Fort-de-France: Société d'Histoire de la Martinique, 1974).

39. Hilliard d'Auberteuil, *Considérations*, vol. 1: 143. Yet, in *The West Indian Slave Laws of the 18th Century* (Kingston, Jamaica: Caribbean Universities Press; Ginn & Company, 1970), 25, Elsa Goveia, noting the extreme contrasts in punishment for the crime of killing a slave and the crime of striking or abusing a white, concludes: "The brutality of the law flowed in well-defined, socially accepted channels."

40. See Gordon Lewis, *Main Currents in Caribbean Thought: The Historical Evolution of Caribbean Society in Its Ideological Aspects, 1492–1900* (Baltimore and London: Johns Hopkins University Press, 1983), 140, for his story of the Abbé Grégoire's account of Hilliard d'Auberteuil's fate at the hands of reactionary colonists in M. Gregoire, *Lettre aux citoyens de couleur et nègres libres de Saint-Domingue* (1791), 9–10. See also Lewis Leary's introduction to the facsimile reproduction of Hilliard d'Auberteuil's *Miss McCrea: A Novel of the American Revolution*, trans. Eric LaGuardia (1784; reprint, Gainesville, Fla.: Scholar's Facsimiles & Reprints, 1958), 9.

41. Gisler, *L'Esclavage*, 32.

42. On Descartes's triple discovery of self, nature, and nation, with New World discovery as backdrop, see Peter Hulme, "The Spontaneous Hand of Nature: Savagery, Colonialism, and the Enlightenment," in *The Enlightenment and Its Shadows*, ed. Peter Hulme and Ludmilla Jordanova (London and New York: Routledge, 1990), 18–34.

43. Descartes, *Meditations on First Philosophy*, trans. John Cottingham, with an introduction by Bernard Williams (Cambridge, England, and New York: Cambridge University Press, 1986), *Sixth Meditation*, 59.

44. Descartes, *Second Meditation*, 18, 19.

45. For the best account of the religious instruction of slaves, see Debien, *Les Esclaves*, 249–295.

46. Pierre de Vassière, *Saint-Domingue: La Société et la vie créoles sous l'ancien régime (1629–1789)*, 80, quoted in T. Lothrop Stoddard, *The French Revolution in San Domingo* (Westport, Conn.: Negro Universities Press, 1914), 24.

47. Père Jean-Baptiste Labat, *Nouveau voyage aux îles de l'Amérique*, vol. 1: 166–167, quoted in Gisler, *L'Esclavage*, 196.

48. Ibid.

49. Carolyn Fick, *The Making of Haiti: The Saint Domingue Revolution from Below* (Knoxville: University of Tennessee Press, 1990), 35. See also C. L. R. James, *The Black Jacobins: Toussaint l'Ouverture and the San Domingo Revolution* (1938; revised ed., London: Allison & Busby, 1980), 12.

50. In *Black Skin, White Masks*, trans. Charles Lam Markmann (New York: Grove Press, Inc., 1967), 216–217, Fanon will deny that freedom can come "without conflict," for it lacks the reciprocity necessary for full self-consciousness. Just as Rousseau ignored that "convention" could not exist between the master and the slave turned into an instrument of profit, Hegel,

according to Fanon, talks of a "reciprocity" that masks the special quality of this relation of domination: "Here the master laughs at the consciousness of the slave. What he wants from the slave is not recognition but work," 220. Glissant, also from Martinique, goes further in *Caribbean Discourse: Selected Essays*, trans. J. Michael Dash (Charlottesville: University Press of Virginia, 1989), 26–35, in his scathing analysis of the proclamation made on 31 March 1848 by Louis Thomas Husson, delegate of the Republic of France, abolishing (but not really) slavery in Martinique:

The goodness of the father. He takes care of his children; it is up to them to be well-behaved, to deserve his attention. . . . The notion of buying back one's freedom, which legitimates the principle of indemnification. (History repeats itself.) You were therefore the *rightful* property of your masters? The equivalence between the status of him who brings the glad tidings and the importance of the latter. The higher placed the delegate, the more news is true and beneficial. The habit that decisions are taken elsewhere. The law *arrives*. (Paris "makes" the law.) The granting of freedom. It is rare that a colonizing country should so develop a theory of "Liberation."

Like the Code, this liberation is a verbal dispensation that says to the slaves: "Until the law becomes official, remain what you are, slaves."

51. Bryan Edwards, *The History of the British Colonies in the West Indies,* quoted in Goveia, *The West Indian Slave Laws*, 35. In *Slavery and Social Death: A Comparative Study* (Cambridge, Mass.: Harvard University Press, 1982), 1–4, Orlando Patterson analyzes the brute force, the violence it takes "to transform free man into slave."

52. Michel-Rolph Trouillot, "Motion in the System: Coffee, Color, and Slavery in Eighteenth-Century Saint-Domingue," *Review* 5, no. 3 (Winter 1982): 336.

53. Charles Frostin, *Les Révoltes blanches à Saint-Domingue aux XVIIᵉ et XVIIIᵉ siècles* (Paris: Editions de l'Ecole, 1975), 138.

54. See Fick, *The Making of Haiti*, 32–34, for an excellent discussion of land allotment to slaves.

55. Sir James Barskett, *History of the Island of St. Domingo: From Its First Discovery by Columbus to the Present Period* (1818; reprint, London: Frank Cass, 1972), 113.

56. See Jean Fouchard, *Les Marrons de la liberté* (1972; reprint, Port-au-Prince: Editions Deschamps, 1988), 92–95, for the most common punishments, other than the whip and the cutting off of ears (both of which had been authorized by the Code), as well as what Fouchard calls "exceptional tortures."

57. Lucien Peytraud, *L'Esclavage aux Antilles françaises avant 1789* (1897; reprint, Edition et Diffusion de la Culture Antillaise, Paris: E. Kolodziej, 1984), 250.

58. I use Orlando Patterson's phrase in *Slavery and Social Death* for the definition of the slave as banished or excommunicated from "any legitimate social order," 5.

59. For another take on Sade's "antimetaphysical position," his "commitment to tracking metaphysics to its physical bases," with an acute analysis of

Sadean sexuality and the reconfiguring of property relations, see Frances Ferguson, "Sade and the Pornographic Legacy," *Representations* 36 (Fall 1991): 1–21.

60. Marquis de Sade, *The Hundred and Twenty Days of Sodom,* trans. Austryn Wainhouse and Richard Seaver (New York: Grove Press, 1966), 16.

61. Beaubrun Ardouin, *Etudes sur l'histoire d'Haïti* (1853–1860; Port-au-Prince: Chez l'éditeur, François Dalencour, 1958), vol. 1: 15.

62. One would like to know more about the "mortgaged plantations in the Antilles" to which Simon Schama refers when discussing the troubles of Louis and Marie-Antoinette in *Citizens: A Chronicle of the French Revolution* (New York: Vintage Books, 1989), 214.

63. Marquis de Sade, *Juliette* (1797), trans. Austryn Wainhouse (New York: Grove Press, 1968), 2: 319, 321.

64. Pierre de Vassière, *Saint-Domingue,* cited in Goveia, *The West Indian Slave Laws,* 44.

65. See Jean Starobinski's comparison of Rousseau and Buffon's methods—with Buffon as categorical ground for Rousseau's speculative daring—in *Jean Jacques Rousseau: La Transparence et l'obstacle, suivi de sept essais sur Rousseau* (Paris: Gallimard, 1971), 380–392.

66. Sade, *Juliette,* 2: 322–323.

67. Gisler, *L'Esclavage,* 81–82.

68. Ibid., 45–47, for a discussion of regulations of work, care, and discipline of slaves, as well as the death penalty for murder of a slave, no matter the pretexts; but Gabriel Debien in his chapter, "Y a-t-il un adoucissement?" in *Les Esclaves aux Antilles françaises* argues convincingly that any improvement in slave treatment only affected a few plantations, mostly the larger ones, 491–495.

69. Lewis, *Main Currents in Caribbean Thought,* 167.

70. Debien, *Les Esclaves aux Antilles françaises,* 410, 494.

71. Gisler, *L'Esclavage,* 118.

72. Ibid.

73. See the detailed reconstruction of Lejeune's case and the story of the two women, both African, named Marie-Rose (from the Congo) and Zabette (an Ibo from the Niger delta) in Jacques Thibau, *Le Temps de Saint-Domingue: L'Esclavage et la révolution française* (Paris: Editions Jean-Claude Lattès, 1989), 17–93.

74. Gisler, *L'Esclavage,* 118.

75. C. L. R. James, in *The Black Jacobins,* 24–25, describes how Abbé Raynal's *Philosophical and Political History of the Establishments and Commerce of the Europeans in the Two Indies* inspired Toussaint.

76. Gisler, *L'Esclavage,* 119–120.

77. Ibid., 121.

78. Hilliard d'Auberteuil, *Considérations,* vol. 1: 130.

79. Ira P. Lowenthal and Drexel G. Woodson, *Catalogue de la collection Mangonès, Pétionville, Haïti,* ARP Occasional Papers, 2 (New Haven, Conn.: Antilles Research Program, Yale University, 1974).

80. *Manuel théorique et pratique de la flagellation des femmes esclaves, d'après le manuscript inédit d'un planteur espagnol (XVIIIᵉ siècle)* (Paris: Librairie Franco-Anglaise, n.d.), 11, 15, 17, 28.

81. Ibid., 11, 13.

82. Sidney Mintz was the first anthropologist to demonstrate how marketing shaped an identity resistant to the degradation of slavery. See, especially, "Men, Women and Trade," *Comparative Studies in Society and History* 13 (1971): 247–269; "Les Rôles économiques et la tradition culturelle," in *La Femme de Couleur en Amérique Latine,* ed. Roger Bastide (Paris: Editions Anthropos, 1974), 115–148; "Caribbean Marketplaces and Caribbean History," *Nova Americana* 1 (1978): 333–334; and *Caribbean Transformations* (Baltimore and London: Johns Hopkins University Press, 1974).

83. Moreau de Saint-Méry, *Description topographique, physique, civile, politique et historique de la partie française de l'Isle Saint-Domingue,* 3 vols. (Philadelphia: Chez l'auteur, 1797; new ed. by B. Maurel and E. Taillemite, Paris: Société de l'histoire des colonies françaises, 1958), vol. 1: 433–436.

84. Ibid., 315–316.

85. Debien, *Les Esclaves,* 371.

86. Yvan Debbasch, *Couleur et liberté: Le Jeu du critère ethnique dans un ordre juridique esclavagiste* (Paris: Libraire Dalloz, 1967), vol. 1: 101.

87. See Arlette Gautier, "Mélange des corps, mélange des sangs," in *Les Soeurs de solitude: La condition féminine dans l'esclavage aux Antilles du XVIIᵉ au XIXᵉ siècle* (Paris: Editions Caribéennes, 1985), 152–154.

88. Moreau de Saint-Méry, *Description de la partie française,* vol. 1: 84–85.

89. Moreau de Saint-Méry, *Notes historiques,* quoted in Pierre de Vassière, *Saint-Domingue,* 318.

90. Judgment of the Council of Le Cap, cited in Gisler, *L'Esclavage,* 95–96, and in Jacques Thibau, *Le Temps de Saint-Domingue,* 210.

91. Thibau, *Le Temps de Saint-Domingue,* 210.

92. In "Motion in the System," *Review,* 331–388, Michel-Rolph Trouillot demonstrates conclusively how the restrictions and harsh treatment of *gens de couleur* after 1760 was triggered by the economic growth of coffee planters, who were primarily *gens de couleur.*

93. For discussions of the workings of the ideal of "respect" for whites, see especially Debbasch, *Couleur et liberté,* 75–77; Gisler, *L'Esclavage,* 90–100; Fick, *The Making of Haiti,* 21.

94. Arrêt of 22 January, Council of Port-au-Prince, cited in Gisler, *L'Esclavage,* 95.

95. Debbasch, *Couleur et liberté,* 53–54.

96. James, *The Black Jacobins,* 41.

97. Frostin, *Les Révoltes blanches à Saint-Domingue aux XVIIᵉ et XVIIIᵉ siècles,* 71.

98. Moreau de Saint-Méry, *Description de la partie française,* vol. 1: 83, 111.

99. Fick, *The Making of Haiti,* 19.

100. Cited in Debbasch, *Couleur et liberté,* 81.

101. Debien, *Les Esclaves,* 373–377.

102. *Une correspondance familiale au temps des troubles de Saint-Domingue: Lettres du Marquis et de la Marquise de Rouvray à leur fille,* 102–103.

103. Fick, *The Making of Haiti,* 19.

104. Moreau de Saint-Méry, *Lois et constitutions,* vol. 4: 342, cited in Sala-Molins, *Le Code Noir ou le calvaire de Canaan,* 201.

105. Hilliard d'Auberteuil, *Considérations,* vol. 2: 77–78.

106. Moreau de Saint-Méry, *Lois et constitutions,* vol. 5: 448, cited in Sala-Molins, *Le Code Noir ou le calvaire de Canaan,* 197.

107. Justin Girod de Chantrans, *Voyage d'un Suisse dans différentes colonies d'Amérique,* ed. Pierre Pluchon (Paris: Librairie Jules Tallandier, 1980), 166.

108. See Debbasch, *Couleur et liberté,* 69–71.

109. Debien, *Les Esclaves,* 72.

110. Jean Fouchard, *Les Marrons de la liberté* (Port-au-Prince: Editions Henri Deschamps, 1988), 228–258.

111. Moreau de Saint-Méry, *Lois et constitutions,* vol. 5: 448, cited in Gisler, *L'Esclavage,* 98.

112. Debbasch, *Couleur et liberté,* 69–71.

113. Fouchard, *Les Marrons de la liberté,* 257.

114. Moreau de Saint-Méry, *Lois et constitutions,* vol. 1: 105, cited in Debbasch, *Couleur et liberté,* 96.

115. George Louis Leclerc, comte de Buffon, *Oeuvres complète de Buffon* (Bruxelles: Chez Th. Lejeune, Libraire-éditeur, 1828–1830), vol. 1: 72.

116. Moreau de Saint-Méry, *Lois et constitutions des colonies françaises de l'Amérique sous le Vent (de 1550 à 1785),* 6 vols. (Paris: Quileau, Méquignon jeune, 1784–1790).

117. Cited in Stewart L. Mims, introduction to Moreau's *Voyage aux États-Unis de l'Amérique, 1793–1798* (New Haven: Yale University Press, 1913), xv.

118. Moreau de Saint-Méry, *Description de la partie française,* vol. 1: 86. See Micheline Labelle, *Idéologie de couleur et classes sociales en Haïti* (Montréal: Les Presses de l'Université de Montréal, 1978), for an important analysis of the ideology of color in contemporary Haiti. Frantz Fanon, in *Black Skin, White Masks,* would be obsessed by *lactification,* or the desire for whitening. Derek Walcott, in his autobiographical long poem, *Another Life,* confesses while looking at the moon in St. Lucia: "he had prayed / nightly for his flesh to change, / his dun flesh peeled white by her lightning strokes!" Michelle Cliff's protagonist Clare, in both *No Telephone to Heaven* and *Abeng,* like Marie Chauvet's Claire in *Amour* or the other-worldly Ella O'Grady Langley in Erna Brodber's *Myal,* suffer the collapse of identity caused by their indeterminate place in a society founded ostensibly on the division between black and white. Liminal, these women are phantoms of a creolized past that haunt the plot of twentieth-century Caribbean novels.

119. Moreau de Saint-Méry, *Description de la partie espagnole de l'Isle Saint-Domingue,* 2 vols. (Philadelphia: Chez l'auteur, 1796), vol. 1: 57.

120. For the best comparative analysis of slave laws in the Caribbean, see

Elsa V. Goveia, *The West Indian Slave Laws of the 18th Century* (Mona, Kingston: University of the West Indies, Caribbean Universities Press; Ginn & Company, 1970).

121. Moreau de Saint-Méry, *Description de la partie espagnole,* vol. 1: 58.

122. Ibid., 59.

123. Natural histories would be instrumental to the civilizing mission in France. See M. Jacques Roger, *Les Sciences de la vie dans le pensée française du XVIIIe,* part 3, chap. 2, 527–536, and Michèle Duchet, *Anthropologie et histoire au siècle des lumières* (Paris: François Maspero, 1971), 229–280.

124. Moreau de Saint Méry, *Description de la partie française,* vol. 1: 101.

125. Pierre de Vassière, *Saint-Domingue: La Société et la vie créoles sous l'ancien régime,* 217–219. Note, however, that previously legally and socially sanctioned marriages in Saint-Domingue, converting "*quarteronnes* into *Whites,*" made it "impossible to verify how many light-skinned people of Afro-European descent crossed over the 'racial' line and happily 'returned' to France or took 'refuge' in the United States during the Haitian Revolution." See Michel-Rolph Trouillot, "Motion in the System," 359; and for an analysis of legal whitening in Jamaica, see Brathwaite, *The Development of Creole Society in Jamaica, 1770–1820* (Oxford: Clarendon Press, 1971), 167–168, and Zora Neale Hurston, *Tell My Horse: Voodoo and Life in Haiti and Jamaica* (1938; reprint, New York: Harper & Row, 1990), 7–9, for a spirited account of "census whites" in Jamaica: "black by birth but white by proclamation."

126. Edward Long, *History of Jamaica,* vol. 2: 489. Many of the ideas discussed here were first formulated in my review essay, "Gothic Naipaul," *Transition* 59 (1993): 158–170.

127. Moreau de Saint-Méry, *Description de la partie française,* vol. 1: 86.

128. Ibid., 90.

129. Ibid., 91–92.

130. Vincent Marie Viennot, comte de Vaublanc, *Mémoires* (Paris, 1883), cited in Yvan Debbasch, *Couleur et liberté,* 62, note.

131. Moreau de Saint-Méry, *Description de la partie française,* vol. 1: 100.

132. Ibid.

133. Ibid., 57–58.

134. Frostin, *Les Révoltes blanches à Saint-Domingue,* 71. See also Baron de Wimpffen, *A Voyage,* 59.

135. Moreau de Saint-Méry, *Description de la partie française,* vol. 1: 79.

136. Buffon, *Oeuvres complètes,* vol. 5: 204.

137. Ibid., 206–207.

138. Peytraud, *L'Esclavage aux Antilles françaises avant 1789,* 249.

139. Buffon, vol. 1: 207–208.

140. Ibid., 207.

141. Moreau de Saint-Méry, *Description de la partie française,* vol. 1: 75.

142. Baudry Deslozières, *Les Égarements du négrophilisme* (Paris, 1802), cited in Sala-Molins, *Le Code Noir, ou le calvaire de Canaan,* 58.

143. Buffon, *A Natural History,* 134.

144. Ibid.

145. See Moreau de Saint-Méry, *Description de la partie française,* vol. 1: 65–69, for complete description of ceremony.

146. "Mémoire sur les poisons qui regnent à Saint-Domingue, 1763," Archives Nationales, Paris, quoted in Sosis, "The Colonial Environment and Religion in Haiti," 183.

147. Hilliard d'Auberteuil, *Considérations,* vol. 1: 137, and 137–138, footnote.

148. Although historians and ethnographers of the African diaspora are all too ready to demonstrate the African retentions in the New World, they do not grant the same survival power to Catholic practices—for example, in Haiti during the disappearance of the Church after independence.

149. Price-Mars, "Le Sentiment et le phenomène religieux chez les nègres de St-Domingue," in *Une Etape de l'évolution haïtienne* (Port-au-Prince: Imprimerie "LA PRESSE," 1930), 126–127.

150. Moreau de Saint-Méry, *Description de la partie française,* vol. 1: 51.

151. Debien, *Les Esclaves,* 287, footnote.

152. Undated manuscript from mid-eighteenth century, quoted in Sosis, "The Colonial Environment and Religion in Haiti," 190.

153. "*Mémoire de la Chambre d'Agriculture du Port-au-Prince, September 23, 1764,*" quoted in Sosis, "The Colonial Environment and Religion in Haiti," 189.

154. Claude-François Valentin de Cullion, *Examen de l'esclavage en générale, et particulièrement des nègres dans les colonies françaises de l'Amérique par V.D.C. . . . ancien avocat et colon à Saint-Domingue* (Paris: Chez Desenne & Maradan de l'Impr. de Guilleminet, 1802), vol. 1: 196.

155. Pierre Pluchon, *Vaudou sorciers empoisonneurs de Saint-Domingue à Haïti* (Paris: Editions Karthala, 1987), 38.

156. "Notice historique," cited in Fick, *The Making of Haiti,* appendix B, 265.

157. Fick, *The Making of Haiti,* 104–105, and Pierre Adolphe Cabon in collaboration with Gabriel Debien, "Les Religieuses du Cap à Saint-Domingue," *Revue d'Histoire de l'Amérique Française* 3 (December 1949): 418–419.

158. Cabon, "Une Maison d'education à Saint-Domingue: Les Religieuses du Cap," *Revue d'Histoire de l'Amérique Française* 2 (March 1949): 565, 574.

159. Cabon, "Les Religieuses du Cap à Saint-Domingue," 418.

160. Moreau de Saint-Méry, *Description de la partie française,* vol. 1: 68.

161. Gisler, *L'Esclavage,* 79.

162. Moreau de Saint-Méry, *Description de la partie française,* vol. 1: 56.

163. "Mémoire sommaire sur les prétendues pratiques magiques et empoisonnements," dated 1756–1758 in Archives Nationales, quoted in Sosis, "The Colonial Environment and Religion in Haiti," 182.

164. Preamble to the "Arrêt de règlement du Conseil du Cap," 18 February 1761, quoted in Peytraud, *L'Esclavage,* 232–233.

165. See Debien, *Les Esclaves,* 286.

166. Peytraud in *L'Esclavage avant 1789,* 226, notes the circular to administrators of Saint-Domingue, Martinique, Guadeloupe, and Saint-Lucia, "indicating that the King obtained diverse decrees from the Court of Rome reducing to ten the number of holidays."

167. Cabon, "Les Religieuses du Cap à Saint-Domingue," 402.

168. See Cabon, "Figures de religieuses à Saint-Domingue," *Revue d'Histoire de l'Amérique française* 3 (June 1949): 77–78.

169. Cabon, "Les Religieuses du Cap à Saint-Domingue," 403.

170. Debien, *Les Esclaves,* 286–287. Lucien Peytraud in *L'Esclavage avant 1789,* 233, lists the five articles of the Arrêt of 1761: 1) Marriages of negroes will take place only with the consent of the parish priests; 2) No priests can delay baptism or refuse as godfather or godmother any black or white person professing the Catholic, Apostolic, and Roman faith; 3) No slaves can assemble in church from midnight to two o'clock and after sundown; 4) No slaves can take on the functions of verger under penalty of the whip; 5) No catechizing.

171. See Jean Price-Mars, *So Spoke the Uncle,* trans. Magdaline W. Shannon (Washington, D.C.: Three Continents Press, 1983), 48–50, and Price-Mars, "Puissance de la foi religieuse chez les nègres de Saint-Domingue dans l'insurrection générale des esclaves de 1791 à 1803," *Revue d'histoire des colonies* (42d year, 1st trimester, 1954): 5–13. See also Price-Mars, "Le Sentiment et la phenomène religieux chex les nègres de St.-Domingue," in *Une Etape de l'evolution haïtienne,* especially 135–147.

172. Peytraud, *L'Esclavage avant 1789,* 234.

173. See Peytraud, *L'Esclavage avant 1789,* 234–235, and Debien, *Les Esclaves aux Antilles françaises,* 282–288.

174. Justin Girod de Chantrans, *Voyage d'un Suisse dans différentes colonies d'Amérique,* 163–164.

175. Peytraud, *L'Esclavage avant 1789,* 286.

176. *Regulation of Discipline for Blacks, Addressed to the Priests in the French Islands of America,* issued by Louis XV in 1764, discussed in Sosis, "The Colonial Environment and Religion in Haiti," 212–214.

177. Unsigned report (April 7, 1794), quoted in Pierre Adolphe Cabon, *Notes sur l'histoire religieuse d'Haïti de la révolution au Concordat (1789–1860)* (Port-au-Prince: Petit Séminaire Collège Saint-Martial, 1933), 25.

178. Cabon, *Notes sur l'histoire religieuse d'Haïti,* 40.

179. Ibid., 41–42, note.

180. Accounts of this ceremony are varied, as demonstrated by Harold Courlander in *The Drum and the Hoe: Life and Lore of the Haitian People* (Berkeley and Los Angeles: University of California Press, 1960), 32–36.

181. J.B. Romain, *Quelques Moeurs et coutumes des paysans haïtiens: Travaux pratiques d'ethnographie sur la région de Milot à l'usage des étudiants* (Port-au-Prince: Imprimerie de l'Etat, 1959), 208.

182. Lorimer Denis, "Le Cimetière," *Bulletin du Bureau d'Ethnologie* 2, no. 13 (Port-au-Prince: Imprimerie de l'Etat, 1956), 4–5.

183. See Rémy Bastien, *Le Paysan haïtien et sa famille* (1951; reprint, Paris: Editions Karthala, 1985), 137–142.

184. Alfred Métraux, *Voodoo in Haiti*, trans. Hugo Chartiris, with a new introduction by Sidney Mintz (New York: Schocken Books, 1972), 257.

185. For lengthy descriptions of this complex ceremony, see Métraux, *Voodoo in Haiti*, 258–259; and Maya Deren, *Divine Horsemen: The Living Gods of Haiti* (1953; reprint, Kingston, N.Y.: Documentext, McPherson & Company, 1989), 46–53.

186. See Métraux, *Voodoo in Haiti*, 302, and Courlander, *The Drum and the Hoe: Life and Lore of the Haitian People*, 98.

187. George Eaton Simpson, "Lou Garou and Loa Tales from Northern Haiti," *Journal of American Folklore* 55, no. 218 (1942): 220.

188. Jean-Claude Delbeau, *Société, culture et médecine populaire tradition-nelle* (Port-au-Prince: Imprimerie Henri Deschamps, 1990), 207–210.

189. René Depestre, *A Rainbow for the Christian West*, translated and with an introduction by Joan Dayan (Amherst: University of Massachusetts Press, 1977), 179–181.

190. Jamaica Kincaid, *At the Bottom of the River* (1983; reprint, New York: Vintage Books, 1985), 9.

Index

Acaau, Louis-Jean, 15, 53, 88
Agulhon, Maurice: *Marianne au combat: L'Imagerie et la symbolique républicaines de 1789 à 1880*, xix
Alexis, Gerson, 130
Alexis, Jacques-Stephen, 27, 47; *Les Arbres musiciens*, 80, 88, 91, 94, 124, 128, 129, 291n60; *Compère Général Soleil*, 47–48, 107, 291n60; on Dessalines, 88, 291n60; *L'Espace d'un cillement*, 80; and Haitian peasant novel, 80, 86, 87, 117, 129; life of, 80–81, 291n60; and male négritude defined against the double Venus, 48; on Rada lwa versus Petwo and Zandò lwa, 104–105, 107; romanticism of past of Haitian peasantry, 86, 87, 88; use of Ezili and Ogou, 107, 128–129, 139
Alourdes (Mama Lola), 132
Alston, Joseph, 165
Alvarez, Oungan, 34; picture of, 35
Ardouin, Beaubrun: on Bois-Caïman ceremony, 29; *Etudes sur l'histoire d'Haïti, suivies de la vie du Général J.-M. Borgella*, 9, 10, 13, 16, 155, 212–213, 288n13, 289n24; on Défilée, 41; his depiction of revolutionary women, 47; on Dessalines's land reform, 26; on Dessalines's murder, 17, 38, 41; on dogs of Donatien

Rochambeau, 155; as Haitian senator, 13, 15–16; as historian of Haiti, 9–10, 15, 16, 288n13; and language and race, 9–10, 16; life of, 9, 13, 15–16; and Soulouque, 13, 15–16; on vodou, 14, 16, 29, 30, 79
Ardouin, Céligny, 15, 16, 29
Aristide, Jean-Bertrand, 49, 261

Baker, Theodore, 80
Barros, Jacques, 81
Barskett, James: *History of the Island of St. Domingo*, 210
Bastide, Roger, 133, 261
Bastien, Rémy: on Haitian peasant women, 133, 137; and land and the lwa, 89; *Le Paysan haïtien en sa famille*, 87, 89, 137; romanticism of past of Haitian peasantry, 87, 89
Bazile, Dédée. *See* Défilée
Beckford, William, Jr.: *Remarks upon the Situation of the Negroes in Jamaica*, 193
Belair, Charles, 158–159
Belair, Sanite, 46, 47, 158–159
Bellegarde, Dantès: *La Nation haïtienne*, 12–13
Bellegarde, Windsor, 42
Benjamin, La Merci, 65, 72; pictures of, 66, 69
Bennett, Michèle, xx

329

Designer:	U.C. Press Staff
Text:	10/13 Galliard
Display:	Galliard
Compositor:	Prestige Typography
Printer/Binder:	Thomson-Shore, Inc.